The Lives of

Danielle Steel

The Lives of

Danielle Steel

THE UNAUTHORIZED
BIOGRAPHY OF AMERICA'S #1
BEST-SELLING AUTHOR

*Vickie L. Bane and
Lorenzo Benet*

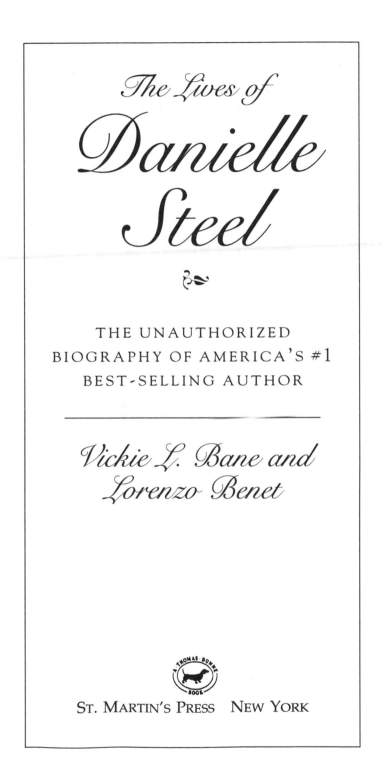

ST. MARTIN'S PRESS   NEW YORK

Authors' Note: In several instances, dialogue has been reconstructed from court documents or the recollections of one of the participants.

Design by Basha Zapatka

Library of Congress Cataloging-in-Publication Data

Bane, Vickie.
    The lives of Danielle Steel / Vickie Bane and Lorenzo Benet.
      p.   cm.
    "A Thomas Dunne book."
    ISBN 0-312-11257-2
    1. Steel, Danielle—Biography.   2. Women novelists,
American—20th century—Biography.   I. Benet, Lorenzo.
II. Title.
PS3569.T33828Z58   1994
813'.54—dc20
[B]   94-19814
                                                CIP

First Edition: October 1994

10 9 8 7 6 5 4 3 2 1

To David G. Bane,
my first-and-only love,
And to Jason and T. J. Bane,
our beloved sons.

To Sarah Benet,
who showed the way.
To Aimee Kravette Benet,
without whom this
would not have been
possible.
And to Hannah Benet,
who made it all
worthwhile.

Acknowledgments

In the year and a half it took to research and write this book, we came in contact with literally hundreds of wonderful people. Without them, it would have been impossible to complete our work. Although contributions varied in depth and scope, our gratitude knows no such boundaries.

Heartfelt thanks to:

Interviewees who so generously shared their recollections, including those acknowledged in the text, those whose words appear without their names (you know who you are), and those we had to leave out.

Librarians Judy Canter, Peggy Emmons, and Richard Geiger.

Attorneys Thomas Burke, Linda Cawley, John Carnes, David Kaye, Paul Sleven, and the law firm of Crosby, Heafey, Roach & May.

Literary agent Madeleine Morel, editor Tom Dunne, as well as Reagan Arthur, Jeremy Katz, Judith McQuown, and Sally Richardson of St. Martin's Press.

And special people who contributed each in their own special way: Arlene Allsman; Michael Arkush; Joseph W. Babnik; Michael J. Babnik; Ken Baker; John and Pat Bane; Doug, Tyann, Alison, and Jennifer Bane; Mike, Mary, Kelsey, and Kevin Bane; Edwin, John, Maria, Pia, and Shaun Benet; Pete and Jonna Benet; Tom Butt; David and Mary Chandler; Anna Cooper; Vera Dawson; Joann Dayton; Tracy Dayton; Troy and Kathy Dayton; Johnny Dodd; Jane, Jereme, Joseph, and Sophia Geller; Todd Gold; Lisa Goldring; Kerry Harris; Jack Kelley; Gil and Mary Kravette; Nick and Cindy Loesch; Vincent Marsh; Liz McDunna; Stan and Kiki Moore; Florence Nishida; Nick Ravo; Monica Rizzo; Jim and Ellen Roller; Marilyn Saltzman; Barry Staver; Bob and Jane Urschel; Dianna Waggoner; Joyce Wagner; and Barry Witt.

The Lives of

Danielle
Steel

1

~

*A*long black limousine glides to a stop in front of the War Memorial and Performing Arts Center in downtown San Francisco. The door swings open, and out steps a large black heel, followed by the slender body of a diminutive woman, clad in a strapless Dior gown of darkest ebony. As she exits the limo, a mink stole drops casually from one shoulder, revealing a diamond necklace encircling her long neck. From her ears hang diamonds that are larger than her red thumbnails.

The woman smiles, red lipstick framing perfect white teeth, as she lightly grasps the arm of her handsome escort, dressed in a black tuxedo with a white bow tie. Her hair is a rich, thick chestnut brown, pulled across the top into a soft knot in the back, and her eyes, as she lifts them up adoringly toward her escort, are a lovely shimmering green.

Danielle Steel, the author, could pass for a movie star or a princess, or even better, a glamorous heroine in a romantic novel. She looks like a fantasy come true—beautiful, beloved, and wealthy beyond belief. But, like the many romantic novels Danielle has penned over the past two decades, there is more to this woman than her cover.

For aspects of Danielle's own secret life, unbeknownst to her millions of fans worldwide, seep through the pages of her novels and, at times, it is more unbelievable than her fiction.

Danielle is the author of thirty-two published novels as well as ten children's books, four books for teenagers, a book of poetry, and a nonfiction work, coauthored with six friends. She has more than 215 million books in print, translated into twenty-eight languages and distributed throughout forty-six countries.

Probably the best-selling author of this century, Danielle is surely one of the richest. Her last five-book contract, signed in 1992 with Dell/Delacorte Publishing Co., commanded $60 million, and her yearly income is reportedly in excess of $25 million.

In between books, she has forged a deal with network television, airing eleven movies based on her novels with at least six more to come.

Given her status as a publishing wunderkind, Danielle has somehow managed to remain a shadow to her work, rarely stepping out to reveal herself. The image she prefers is that of a wife and mother whose days revolve around her husband, her children, and then her writing.

French by persuasion if not by birth, what she has unveiled about her life seems to manifest itself in the French expression *corriger la fortune*, which means to correct one's fortune by disavowing the past. In interviews given by her since 1979, Danielle has evaded, avoided, and in some cases simply failed to tell the truth about her life.

Much of what follows is missing from her official press biography. What follows is the untold story about the lives of Danielle Steel.

2

wo years to the day after Japan surrendered, bringing an end to World War II, Danielle Fernande Dominique Schuelein-Steel was born in New York City. On August 14, 1947, the seven-and-a-half-pound baby girl made her debut. The only child of John Schuelein-Steel and Norma da Camara Stone des Reis, the newborn Danielle was labeled by family members as "exceptionally pretty."

Baby Danielle was the daughter of immigrants. Like scores of other Germans of Jewish descent, her father's family had sought passage on crowded ships during the late 1930s and early 1940s to escape the Nazis. Her mother's family had already arrived in the United States from Lisbon, Portugal, and the Azores Islands, a Portuguese colony located in the Atlantic Ocean some 740 miles west of Europe.

Danielle's paternal grandparents were born in Munich, Germany, and raised in well-to-do families. Her great-grandfather, Josef Schuelein, was a giant of a man for that era, over six foot two, who married a woman four foot eleven. Together, Josef and Ida had six children: four sons who were all under five-foot-two, and two daughters.

Josef founded the Union Brewery Schuelein and Company in 1895, later merging it with another brewery to form one of the five largest breweries in Munich. Of his sons, Julius, Hermann, Fritz, and Curt, only Hermann, who held a doctorate in both economics and law, would remain active in the family business. Through Hermann's leadership, the company was able to complete a successful merger with Löwenbrau in 1921, creating the largest brewery in Bavaria.

In many interviews over the past two decades, Danielle has described her father, John, as having "lower-echelon connections to the Löwenbrau brewing dynasty." In fact, it was her grandfather's brother Hermann who created that connection. A close family member maintained, however, that there never was a "dynasty," and that even Hermann, as director of Löwenbrau, was just an employee after Josef sold his shares in the brewery and bought the Kaltenberg Castle in Bavaria. There was, the family member said, no Löwenbrau fortune to inherit.

Danielle's grandfather Julius, like his younger brother Hermann, was short in stature but long on intellect. Julius earned degrees in law and chemistry from the University of Munich before marrying Danielle's grandmother Minni L. Kahn. For many years Julius practiced law in Munich. Then, in 1914, at the start of World War I, he changed from lawyer to chemist-inventor, developing vitamins and food products from brewer's yeast.

Like his granddaughter-to-be, Julius was also a writer. He wrote several detailed works about his vitamins while heading a company that manufactured the supplements and marketed them throughout Europe and Japan.

Julius and Minni produced one child, John, born in January 1914. A blue-eyed blond, John was described as a "bright boy," who would grow to be taller than his father, nearly five foot six in height. He lived with his parents in what one family member remembered as a "lovely apartment in a very nice neighborhood, right in the middle of Munich."

Unlike his own father, John didn't earn a degree from the university, but rather graduated from a gymnasium, which was more difficult than an American high school. Eventually he was sent by his father to Japan, to help with the marketing of their vitamin products under the name Presco-Vegex.

As Germany was coming under the dominion of Adolf Hitler, changes were being forced on the Schuelein family. By 1933, Jews were beginning to be excluded from business leadership in Germany, and the executive committee of Löwenbrau sought to remove Dr. Hermann Schuelein, ostensibly to keep him out of the Nazi line of fire. Hermann turned over his title as director, or president, of the company.

Later that year, after reading Hitler's *Mein Kampf* and realizing what the Führer had in mind, Hermann saw the urgency in getting his family out of Germany. He drove with his wife, Luise, and young daughter, Anne, to the border, hoping to cross into Switzerland on a "business trip." Hermann was arrested at the border, and while Luise and Anne were set free, they feared he would end up in a concentration camp. The police detained Hermann for three days before he was finally returned to Munich.

By 1936, the situation in Germany had become so dangerous for Jews that

4

Hermann bought his way out of the country. He was able to get official permission for his family to leave, but at tremendous cost. Jewish emigrants had to leave three-quarters of their fortune, which the Nazis then confiscated. The other one-quarter, said a source close to the family, was converted at ridiculous rates: a hundred thousand German marks for eight thousand U.S. dollars. After buying passage for himself and his family, Hermann had little money left.

In 1938, Josef Schuelein died in Germany and his castle was confiscated by the Nazis. During the next few years, the rest of the Schuelein sons fled to the United States, aided in large part by Hermann.

In years to come, Danielle would sprinkle in bits and pieces carved from the lives of these colorful ancestors into her books, telling writer Jean Ross in 1985 that "I have a real pull toward the era of World War II." For example, her 1980 best-seller and first hardcover, The Ring, begins in Germany several years before the start of World War II. A San Francisco Examiner article written in 1979 reported that this book was "based on an incident in the life of her grandmother."

The Ring commences with the story of a successful Jewish writer, Dolff Sterne, who can no longer publish his books in Germany. In a moment of anguish, Dolff explains to his lover, the wife of a wealthy German banker, why his homeland will ignore his accomplishments: "A Jew isn't supposed to be successful, isn't supposed to win national awards. There will be no room at all for Jews in the New Germany, if Hitler has his way," Danielle wrote.

And, although clearly not the same escape, one of Danielle's characters would take flight to the Swiss border just as Danielle's relatives had done. Both in fiction and in fact, they were attempting to flee the tyranny of Nazi Germany.

After arriving in the United States, Julius got a job with Standard Brands, Inc., in Peekskill, New York, which at that time was the world's largest yeast plant. Within a year, Julius helped set up facilities to manufacture his supplements through Standard Brands. He would later become an executive of that company.

Wanting to participate in the distribution of his father's products, Danielle's father worked briefly for Standard Brands before creating Vegex, his own company in New York. He was eager to fit in to his new country, so he changed his name to Steel. "He thought Schuelein was too German for him. It was during the war and he was afraid people would be antagonistic [toward him]," said a family member. After the war, John would begin to use the hyphenated Schuelein-Steel instead. (He may have dropped the first e in Schuelein, although most legal documents use the traditional spelling.)

Thus, rather than heirs to a massive brewery fortune, family members said the Schueleins of New York were actually middle-class businessmen.

In a 1988 interview with the *Los Angeles Times*, Danielle would describe her father as "a playboy who preferred going to the opera in white tie and tails to work." "This," she went on pointedly to tell the *Times*, "was a matter of great concern to his family."

Family members and friends do remember a dapper, debonair John, who always wore a carnation in his buttonhole and leaned toward the "eccentric" in dress. "He liked to wear very flashy vests and suits," recalled one source. "But a playboy," they said, "is a matter of opinion."

In the meantime, the lovely Norma da Camara Stone des Reis, born in Massachusetts to a Portuguese-American family, was already living in New York.

Her father, Gil da Camara Stone des Reis, emigrated from the Azores Islands in the early 1900s, settling in Cambridge, Massachusetts, and playing soccer for a Portuguese club in nearby Hudson. During the 1920s, he moved his Portuguese wife and young daughter into an established Portuguese-American community in Newark, New Jersey. Stone, as he came to be known, would become a writer, working for the Portuguese-American newsweekly *Luso Americano*.

In 1939, the World's Fair came to New York City, and after the fair ended, the Portuguese government wanted to maintain a commercial presence in the United States. To that end, they created Casa de Portugal, the Portuguese national tourist office.

Again, in interview after interview during the 1980s, Danielle would describe her mother as the daughter "of a high-ranking Portuguese diplomat."

"Mr. Stone was one of three gentlemen on the staff of Casa de Portugal, and later on he became director," remembered Maria Theresa Braga, who served as his assistant for many years. "He was not a diplomat," explained Braga, although he worked for the Portuguese government. A representative of the Portuguese embassy who once knew Gil Stone concurred. "It was not a position with diplomatic status," she said, even though Stone was friends with then-Ambassador João de Bianchi.

"Mr. Stone was a wonderful man. He used to see that a long-stemmed red rose was placed on my desk each morning. It became a trademark. That was the type of person he was," said Braga.

Reportedly caught in an unhappy marriage, Stone, then forty-seven, wanted a divorce from his first wife to marry Tekla Alicanti, a thirty-seven-year-old American of Italian descent who was a social worker in New York. Although both he and Tekla were Catholic, Stone was ready to forsake his church and get married by a justice of the peace before his first wife relieved him of that responsibility by dying in early 1945. In June he traveled to Washington, D.C., with his only child, Norma, to marry Tekla in St. Thomas Catholic Church.

Danielle's parents, John and Norma, met in New York City as World War II was reaching its peak. Although both were fluent in several languages, their common tongue was English. They married in New York in the mid-1940s in the chapel of St. Patrick's Cathedral. John converted from Judaism to Catholicism, said a source close to the family.

Some time after Danielle's birth, the family moved into an apartment on East 45th Street off Lexington Avenue in New York City.

Indeed, Danielle would later write in a November 1985 *Cosmopolitan* article about her own sad childhood. "There were few children in my life until I had my own. My parents were enormously sophisticated people at a time when it wasn't fashionable to have children around; children were meant to be seen and not heard, and preferably neither. Actually, my parents let me hang around with their friends, but there were no other children present. I was an oddity. . . ."

Danielle would later tell her second husband that when she was just five years old her parents sent her to a summer camp in Colorado for two months to help "toughen her up." "It was very lonely for her," recalled her second husband, who said that Danielle didn't bond with the younger children, but rather with two girls, one twelve or thirteen and the other sixteen. "They more-or-less adopted her, and called her 'Pixie' because of her size."

Danielle would also reveal to reporter and friend Pat Montandon in the now-defunct San Francisco-based *Scene* magazine, a high-society publication, that even when she was five years old her parents didn't go with her to visit the dentist. "I had a disastrous childhood," she said to Montandon. "A lonely, heartbreaking, no-one-wanted-me kind of growing up."

3

~

Once questioned by a reporter about her parents' marriage, Danielle characterized it as "noisy."

She described her mother to Gary Goldberg in a *Cosmopolitan* interview as being "absolutely beautiful and very flirtatious."

And her father, Danielle said, "was sort of a great international playboy; that was his work—even after he got married."

The marriage officially ended when Danielle was seven years old. Asked by Goldberg why her parents split, Danielle would confide, "My mother was very young and wanted to be free."

This was obviously a subject of great emotional pain for Danielle, and she has refused in countless interviews to discuss her mother. She would, however, tell Nikki Finke of the *Los Angeles Times* that, after their divorce, her parents "flipped a coin and he won." "I saw her over the years," Danielle said. "I didn't see a lot of her, but I saw her [occasionally]."

A source close to the family added to the story: "Norma was very beautiful. She met a man on the subway. I'm not saying there's anything wrong with that; you can meet some very nice people on the subway. Anyway, she married this man, then divorced him a year later."

A family friend said that after her divorce, Norma lived in New York City and worked "in a wholesale gift place on lower Fifth Avenue that was nothing very glamorous."

The source also revealed that John didn't want the divorce from Norma and "was upset that he would lose his daughter." Determined to keep Danielle, her father reportedly fought for custody and won.

Regardless, it was evident that she felt abandoned. In a 1981 interview with her friend Pat Montandon, Danielle would describe herself as an "unwanted child."

"It was the way I grew up—alone with my father. I had two self-indulgent parents," she said to *Woman's Day* in 1990. "They weren't what I would consider serious people."

While her father traveled extensively for his company, called Vegex, Danielle has said she was shuffled off to stay with various relatives, including her paternal grandmother. Minni Schuelein, whom Danielle called "Omi," was the most wonderful and significant person in her childhood. Danielle described her tiny grandmother to her second husband as "the only person who ever made me feel tall."

A source close to the family said that when Danielle's father or grandmother couldn't pick her up from school, the cook who worked for one of the Schuelein uncles would perform the task.

Danielle divulged to Glenn Plaskin in a 1988 interview that "the most important things my children have are not ballet lessons or nice clothes, but two parents who really care about them, and who are there for them and love them and want to be with them—which I didn't have."

Danielle also revealed to her second husband, verified in letters she wrote to him, that her parents would forget her birthdays, and that Christmas was not very eventful. Danielle and her father would generally have dinner with her grandmother, and then, very late, celebrate with friends at a party on Christmas Eve. She would later describe her youth to her second husband as being rather like a Fellini movie.

Danielle said she would spend her summer breaks with her father in places like Capri or Rome. "He'd give two or three parties a week—big, wild wonderful bashes with lots of food, lots of music," Danielle reported to Gary Goldberg in *Cosmopolitan*. "It was always very dressed up," Danielle continued. "My father's idea of an informal evening was black tie for dinner."

"I was very shy," Danielle divulged in another interview. "Besides, nobody was going to talk to an eight-year-old. So I became sort of a fly-on-the-wall observer at an early age. Looking back on it now, I think it's probably what made me a writer."

A close family source confirmed that John Schuelein-Steel was indeed an avid party thrower, but the New York parties weren't quite as elaborate. "He would give two or three parties a week at his New York apartment with a little wine and not a lot of food," remembered a close family source who attended several of the events. "He tried to be some kind of a dandy."

At an early age, however, Danielle said her family instilled in her the concept of noblesse oblige. It was her moral obligation always to conduct herself honorably and responsibly. Certain activities were taboo. For example, she reportedly wasn't allowed to watch television until she was twelve, or to chew gum until after she was married, or even to wear blue jeans until long past her teens. The philosophy of noblesse oblige, which surfaces repeatedly in her books, would resurface in her life as well.

Because she was raised primarily around adults, she had few friends as she was growing up, Danielle told her second and third husbands. She attached herself emotionally to her first dog, a purebred pug, described in *Having a Baby* as "the love of my life." The dog died when Danielle was nine, "which almost broke my heart," she wrote. Even though her father attempted to fill the gap by buying her another dog, Danielle said "he never took the first dog's place."

Over the years, Danielle has talked vaguely about being schooled for a time at a "Swiss boarding school," although never, in any interview, giving that school a name. However, according to a family source who lived near the Schuelein-Steels in New York, Danielle was educated primarily in New York.

When she was eight, her father enrolled her in the exclusive French private school Lycée Français de New York in Manhattan. Tuition at the school was a costly $625 per year then, and $5,500 today.

From the outside, the gray-brick Lycée Français building with arched windows and doorways and two flags flying from the second-story balcony, resembled an embassy more than a school. Founded in 1935, it catered from its inception to the French-speaking population in New York, as well as to well-to-do families who were looking for a rigorous academic program for their children.

The primary language of instruction was French, and students were required to take a variety of courses including math, science, history, geography, French, English, modern and classical languages, the arts, and physical education.

Uniforms were required at all times, and young Danielle, like her cohorts, wore a navy blazer, white blouse, and dark gray skirt or tailored pants. Her school day began at eight A.M. and, as she got older, classes could continue until five or six P.M., followed by several hours of intensive homework.

Danielle once told a *People* reporter that the discipline that allowed her to turn out books in two months began when she attended the Lycée Français. She would say she was "obsessed by her studies," completing "sometimes eight hours of homework a night."

While she excelled in the humanities, Danielle would admit to a distaste for both math and chemistry. A "bright" student, Danielle did especially well in languages. Danielle could attest to speaking three languages fluently: English, French, and Italian. She was conversant in Spanish and German, and could understand some Finnish and, later, Japanese.

She liked poetry, but her escape was literature. Danielle's favorite author was Sidonie-Gabrielle Colette, France's most-honored female writer of her day, who died in August 1954, just shortly before Danielle's seventh birthday.

Like the author she would later inspire, Colette penned a series of contemporary novels from the early 1900s through World War II, many of which centered around the theme of love and betrayal. Married three times, first to a man fourteen years her senior, Colette was also an admitted bisexual, whose works were sexually frank as well as descriptive. Reviewers found Colette's works to be both "evocative and sensual." Danielle delighted in her prose.

Danielle was so "bookish" that she once told a reporter she was kidded in school about "walking into walls" while reading.

While intellectual pursuits came easily, athletic endeavors did not. During her school years, she played basketball, volleyball, badminton, and golf, but would later joke that her classmates drew lots to see who had to take her on their team. Her lack of athletic prowess would dog her into adulthood, where she would admit to being "unathletic," even though she would ride horseback and occasionally ice-skate with her daughter Beatrix.

When she wasn't at school or studying, Danielle began to take control of her father's household. "I ran his house," she revealed to *Woman's Day* in 1990, "made his appointments, took care of everything. I thought that was what I was supposed to do." It would also teach Danielle good organizational skills. She later commented that by running her father's house, she "learned to economize on time and minimize physical effort."

Unfortunately, their relationship was far from reciprocal in terms of care and concern.

Danielle was almost completely deaf in her right ear and was always sickly. She went through a series of hospitalizations for a variety of ailments. She had asthma and allergies, and, at age twelve, contracted polio. She would later confide in her second husband that she was often sick and alone in the hospital. And, although her bout with polio was relatively mild, it did affect her back, which necessitated three years of intensive physical therapy. Even her vacations were punctuated with illness. At fifteen, while on a trip, she got hepatitis from something she ate.

Given Danielle's own parental role models, it's no wonder that in nearly two-thirds of her novels, the heroine's parents are somehow persona non grata, ending up either dead or in conflict with the main characters. If family does appear, as in *Thurston House* or *Daddy*, the plot often revolves around the mother abandoning her child (or children) and relinquishing control to the father.

A case in point is Danielle's 1980 novel, *Loving*. Heroine Bettina Daniels's mother dies when the girl is only four years old, leaving Bettina alone with her father, Justin. Through the years, Bettina begins to manage the household for Justin, who is a successful writer.

In what could almost be a description of her own sad childhood, Danielle wrote about Bettina's father:

> He had failed her and hurt her, he had forgotten to be at school for almost every important moment, had never shown up for a race or a play. He had assured her that young people were boring, and dragged her along with his friends instead. He had hurt her over the years, mainly in the pursuit of his own shimmering dreams. It never occurred to him that she had a right to a childhood, and picnics and beaches, birthday parties and afternoons in the park.

Still, by page twenty-seven, Justin dies of a heart attack, leaving a nineteen-year-old Bettina free to pursue her own writing career.

Besides her characterizations, Danielle has also tended to overlook her parents in book dedications. In thirty-two novels printed to date, only one mentions her mother (along with fifteen other people) and two her father (again, not alone).

Danielle graduated from Lycée Français when she was nearly fifteen, in what would have been her junior year of high school. She told her second husband that she scored "very high" on college boards, but at that time was most interested in making fashion her career.

In 1963, Danielle began her studies at the prestigious Parsons School of Design in New York City, bent, she would tell several interviewers, on becoming "the new Coco Chanel."

Frank Rizzo, the current chairman of fashion design at Parsons, was a teacher there in 1963. Although neither Rizzo nor David O. Levy, then director of admissions at Parsons, who is now chairman and president of the Corcoran Museum of Art and School of Art in Washington, D.C., remembered Danielle, they did recall the rigor of the program.

"Parsons was in a little jewel of a warehouse on East 54th [Street]," Rizzo remembered. "It was a big building, a quarter of a block long near the river . . . but an incredible environment with people who had this thirst for knowledge. It was still small and very private, although the amount of talent coming in was just astounding. The classes were tiny, so there was a lot of real contact between the professional staff and the student body."

In those days, Rizzo said, Parsons was strictly a three-year certificate course. If students wanted a bachelor's degree, they took liberal-arts courses at New York University. Parsons was tough to get into even then, and applicants were required to submit a portfolio of their work, which didn't have much to do with fashion. "It was more about doing collages of color and cut-out shapes, and going through current magazines and pulling out a wardrobe to see how you put things together," explained Rizzo, who said that each applicant also had a personal interview with the chair of the department.

"We deliberately kept enrollment small," said Rizzo, "selecting around seventy students. Of the seventy who started, you were lucky to get twenty to twenty-five who graduated."

"The fashion design department at Parsons was murderous," Levy confirmed. "The dropout was huge, and if you didn't drop out, the chances were they threw you out. This is a field [fashion design] in which the survival rate is very, very low. The chair back then decided she was going to make the department as hard or harder than the field."

For students like Danielle, the days were long and arduous. Classes started at nine A.M. and ended at four P.M., although most students would stay until six or seven at least four days a week. And always, always, there was competition.

Danielle's sojourn at Parsons lasted less than a year. She would develop a stomach ulcer and decide to leave the program on her own, enrolling instead at New York University.

However brief her studies in fashion design, they would come back to help Danielle with her own sense of style as well as in her writing. Danielle Steel heroines are traditionally fashion conscious, decked out in the latest from Dior or Chanel.

In the winter of 1963, her father married for the second time, taking as his bride a lovely Japanese woman named Kuniko Nakamura, whom Danielle adored. From the beginning, she would describe Kuniko as a "ray of joy and sunshine" in an otherwise-difficult household. An artist herself, Kuniko was interested in intellectual pursuits, unlike Danielle's own mother, Norma, who wasn't particularly scholarly. Danielle would later report that her father used to say Norma "knew about World War II only when the hemlines changed."

Danielle began her own university career as a French literature major with a minor in Italian, living at home rather than in the dorms at NYU. And, since she was dating someone who had already graduated from college in California, even her love interest was far removed from the campus.

Danielle dropped out of NYU about four months before she graduated. "It drove her parents crazy that she was that close and didn't finish," reported her second husband. "Danielle always told me she got the education out of it and didn't need the diploma."

In years to come, however, Danielle would find she still had more to learn.

4

இ

*D*anielle's first love came into her life when she was only fourteen. Claude-Eric Lazard was eight years her senior, the somber youngest son of an international banking family. They were reportedly introduced by friends.

At five foot ten, Claude-Eric towered over Danielle's five-foot-one stature, forcing her to look up to him in more ways than one. A brown-haired, brown-eyed French aristocrat, Claude-Eric was educated in Paris at the Lycée Louis le Grand, and at that time was about to graduate from Stanford University in California, with a major in economics.

Characterized by friends as "intense and very private," Claude-Eric had lived off campus at Stanford and was not a member of any fraternity. He was, however, appointed to the Fundamental Standard Commission, whose purpose was "to educate students about fundamental standard and the honor code." Later newspaper and magazine articles would depict him as "conservative and reclusive."

After graduating from Stanford, Claude-Eric enrolled in Columbia University, where he received a master's in business administration, soon thereafter going to work at Bankers Trust Company in New York City.

By all accounts, Claude-Eric was a "good catch." His father, Claude Lazard, was the son of a former partner of the international banking firm of Lazard Frères of Paris, and his mother, Esther, was the daughter of Sidney M. Ehrman, a San Francisco attorney and University of California regent, respected as both an art patron and a philanthropist. Esther's maternal grandfather was Isais W. Hellman, who, in the early 1900s, was labeled "the richest man in California."

In addition to a spectacular mansion on the rue de Varenne in Paris, whose facade of the house was reportedly so historically significant that art lovers from all over the world would come to see it, the Lazards owned the Château de la Couharde, a country estate about thirty-five miles outside of Paris, and later a home on Telegraph Hill in San Francisco.

On Claude-Eric's mother's side, the Ehrmans were a pillar of California society. They owned a mansion next to the historic Presidio in San Francisco, and a 1,977-acre estate in Lake Tahoe on Sugar Pine Point, complete with a mile and a half of beachfront on Meek Bay. In 1932, Claude-Eric's parents were married by Catholic Archbishop Edward J. Hanna at the Ehrman mansion in what was termed in newspaper accounts "the most brilliant wedding of the social season."

A first lieutenant in the French army, Claude Lazard saw action against the Germans in World War II as part of the Brenton regiment of motorized cavalry. When France fell, he joined the Free French forces and eventually became an officer in the U.S. Army. In the meantime, Esther and their children had escaped France just ahead of the invading Germans and made their way from Bilbao, Spain, back to San Francisco. In the United States, she was chairman of American Relief for France and one of only 1,277 Americans awarded Britain's King's Medal for war service in the cause of freedom.

Indeed, Danielle was impressed with the Lazard family and would later intersperse episodes in her World War II–era books like *Crossings* that were similar to those experienced by Claude and Esther.

For example, a *San Francisco Chronicle* article from 1946 talks about Esther Lazard, an American heiress from San Francisco, being in France with her husband "until his troops went into action against the invading Germans. She escaped [with her children] to America after harrowing experiences." Similarly, Liane de Villiers, Danielle's heroine in *Crossings*, is an American heiress from San Francisco, married to a French diplomat who stays behind to help his country during World War II. After the German army overruns Paris, Liane and her children are spirited out of the country through "back roads in a borrowed car with their headlights off," writes Danielle, and whisked aboard a freighter bound for New York.

From the beginning, Danielle seemed to have liked Claude-Eric's parents more than she liked her own. The Lazards, she would say, made her feel not as lonely, almost like a younger daughter. Danielle would also reveal that the senior Claude Lazard and his namesake son had trouble getting along and the father usually took Danielle's side.

Claude-Eric and Danielle courted, officially and unofficially, for nearly four years. It was during this time that she went through one of her most devastating illnesses. At sixteen, doctors discovered a tumor on her ovary. Surgery to remove the tumor revealed cancer, and Danielle lost her left ovary.

Sadly, once again Danielle's parents demonstrated little support for their daughter. She would divulge to socialite columnist Pat Montandon in a 1981 article in *Scene* magazine that at age sixteen she was "very ill and hospitalized for months. All during that time, my parents never once came to see me."

Claude-Eric, on the other hand, was very attentive. She would even tell a *People* magazine reporter in a 1979 article that she thought Claude-Eric "married me because of my illness—he probably felt sorry for me."

The couple announced their engagement in May 1965. San Francisco newspaper accounts of both the engagement and subsequent marriage note that Danielle made her debut in December 1964 at a Greensleeves Cotillion at the Delmonico Hotel in New York. It was evidently a cotillion of little importance because it wasn't covered by any of the big-city newspapers, nor was it remembered by the Junior League, the *Social Register*, or even the New-York Historical Society.

Then, on September 25, 1965, guests from Europe and the States gathered for the morning wedding of Claude-Eric and Danielle at the stately St. Ignatius Loyola Roman Catholic Church on New York City's chic Upper East Side.

The *San Francisco Examiner* account of the wedding noted that the bride, who was given in marriage by her father, "wore a very feminine gown of white organdy, styled with an empire waistline and ruffles at the cuffs and around the neckline. [A] Tiera [sic] of ruffles formed her train, which began at the shoulders. A white organdy pill-box held her tulie [sic] veil, and she carried a bouquet of lily of the valley, gardenias and white tea roses." Danielle's mother was never mentioned.

Danielle chose as her matron of honor Florence de Lavalette, Claude-Eric's sister, and two friends from Lycée Français as her attendants, all bedecked in beige silk dresses with matching organdy hats and carrying red roses entwined with ivy. Claude-Eric's brother-in-law, Bernard de Lavalette, served as best man, while his older brother Sidney, then an ABC newsman, was an usher. The Lazards' older sister, Christine, an acclaimed artist who was married to André Paul Peyromaure de Bord, and grandfather, Sidney Ehrman, were in San Francisco and missed the nuptials.

They selected the quietly elegant Hotel Carlyle for their wedding reception, which included a sit-down dinner. It was the same hotel that Danielle would mention in many of her novels.

Asked why she wed so young, Danielle would laugh to a reporter in years to come that some people thought she was getting married because she was already pregnant. "I wasn't pregnant, contrary to what everybody was hoping to discover at the wedding," Danielle told *Women's Wear Daily*. "As we were standing in the receiving line, I remember hearing these two old bags say, 'I want to see her in three months.' "

Then the bride, who had just turned eighteen, and her twenty-six-year-old groom flew to San Francisco to begin an extended honeymoon that would also take them to Venice and Paris.

According to a source close to the family, Claude-Eric and his bride moved first into the Stanhope Hotel on Fifth Avenue, then to a series of Manhattan apartments before finally settling in an elegant, eight-room co-op on 655 Park Avenue, which they decorated with French antiques that had belonged to the Lazard family. A friend of Danielle's would depict the flat as "terribly grand in the Old World way. It was," she said, "done in pale yellow brocades . . . and filled with pale yellow roses and fresh-cut flowers. Totally other worldish."

Mona Skager, an acquaintance of Danielle's from both New York and San Francisco, remembered attending cocktail parties at the Park Avenue co-op. "The apartment was beautiful," recalled Skager, who now writes films freelance and is a real-estate broker in California. "It was one of those Park Avenue numbers with high ceilings; a little formal. I don't remember any spectacular view, but it was in a great location."

As the wife of a wealthy banker, Danielle led a hectic life, traveling constantly. For a while, she tried to keep up her work at NYU, but dropped out four months before she would have graduated.

Danielle found herself married to a man she would characterize to others as strange, solitary, and lonely. Using Danielle for verbal target practice became second nature, she would say.

Claude-Eric was also reportedly frugal. A source close to the family (and confirmed by Danielle's third husband, who met the jeweler) said it was Danielle who picked out her own eight-carat diamond-and-emerald ring before their wedding, after finally convincing Claude-Eric that it was a good investment.

Because of Claude-Eric's family, Danielle had homes in Paris and San Francisco, as well as their own apartment in New York City. "I was very bored and disenchanted with the comfortable world I grew up in," Danielle said. "I saw the hypocrisy."

It would be the kind of existence she could describe with authenticity in *Summer's End*, in which her heroine, Deanna Duras, is dominated by her husband, Marc-Edouard, a rich French businessman who takes away her identity as a person.

Danielle would write:

And by then she understood what she had done. She had married a country as well as a man. A way of life. She would have to be perfect, understanding—and silent. She would have to be charming and entertain his clients and friends. She would have to be lonely when he traveled. And she would have to give up the dream of making a name for herself with her art. Marc didn't really approve.

Similarly, in another Steel classic, A *Perfect Stranger*, the beautiful Raphaella de Mornay-Malle y de Santos y Quadral marries an elderly multimillionaire. "What was wrong with her?" Raphaella would ask herself. "Why was she suddenly chafing at those traditions? The other women she knew in Paris and Madrid and Barcelona, they had the parties, and the amusements, and the gala events that made the years drift by."

"Noblesse oblige" was a concept that she knew well. In *Passion's Promise*, Danielle wrote:

The words meant "Nobility obliges"; she'd grown up with it all of her life. The obligation to keep your chin up, no matter who sawed off your legs at the knee; the ability to serve tea with the roof coming down around your ears; the charm of developing an ulcer while wearing a smile. Noblesse oblige.

She was also reportedly beginning to bubble and boil internally over the control her husband exerted over every aspect of her life. "It was like he was the father figure and she was the little girl. She needed permission for everything," her second husband said about her relationship with Claude-Eric. Danielle supposedly had to ask Claude-Eric if she could do simple things like open a window, and also had to justify every dollar she spent. Sometimes, she said, he would withhold permission just to taunt her.

Once, for a six-week period of time, Danielle went to work as a sales clerk in a fashionable ladies' store for five dollars an hour, but would confess to spending all of her income on clothes before she brought home the check. At another point she tried tutoring in French, but gave that up as well.

Danielle spent a good part of her time in San Francisco, staying with Grandpa Ehrman, whom she "adored." Grandpa Ehrman would be described to friends "as more like her father than her real father." He, too, would later find himself woven into the chapters of Danielle's fiction.

Charles Flowers, one of her longtime writer friends from New York and California, recalled visiting with Danielle at the huge Ehrman mansion at the edge of the Presidio, overlooking the bay.

"We walked into this house, which was enormous," Flowers remembered.

"You came to a winding staircase and looked up three stories to a skylight. Looking to one side or the other, the rooms were like Henry James novels because they were so huge, with groups of chairs to sit in and early Italian Renaissance paintings on the walls. They were ballroom-size rooms with lots of red velvet. We went through this grand house, which had four- or five-room apartments for each of the family members to use when they came to visit. Then we got up to the top floor and in this tiny room, sitting in his wheelchair, watching a small black-and-white television set, was old Mr. Ehrman. Across from him in the kitchenette was his nurse, making some appalling concoction of cold cereal, banana, and honey. He was very old at that time. It was the most extraordinary scene to go through that grand house and come up to these rooms. He was sharp as could be, although physically debilitated, very funny and charming, and kind to me and to her. We sat there in this little room, talking about the world and looking out all over San Francisco. I don't know [her] books well enough to guess where he appears, but I'm sure his traits appear often in characters."

As does the house.

In her 1983 best-seller, *Thurston House*, Jeremiah Thurston builds a Nob Hill mansion for his new bride; it is described as "a veritable palace, with a stained-glass dome gracing the central part of the house over the main hall."

Happily, in 1967, Danielle discovered she was pregnant. In the 1984 book *Having a Baby*, Danielle would reveal that she "felt nauseated in the evening," and would "gain roughly fifteen pounds with the pregnancy." Many years after the birth, in a *Ladies' Home Journal* article, Danielle would detail an experience that stuck in her mind from that time:

> I stood on a street corner in New York, seven months pregnant, pigtails framing a childlike face, and a cabbie shrieked to a stop, sneering and shouting, "What happened to you, sweetheart, ya get raped?" . . . and raced off again. Even though his words were coarse, his attitude was not that unusual. It was the late sixties, a time when it was no longer considered fashionable to have babies.

5

༄

The year 1968 was one of intense political upheaval in America. It saw the assassinations of both Martin Luther King and Bobby Kennedy. It was also a year of personal upheaval for Danielle.

Just twenty years old, she became what she always wanted to be: a mother. A dark-haired, seven-pound, fourteen-ounce daughter slipped into Danielle's world at 4:13 A.M. on January 10. Danielle would later write about this first birth: "They gave me scopolamine and several other drugs, and I remember absolutely nothing, except waking up feeling like hell, with a baby and double vision." And, although she didn't discuss it publicly, she was also feeling pangs of guilt, she would tell a subsequent husband, for not having produced a male heir for Claude-Eric.

Four days after the birth, Danielle and baby Beatrix returned to their Park Avenue co-op. From the beginning, a nanny was hired to help care for the baby. In *Having a Baby*, Danielle remembered coming home and suffering from "a little postpartum depression. I mean I wasn't in a black funk, but, looking back, I don't think I was ecstatic either," she wrote. "For one thing, I really never got to have the baby. I had been through this major experience alone, barely got to hold the baby, never got to share her with my husband, and then I went home and gave her up to a nurse who took over."

Although Danielle remembered being appreciative of the nurse's knowledge and skills, she wrote that "there were also times when I felt shut out by her. Or perhaps because of my own ignorance about babies, I knew so little that I took a backseat to everything and the nurse almost became the baby's mother, and it was only when she left us that I really came to know my child."

Expressing remorse at what she missed, Danielle concluded, "But I was a baby myself and knew nothing about my own baby. And what I lacked most of all was self-confidence."

Not surprisingly, Danielle was ripe for new experiences. While on a trip to San Francisco several months later, she was watching "The Tonight Show" when two guests came on who would help change her life.

Danielle would later talk about watching Johnny Carson interview two young women who had started a public relations/promotion firm called Supergirls. It was the kind of excitement Danielle craved: two young women marketing their energy and creativity, doing "anything as long as it's legal." Intrigued, Danielle called the Supergirls office in New York the next morning to apply for a job.

Claudia Jessup and Genie Chipps-Henderson, founders of Supergirls, both remembered that first call.

"She saw us talking about our business when we were on 'The Tonight Show' with Johnny Carson, and called the very next morning to ask if she could work for us," remembered Jessup, who is now a successful novelist living in Santa Fe, writing under the pen name Meredith Rich. "We didn't need any more employees and told her so. But she wrote a long letter listing her qualifications and strengths and kept bombarding us with phone calls. We finally agreed to see her just to get her off our backs."

Genie Chipps-Henderson, of East Hampton, New York, another successful author who writes novels under the pen name Georgia Hampton, saw it as a time when women were coming out of their 1950s shells. "Millions of women had come through college, gotten jobs at entry-level positions, and dropped out in the sixties. This wasn't Danielle's style. She thought one should be doing something more fun, something more amazing, and Johnny Carson made us seem all the more glamorous," Chipps-Henderson believed.

She, too, remembered Danielle's persistence: "We got letters from Danielle, postmarked from all over the world. I suppose she was traveling quite a bit with Claude-Eric."

Finally, Jessup and Chipps-Henderson met with Danielle in person and were so impressed with her energy and enthusiasm that they hired her to fill in temporarily while an employee went on vacation.

"Danielle had . . . astonishing energy, and a high metabolism: about five feet tall and eighty-five pounds," Jessup recalled. "She had very short hair when she first came to work at Supergirls, and she reminded me a bit of the young Audrey Hepburn, with her large eyes and diminutive frame."

Jane James, who started working for Supergirls a year later, also remembered her as a person of tremendous energy. "She sort of never stopped," said James, now an executive recruiter in New York. "I was never quite sure of all that she was doing, but it just seemed to be terribly important. She was an ongoing bubble of energy."

From the start, the Supergirls knew Claude-Eric was less than pleased with Danielle's new position because she couldn't use her married name, becoming instead Danielle Steel. In *Supergirls*, a book Jessup and Chipps-Henderson wrote in 1972, they said:

> Danielle was married to one of those wealthy, prestigious, and familied French who like to keep their grand old names out of places with suspect names like Supergirls. So, in the beginning, Danielle had a bit of a thing with names. To business people she was Danielle Steel, and to personal people she was her married name.

Jessup and Chipps-Henderson also wrote that Danielle was the last person who needed to work. "Her weekly florist bill came to more than her salary, and the amount she paid her daughter's nanny was more than she could ever hope to earn at Supergirls."

"I think if you look at her whole life, it started with coming through the door at Supergirls," said Chipps-Henderson. "It was a giant step out of what had been preordained for her. She had the child and the husband and all the trappings of this life, and suddenly she goes to work for this kooky agency down the street. In a way, this was an amazing thing for her to do. She had to reach to get out from under them, and then take the next step and the next."

Danielle approached her new duties with unbridled enthusiasm and arrived each morning dressed impeccably. "Unlike many petite people who are often described as cute or pert, Danielle was elegant: her hair and makeup were always perfect," Jessup said. Danielle, she said, wore "only black or white" and was accessorized perfectly. "She was so tiny that she had trouble finding clothes that fit properly. I'm sure she had a lot of things made, but once she bought a fur coat from Bloomingdale's children's department," Jessup remembered.

Supergirl Jane James, too, saw Danielle as a woman with a unique flair for fashion. Arriving a bit early once for a party at Danielle's, James said she found her in the bathtub. "We sat and chatted while she finished her bath," James said. "She was terribly calm about this ensuing party. Then I followed her into her bedroom, chatting about whatever, to select what she was going to wear. She had a gob-full of clothes, but sort of pawed through a whole pile of things, very undecided. Meanwhile, the doorbell is ringing and people were kind of filing in, and she was still standing in her bedroom trying to make her decision on clothes. Finally, she pulled out some sort of black, fringed shawl, which she proceeded to use as a skirt. She wrapped it around herself and crossed it over on the side. In those days it was the fashion to have these clip-on bows on your shoes. She pulled a couple of these clip-on bows off her shoes and put them on this shawl that is now a skirt, kind of on sideways, fastened it with a belt, put on a blouse, and looked as if she had just slipped on the latest creation from Bergdorf's. Then she put what looked like a cheap plastic ring on one hand while she had an eight-carat diamond ring from Claude-Eric on the other hand. Her ability to just pull things together—it was a sense of style that I, at that time, did not know about or have. It was a sense of sophistication that I was not used to at that age."

As Supergirls had more titles than money, they named Danielle director of public relations and vice president in charge of marketing. She went to work using her contacts and cultivating more to bring business into the firm. In their book, the authors noted:

> She carried the Supergirls gospel to Big Business shrines with a religious zeal. In fact, every once in a while, when Genie and I were about to see a client, with Danielle in tow, she would slink into the office like a guilty dog and allow as how this particular client "somehow has the impression that I own the business." "We were not," she said, "to be upset if he directed all the questions to her."

In addition to her ability to bring in new clients, the Supergirls remembered Danielle's organizational abilities. "Danielle was always extremely organized," Jessup said. "In order to keep her work and private life in order, she was a compulsive list-maker. She would fill one notebook page with myriad lists, in a different color ink for each category. As she accomplished something, she crossed it out, in its proper color ink. She *never* went on to a new page until the old page was so crammed full that there was no more space to write, or until every last item on each list had been seen to.

"Danielle was on top of everything," Jessup continued. "She sent thank-you notes after business appointments, and flowers for social occasions. She was very thorough, and also thoughtful and generous.

"Once when we were celebrating landing a particularly big account, she breezed out of the office, which was only a couple of blocks from her apartment, and returned with two bottles of Bordeaux, 'borrowed' from her husband's wine cellar. The wine happened to be Chateau Lafite-Rothschild, which has been described as 'the wine for intelligent millionaires.' "

James, too, remembered Danielle's generosity. "Danielle could meet somebody on the street and say, 'Hi, how are you?' and send flowers and a thank-you for meeting them on the street. Her flower bill was more than my rent."

For Danielle, the day would start with a call to a nearby coffee shop for a delivery of coffee and rolls. She would reorder from the shop at various times during the day, even ordering up, on occasion, a pack of Marlboro cigarettes. Used to being waited on, Danielle considered it tacky to bring in her own food.

"She chain-smoked, and with her constant energy, she was always in motion, typing a mile a minute or talking on the phone in a rapid mix of French and English," said Jessup. "She was also into needlepointing at the time, and needlepointed pillows as fast as Madame Defarge could knit. She even made little items to brighten the Supergirls office, such as pencil holders and coasters."

Since it was a small office (only five people), each person was asked to take a turn at cleaning up. Jessup reported in their book that "Danielle's idea of cleaning the office was to breeze out the door, then run back in with a pseudo-earnest wail: 'My God, I forgot. Today's my day!' Then she would stay long enough to dump one ashtray into a wastebasket before rushing out in total satisfaction."

Chipps-Henderson recalled that "the phone seemed to grow out of her ear. She interviewed, wrote letters, always on the phone. She was either making client calls or making plans for a dinner party."

Even then, Danielle was attached to manual typewriters. In *Supergirls*, the authors wrote:

One thing we never figured out about Danielle was her obsession with typewriters. When she first came to work for us, we had three machines, and she never failed to change typewriters, always in utmost urgency, at least several times a day. There was never any particular pattern to her quirk. She would just go up to someone and say, "How much longer are you going to be typing? I need to do this up." Then she would stand there, tapping her foot and breathing down her prey's neck, while another typewriter would be sitting idle.

Although both Jessup and Chipps-Henderson said Danielle wasn't doing creative writing at that point, she did type her own letters and reports. "It would be shooting out of the typewriter," Chipps-Henderson recalled with a laugh. "How she got to be such a good typist, I'll never know. She was ten times more efficient and faster than anyone I know."

Because of Danielle's ability with languages, the Supergirls decided to take advantage of her skills by contacting the foreign consulates. In their book, the authors said:

Danielle wrote one of her perky little letters to each place. In its own language. In one day flat, she whisked off letters in French, Spanish, Italian, and Japanese (her stepmother was Japanese). We were all so pleased.

The first response came from the Italian Consulate. They sent her letter back with three grammatical errors rudely circled in red. Attached was a snippy note, "If you are going to write us in our own language, please write it correctly." And to think that these *villani* were supposed to be diplomatic. Danielle's ego was so desperately bruised that we all rallied around, making elaborate plans to blanket their courtyard with pasta. But she insisted on sending them a ladylike apology, which may have done her sense of honor some good, but it brought in no further reply from the Italians.

In 1969, after their initial onslaught of publicity, Supergirls was struggling to make a profit. They needed a new direction. While previously they had taken whatever jobs came in, Supergirls decided now to concentrate on working for companies. Cuts in pay were also in order, and Danielle agreed to work for less base but to get a commission on business she brought into the firm.

Still, it wasn't always easy, even with Danielle's connections and tenacity. In their book, the authors recalled giving Danielle the title of "Executive in Charge of Drumming Up New Clients." "Every morning armed with a few Supergirls press clippings and an off-the-cuff presentation, Danielle would set out to dazzle Big Business. Every afternoon, she would stagger back," they wrote.

But Danielle was always looking for business. At a dinner party one night in the summer of 1969, she met Fred R. Smith, the new editor of *American Home*, who was in the process of rebuilding a staff. Danielle was there with the answer to his interim problems: hire Supergirls.

Smith, now successfully retired but still writing free-lance articles for publications like *Smithsonian* magazine, remembered those days: "These were pretty connected kids in their early twenties . . . well-heeled," Smith said. "They knew an awful lot of people. Danielle was full of beans. She was coming up with all sorts of ideas when we needed to do a party or scout out new locations."

Although Smith said she didn't write for the magazine, he did see her writing in the form of memos. "Any time she wrote a memo, it went on for thirty pages," he said. "It was not always the most grammatically correct, but it would be full of ideas and suggestions.

"She once wrote for me what she considered a path I should follow for editorial and social success," remembered Smith, who had come to *American*

Home from notable stints at *Sports Illustrated* and *Life* magazines. "I ignored it completely," he laughed.

Her personal experiences with *American Home* would also serve as grist for a later Danielle Steel novel, *Mixed Blessings*, where one heroine, Samantha, is senior editor for a magazine called *Today's Home*.

At the same time, Danielle won the notice of another publisher, John Mack Carter, then with *Ladies' Home Journal*. "She met him through making sales calls," said Chipps-Henderson. "He was captivated by her, and employed her and Supergirls to do a whole press thing. It was billed through Supergirls, but this was her baby."

In later years, Danielle would credit Carter, on numerous occasions, with starting her on a path to writing. In a *Contemporary Authors* interview in November 1985, Danielle would tell interviewer Jean Ross that she came to writing through her PR and advertising work. "I had done some writing," Danielle told *Contemporary Authors*, "and the editor of *Good Housekeeping*, John Mack Carter (he was at *Ladies' Home Journal* then), encouraged me. He was one of our clients (at Supergirls). He suggested that I should try writing a book and I did."

Modestly, Carter takes credit for "shoving" Danielle into writing. "Giving someone a shove deserves credit but only a limited amount of credit," Carter said. "I shove a lot of people."

Carter remembered Danielle as a "super facilitator. At the time she was not writing, but she was getting the job done. She did some research. She didn't do the final writing, but out of that, talking with her and knowing how she did the research, you knew that here was a very lively individual who had these passions and convictions and enthusiasm which made fascinating copy whether she was writing a simple research report or writing to explain one of her projects. I remember suggesting that one of the first things she should get into is writing verse and poetry because of the emotion she was putting into her work. I thought poetry would capture this and give her a chance to explore that, give her a chance to begin to put her passions on paper. This was an easy form for her because it doesn't take five thousand words. You can rearrange fifty words until they come out. Most people can't do that. She could do that and did do that."

Although Carter said he didn't predict the tremendous success Danielle would later have as a novelist, he did know from the beginning that she was a person "who was going to get it done. Getting it done is the hardest part of writing."

But what Danielle wanted most at this juncture was a stake in the Supergirls' business. "She wanted to become a co-owner," Jessup recalled. "Her husband, she reported, thought it was déclassé for her to work for someone else. But Genie and I had conceived and started Supergirls together. Although it would have been nice to a have a bit of Danielle's capital injected into the business, Genie and I decided that, in our case, two was a company, and three owners would be a crowd. We turned down her offer, and I think it pissed her off, although outwardly she took it graciously. In years since, however, she's said in magazine interviews that she once owned a P. R. agency in New York called Supergirls. Oh, well."

While Danielle's career was taking new directions, so was her personal life. "She seemed to be happily married in the beginning, but he had an Old World attitude," Chipps-Henderson believed. "He really controlled her. And to control Danielle, who bubbled up at all times with energy and enthusiasm, wasn't all that easy." Chipps-Henderson said she met Claude-Eric on several occasions and thought he was "charming."

Danielle told the *Los Angeles Times* in 1988 that the transition was hard for Claude-Eric. "It's like if you buy a puppy not quite knowing what it is and you take it home and it turns out to be a giraffe. When we met, I was going to school. I was very well behaved. And then I did everything to the poor man but grow two heads."

Danielle repeated the same message to *Women's Wear Daily* in 1986, saying: "I changed so radically between the ages of seventeen and twenty-one. My great act of defiance came when he'd [Claude-Eric] been away for a month or two. He came back and said, 'Open the Window,' and I said, 'No. I won't,' and thought that I'd invented the wheel. I got sent to my room a lot."

What she didn't say then, but would be repeated by Danielle to husbands, in-laws, and friends over the next decade was that Claude-Eric was also not as attracted to her as she wanted. "Danielle said she tried everything to please him . . . gaining weight, losing weight, dressing differently, switching perfumes, complying with everything . . . and still it [their marriage] was all a bad joke," said her second husband.

At the same time, Danielle was crazy about her daughter. Jessup said she would jokingly refer to Beatrix as "the Beast" or "Beastie." Chipps-Henderson, too, described Danielle as "a wonderful mother. The child just adored her. I remember her [Beatie] racing in from the park and right to her mother's arms."

By all accounts, Beatie was a darling, pixyish child with big brown eyes and pretty brown hair. Still, unlike what she did with future children, Danielle didn't spend much time with Beatie during her early years. In the foreword she wrote to the book *After Having a Baby*, Danielle would reveal her guilt over missing Beatie's early years. "When Beatrix was born I wasn't working yet, but got a job within the first year. I traveled a great deal, and was out a lot, and I was also very young, so more outwardly directed than I am now. And I felt guilty about it even then, but I don't think it affected her as much as I feared."

Following a bout with a kidney disorder that Beatie would undergo, Danielle saw the unhappiness of her marital situation come to a head. She would separate, although not legally, from Claude-Eric in 1970.

Both Jessup and Chipps-Henderson said they did little "socially" with Danielle, but even then they sensed she was "in love with romance."

"She read romances by the trillion—one of her favorite writers at the time was Georgette Heyer," Jessup recalled.

Jessup also remembered what she called "a great deal of marital unrest around the Supergirls office, and Danielle joined right in. I was not part of it because I was still a newlywed and Genie was still single."

On this, too, Chipps-Henderson concurred. "I think she was madly in love her whole life. She pours it into the romance of her books where her heroine always meets the love of her life."

Chipps-Henderson remembered that Danielle was always getting strange phone calls from people who were from every known walk of life. "People were banging at the door in love with her." Chipps-Henderson also said Danielle had many "gentlemen callers" who would send her flowers and candy. "Her life seemed to be bubbling with romantic intrigue at all times."

The decade of the 1970s became one of new beginnings for Danielle.

Having taken John Mack Carter at his word, Danielle had acquired an agent. In 1982, Danielle would tell Loretta Noffsinger, a reporter for the Associated Press, that her "first manuscript, composed at twenty-two, was single-spaced with no paragraph indentations and little punctuation." Her first agent, she said, "told me to go home and learn how to cook. I never did learn how to cook."

"Danielle said this agent let her work sit for over three months and then told her the book wouldn't sell. He said she should go home and have more kids," said one old friend. "Then she matched up with Phyllis Westberg, and that's when she sold her first book."

That book was *Going Home*, which was written during the summer of 1971, when Danielle took Beatrix and left New York for San Francisco. She told *People* magazine in 1979 that she holed up for three months to finish the book. "The concept was that every woman falls in love with a bastard at least once in her life," she said.

"When she came back, she no longer wanted to work for us," Chipps-Henderson said. "She was in love with somebody, a very sort of serious romance with somebody."

Danielle herself would describe her romance in the most general terms to her second husband, saying he left her after a few months to marry someone else, which hurt her deeply.

"She told me that the guy left her on a street corner one day, saying he was going to marry someone else," her second husband relates. "He said something like Danielle could take hard knocks better than the other girl."

Danielle turned in the *Going Home* manuscript in January 1972. Initially, she would receive just $3,500 for her book, which was bought by Pocket Books, a division of Simon and Schuster. Published in October 1973, it marked the first and only time one of her published novels was written in the first person. It wasn't one of her favorites, and Danielle told her second husband that the book was revised so many times, she hardly recognized it as her own.

The story of a single mother who leaves the security of New York for the freedom of San Francisco to start a new life, *Going Home* marked Danielle's official separation from Claude-Eric. In the book she writes a description of her character Gillian Forrester's ex-husband, Richard, coming to pick up their daughter for a visit. Interestingly, the description in her book bears a striking resemblance to Claude-Eric.

> . . . he arrived promptly at two-ten, looking painfully neat and well put-together in a dark gray suit, with a navy and white striped tie, white shirt, and highly polished black shoes. It was an odd feeling to watch him come in the door and realize that this had been the man I had been married to and had once gone home to the end of each day. He seemed like someone from another world. And I suppose I did too. I was no longer the Gillian he had known.

On January 10, 1972, Danielle staged a festive party, complete with a magician, for Beatrix's fourth birthday. The next day, she left her child in New York and headed again to San Francisco for a month, this time to do research on a mystery novel she wanted to write.

With her typical enthusiasm and energy, Danielle spent countless hours with police detectives in the Bay Area, trying to capture a sense of how they worked to portray them in her novel. Titled *In the Fog*, the book was centered around a policeman solving a murder mystery. It would become the first of five books that Danielle was not able to get published.

She stayed for nearly a month, returning to New York determined to change her life by making a permanent move to San Francisco.

On June 28, 1972, Danielle legally separated from Claude-Eric although they had been living apart for nearly two years. In the agreement, Danielle would gain custody of Beatrix and live in their Park Avenue co-op. Claude-Eric would also provide both child support and alimony, although he reportedly wasn't at all pleased about the prospect of divorce. Danielle told future husbands that Claude-Eric would suffer from the "Catholic guilt that stems from divorce."

Danielle continued to fly back and forth to San Francisco, researching and writing. She garnered a commission from *San Francisco* magazine for a nonfiction article on a group of street musicians called the San Francisco Strutters (eventually published in July 1973), and continued to write her poetry, selling poems and articles to both *Cosmopolitan* and *Ladies' Home Journal*. In a 1986 interview, Danielle would reveal that those writing assignments weren't always fun. "I did a thing for *Cosmo*, 'The 40 Most Prevalent Sexual Hang-ups of Women'; I hated things like that," she said.

And then, once again, Danielle's body sent her life into a tailspin. She discovered a lump in her left breast.

6

_____

ào

*H*aving gone through lengthy hospital stays with polio, hepatitis, pneumonia, and losing an ovary to cancer, Danielle was panicked over finding the lump. Even though her doctor wanted to operate immediately to remove it and perform a biopsy, Danielle put him off. Instead, in September of 1972, she scheduled a brief trip back to San Francisco. She would tell friends later that she didn't want to think about the lump just then, even though she knew she would have to deal with it when she returned to New York. For now, she just wanted to experience, once again, the roller-coaster hills overlooking the bay in San Francisco.

This time she stayed with the San Francisco Strutters, a group of street musicians she had interviewed earlier that summer for a *San Francisco* magazine article. Living in what Danielle described as a commune with other musicians and writers, the group may have appealed to her need to rebel against the confines of a structured life as a child, a young adult, and a teenage bride. Danielle would later describe herself to her second husband as a "conservative rebel," whose parents considered her a "hippie" because she wanted to be a writer. Even her language and her letters were peppered with four-letter words, another outward manifestation of her rebellion.

A group of three male musicians and a female singer who Danielle would portray in her article as a "tiny blonde dynamo [who] sings and tap-dances on the pavement in high-heeled silver shoes and a 1930s dress," the Strutters were pure jazz and swing. Using the street for their stage, they would set up shop in front of theaters, performing during intermissions. Danielle claimed the group could attract "a mob of two hundred in a matter of moments." Indeed, they also attracted the attention of a production person for a major Hollywood studio and ended up doing brief spots in two movies, *The Conversation* and *The Laughing Policeman*.

With the commune, Danielle could live on the edge without stepping off, reveling in the group's exploits without becoming one of the revelers. More restrained, Danielle was titillated by their freedom, but stopped short of joining in when it came to being "branded" on the thigh with a communal design or even having her ears pierced.

Nonetheless, Danielle had already made the decision to move to San Francisco sometime in 1973. She used the commune as a base from which to look for a place for her and Beatie to live when they returned.

Charles Flowers, a writer friend from New York whose sister, Nancy Eisenbarth, is Danielle's researcher, hailed Danielle's decision to move to San Francisco as very important in terms of her career as a writer. "In New York she had a certain image," Flowers explained. "She was, of course, Claude-Eric's wife, and the daughter of the Schuelein-Steels and had friends from prep school, people coming over from Europe, people who had worked at Supergirls and all that. After the first novel, she decided she had to get away from all those distractions. When she went to San Francisco, she did love the city and did know some people. She had remained close to Claude-Eric's wonderful grandfather. But essentially she had made the decision, I think, that she had to get off to that city where it would be quieter and less expensive and with fewer people she knew so that she could concentrate on her novels and possibly her personal life as well. That was really a tremendous decision. She was leaving the linkage between Europe and America behind, the sort of Paris–New York connection and all that it meant.

"There were friends who thought she would not be able to stick it out," Flowers continued. "They thought after a year or two she would long for the life and companionship in New York City. They didn't realize that the guiding principle in her life was to make those books work, make that career work, and then use that to build the stable, comfortable family life she wanted."

Besides looking for a new home, Danielle also planned to spend time with Bruce Neckels, an actor friend she had met in New York two years earlier. Neckels had gone to prison as a conscientious objector. It was the fall of 1972, and while the last U.S. combat troops had left South Vietnam on August 12, the Vietnam War was still very much alive in the minds of most Americans, and Danielle wanted to interview Bruce for a possible magazine article.

During Neckels's imprisonment, Danielle had written him almost-daily letters of encouragement.

"While I was in prison, she was a real source of emotional survival for me," recalled Neckels, who now lives in Los Angeles and is a writer, producer, and associate director for television. "I probably got one or two letters a day from her during the time I was there. She alone could have kept my spirits and hopes alive."

Although Neckels said the two were never involved romantically, they shared a close friendship. "It was one of those things where we trusted each other and could discuss anything," he said. "It was a sharing of frustrations and loneliness."

In addition, Danielle had been attempting to free Neckels from what she considered an unjust sentence by asking an attorney friend in New York to write to influential people in Washington, D.C.

In September, Neckels had been moved to the U.S. Public Health Service Hospital in San Francisco to complete his sentence by volunteering to be a "human guinea pig" in a research project for NASA. Neckels said the study involved three months of total bed rest so researchers could collect data on bodily functions in an attempt to discover why astronauts lost calcium in space.

While Neckels was in the hospital in November 1972, and Danielle was in San Francisco, she came to see her friend almost every day.

"Even though we had to be in bed, flat on our backs, we could still transfer onto a gurney and sort of paddle around the hallways if we wanted to," Neckels recalled about his hospitalization.

Neckels remembered a prisoner in a neighboring room on the sixth floor, one Danny Eugene Zugelder, wheeling by on his gurney and coming in to find Neckels talking with Danielle.

"After Danielle left," said Neckels, "Danny came by again and said, 'Is that your girlfriend?' Had I known what was going to happen subsequently, I would have said, 'Yes. We're in love. We're engaged and we're going to be married.' But instead, I said, 'No, she's just a good friend of mine.'

"He asked if there was any chance of getting her phone number, and I said, 'I don't want to give out her phone number, but I'll call her and if it's okay with her, then you can call.' So I called Danielle and I said, 'Listen, there's a guy from Lompoc doing a study with me next door and he got a glimpse of you and he would really like to meet you and talk to you. His name is Danny Zugelder and he wants to know if he can call you.' She said, 'Sure, you can give him my number,' and so I did.

"She always came back to see me," Neckels continued. "She would pop over to say hello to him and then leave. After a while, I would pick up the phone to call Danny and talk to him and the line would be busy. I mean it would be busy from like ten at night until two in the morning. They would carry on the longest conversations."

34

According to a letter written in February of 1993 by Danielle's attorney, Charles O. Morgan, Jr., she met Danny while going to see a friend in the hospital. Morgan's letter claims that Danielle didn't know Danny was "on leave" from prison, and that she didn't speak with him until he called her, after getting her number from her friend. Danielle told Morgan that Danny was "pursuing her," all the while "concealing" his past as a "convicted felon."

Before Zugelder left Lompoc for the NASA project, he laughingly told his friends he was going to San Francisco to "find a rich woman and make her fall in love with me." "I'd like to say this [meeting Danielle] was part of my plan, but it wasn't," contended Zugelder. "Out of the clear blue she comes waltzing into the room. Yeah, I actively pursued her."

Wheeling by Neckel's room on a gurney, with his naked chest exposed under a white, hospital sheet, Danny was an impressive sight. At six-foot-six and 220 pounds, the blond-haired, green-eyed Zugelder had lots of chest to expose, including two tattoos that were mementos of his youth: a fly on his left arm and on his right shoulder, a heart, fortuitously etched with two Ds, which were actually a reminder of an adolescent sweetheart.

Just turned twenty-two, Zugelder was serving the second year of a six-year sentence for bank robbery when he volunteered for the NASA research project. He had been at the San Francisco facility for just two months.

More than twenty years later, Zugelder said he still will never forget the day they met face-to-face. "She was beautiful," recalled Zugelder. "Danielle was twenty-four or twenty-five, with the biggest green eyes you ever saw, and when she smiled, well, it just lit up her face. She came in the room and it was like a burst of sunshine."

Zugelder contends that Danielle knew from early on that he was a prisoner. "We talked about it," he said. "Her friend [Bruce Neckels] was a prisoner too. We were all prisoners [in the research project]. I think it really excited her that I was this dangerous person and yet so nice and pleasant," he added.

A self-described loner from a poor family, Zugelder grew up dangerous.

"My real father was a migrant farm worker and an alcoholic," he said. "My mother chased him off after he got drunk, threw me in the middle of a reservoir, and drove off." Only three and a half at the time, Zugelder said he would have "dreams of bubbles and circles, and trying to claw my way to the surface." Wet and muddy, he not only made it out of the water, but even managed to walk home alone. "After my mother saw me," he remembered, "that's when she threw him out."

Zugelder started his criminal career, innocently, at age four, taking toys from a local toy store. And, even though he said his mother made him take those back, she had lost total control of him by age eleven, when he started smoking pot and drinking alcohol.

"I was drinking actually when I was a baby," explained Zugelder. "My . . . father used to put whiskey on my lips."

In his teens, Zugelder moved into more serious crime, stealing cars. "By the time I was thirteen, I had stolen over a hundred cars and burglarized a hundred and fifty homes," he revealed.

At age seventeen he graduated—not from high school, but to robbing banks. "The first bank I ever robbed, I was loaded," he said. "It was lunch hour at high school. I was using marijuana and reds [barbiturates—a depressant] and was making a wine run because I was the only one who looked old enough to buy liquor in a store. I was driving to make the wine run when my car broke down by a shopping plaza. I walked into the grocery store and got a bag out of it, and then I turned around and walked into the bank next door. I wrote them a note that said I had a bomb and if they didn't give me the money, I'd blow them up." Running to a park near the high school, Danny opened the bag and discovered "between $4,700 and $5,400, which was a lot of money back then." But he added, "Still, to this day, I don't know why I did it."

Zugelder said he used the money to buy a car—"a '66 canary-yellow Chevette with black interior and bucket seats"—keeping the purchase a secret from his parents. Of course, for Danny, that wasn't the first time he had a car that he kept a secret from his parents. At age twelve, Danny, who was then approaching six feet in height, stole a '47 Chevrolet that he parked a few blocks from his parents' house. "I'd get up in the morning and ride my bike to the car, put the bike in the trunk, cruise the junior high in the car, and then go to grade school."

Over the next three years, Zugelder admitted to pulling "seventeen to twenty heists," upgrading his sales technique from handwritten notes to dynamite.

"I had a little experience with construction work when I was very young," Zugelder explained. "I would walk into a bank dressed well and carrying a briefcase. I'd sit down with the manager to discuss opening an account under the pretext of starting a subdivision in the mountains. Then, when I saw the dollar signs in the manager's eyes, I'd show him what was in the briefcase." What was in the briefcase was "three sticks of dynamite with a blasting cap and a small nine-volt battery with a wire attached to the blasting cap and the dynamite and a wire attached to the battery with one single wire loose where I could just touch it to the battery to make it explode."

After showing the dynamite package to the bank manager, he would walk the manager into a vault, and they would get the money. "It worked every time," he said.

"My mother said my biggest problem was I hated being poor," Zugelder remembered, folding his hands together quietly. "I hated people who looked down on me."

He recollected living in nineteen or twenty different houses by the time he was eighteen. "I lived in more places than I had years as a child," Zugelder said. "My family was very, very poor. I was always doing things on my own. My stepfather would take me and drop me off for the whole day to hunt or fish. I became very independent very young. And being larger than everyone, I always ran with people much older than myself."

Staying at that time in Riverside, Zugelder, then eighteen, met a sixteen-year-old girl. "She ended up getting pregnant and I got busted for statutory rape. I went to jail for that," Zugelder revealed. "Anyway, I went to her parents and said, 'Hey, I want to marry your daughter. I love her.'" Zugelder said they lived together, as common-law man and wife, for two years. She left him after his arrest for bank robbery, Zugelder said.

It was November 7, 1970, and Danny had just gotten paid. He used the money to get drunk and impulsively robbed a bank. Giving the teller a note demanding money, Danny didn't think about the dark work clothes he was wearing that had the name of his employer on the shirt.

After pleading guilty to bank robbery, the twenty-year-old Zugelder was sent to Lompoc Correctional Institution in California, where he served nearly two years of a six-year maximum sentence before volunteering for the NASA research project that brought him to the U.S. Public Health Service Hospital—and Danielle.

Smitten from the moment he first saw her, Zugelder said he "browbeat" Neckels into giving him Danielle's San Francisco phone number. "Bruce didn't like me," he said. "He thought I was just a hard-core, killer-type bank robber."

The next time Danielle returned to the hospital, Danny arranged with his roommate to be gone so they could be alone. "She reminded me of a wild mare, real skittish and scared," said Zugelder, smiling. "She later told me she felt that something was happening there, between us, and she was afraid of the relationship. We laughed and made small talk. Then, just before she left, she reached over and touched my hand."

Subsequently, the song "Wild Horses," by the Rolling Stones, would become "their song," and "Danielle," said Zugelder, "would play it over, and over, and over again."

When Danielle flew back to New York, Danny got her phone number, calculated the length of time it should take her to reach her apartment from the airport, and dialed. "I called her as soon as she walked in the door," said Danny, laughing and pushing big hands through his long hair. "It was funny, because on the plane going back to New York, she told me she had written a letter to me. We started a coast-to-coast romance over the phone, talking almost every day. We got pretty mushy and pretty graphic over the phone."

Zugelder termed it "phone sex" and said it began about a month after their first meeting. "This was a masturbation sequence," he claimed. He would slide down the stairs at two or three in the morning to a phone booth at the hospital in San Francisco and call Danielle in New York. They even had names for each other's sexual organs. "Danielle had nicknames for everything and everybody," he said.

In addition to the phone calls, Zugelder said Danielle wrote him hundreds of letters, sometimes two and three a day, which he still has in his possession. They confirm much of what he said about their relationship.

On Thanksgiving, just days after her return from San Francisco, Danielle's thoughts were still on moving to San Francisco permanently. She had looked at a small house with an overgrown yard and a studio for her to work in, but had not finalized arrangements.

Danielle prepared a chicken for Thanksgiving, just for herself and four-year-old Beatrix. Having been raised by a father who was European by origin, she wasn't caught up in the American tradition, and, although her parents were both in town for the holidays, Danielle informed Zugelder that they had plans. "They had their own lives," recalled Zugelder, who said Danielle preferred it that way. "She wasn't particularly close to either one of them."

For now, however, the most important thing on Danielle's mind was the lump in her breast. She became sick between Thanksgiving and Christmas, suffering from a bout with bronchitis and a flare-up of asthma. The doctors set the operation to remove her lump for the day after New Year's.

In December, Zugelder was returned to Lompoc from the hospital to serve the remainder of his sentence. "I got hepatitis from a dirty drug needle, and they took me out of the [NASA] program," he explained. He managed, however, to weave a green-and-red scarf for Danielle, and sent it to her as a Christmas present. He also sent her a box of his personal belongings to hold for him, including an extra-large white sweater, trimmed in navy blue, that Danielle wore constantly around her New York co-op. "She told me it made her feel closer to me," Zugelder said.

Danielle continued to shower Zugelder with letters. "It used to be embarrassing sometimes to go to mail call at Lompoc," he laughed. "It would be 'Zugelder, Zugelder, Zugelder.' I'd get two or three or five a day, and once a record seventeen. Not just letters but cards. I wrote her every day, but not as much as she did."

Shortly before the holidays, Danielle revealed to Zugelder that she had been to an astrologer. "She told Danielle that I was very intelligent and would be a writer," he said. "Danielle, even then, was trying to push me into a 'proper profession.' " In addition to her musings about Zugelder, the astrologer also told Danielle she would be married again in two years and would conceive twins. Both, amazingly, would later prove to be true.

Just recovered from her illness, Danielle spent a quiet Christmas Eve with Beatie, seeing her father and stepmother, but not Claude-Eric. Lonely, she called Lompoc after Beatie went to bed and, surprisingly, got through to Zugelder.

"It would blow my mind," Zugelder recalled, shaking his head in disbelief about her calls to him in prison. "I'd be sitting up in the dorm . . . and the guard would come up and say, 'Zugelder, they want you in the office to make a phone call.' I'd go over there and Danielle had left me a message to call and they'd let me call! No one got to do that! I used to sit there and say, 'How does she do this?' "

Zugelder believed it was Danielle's "persistence and name-dropping" that probably made the difference. "She would use whatever names she felt would work," he said. "They all had a basis of legitimacy to them."

She spent Christmas afternoon with her mother, surprised, said Zugelder, at one gift for Beatie: "It was some sort of book on sex education. Danielle thought that was especially funny since she said her mother couldn't even tell her about the birds and the bees when she was engaged to marry Claude-Eric."

Danielle was glad to be putting the holidays behind her. She would tell Zugelder that Christmas was for Beatie and that she had never enjoyed a special Christmas, even as a child. "We both associated Christmas with bad memories," Zugelder revealed. "She didn't start enjoying Christmas until she had Beatrix." And weighing on her mind was the upcoming operation to remove the lump in her breast, the move to San Francisco, and, now, Danny.

Shortly after New Year's, Danielle checked into a New York hospital with Danny's scarf tucked around her neck and visions of losing a breast to cancer running through her head. Zugelder recalled her talking about it a lot. "She was paranoid that she was going to wake up and her breast would be gone," he said. "I told her, 'You don't have any breasts anyway, so you know it doesn't matter if they knock one off.' Joking with her, you know, to try to put her mind at ease."

Danielle was elated the next day, following surgery, when she awoke with two breasts. She would happily reveal to Zugelder that her lump was just a benign cyst. "They [the surgeons] left the lump in rather than cut further into her breast," Zugelder recalled. "She was giddy, she was so happy."

In the early 1980s, Danielle would lose a close friend to breast cancer and write about the experience in her novel *Fine Things*. Although she would tell the *Ladies' Home Journal* in 1987 that the book was written for her friend, she must also have been remembering her own thoughts going through those trying weeks of not knowing. Calling it a "draining experience," she told the interviewer that "seeing someone so much like me with a fatal illness was terrifying."

Now, however, she could concentrate on moving to California and visiting Danny.

Within days of her release from the hospital, Danielle was busy checking on schools in San Francisco for Beatie and searching out job opportunities. "She didn't want a full-time job because she wanted time to write," Zugelder remembered. And, thanks to the separation agreement with Claude-Eric, Danielle's alimony and child support of about $2,400 per month would afford her the luxury of part-time employment.

Even though Danielle complained to Zugelder continually about Claude-Eric's "moodiness," she was delighted that he had not fought her decision to move to San Francisco. "If he wanted to, Claude-Eric could have prevented Danielle from taking Beatie out of the state to live," Zugelder revealed.

Danielle planned to return to San Francisco in the beginning of February to interview for a job, find a place to live, and visit two schools for Beatie: one Catholic and one French. At the same time, she planned her first trip to visit Danny at Lompoc, down the coast several hundred miles from the city.

Although Danielle was to arrive in San Francisco on February 2, bad health would once again alter her plans. This time, she caught the flu, which delayed her departure one week. When she finally did get out, she left Beatie behind with her nanny and Danielle's stepmother, Kuniko, looking in on her.

"Danielle always had a nanny for Beatie," said Zugelder, who remembered "at least four or five" different nannies Danielle hired while they were together.

As before, Danielle would stay with her friends from the commune. Her main concern, she would tell Zugelder, was to find a place for Beatie and her to live. In between times, she interviewed for a part-time job at various magazines, selected Sacred Heart Catholic School for Beatie's schooling, and started searching for a way to be involved in prison reform.

From New York, she had called about a program started by Mark Dowie called Transitions to Freedom, Inc. Dowie, an economist who would later go on to edit *Mother Jones* and become nationally known for his investigative reporting, created Transitions to Freedom in 1969 with "one simple objective: to improve the employment situation for convicts coming out of prison."

40

Dowie still remembers the first day he met Danielle: "She walked into my office on a fairly warm day in a fur coat," he revealed. "Fur coats were just unheard of in San Francisco. No one wore them even in the winter. There she was standing in my office with a fur coat saying, 'I want to help.' Here was this wealthy-looking woman who wanted to help out and I said, 'Come on in.' There were not many people who wanted to get involved with convicts in any way at all, and she was bright and articulate."

And, although Dowie said they didn't decide that day what she would do, they made arrangements to meet again.

On Saturday morning, Danielle boarded a small aircraft for the flight to Santa Maria, and then drove approximately another half-hour from there to Lompoc. It was, for Danielle, an act of love; she hated flying in small planes.

Lompoc Correctional Institution was a minimal-security facility. The visiting room was large and airy, opening up to a fenced yard where visitors could sit on the lawn or the terrace and picnic.

Zugelder said he was once again in the throes of hepatitis, but afraid to check into the prison hospital for fear he would miss seeing Danielle. It was their first face-to-face visit since November, and both Danielle and Danny were anxious.

Danielle arrived in the early afternoon, dressed in slacks and a red-checkered shirt. "She always wore slacks or long wraparound skirts because she hated her thick legs and ankles," Zugelder recalled. "She used to say, 'Between the thick legs, the big ankles, and the big feet, it's like the body just went so far and decided it was going to quit growing.'"

"She was scared and nervous," Zugelder remembered. "I remember when she saw me she was looking up at me, batting her eyes and blushing beet red. I immediately grabbed hold of her and then—she was so tiny—I just picked her up like she was a feather, and gave her a big hug and kiss.

"She was rattled, really talking fast, chit-chatting about the drive up. So"—he smiled, ducking his head and almost blushing himself—"as soon as we sat down, I took her hand and I placed it in my pocket, which was cut out, and on my penis. She turned just scarlet. It kind of broke everything loose to where she was comfortable. I know that sounds strange to say, but once you have done the worst thing that a person can possibly anticipate happening on a visit, the rest is gonna be easy, and that's pretty much how it worked out."

Zugelder said the first visit lasted only a few hours before Danielle had to get back to San Francisco for her return flight to New York.

"The day after she left, I went to the clinic and said, 'Hey, I think I've got hepatitis,' and they put me in the hospital for a month," Zugelder said.

Meanwhile, Danielle was back in New York, packing for her move to San Francisco. By early March, she and Beatie would be on a plane headed west; a permanent move to a new life on the hills overlooking the bay, although not the prescription for happiness that Danielle might have hoped.

7

*D*anielle arrived in San Francisco on March 5, 1973, with three trunks, four crates, fourteen suitcases, and the desire to build a new life. The trip from New York to the city by the bay had been her flight to freedom, both physically and mentally. Grasping Beatie's tiny hand in hers as she left the American Airlines plane, Danielle, not unlike the character in her first novel, was elated to be going home.

In fact, her book, *Going Home*, which she had already completed, started with single mom Gillian Forrester and daughter Samantha's exodus to the same city. "We had left New York one grizzly, rainy day, like pioneers off to another world," Danielle wrote. "I was twenty-eight, she was almost five, and I think we were both scared. Brave New World. And off we went. To San Francisco, where we knew no one, but it was pretty and it was worth a try."

A great admirer of Victorian architecture, Danielle had rented a flat in that style in Pacific Heights, one of the most fashionable areas in the city, and, ironically, not far from the famed Spreckels mansion she would later purchase. Situated on a hill overlooking the bay, the two-story gray Victorian duplex was fully furnished. The French antiques that had graced her New York flat belonged not just to another era but to Claude-Eric, who in nineteen months would become her ex-husband.

The first home Danielle had ever rented entirely on her own, it was located across the street from a Mormon church and two blocks from a park, rich in foliage, palm trees, and playground equipment. The backyard had a small garden and a huge tree with a rope swing for Beatie. On the main level was a good-sized living room with parquet flooring, a dining room, a kitchen, and a bathroom. Upstairs was the large master bedroom, complete with a fireplace and bay window, Beatie's room, a room for the nurse, a bath, and the den.

Even with the den, it was in front of the drapeless bay window in the master bedroom, with its view of the bridge and Sausalito out beyond, where Danielle planned to set up shop. She installed her manual typewriter on a small table, leaving room for an ashtray and her writing paper on the side.

And, from the beginning, she also left room for Danny. Danielle, said Zugelder, described the duplex to him lovingly in phone conversations, saying she had space for his clothes in the closet and had not touched the high shelf in her cocoa-brown bathroom. It was waiting for him, and so was she.

Within days of moving in, Beatie had made friends with their duplex neighbors, Dan Talbott and his girlfriend, Linda. Talbott remembered Beatie as a "very precocious, wonderful little girl," and Danielle as a "beauty." He recalled, "She had a lot of background, backbone, and a tremendous amount of energy."

From the beginning, Talbott was impressed with her dedication to her child and to her writing. "To my mind she was one of these people who had all of her priorities in the right place," Talbott said. "Her first priority was [being] a mother. Synonymous with that was [creating] security for herself and her family. Whatever she had to do to provide for her family . . . her family was Beatie . . . that was her priority."

Talbott was also impressed with Danielle's positive outlook on life. "She didn't spend time impressing me or anybody else that I know of about where she had come from or about her socialite ex-husband," Talbott remembered. "She concentrated on the here and now, and I always admired her for that."

Even now, Talbott's clearest recollection of Danielle was pounding away on her typewriter every night.

"Our bedroom was on the second floor facing the street, and her bedroom was on the second floor," Talbott recalled. "The only thing that separated us was this wall that they had put up, and you could hear her banging away on the typewriter until three, four, or five o'clock in the morning. It sounded like a machine gun, like part of the background noise. I mean, it wasn't stop and go, stop and go. She had her mind, her vision of her story, and she never lost sight of that. It was incredible, just incredible."

Initially, Danielle didn't reveal her true involvement with Danny to her new neighbors. Talbott said he thought she was doing "service" by visiting convicts. She was, however, already deeply involved with Zugelder. Danielle would reveal in a letter to the County Probation Department in 1974 that they "corresponded daily" and that she "visited [Lompoc] weekly" prior to his release. According to Danielle, they had "no secrets."

So, within a week after her arrival in San Francisco, she was already mapping out her next official trip to Lompoc. Danielle had arranged for Beatie to spend the weekend of March 16–18 at the beach house of a friend while she traveled to the prison for a three-day visit.

She would fly to Santa Maria and drive some twenty-six miles south to Lompoc. Arriving in time for visiting hours, she would spend her days with Danny and her nights at a local Motel 6.

The Sunday before leaving to meet Dan, Danielle took Beatie to church, although not the Catholic Church of her upbringing. It was the Glide Memorial United Methodist Church on Ellis Street. "She thought this was the greatest church she had ever been to in her life," said Zugelder. "They would get up and dance and clap their hands and praise the Lord. As opposed to her Catholic upbringing, this was just the greatest thing that she had ever seen." Even though she had enrolled Beatie in the Sacred Heart Catholic School, Danielle herself was pulling away from the church of her youth. And, although she continued to read passages from the Bible on a regular basis, Zugelder said she was searching for a faith with meaning for her. "And Beatrix loved it," Zugelder added. "Beatrix was used to being in a Catholic church, and when she went to the Glide, she couldn't believe it. In a Catholic church you can't have fun. She could be a kid there [at the Glide]."

That weekend Danielle arrived at Lompoc with a bag of groceries to prepare a picnic lunch for Danny and her in the grassy outdoor visiting area surrounded by lofty elm trees. As a minimum-security prison camp, Lompoc allowed prisoners and their families the use of lawn chairs and small tables situated above outdoor electrical outlets where they could plug in electric skillets for cooking.

After a month in the hospital with hepatitis, Zugelder weighed only 190 pounds. His prison garb—tan pants and a tan short-sleeved shirt—hung from his massive frame. Conversely, Zugelder remembered, Danielle looked wonderful, dressed in blue bell-bottom jeans and a long-sleeved white top that clung to her slender body. She was wearing her long hair the way Dan liked it: parted down the middle, with colored barrettes holding back thick waves from her face.

As before, Zugelder said Danielle was flighty and nervous when she first arrived, gibbering incessantly about her trip. Once again, a bearlike hug from her own "Pooh Bear" would break the ice.

Ever the writer, Danielle was, however, fascinated by the other inmates in the facility, Zugelder said.

"She made mention that she was a hippie—well, to her this was just the ultimate thrill. Here was a convicted bank robber, and all my friends were either bank robbers or drug smugglers, flying planes and doing all this wild stuff.

"When we first started getting this thing together, I said, 'Listen, there are a few ground rules we have to go by: you don't stare at people, you don't make any comments about people, because any comments that you make or any staring that you do can reflect on my life once I leave the visiting room,' and I told her, 'Don't ever tell me that you will do something and then not do it.' I told her I can accept and handle a no, but telling me you're going to do something and then not doing it [can have] repercussions on me."

Still, Zugelder remembered Danielle asking lots of questions. "She would say, 'Who is this guy over here, what's happening here?' She was always asking questions.

"Actually, the whole visiting time would be one big party because a good two-thirds of the people doing time out at that camp were drug smugglers. I chewed cocaine leaves, everything. That place [Lompoc] even got busted by the FBI while I was still there.

"I was out on the [prison] golf course at the time," he remembered. "We had these kind of, like, rifle pits built. We'd put sod in them and water them so you could lay down in them and get high and sunbathe. Every now and then you'd poke your head out and look around. The day we got raided, I raised up my head [from the pit] and I saw four or five tan-and-green Plymouth sedans coming at us, and I said, 'Geez, if I wasn't in prison, I'd think this was a bust,' and all these guys in suits got out and rushed into camp, and it *was* a bust. They were mostly after two brothers who were Mafia guys."

Most of Danny and Danielle's visiting time was spent walking the compound and talking, planning for the future. It was on one of these walks, said Zugelder, that he and Danielle concocted plans for their first sexual interlude in a prison bathroom.

During a visit in late April, Zugelder said, Danielle, wearing green slacks and a red-checkered shirt, made a trip to the women's bathroom.

"The women's bathroom led out into the visiting room, and there were two doors going into the bathroom," Zugelder explained. "You would go in one door, and then you would have to go into another door to actually get into the bathroom itself. It had a toilet and a sink, and that was it."

By prearranged signal, one prisoner kept the guard in conversation while Danny slipped into the bathroom. Meanwhile, Zugelder continued, the wife of another prisoner would "hold point on the door," to make sure no other inmates or visitors came in.

"There was a high window, a high, high window in the bathroom that led out to a side wall outside the building," said Zugelder. "Right in the middle of the, you know, the act, I heard keys jingling and there was a guard.

He is right there outside the window, and that doesn't do much for your excitement."

Although Zugelder said they consummated their relationship that day in the Lompoc prison bathroom, it wasn't particularly enjoyable. "We tried it once. We did it once, and it wasn't that great. I mean, you know, we've got pants flying everywhere and just hurry up, let's get it on. In fact, I think she had to take a Valium before she could go in there."

Even though it was a less-than-auspicious occasion, it produced remarkable results, Zugelder said: Danielle got pregnant.

Danielle's attorney, Charles O. Morgan, Jr., claimed in a February 24, 1993, letter that she "did *not* engage in any 'sexual liaison' " with Danny in the women's bathroom at Lompoc. Morgan added that looking at the facility would show it was "impossible."

Lompoc, which still remains a minimum-security institution, has undergone structural changes in the visiting area since 1973. Still, according to Dan Dunne, assistant public information officer for the Bureau of Prisons in Washington, D.C., conjugal visits were never allowed at Lompoc, even for married prisoners. Dennis Grossini, executive assistant to the warden at Lompoc, says that "furloughs were granted for the purpose of strengthening family ties, establishing employment and crisis situations such as a death or bedside vigil for a verified family member." Grossini adds, however, that "girlfriends could not sponsor a furlough." Zugelder and his sister both affirm that after he was sent back to Lompoc from the NASA research program, he didn't apply for or receive a furlough for any purpose.

In a letter written to Zugelder's attorney on May 21, 1974, which is part of court records, psychiatrist Richard Komisaruk makes reference to the fact that Danielle got pregnant by Danny during a visit to Lompoc. And, in twenty-two different letters written by Danielle Steel to Zugelder from May through June 1973, when Danny was finally released from prison, she herself documents this pregnancy.

As they walked around the prison visitors' compound, Danny and Danielle had discussed their mutual love of children. "I wanted enough kids to fill a baseball team," recalled Zugelder, smiling, and even though Danielle was using protection at the time to prevent pregnancy, neither she nor Danny was sorry she got pregnant. In phone conversations and in letters she wrote to Zugelder, he said she would refer to their child-to-be as "Irving Bullfrog."

"She used to think she was French," Zugelder explained. "I would kid her about the French being 'frogs' . . . French frogs. That's how she came up with the Irving Bullfrog thing."

Danielle, said Zugelder, would come down almost every week to visit, sometimes driving with the wife of another prisoner and sometimes coming alone, staying with Beatrice Baer on a ranch about fifteen miles from Lompoc. A confidant of Danielle's longtime friend Charlie Flowers, Beatrice was also a writer who had shared, at one time, a romance with the late actor Walter Pidgeon, according to what Danielle told Danny. Intelligent as well as intellectual, Baer greatly impressed Danielle.

"She [Beatrice] lived in an area called Santa Rosa Road that is out northwest of Santa Barbara, and that road goes into Lompoc. It was settled one hundred years ago by people from the East, including Beatrice's grandfather," explained Charles Flowers, who said Beatrice's family originally brought in sheep, then cattle, and finally got into growing walnuts. "They called it a walnut ranch," he said.

"Beatrice's husband died young. Beatrice, until her death, which came too early, worked on the ranch with the hands, selecting walnuts and going off to do whatever you do with the trees in the spring, and had gone through years of not having very much money. She had to run the whole ranch for years and take care of two sons. In many ways she was like Danielle . . . a survivor.

"And," Flowers continued, "like Danielle, she [Beatrice] was great company. She would chatter away for hours on any topic."

Danielle would later use Beatrice, affectionately, as the basis for supporting characters in at least two of her books, *Now and Forever* and *Palomino*. Both books had built into their plots wonderful, warm older women who own ranches.

In *Now and Forever*, the character was Bethanie Williams, whom Danielle would describe as "peppery as all hell, but the blue eyes were gentle and the mouth always looked close to laughter." And in *Palomino*, Danielle would name a similar character Caroline Lord. "She was a superwoman," Danielle wrote. "She was brilliant and amusing, attractive, kind, compassionate, intelligent."

From the beginning, Danny and Danielle decided it would be better if Beatie didn't visit Zugelder in prison. "I fought that [Beatie's coming] at first because it wasn't a suitable place, and I was always conscious of not giving Claude-Eric the ammunition to try an take Beatrix away from Danielle." Beatie and Dan had corresponded by letter, they had talked on the phone, and Dan had made her a macramé necklace, but they had never met face-to-face.

Then, a month or so before Dan's release, Beatie and her nanny were on their way to Los Angeles and dropped Danielle off at Lompoc. "We were going to wave at each other from the car and everything, and instead it ended up we had like a family visit. It was just great," Zugelder said.

At the same time that Danielle and Beatie were developing a routine around visiting Danny, they were also settling nicely into a conventional

48

life in San Francisco. One of Beatie's previous nannies from New York had joined them after a three-week vacation. Beatie was happily involved in school. And Danielle was spending her evenings writing her novels.

In addition to *Going Home*, which was due to be published in October, Danielle had already written a mystery entitled *In the Fog*, and several others, including *Drea, To Kill a Son*, and *Savage Kind of Loving*. She also had finished a screenplay called *Give Me Some Slack, Mama*, but she was most excited about a new work in progress, *Passion's Promise*.

"She started just before I got out of Lompoc," recalled Zugelder. Danielle reportedly told Danny that she was basing the main character on him. "It was the story of a socialite who fell in love with this ex-con who was into prison reform," explained Zugelder. "She would ask me about dialogue and slang and expressions that were used in prison and stuff.

"I actually used a lot of prison slang because, being a writer, she wanted to hear all that. When I'd talk to her, I might make mention of 'Yeah, I had to go throw chingassos with this guy.' She liked that term [slang for fisticuffs or fighting], and started using that when she wrote to me."

Zugelder admitted that the characters based on him in this and other books didn't always have his exact features. "She always made me tall," he claimed, "but sometimes changed my hair to black and my eyes to blue. And she always wanted her [character] to be a tall, winsome blonde, with long, shapely legs."

In addition to her novels, Danielle was writing poetry. *Cosmopolitan, McCall's, Ladies' Homes Journal*, and *Good Housekeeping* all continued to purchase her poems, which she generally sent first to Danny at Lompoc. Often she would refer to it as her "prison poetry."

As a favor for a friend more than for money, Danielle also did a small modeling job. After a model failed to show up for an assignment, a photographer pal called Danielle at the last minute to take the model's place. But instead of immortalizing her face or figure, Danielle had her hands photographed for an IBM advertisement.

Throughout, Danielle had continued to search for permanent work. In May, she took a part-time position with the San Francisco branch of Grey Advertising, a New York–based agency.

As a free-lance copywriter for Grey, Danielle was paid two hundred dollars for three eight-hour days of work, which she could sometimes complete at home. Danielle was elated with the position. She would prattle on to Danny over the phone about writing copy for Knudsen Yogurt, Bank of America, and anti-drug-abuse commercials in her office on the thirty-fourth floor overlooking San Francisco. She even built an office calendar around Danny, with a countdown to his release date. "While she was waiting for me to get out," Zugelder remembered, "they kind of made a lit-

49

tle office calendar that said 'Danny will be home in seventeen days' . . . and so on."

In between, Danielle was working with prison reform. During the middle of May, she would host her first and last support group for wives and girl-friends of prisoners. She laughed with Danny on the phone about the two women out of eight scheduled who showed up for "tea and cookies." "One," said Danny, "was a five-foot-ten two-hundred-pound toughie, and the other looked retarded." Danielle described the whole meeting as "a hundred and ten minutes too long" and a "bloody bore."

She was, however, a strong advocate of Delancey Street Foundation. In 1973, when the program was searching for new quarters to house its bur-geoning residential population of one hundred ex-cons, Delancey Street caused a major uproar after it bid on the old Russian Consulate building in Pacific Heights. The fifty-room building was located on Divisadero Street, just a few blocks east of the house owned by Claude-Eric's grandfather. Many neighbors were not amused by the prospect of having a group of one hundred recovering heroin addicts move in next door and a major battle ensued to block Delancey Street from acquiring the property.

"The neighborhood went totally crazy," recalled Dr. Mimi Silbert, one of the two founders of the program. "In those days, it was a new thing for a program like this to be in a community, and to have picked the poshest section of San Francisco! There were raging cocktail-party fights over this. People threw food and drinks at one another; it divided the community."

Danielle, who had not lost her newfound flare for rebellion, sided with the foundation, even lending her prominent married name of Lazard to a petition in support. It was a gutsy move, especially since the names of those signing were to appear in a newspaper advertisement. It was also a move that ultimately would earn her a visit from Claude-Eric's aunt, admonishing her for bringing down the property value on a house that her own daughter would one day inherit.

"This was a seriously hot issue, and it took courage for Danielle and a handful of other people to stand with us," Silbert said. "They went against relatives and, even more, the power base of the neighborhood."

Thereafter, Danielle concentrated on fund-raising for a prison-reform pro-gram called Connections and Mark Dowie's prison reform group, Transitions to Freedom, helping to find jobs for felons who were soon to be released. But her favorite project was Danny and trying to get him work.

"She was trying to find me a job in counseling," said Zugelder. "I've always wanted to be a counselor or work with kids. I've always been fairly intelligent and had enough common sense to realize the things that were wrong with the system and why kids ended up like myself. She found out ex-cons couldn't work with kids, so she started shifting her focus into programs for adult ex-cons.

"Danielle was the type of person that if you gave her a grape seed, she would try to grow a bush out of it and make wine," Zugelder said with a smile.

In addition to the writer she initially hoped Danny would become, Danielle later would offer to pay for pictures so he could look for work as a male model.

Between her almost-weekly visits to Lompoc, her work, and Beatie, the time passed quickly for Danielle. Fascinated with the ocean, they would spend hours at the beach, swimming and sunning at Marina Beach near the St. Francis Yacht Club. It was there that Danielle attracted the unwanted attention of a man who became so obsessed watching her and trying to talk with her that she eventually asked the police to keep him away. He turned out, she would tell Danny, to be a pushy gentleman with a little money, a lot of time, and a big ego.

Danielle rarely went to parties, although she did find time to attend a "terribly posh-posh" dinner given by the publisher of *San Francisco* magazine. In attendance, Danielle reported to Danny, were Dr. and Mrs. Jonas Salk; Jack Warnecke, a renowned architect; Herb Caen, the San Francisco gossip columnist; Herbert Gold, the writer; the Gettys; and an Italian count. Even by Danielle's standards, this was an illustrious group, and, for a change, she told Zugelder, they talked about her books instead of her well-known mother-in-law.

Otherwise, she would tell a reporter in 1988 that this was a "a very quiet life. A solitary life. Friends would say, 'You have to go out more, meet people,' and here I was alone in my house, with my child, writing books and never meeting anyone. And I was always saying that I'm waiting for Prince Charming to come up and knock on my door."

In reality, Danielle was about to ride to the rescue of her own version of Prince Charming. Danny was due to be released on June 18, 1973, and Danielle planned to pick him up in the 1969 white four-door Ford Cortina she had bought for $550 in March.

Again, Zugelder remembered those days well:

"She came up one or two days in advance and stayed with Beatrice Baer up until the night before and then rented a motel room," he said.

"That morning she picked me up, I think it was five-thirty or six A.M., it was still dark," remembered Zugelder, who said he barely slept at all that night. "They would let you leave as early as the people got there."

Danielle had bought Danny a pair of tan Frye boots, and he was wearing them, along with Levi's and a long-underwear-type shirt that buttoned up the front.

"She was dressed in a pair of Levi's, too. She knew I loved the way she looked in Levi's. Red was her favorite color, and she used to wear this red-checked shirt a lot, a long-sleeved shirt with a red V-neck, long-sleeved sweater." Danny remembered that Danielle "looked terrific."

And, for once, Danny remembered being nervous, too. He climbed into the driver's seat and gave her a big kiss, and they drove to the Motel 6, where she had rented a room the night before.

"We go into the motel room, and she was fidgeting around and pacing and looking at me with those scared doe eyes. I was nervous myself," Zugelder said.

They had jittery little snippets of conversation that he said "didn't mean anything." They popped a bottle of champagne that Danielle had bought, but barely sipped from their glasses.

"It was kind of like a chase because she is edging away from me and she's scared to death," he said. "At one point she was standing up on the bed kind of bouncing up and down. This was all kind of like play, but you could tell she was totally terrified. I think she made a joke, like, 'Why don't we take you back to Lompoc?' And I said, 'No way, Jose.' Somehow or another, it's kind of hard to describe the exact moment when we started taking clothes off and things, but somehow or another I got her calmed down and started taking it real slow and we started making love."

They spent about three hours in the motel before check-out time at eleven A.M. Then they packed the car to leave Lompoc, heading south to Riverside, where Danny's mother and stepfather lived and where he was supposed to meet his parole officer.

"After we got the initial animalism out of the way, everything was fine," said Zugelder. Danielle had changed into a yellow sundress with flowers on it and they took off.

"We get just outside of Lompoc, heading down toward Santa Barbara, and a bee flew in the window. We were both trying to get it back out the window and she tells me, 'I think it stung me.' I said, 'Poor baby' and all that. I had no idea she was allergic to bee stings. So she tells me we're going to have to turn back around. She says, 'I'm allergic to bee stings and I have to get a shot.'"

Danielle's right arm where she was stung began to swell, so Danny turned the car around and headed back to the emergency room at the hospital in Lompoc. "She had the shot, and forty-five minutes later she was fine," remembered Zugelder, who said, once again, they got in the car heading south, stopping for lunch at a fast-food Mexican restaurant.

"Leaving Lompoc, the highway goes inland," Zugelder continued. "I don't know the name of it anymore, but there's a stream that runs alongside of it, and the stream runs down to the ocean. I'm free and can do anything I want, so I make a turn out and then I said, 'Let's stop here for a while. I want to go play in the stream.' And so we stopped."

They climbed down the embankment about thirty feet off the road and down another thirty feet, enjoying the warm afternoon sunshine.

"I sat down when we got there, took off my boots, my socks, rolled up my pants, and started walking in the water. Then she followed suit, and we started giggling and laughing and throwing water at each other. The next thing you know, we were rolling around in the grass."

Forty-five minutes later, they were once more on the road, this time driving to Malibu and checking into a motel on the beach. "It was probably four or five in the afternoon," said Zugelder. "We could have made it to Riverside—no problem—but we didn't have any desire to make it to Riverside.

"When we got into Malibu, I remember it was a real nice motel that had a little deck that sat on the beach and you could leave the deck and walk on down to the ocean itself. When we got in there, I brought her suitcases in and I kicked back on the bed. She went into the bathroom, and when she came out, she jumped my bones.

"You know, I knew her from all the letters, and all the visits we had, how she was, how tentative, and shy and insecure she was with a lover, with a man she loves, in that type of relationship. I was really surprised that she turned into such a tiger, but it wasn't like I'm shocked and appalled, it was like, 'Whoa, I like this.' Once we broke the ice that first time that day, it was like she was a kid who had ice cream for the first time."

Afterward, Zugelder said they went down to the beach, walked along the sand, and watched the sun go down. "I believe we made love on the beach, too. There was nobody around. Everything that day was like going to Disneyland. I'd look at the sea gulls, look at the waves, I'd jump in the water. I was like a kid experiencing many things for the first time."

The next day they headed once again toward Riverside, stopping along the way to sightsee, and finally checking in, once again, at an emergency ward. "I was teasing her," recalled Zugelder, "but I was also scared because she was hurting that day from all the lovemaking. She was walking bowlegged. I mean, she's bowlegged naturally, but the reason why we stopped at the hospital was to see if she was actually seriously hurt or not." According to Zugelder, the doctor gave Danielle a prescription for a vaginal ointment, and they drove to Danny's mother's house.

Donna Monroe, Zugelder's younger stepsister, vividly recalled the arrival of Danielle and Danny: "I remember that he didn't come right home. My mom was kind of hurt over that I think. [But] I realized he wanted time alone with Danielle before he came down."

"I remember her looking so funny beside Dan," Donna continued. "He was so tall and she was so short. They were so mismatched from the beginning . . . culture, height, everything."

Danielle, reported Donna, had been corresponding by letter and phone with Danny's folks for several months before his release, and had sent pictures as well.

"She was nervous," Donna said about her arrival. "But she hugged everybody and tried to put everybody at ease."

Zugelder's older sister, Sharlene Sweet, had also driven in to see Danny and meet Danielle. "She [Danielle] was pregnant when he brought her for the first time to my mom's house," recalled Sweet, who wasn't crazy about Danielle from the beginning.

"She unfortunately . . . this was awkward for both of us . . . had to stay up in my room with me and Dan had to sleep downstairs on the couch," Donna continued. "My [step]sister and brother-in-law were in from out of town and it was only a two-story, three-bedroom house. Anyway, she [Danielle] goes sneaking downstairs in the middle of the night. The living room is outside my parents' bedroom. They [Danielle and Danny] were going to make it right there in the living room. Needless to say, being seventeen, I went right to my sister's bedroom and said, 'My God, Shar, Danielle just went downstairs.' Well, Sharlene didn't like Danielle right off. She went down the stairs and hauled Danielle's butt right back upstairs. She said [to Danielle], 'You won't do that in my parents' house.'

"Danielle was not happy is the only way I could put it," Donna continued. "She was very quiet. I remember that better than almost anything else because I was trying not to laugh."

Jarrie Monroe, now Donna's husband but her boyfriend in 1973, recalled that Danielle and Danny always sat together during the time they spent in Riverside. "She was either as close as she could get to him or sometimes in his lap with [their] arms around each other," said Jarrie. "They were real loving."

Jarrie and Donna also "double-dated" with Danielle and Danny, driving Donna's 1965 Mustang fastback to "cruise," and then later to take in Danielle's first drive-in movie.

"Danielle wasn't all that impressed with cruising Magnolia. It was something Dan had done as a teenager," explained Donna, who said Danny wanted to show Danielle all his "old haunts." "There were a lot of kids out doing it [cruising], but let's face it, she was a little past that."

On the other hand, Danielle was fascinated with the drive-in. "She thought it was really strange that you would drive your car in, park, take the speaker out, put it inside the window, and then they would show the movie," Zugelder related. "And then that you would walk all the way down to the concession building and buy popcorn and stuff. It was just totally alien to her—she had never seen anything like it in her life."

"Danielle thought the little speaker was to talk into," Donna added. "My brother told her she could talk in it to the people next to us. He was always pulling stunts on her like that because she was so naïve. She believed him."

The visit continued, uneventfully for a few days, until Danielle got a call from her nanny in San Francisco. The nanny was leaving for an emergency and she needed to drop off Beatie.

Both Danny and Donna remembered them leaving to pick Beatie up at the airport. "We picked her up late at night, probably ten or eleven in the evening. It's about an hour or an hour-and-a-half drive back to Riverside, so we just checked into a motel," said Zugelder.

The next morning, they drove back to Riverside to Danny's parents. "Beatie stayed in my room, too," Donna remembered. "She [Beatie] was sweet and well mannered, but very busy, like any normal child. She [Beatie] absolutely adored Danny. She wouldn't hesitate to run up and hug him, or if he were sitting down, she would run up and kiss him and put her arms around him. He adored her, too."

Shortly after his arrival in Riverside, Zugelder said he and Danielle went to meet with his parole officer. "I introduced her to him and told him that we were going to get married, and that I really didn't want to live in Riverside, but I wanted to move in with her in San Francisco," Zugelder said. "We were expecting that I would have to stay there for two weeks, and then he said, 'Fine, you can leave any time you want. Just tell me when you want to leave, and I'll type up your transfer and travel papers.'"

So, within a week of his release, Danny was once again on the move. He, Danielle, and Beatie climbed into the Cortina and headed north toward San Francisco.

For Zugelder, the drive would be one of the most memorable and loving of his life. "We drove straight through," he recalled, explaining that he drove, Danielle sat in the passenger's seat, and Beatie sat in the back. "I would be driving and she [Beatie] would reach around and grab hold of my hand," he remembered, smiling. "I had to drive for the longest time, just holding on to her hand."

8

—————

ફ્જ

It was nearly three A.M. when Danny Zugelder caught his first glimpse
of what life would be like living with Danielle Steel.

As he pulled the Ford Cortina in front of the flat in Pacific Heights after
their drive up from Riverside, even in the dim shadows of a streetlight,
Danny was impressed.

Zugelder said his first reaction was "Oh, geez, look at this place. We only
had half of it, but it was a huge Victorian that sat high up on a hill. It had
these stairs out of concrete. It was a hell of a walk just to get to the house
itself, let alone open the door and go on in," he remembered. "When you
walked in the door, there was this big fireplace in the middle of the living
room. There was a bar up against the wall, and a suit of armor in the corner.
A suit of armor! I just went, 'Whoa!' "

When their neighbor Dan Talbott met Danny shortly after he moved in,
Talbott saw him as "full of wonder. The only way I can describe it is like
taking somebody from East L.A. and dropping them down in the middle of
Disneyland. This was a world he had never known. This guy came from a
land that Danielle couldn't relate to, and Danielle came from a place he
couldn't relate to."

Nonetheless, they attempted to settle in as a family. They spent the first
few weeks in what Danny would call a "honeymoon period." They took
frequent trips to Stinson Beach and to the Marina Beach near the St. Francis
Yacht Club, where Danielle would sun herself while Danny, an avid fisherman, threw his line off the dock. "We went for picnics at Mount Tam-

alpais. We'd go to the Steinhart Aquarium, the zoo, and the theater," recalled Zugelder, mentally ticking off their travels.

In a previously mentioned letter, which was written on February 26, 1993, by Charles O. Morgan, Jr., Danielle's attorney, he claims that Danny did not "move in" with Danielle.

Not only have more than eleven different neighbors, friends, and former relatives (Dan Talbott, Mark Dowie, Bruce Neckels, Sharlene Sweet, Donna Monroe, Jarrie Monroe, Emmett Herrera, Ann Dowie, Joan Patricia Tuttle, and two psychiatrists) documented through both interviews and letters that Danny lived with Danielle, she herself admitted it in a June 3, 1974, letter to the probation department, which is part of court records. Danielle wrote that Danny "moved in with me" one week after he was released from prison. "Everything was mine," she continued, noting that Danny found a job at Whisler-Patri two weeks later and tried to "adapt" to her lifestyle.

"Sitting in prison is a safe relationship," Zugelder agreed. "You have your dreams of how things are going to be and what you are going to do, and then the actual nuts and bolts of that is kind of scary. I didn't have enough sense to be terrified of entering a whole other arena. I didn't see the problems we were going to have. I just assumed we would move into together and we would live happily ever after."

Three weeks out of prison, with freshly trimmed hair and new clothes purchased for him by Danielle, Danny started work for Whisler-Patri, a well-known architectural and interior-design firm in downtown San Francisco.

Emmett R. Herrera, an interior-design architect who at that time was employed by Whisler-Patri and later became a friend of both Danny's and Danielle's, still remembered the first day he met Danny.

"Danny showed up one day," Herrera recalled. "He's got a presence about him. I walked into the office one morning, and I look up and here's this Adonis standing there, and from twenty paces I went, 'Oh, boy—he's fresh out of the joint.' "

Herrera said one of his first questions to Danny was "How did you get here?" And Danny replied honestly that his girlfriend was a big socialite who got him the job and helped get him out of prison.

"I said, 'Do you have time for a drink after work?' and he said, 'Absolutely!' " Herrera recalled. "That was a sign I should have caught right off. After work, he sits down and drinks only vodka. I mean, he could drink bottles of vodka."

Still, according to Herrera, not many people in the office knew about Danny to begin with, although everyone knew that the owners, Piero Patri and Francis "Bud" Whisler, helped people in trouble. "They are just big hearts," Herrera said. "They had a history of risk taking when it came to helping people who normally didn't have a lot of opportunity."

Primo Angeli, who owns a prestigious design firm in San Francisco, was at that time sharing space with Whisler-Patri and recalled spending time with Zugelder and the two other ex-convicts employed by the firm.

"I thought he [Danny] was an extraordinary guy," Angeli revealed. "The guy was on the edge. Danielle probably found him fascinating just because of lifestyle. She being a writer, interested in people, I could see where there would be an attraction. He was a nice-looking guy, and she was a very exciting woman. I liked them both."

Zugelder, whose formal education and work history were scant, at best, was called the "office expeditor." In essence, Danny said, his job was created for him. "They took everything the architects and interior designers and draftsman didn't like to do, and incorporated it into one job—photographing job sites, measuring buildings, copying documents," Zugelder explained. And, since there were no official company cars, if Danny was going on a company errand, he would generally use the little Jensen convertible that belonged to one of the partners.

"A lot of times during the week, I had to go to work earlier than she [Danielle] did," Zugelder said. "So I would wake her up and we'd growl at each other. I'm not a morning person and she wasn't either. She would burrow back down in the covers, in this tight little ball right in the middle of the bed and tell me to go away.

"Her biggest idiosyncrasy was that she talked in her sleep. I mean, she would go to sleep and I would lay there. All I would have to do is say a couple of words in French, German, or English, and she would take off talking. She would hold whole conversations."

Zugelder remembered a thin-blooded Danielle who was always cold, going to bed with socks on, "big, old, long droopy socks that would go up to her knees. She would slouch around in her socks and her nightgown with her Sanka. She had to have a couple of cups of Sanka before she would get around to getting dressed. She wasn't the type of person who would get up at six to be at work at seven. She would have to get up at seven to be to work at nine. Times that she had to get up and I didn't, she would get up, go downstairs and make a cup of Sanka, and then come back upstairs and get her wardrobe ready, putting it on the bed. I'd check her in the bathroom, and she would be putting on her mascara. Then, when she had her makeup on, she would go ahead to the bedroom and get dressed.

"She was methodical to the point where she would lay out the ensemble she was going to wear. Everything would be right there, including the shoes, and if she didn't like it, she would get cranky and start going through the closet," Zugelder said. Even then, Danielle had a love of good shoes, he said, collecting over fifty pairs.

Zugelder said Danielle would usually take a cab to her office. "We only worked like blocks away from each other in the financial district of San Francisco. We would actually take the same route to get to work. She was on California Street. I used to enjoy taking the cable car to work. The only time she ever did that was with me.

"The whole time we were together, she was just terrible at managing money. Rather than go to Safeway and buy dinner, she would pick up the phone and call the neighborhood grocery store and have them go pick up dinner. Everything was delivered by the dry cleaners, the druggist, the grocer. If she wanted a pack of cigarettes, she would pick up the phone and call the druggist and have him bring her a carton."

And then there was the expense of a nanny for Beatrix, a Chinese cleaning lady who would come two or three times a week, and since Danielle rarely cooked anything besides lamb chops or shrimp curry, the cost of eating out, said Zugelder. "She loved Chinese food," he added, as well as eating peanut butter from the jar, and she hated Jell-O.

She also set up accounts for Danny. According to what Zugelder told Herrera, Danielle let Danny run a tab at several places, including the neighborhood grocery store. She would take him to Brooks Brothers and other exclusive shops to buy clothes for him. "Even my Levi's were dry-cleaned," Zugelder remembered.

Still, in the first month, Zugelder believed they didn't really have any troubles. "She was still showing me things she liked to do and I was showing her things I like to do." He recalls lazy Sunday mornings when he would rise to fix omelets for everyone, and the hours they would read together or sit and talk. They even discussed buying a little bookstore. "I was a fairly avid reader—Robert Ludlum and Stephen King," he said, while Danielle was into reading magazines and the best-sellers, "to see how they were writing their books.

"When she wanted to read something [for pleasure], she would read something deep—the great French writers like Voltaire. We used to talk about philosophy. That's something she loved to do," he said, although admitting politics was not their forte. "She claimed to be a Gaullist," he added, "but she wasn't politically active. I don't think she even voted."

A mutual love for both Danielle and Danny surfaced in the form of six-year-old Beatie. "My recollection is that she tried to include him in everything that she did," believed Dan Talbott. "And that ranged from putting absolute trust in him with his relationship with Beatie, in spite of his background."

Like nearly everyone who remembered them in that period, Talbott felt that Danny and Beatie adored each other. "I think Beatie thought the world of him at that time," Talbott said.

Herrera agreed with Talbott. "He was excellent with Beatie. He had this innocent side of him, this genuine person that was for real."

"Danny was very good to Beatie," concurred Mark Dowie. "I think Beatie was hoping for a male figure . . . really like Danny."

At the same time, Beatie was spending time with her father, Claude-Eric, as well. Claude-Eric would take her with him to a beach house for nearly six weeks during the summer months. And, in the months between the move to San Francisco and the time Danny got out of prison, Claude-Eric visited his only child nearly every month and called often.

"She [Beatie] would be excited to see her father when he was being talked about," Zugelder said. "The closer she got to actually seeing him, the more into a shell she would go. I'm sure she warmed up once she was with him for a while, but you'd just see the tension. It was probably because of the estrangement and having to get used to him all over again each time.

"Danielle and Beatrix had a conversation about the fact that Claude-Eric was her father, and that it was okay to love him and love me, too. In fact, I talked to her about it, too. I wasn't trying to replace her father, but I would be a daddy to her while he [Claude-Eric] was in New York, but that he was her father."

"To me Beatrix was my child, too," Zugelder believed. "I was her stepdad. I always had time for her. I'd come home from work and we would go do something, watch cartoons together, go to the park, ride the cable cars, whatever. I loved her. She was 'The Bink' or 'Binky.' "

They also had a nighttime ritual, he said, where after the nanny gave Beatrix a bath, she would come to their bedroom to say good night and stay "for a tickle." Afterward, Danielle would lead her back to her bedroom, Danny would stop by for a good-night kiss, and Danielle would talk for a while or read her *Babar*. "That was back when *Babar* was just in French," Danny recalled.

And then, late at night, like a hermit crab coming out of its shell, Danielle would fold her mass of hair on top of her head, secure it with pencils, slip into a bright canary-yellow terry-cloth robe, and begin the process of writing.

Zugelder revealed, "Most nights, if she was feeling good, she would write. We would go to bed about eleven or twelve. We would have sex, and then just when we would start to get all comfortable, she would say, 'Well, I've got to go write.'

"When we first started living together, she would go down to the library [den], and she would write there. Our [bedroom] windows overlooked the bay. You could see the ships and the lights and the fog. She used to like to sit there, looking out the window, and type. I got to where I could sleep with the typewriter going a hundred miles an hour.

"Her writing habit was to take all of her hair and pile it up on top of her head with a pencil in each side, and grab a cup of Sanka and maybe some cookies—Oreos when I first met her, and then she switched to Pepperidge Farm. She would pull a pencil out when she was going to erase something, but it would immediately go right back up. She had her own kind of paper she used, and she would roll the paper in. She would sit and stare out the window and then an idea would hit her and she would type."

It was the same picture Talbott had of Danielle as well. Talbott remembered seeing her sitting next to the bay window late at night, with pencils in her hair, typing. "That's the recollection I have of her," said Talbott. "This wasn't sometime. This was every night—every night."

And while she typed, she chain-smoked Marlboros. "She had a ceramic ashtray [next to the typewriter] that had been fired and glazed," said Zugelder. "She would let the butts pile up until she couldn't put any more in, and then she would throw them in the fireplace. I told her not to because they are hard to clean up and the poor old hired help had to clean the fireplace. It was just a habit she had; someone else will have to clean it up."

Normally very generous, Danielle was extremely possessive of her typewriter. Zugelder said he started to use it once to type a letter to his parents, and Danielle got furious. " 'Don't use that. I didn't say you could use that,' she said to me," he recalled.

She also was an obsessive note taker. "She would take notes everywhere we went," Zugelder said. "She used to keep one of those wire binders around the house and in the car. She would make little notes on this and that— like if she had a thought she would write down the thought and she would incorporate it into whatever she was writing."

And, although Danielle didn't always discuss what she was writing with her friends, she did with her lover. When Danny was still in Lompoc, she had sent him a copy of her manuscript *In the Fog* to read. *In the Fog*, one of the four books Danielle would write from 1972 on that were rejected for publication, was her first-and-only attempt at writing a mystery.

When they first started living together, Danny said Danielle was working on a variety of projects. "She was working on rewrites and cleaning up the galleys on *Going Home*, as well as trying to get a movie deal on it." And she was still working on the book she had started while Danny was in Lompoc, *Passion's Promise*.

"She told me one time, 'This is how I'm going to get rich if I work my fingers to a nub doing it,' " Zugelder remembered. "She also said the books she wrote from experience, the stuff she really knows, were easiest for her to write."

On the Fourth of July, 1973, Danny went to his first social event with Danielle. They had been invited to a party given by the creative director of Grey Advertising in a home that overlooked the Cow Palace in San Francisco and, as Zugelder remembered it, there were lots of people in attendance.

Dressed in jeans and a sports jacket Danielle had bought for him, Zugelder recalled being extremely uncomfortable. "Everyone was a professional or an artist or a writer, and I was this crass bank robber from Southern California," he said. "I was mingling and talking with everyone, and they would say, 'I'm into this and into that,' and I would say, 'Well, I'm into banking.' They would say, 'What kind?' and I would say like, 'Making withdrawals from Bank America.' "

On edge, Zugelder made up for his nervousness by drinking more. "That's how I started handling our differences and my being uncomfortable in that environment," he said, truly believing that no one could tell he was drunk. "The drunker I get, the more I fight to stay in control."

Still, Zugelder said he didn't tell Danielle how uncomfortable he was because "I didn't want to admit it. You have this relationship where for months you have been playing the game through these letters, and all of a sudden reality. It wasn't until later on that I would admit that I was having trouble coping with it."

In a 1974 letter to the probation department, Danielle would acknowledge Danny's early problems with both drinking and drugs, which continued in Lompoc. She said, however, that she had "no doubt" that it would stop when he got out and began his new life. Unfortunately, she said they didn't realize "the pressures he would face." Danielle wrote that during July she sought the help of a psychiatrist in hopes of dealing with the adjustments they both had to make.

Even then it was apparent to many of the people who knew Danielle that, despite the difficulties, she was fanatically and irresistibly drawn to this man.

"It seemed to me," said Mark Dowie, "that they were, by some definition, in love with each other." Dowie believed Zugelder was obviously smitten with her and she—"Well," he said, "there is a type of woman who is really turned on by the outlaw and the outlaw mentality. They like convicts and they like the mystique of the bad guy . . . the *really* bad guy. I think Danielle was definitely caught up in the mystique. At least for a while."

"They held hands a lot," remembered Danielle's friend Bruce Neckels. "They were real affectionate. I know I went to a few parties that she threw when Danny was there, living at her house. They [the guests] were from all different walks of life. She had a great variety of friends, a fabulous variety. She just never left him [Danny] alone. She always had time to go up and give him a kiss, hold his hand, and sit next to him or sit on his lap. She was not so rigid that she wouldn't allow that to be seen."

At the same time, Danielle was feeling stifled by Danny. "Basically, she wanted some freedom," Zugelder said. "She thought that I was overly clinging and I felt that she kept pushing me off is where our problems began. She would push me off because she couldn't deal with the intimacy we shared, and I imagine I was being clingy because of the insecurity of the lifestyle that I was in and her having all the money."

As the "office expeditor," Danny was making around $130 a week. "My [monthly] check wouldn't even pay the rent on that place [the duplex]," Zugelder said. "We could spend more on a night on the town then I could contribute to the household. This is when I really started saying I was a kept man, I'm just a gigolo. She wouldn't say anything. It was just the little glances and the way, like I say, at a restaurant, she would slip me forty or fifty dollars underneath the table to pay for something."

Danny continued, "I have to admit I would be jealous when she would say that she wanted to go to the French embassy for dinner and not take me."

Indeed, the society columns from that period indicate that Danielle was going to social functions without her live-in boyfriend. At a black-tie Bastille Day celebration at Cercle de l'Union (a private club that the *San Francisco Examiner* described as "so elite each member has his own liquor locker"), Danielle showed up on the arm of a well-heeled state Republican Party leader and businessman named Edward Osgood. Ironically, Osgood's former wife, Jane Hewlett, had a sister, Marion Hewlett Pike, who at one time had painted portraits of Claude-Eric Lazard and his siblings.

Zugelder remembered quarreling with Danielle about Osgood. "He was one of the most eligible bachelors in the San Francisco area," he said. "Here I was living with her, and she wanted to go to these affairs with this guy Osgood." Danielle even introduced Danny to Osgood as a "friend."

"That was one of the things that bugged me," he added. "She would always introduce me as her friend Danny."

And Osgood wasn't the only one. Zugelder remembered a well-known San Francisco newspaper columnist who was also in pursuit: "I copped a real bad attitude about that. When we started living together, I would come out, and there would be a rose . . . one rose and his card with some crap [written] in French . . . on the windshield wiper [of the car].

"I got the idea from her pretentious friends that I was just a slight flame that she would get out of her system, and since I was from a different class, it was okay to talk about me in my presence, and that would set me off."

Herrera recalled those situations as well, noting that when Danielle had a party, they were 98 percent her friends and the rest Danny's. "He didn't really have that many [friends]," Herrera explained. "Most of his revolved around work and those friends were involved with my friends. I pulled him into my circle and my circle accepted him. We would go to these parties [at Danielle's], and there would be us and them. It got to a point where he couldn't handle it.

"I gave a shit about him, but a lot of people instead . . . really kind of looked at him as an albatross or an oddity that might do them some good, you know as tidbit conversation at cocktail parties or whiplash gossip here and there. It was really disgusting. He started to feel it."

"She would include me," Zugelder continued, "but there was always the class difference and the idea of whether I would be included if she got angry with me for any reason. All the relationships I've had before were the more submissive type. I was from a lower class. Every time we would have the slightest misunderstanding, she would drop the class thing. All of a sudden her tone would turn condescending, and then I would really blow up."

Danielle would admit as much in a letter written to the courts in 1974. She said she was "unwilling to effect the changes" and acknowledged that if she would have been smart enough "to modify my lifestyle" it would have helped. Danielle wrote that instead she expected Danny "to conform."

Toward the end of July, Danielle's father arrived in San Francisco to visit, stopping off after a business trip to San Diego. He didn't stay with them, but rather at the Fairmont Hotel. John also didn't bring his second wife, Kuniko, who was recovering from another round of surgery after being hit by a taxi several years prior.

John Schuelein-Steel was a blond-haired, blue-eyed German who made up for his small stature by his posture. "He was the kind of guy who wore a diamond stickpin, carried a cane—the whole nine yards. He was a trip. I liked him," said Zugelder, who also felt the feeling was mutual.

Conversely, Danielle's relationship with her father was visibly strained, even on this short visit. "He was real aloof, with no show of affection," Zugelder said. "I always got the impression he felt women had their place in the home as an ornament. There are things you don't do, and then there are things that you have to do. All of her life Danielle was rebelling against those things. Like her being a writer didn't count for squat. It was like, 'Oh, is this a little hobby you have?' The fact she was a writer, well, it didn't make any difference to them that she was published or that she was making money from it because it was beneath their station for her to be a writer."

By then, Danielle's father was a free-lance photographer, and Zugelder said they took him to a Japanese tea garden so he could take "nature shots."

While Zugelder felt Danielle's father liked him, he was equally positive that her mother did not. Visiting that summer, Norma was as critical of Dan as she was of Danielle. "She stayed with us for a week," Zugelder said. "Her mother would put on this face for me, sit there and look me right in the eye and tell Danielle something really crude about me in French. But she would be smiling all the time, and since I couldn't understand French, I didn't know what she was saying. It was really, really beneath her dignity to even be associated with me.

"Her mother believed that you did not come down the stairs unless you were totally dressed," Zugelder continued. "That was with the earrings, the necklace, all that kind of stuff. Her mother would get up in the morning when she stayed with us and would be impeccable, dressed to a T, before she would ever come down. That was one of the biggest things she had against me and against Danielle was the fact that we would come down in bare feet in a sweater and pants or whatever we had handy and get into the morning— slowly. She hated that."

Danielle told Danny that her parents had wanted her to marry a wealthy man, and once she was married to Claude-Eric, they wanted her to stay with him. Norma would tell Danielle that she should go back to Claude-Eric. "Why are you doing this to yourself?" she would say.

Yet, Zugelder marveled, her mother never complimented Danielle on anything while he was around. "It was 'Your hair looks like a rat's nest,' or 'Look at this nurse. She doesn't look like the kind of person we want to take care of Beatrix.'"

Then sadly, around the beginning of August, almost four months along in her first pregnancy with Danny's child, Danielle miscarried.

"I was at work and she was working, and she started getting cramps and spotting," Zugelder recalled. "By the time I got to the doctor, she had already had what was called a spontaneous abortion."

Danielle, who admitted in *Having a Baby* to not liking hospitals, didn't stay long after the miscarriage. "They packed her and, at her insistence, she left," Zugelder said. "They wanted to keep her in the hospital, but she wouldn't. During all the miscarriages [they would go through several others together] she wouldn't stay in the hospital. She was crying. It was just a sad, sad thing in our lives because we both wanted children."

Once again Danielle and Danny were bound together by misfortune. But, within that month, Danielle became pregnant again. "I never lived with Danielle," claimed Zugelder, "that she wasn't pregnant or just recovering from a miscarriage. I mean we used everything—IUD, the diaphragm, foam—and this woman would still get pregnant."

To this day, Danny can't recall the exact number of miscarriages Danielle suffered through, only that it was "more than five and less than eight." "When you take into account the fact that she was insecure anyway," he said, "then add the hormonal change that's going on with the body repairing itself from being pregnant, then turn around and, right on top of that, before the body even knows what's happening, be pregnant again; there was just this constant hormonal change going on. It's no wonder she was driving me crazy and I was driving her crazy."

Indeed, an article in the September 3, 1993 *Rocky Mountain News* reported a study conducted by the American College of Obstetricians and Gynecologists and that said "women who suffer miscarriages often experience stages of grief: guilt, depression, anger, failure, anxiety, loneliness."

During the summer months, Danny's stepsister Donna and her boyfriend, Jarrie Monroe, came to visit along with Danny's older sister, Sharlene Sweet, and her husband, Jim. The couples went out together for dinner at Danielle's favorite Chinese restaurant, the Far East Café. "They didn't seem like they were having problems," recalled Donna of the visit to San Francisco. "When I look back on it now, it was like she was trying to show off with everything. She knew everybody, all the waiters and everything."

Donna also remembered the tension level between Sharlene and Danielle being extremely high. "They never exchanged words or anything, but it was tense because my sister would just not accept her at all."

"I didn't really like her," Sharlene admitted. "I don't know why." Still, Sharlene acknowledged that her brother obviously cared deeply for Danielle.

But Danny continued to have problems. His drinking was increasing in his daily life, and he began to resent the fact that Danielle was writing and rarely wanted to go out.

"She was very set in her routines," Zugelder said. "I would say, 'Hey, let's go for a drive,' and unless we had a specific place in mind to go where she had been before, she really didn't want to. She wanted to stay home."

Herrera, too, recognized Danielle's devotion to her writing: "If anything was sacred, it was her writing. I don't know if writers go into a fantasy world in order to avoid what's really going on in their life. It was like she could close her eyes and be gone in her typewriter."

Nevertheless, Herrera and others believed Danny used Danielle's lifestyle as an excuse to drink and cheat with other women. "He was a finger pointer. He was a victim," Herrera believed. "His stand was he couldn't fit in, regardless of what he did. He couldn't possibly do what she wanted him to do. What was interesting is she never asked him to be that [something different than he was]. As he demanded of her to respect him for who he was and what he was, in truth, she was only asking the same thing."

Talbott also recalled seeing the first glimmerings of trouble at Pacific Heights. "Maybe six months after they [Danielle and Beatie] arrived, we moved to Piedmont and we saw less of them, but it was about that time the fighting started," said Talbott, who said he got phone calls from both Danielle and Danny.

66

According to Talbott, Danny would call "complaining that he was not a priority in Danielle's life, that she spent too much time writing, that he was an ornament and he was window dressing for her, and made her look good. Nothing could be further from the truth. He was never considered window dressing. He wasn't exactly a Rolls-Royce she was riding out of town. That was an illusion on his part. She, at that time, genuinely loved him.

"We tried to give him [Danny] affirmation. We tried to reaffirm, and we tried to convince him that he was wrong. He was obviously a very important part of Danielle's life. 'Jesus, Danny, where are you living? How did you get the job? What are you doing and who are you with?' He wouldn't be there if she didn't care."

When Danielle called, Talbott said they tried to encourage her to "be patient." She said, 'I just don't know what else to do to help this guy. He's missing work, he's drinking a lot, he's very angry, he's jealous of my writing.' "

In September 1973, the month before the scheduled release of her first book, *Going Home*, Danielle arranged a trip to New York on business that didn't include Danny. In addition to a luncheon with her publishers and meeting with her agent and attorney, Danielle planned to spend time visiting friends and relatives. She and Beatie were to stay in Claude-Eric's co-op on Park Avenue, Danielle sleeping in the nurse's old room. Although Claude-Eric was well aware of Danny's existence in her life, and had been since before his release from Lompoc, Danielle wasn't eager to bring them face-to-face.

Danny took Danielle and Beatie to the airport on a Sunday morning. He was supposedly taking a short trip to see his family in Riverside, but otherwise staying at the Pacific Heights house while Danielle was gone. By all accounts, it was a tense departure, with Danny remaining aloof and hurt, and Danielle feeling overwhelming pangs of guilt for going away without him.

"She wanted her independence and to be able to fly to New York and take care of things, which I had absolutely nothing against, but I was hurt because of the way she treated me," said Zugelder. "She wouldn't want me with her [in public]. I knew she loved me, but she was never up front in dealing with that. I really treated her cold at the airport."

During the ensuing ten days, Danielle would send him five letters, including one she started writing before the plane even left San Francisco International Airport, proclaiming her love, regardless of how much the two would fight.

Meanwhile, Danny was exacting his own revenge. From the airport, Danny said he headed downtown to the Hyatt Regency Hotel to have a drink. Sitting at the bar that afternoon, he watched with interest as two beautiful young blondes made their way through the hotel, accompanied by a handsome black youth.

"He was a pimp," Zugelder revealed. "I watched his action for a while and then went up and bought him a drink and we started talking. You know, I was twenty-three years old, and I thought being a pimp must be great. So I invited him and his ladies to the house in Pacific Heights."

According to Zugelder, the foursome "partied all night" in the bed and bedroom he had shared with Danielle just the night before.

"After doing cocaine, drinking, smoking grass, and making love to these girls all night, [the pimp] invited me over to where he was living in Oakland," continued Zugelder, who dropped by a few days later to find one of the girls was sick with the flu. "The younger of them," he said, "loved being a hooker. She wanted him [her pimp] to take her to San Francisco to work. He said, 'Danny, why don't you take her so she can turn some tricks?' I thought that was great. So here I was playing the pimp down at the Hyatt and drinking. She's turning tricks and I'm having a good time. I started getting kind of drunk and she didn't want to quit. It was like midnight, and I tell her I'm going home and to call me when she got done. About an hour later, she calls me and tells me that the vice have made her and that they are after her. I tell her to go over to this place and stay and I'll come get you. So I went down to get her and she wasn't there. They had busted her. I went down to bail her out, and come to find out this girl is only sixteen. I had no idea that she was sixteen; I was really sweating, man. I could just see the headlines, 'Danielle Steel's lover arrested for pimping and white slavery.' "

Luckily, Zugelder said Danielle never found out about this escapade. It wasn't the first time nor would it be the last time that Danny cheated on Danielle. But for Danny, his day of reckoning was almost at hand.

9

$\mathcal{T}$he same month Danielle returned from her New York sojourn, she asked Danny to move out for the first time. In the 1974 letter Danielle wrote to the probation department, she acknowledged that Danny's drinking problem "grew" as he tried to fit in to his "new role," and that she asked him "to move out" of her flat "in September." Danielle said that was Danny's "greatest fear." Although she wrote that Danny didn't drink in front of Beatrix, she still felt she "had no choice" in asking him to go. At that time, she said she thought his problem was "immaturity" rather than "alcoholism," but later realized he was relying on the liquor to "survive the shocks of readjustment."

Several events precipitated Danielle's move, two of a physically destructive nature.

Danielle and Danny seemed to thrive on verbal battles. "It was like the only time she felt secure was in a crisis situation," Zugelder complained. "She would create a crisis. If everything was going along smooth, she would feel insecure about it. She would start creating these little minor crises to get me to go off or whatever. And then, once the crisis had developed, we could get back together and make love and everything would be fine for a week or two.

"It got to be a pattern. I wouldn't know what was going on. I'd say, 'Why are you acting so snobbish with me? What the hell is going on here? Do you want me to leave? Do you want me to just pack up and leave?' I never would get an answer. And then I'd start to leave and she would stand at the top of the stairs and tell me, 'You can't leave—you're not leaving.' I never would touch her. But one time I did put a hole in the wall with my fist when she was blocking the stairs to keep me from leaving."

Bruce Neckels remembered seeing the fist indentation. "I came over to see Danielle one day, and Danny was at work. I walked in and I remember looking at a wall and there was a fist mark, a big hole in it, and I remember saying, 'What the hell happened here?' Danielle just said, 'Well . . . '

"I think he was quite jealous because of the people she knew, where she was going, what she wanted in her life," Neckels concluded. "Danielle is just so talented and so bright and so willing to put herself out there. There was no doubt she was going to make it . . . this lady was going all the way."

Mark Dowie, then head of Transitions to Freedom, recalled sending a crew from his labor pool to Danielle's to fix the hole. "The story was that they had moved some furniture around, and the leg of the table or something had gone through the wall. I got there, and there was this hole in the wall in the stairwell going up the stairs. It was exactly the shape of a fist. You couldn't have made a better imprint yourself. And Dan's hand was all band-aged up."

Ann Dowie—Mark's sister, former copy editor of the *San Francisco Examiner*, and now a successful free-lance photographer—met Danielle through her brother and once took formal pictures of Beatie. Ann admitted that she never liked Zugelder, describing him as a "big oaf" who got violent when he was drunk: "If he had any charm, I missed it. He would posture himself as helping her [Danielle], taking Beatie by the hand up the stairs, but basically he was a good-for-nothing."

Danny continued to leave his imprint in other arenas as well: "When I was working for Whisler-Patri, I would get up in the morning and walk to the grocery store. It was a half a block away from our house. We had a charge account, and every morning I would walk there to get half a pint of vodka and a quart of grapefruit juice and a pack of Camels. That would be my wake-up. The people that owned the grocery store put a trash can right outside by the curb just for me to throw my empties in when I walked away."

He was drinking at work as well, taking extra-long lunches. "I've never been very good at saying, 'Whoa,' so when everyone else would quit, I would just keep going," Zugelder said. By now, according to his own estimates, he was consuming a quart of vodka and a case to a case and a half of beer every day.

Herrera confirmed Zugelder's words: "He would perspire. Every time you would look at him, he would be perspiring. He would perspire at nine o'clock in the morning, and he would perspire all day long and all night long. That's serious drinking."

Danny, however, was adept at hiding his drinking problem from most people. In a letter the president of Whisler-Patri would write to the probation department on Zugelder's behalf, Francis Whisler said they all thought he was "rehabilitated," and believed he was "a very trustworthy and capable employee." Whisler wrote that he helped Danny find other part-time work, and never was cognizant of his "apparently . . . serious problem with alcohol."

One of the final straws for Danielle and Danny came in late September. "We had an argument about going out," he recalled. "I wanted to go out and do something . . . and she didn't want to. So I got mad. I had a set of keys to her car, so I took her car. I went to Union Street and started partying. This Cortina, you really had to punch it out to make these hills. I had taken this street I wasn't really familiar with. I thought it was a straight shot all the way to the top of the hill where we lived, and it wasn't. It had a stop sign obscured by a bush, and I didn't see it. So I'm flying as fast as this little car goes to make it to the top of the hill to turn on our street, and I slammed into a big old Chevy Impala, broadsided it. It just totaled out the Cortina."

Convincing the police that the other driver pulled out in front of him, Zugelder wasn't ticketed, but it did require a tow truck to bring home the Cortina.

"It was really sad because Danielle was down at a friend's and the wrecker drops this car off right in front of the house," he said. "She comes strolling out of her friend's and looks down the street, and here's her car with absolutely no front end. I mean it was just totaled out. She sat down in the street and started crying. I really felt bad, geez, I felt bad. It was the first car she had ever owned."

When Danielle asked Danny to leave, he moved to a residence hotel, but still visited Pacific Heights often and called constantly. Danielle would write in her 1974 letter to the courts that because he was so lonely, Danny "drank more," and she didn't want him moving back to her duplex nor "under the circumstances" would she marry him. Still, she said she was "unhappy" in November when he told her he might be moving to Lake Tahoe. He drove to the Nevada resort and, she said, called her "several times that night." She told the court she believed "the Reno incident" happened because of "his frustration" that they couldn't "solve our problems."

"The Reno incident" Danielle referred to in her letter to the probation department was Danny's first arrest since prison. He had been out of jail less than five months.

"Actually, it was just like a chess game between her and me," Zugelder explained. "It's like, I'm trying to get her shocked into straightening up her act. She was such a loving woman, but these insecurities would just creep into her life and just screw up everything. She's got some severe insecurities.

She is a real worrier. It's like her life is a play. As long as everybody says their lines, she's fine. When they start ad-libbing, it scares the hell out of her.

"The biggest problem of all this, the reality is never as good as the fantasy. That is what was happening to us. When we were just writing letters and seeing each other in a controlled environment on visits, it was totally different, because you're on your best behavior. And then when you're actually living with someone . . . well, it was just a volatile situation all the time."

Still, moving to Reno, Zugelder would reveal, was nothing but "an empty threat. I wasn't going up there to really look for a job, I was just going up to party. I called her [from Reno] and said, 'I think I have a job here and I'm going to be moving up here.' She didn't take that well at all. She was trying to give the impression that it didn't make any difference to her. It was just another part of the psychological warfare that we managed to engage in."

Zugelder said he was wasted on Valiums and grass when he stopped at a casino in Reno to play blackjack. "I'd give the girl a five- or ten-dollar tip and tell her any time you see my glass empty, fill it up. By that time I was drinking vodka pretty much exclusively."

On November 15, drunk and losing badly, Zugelder left the casino and, on the spur of the moment, mugged an older woman in the parking lot, stealing her purse. He was arrested shortly thereafter.

"I get involved in this stupid stuff," Zugelder related. "I go to jail and I call her [Danielle] up. Immediately she calls the lawyer. He calls, and I'm out of jail in two or three hours."

Danielle would write in her 1974 letter to the courts that following his release from jail, Danny "moved back into my home." She said they were frightened by the thought he could go back to jail, and "sought psychiatric counseling" for him.

"At that time I'm twenty-three years old," Zugelder countered. "I'm big. Because of my size and the way I carry myself, people gave me a lot more credit emotionally than perhaps I had coming. Getting involved with her . . . I moved too fast. She used to tell me, 'I know guys thirty years old who don't know what to do with their lives and don't worry about it. It's all going to come to you. You'll find a career.' Now, what the hell was I going to do? I'm a high-school dropout, but about the only thing I ever felt I was good at was bullshitting. I can talk to people and make things get done. I'm a manipulator."

Even with all the difficulties they were having personally, Danielle went ahead with a November 19 fund-raising party she had planned for one of the prison reform groups she was supporting. The party was for Connections, a group that Carol Parker, one of the cofounders, characterized as an organization founded primarily to deal with the wives and girlfriends of prisoners. "One of the things we were known for was transport [transportation for family members]," explained Parker. "We were also raising consciousness. We were wanting to change the prison system in a more radical fashion."

Parker called Danielle a "connector." "She helped to arrange a benefit for us and introduced people she knew in her other world . . . people she knew who might help us," added Parker.

And, on November 19, Parker remembered Danny Zugelder standing at the door of the Delancey Street restaurant with Danielle, greeting guests as they arrived for the benefit. Ironically, considering the fact that Delancey Street was a drug-rehabilitation program, it was a cocktail and hors d'oeuvres fund-raiser.

Parker believed Danielle was "gaga" about Danny. "She was somebody who went all out for those people she cared for. And, on the reverse side, she was very vulnerable for anybody able to manipulate her, which I'm sure Danny did."

Dan Talbott, too, felt Danny was a successful manipulator. "She was a very loyal person. She had a very warm heart. In her mind, there was nothing she couldn't do, and she was capable of doing most anything. But the one thing she couldn't do, she couldn't change him any more than anybody in the world has ever been able to change an alcoholic. She's not a professional counselor, and he was in denial. We didn't know then what we know now, but the fact is that she had as much chance of turning him around as giving birth to a whale. It's just not going to happen."

As Danielle and Danny settled back into their life in Pacific Heights, the pressures, with a trial in the works, were staggering.

Danny continued to drink, and in her 1974 letter to the probation department, Danielle wrote they had "found no solutions" to past concerns about their relationship. She also told the court that when he came back from Nevada, she "discovered that I was pregnant," but added that she "miscarried" the next month.

As before, Danny was there to comfort Danielle after her trip home from the hospital. "I would kind of climb in bed with her and hold her in my arms and let her cry on my chest," revealed Zugelder, "She was wasted on Valiums and whatever else they had given her. It wasn't like we were planning [either the pregnancy or the miscarriage]. I would tell her, 'Look, you can't do this again. We can't afford this up here—psychologically—it's too hard. Whatever it takes for you to not get pregnant is what we've got to do.' See, she was having trouble with this IUD, getting turned wrong or something. I don't know. I want to say 'birth-control pills,' but she was really against birth-control pills. With her body being in the shape that it was, and all the problems she was having anyway, it was like, 'Sure, let's take birth-control pills, and that will really screw me up.'

"It was also a strain on sex—not to where we would totally abstain or anything—but I mean it would definitely make us gun-shy about the whole thing and nervous. I mean, it was like, okay, we are going to make love tonight, so we know that in a month you are going to miss your period and we would be back on the roller coaster."

Together, Danny and Danielle were attempting some degree of normalcy. With Emmett Herrera and a friend of Danielle's whom she had "set him up with," they took Beatie to a Christmas fair in San Francisco. "Danielle was a 'Yentl,' a matchmaker," said Herrera in commenting about the date. "In those days she used a lot of Yiddish terms."

Danny would celebrate Christmas Eve, his first outside of prison in three years and his last for the next two and a half decades, with Danielle and Beatie. For Zugelder, it remained one of his fondest memories. "We got a Christmas tree and put it up by the fireplace in the living room and bought presents for all of us. The ritual [of opening gifts] was for Christmas morning. Christmas Eve we played Santa Claus [for Beatie]." Danielle would buy him an expensive deep-sea rod and reel. "It was just a fabulous rod and reel," he said, adding that he bought her a crystal frog in memory of their "Irving Bullfrog" experience while he was in Lompoc.

On Christmas Day, Danny traveled alone to nearby Cupertino, outside of San Jose, to share Christmas dinner with his sister Sharlene and her family. Danielle, who didn't get along well with Sharlene, begged off, but sent homemade brownies with Danny. Instead, Danielle took Beatie to be with her father, Claude-Eric, who had flown in from New York to visit with his only child.

Zugelder said he and Danielle brought in the new year making love, but three days before his January 6 birthday, they were fighting again. The next morning Danny left to go fishing.

"We argued over my drinking," said Zugelder, who remembered arriving home on his birthday after two days of fishing. "I hadn't shaved. I was wearing a tank top, Levi's, and sandals. I come in, and she's dressed to the nines."

At first, Zugelder said he thought she was going out. And then, not; "Here's all these people, hiding behind the fireplace and everywhere, jumping out and yelling, 'Surprise!' " It was his first surprise party, and what he called his best birthday ever. Danny hugged and kissed Danielle and ran upstairs to shower and shave. "I felt great," he said. "I kind of felt like I was going to make it."

Less than two weeks later, they were back at it; Danny was drinking and cheating on Danielle, now more than ever.

"I was on an errand for the architectural firm and saw this gorgeous girl on a ten-speed bike," he recalled. "I got her phone number, and when Danielle didn't want to go to this party [at Emmett's], we got in a spat and I said, 'Well, fuck it, I'm going to the party.' I called this girl up and asked her if she wanted to go with me. She only lived a block away from where we did, almost right next to the Hippo [a hamburger place], where Danielle always took Beatrix. I ended up spending the weekend with this girl. We never had sex or anything, we just shot heroin. Danielle never would believe it. When I told Danielle about this and said, 'Hey, I never touched this girl. I just spent the weekend with her and we got loaded, and that was that,' she wouldn't believe that was true."

Once again, Danielle would ask Danny to move out, this time arranging for him to sublet the apartment of one of her friends.

Danielle affirmed in a 1974 letter to the courts that she asked Danny to leave in January, because their relationship had worsened. She said that the doctors had given them "insights" but they "needed . . . total re-education."

Writing that "January was a nightmare," Danielle said they both "retrenched into . . . negative behaviour (sic)." According to Danielle, Danny went to court on January 28, and four days later they had what she thought was their "final argument." She said "the assault" took place later that evening.

The "assault" was a vicious attack, not far from Danielle's home, on a woman who was walking home alone. From out of an alcove, a man grabbed the woman and beat her about the head and body with a billy club before running away. Danny would later be charged with the crime.

Danielle told the court in her letter that she "did not see" Danny after the evening of February 1. He moved into a flat on Larkin Street but continued to call Danielle. She admitted in her letter that they "spoke often on the phone" during the next two days, and that Danny felt "his world" had ended.

Herrera agreed. "This boy," he recalled, "was a walking mess." Herrera said that on February 4, 1974, he received a phone call from Danielle. "She was stressed out big-time, and she said, 'Danny is really out of it, Emmett— today he is really out of it.' "

Instead of carrying on their conversation over the phone, Herrera said he left work early and went to Danielle's house in Pacific Heights. "I go up to ring the buzzer on the intercom," he said, "and it's smashed in about five inches—on a concrete wall. I mean bashed in. Danny had pushed it in with his fists. Apparently, that afternoon he had gotten drunk and he went over there. She wouldn't let him in because he was obviously blazing. He started calling her names and everything and she was obviously scared to death.

"If ever there was a woman who was truly faithful, devoted to someone," Herrera believed, "it was her to that man. She loved him. They write songs about the way she felt about him.

"That day she was crying. She was hurting bad, and it wasn't a hurting from fear, it was a sad hurt. She was really crushed that her man was falling apart in front of her and she had the sense not to let him get in front of her [let him in the house]. All she could do was to hold him out, kind of like a prison, only she changed places with him. She wouldn't let Danny come in and destroy their love because it meant everything to her.

"I was blown away with the level of true, faithful, devoted, real feelings she had for this guy. Totally undeserved, but it was there."

Herrera said he talked to Danielle for quite a while and then went back to work late that evening. After he left, Danielle received a call from Danny pleading for help.

Danielle would later write a letter to the probation department acknowledging that Danny had finally admitted to her how much he was drinking and told her he was calling his psychiatrist to find "immediate counseling." When the psychiatrist wasn't available, she wrote that he called Alcoholics Anonymous, making an appointment for the next day.

Unfortunately, Zugelder wasn't out of the haze yet. Sometime much later that evening, after Herrera had returned to his office to work, he got another call.

"Right across the street from the office was this bar where all of us professionals would go to drink after work," Herrera related. "I get a call from the bartender, who knew me and Danny. He said, 'You've got about two minutes to get down here and get this son of a bitch out of here. He's got my whole bar backed up. He's losing it. He's drunk out of his mind. He's going to tear this place apart.' I said, 'Danny?' and he said, 'Yeah,' and I said, 'I'll be right there.'

"I walked into the bar and there's Danny standing there with two cue sticks in his hand. He's got a group of guys, six or seven guys facing him . . . big boys . . . yet he would have taken them out, and they knew it. It was still pretty quiet. I walked right up to him and said, 'Give me those cue sticks.' I grabbed him by the arm and said, 'You come with me.' I turned around to the other guys and said, 'Back off . . . I'm sorry . . . no problem . . . it's handled . . . don't call the cops.' We walked out, turned the corner, and I started chewing his ass out.

"He was drunk out of his mind, sweatin' like a big guy, his eyes were blazing. We started walking up the street toward my car. I'm chewing his ass out, and I turn around, and he's gone. He had stopped about ten feet back. He was looking at this sign in front of this sunken parking lot, and he starts slugging this sign, and he bends this sign over. I go, 'Danny, put that back,' and he starts to bend the sign back. And then I threw him in my car."

Herrera took Zugelder back to his own apartment. "I said, 'You fucked up bad, man. You got your woman out there all torn up. You're callin' out bars. Jesus Christ, what in the hell is going on with you? Obviously you're drunk, and obviously it's out of control, man. You're drinking too much. How much do you drink?' He said, 'At least a quart a day.'

"I said, 'You're killing yourself, man,' and he said, 'Well, what the hell do you expect.' He starts getting mad, real mad, and then he starts fooling with his leg. His whole face gets distorted, and he slugged his fist as hard as he could into his [own] leg. He slugged his leg six times, I counted them off. He slugged so hard that it would have crushed anybody else."

Herrera said he continued to badger Danny to open up to him. "He just looked at me," said Herrera, "and he said, 'My father.' And he just closed right up again. I knew I was dealing with something big-time then. He got real depressed, big tears welled up in his eyes. Here is a guy so drunk he can't even see, but he had it bad enough [that] tears welled up in his eyes. He couldn't say another word. I said, 'You just lay down over there, and I'll see that you get up for work; you got to go to work.' He laid there and just fell asleep in seconds. He was sweating.

"When he broke the sign, he was a kid, and when he had the guys backed up [in the bar], he was just a punk. But I saw his eyes. He hated being like that. He hated what he did."

The next morning, Herrera got Zugelder cleaned up and ready for work. Shortly after arriving, Herrera remembered two men talking to the receptionist. "I walk over like I'm getting something out of the 'in' basket," Herrera revealed, "and I listen to this detective talking—you could tell he was a cop. I looked down the hallway, and there was a uniformed San Francisco policeman standing by the elevator, and there was another one by the stairwell. I went, 'Oh, baby, this is it.' "

Herrera said Danny saw them, too, and that a "look of panic" came into his eyes. "Then I said, 'Don't do anything. They've got the whole place covered, man.' I said, 'It's time, man, you've got to hold it together. If you have any sense of obligation, maintain the dignity of this office. Don't go crazy. You go crazy and you will die. They will kill you, because this man is as serious as a heart attack,' " Herrera remembered.

Within minutes, the detectives entered the office, handcuffed Zugelder, and led him away. The charge: rape.

10

Danielle was never as tall as when she stood to face adversity. "It seems," Danielle would tell a reporter for the *San Francisco Examiner,* "that every time you reach a comfortable spot, life kicks you in the ass, and you have to grow, or something."

Danny's latest arrest was just such a "kick." Within hours of his booking in San Francisco City and County Jail on February 5, 1974, Danielle forgot her own apprehensions about Danny's drinking and drug use and visited her lover in jail.

Danielle hurried into the visiting room, Zugelder remembered, wearing a wraparound skirt and a blouse. "She had already heard what I was in there for; she knew what had happened. She didn't believe for a moment that I raped this girl. So her reactions were pure anger that I was messing around on her, that it got me in trouble, and that I was in jail. Then once she got it off her chest what an asshole I was, there was hurt and tears, and finally [she said], 'I'll get you out of here. We'll get this taken care of.'

"It's like our relationship was always better, very honest, when we were in the middle of a crisis. We were pulling together for one cause," Zugelder explained.

Danielle immediately spun into action to set him free. She called an attorney to represent Danny and found $25,000 for his bond. Zugelder said Danielle left as collateral the eight-carat diamond-and-emerald ring Claude-Eric had bought her when they married. As one of the court conditions for his release, she also helped arrange to have Danny placed in a drug-rehabilitation center. In addition, she organized what was called ZDL—the Zugelder Defense League—notifying friends so that Zugelder would have visitors and support while he was imprisoned.

Believing as she did in Danny's innocence, Danielle reportedly could not understand why the victim, Kathy G., was pursuing Danny's case.

Within days of Danny's arrest, Danielle called their mutual friend, Emmett Herrera. "I came over to her house," recalled Herrera, "and that's when she asked me if I would go talk to the victim and see if I could get her to drop the charges. Actually, she put it a little bit clearer than that: she begged me to do what I could do or had to do to get her to drop the charges.

"Danielle would do whatever was necessary to get Danny out of this. At that point there was nothing else that could be done other than her dropping the charges," he added. And, because it was Danielle, Herrera said yes. An attorney friend, who asked not to be identified, also said that there "was some discussion about approaching the victim."

To this day, Kathy G. doesn't remember actually meeting Herrera, although he believed he talked with her in person, but she did remember getting at least three telephone calls prior to the first preliminary hearing. It was, said Kathy G., a female caller: "The voice said not to take it to court or I would be sorry. It said, 'You're barking up the wrong tree.' It scared me."

Kathy G. reported the calls to the police and also to the assistant district attorney, who she said asked her to place a tracer on her phone. Although they recorded one of the telephone calls on tape, the call didn't last long enough to trace the phone number or identify the caller.

"The first call came at work," remembered Kathy G., at that time a secretary for a San Francisco television station. Frightened, she said she called a friend to meet her at the bus stop on Van Ness, and she went outside the front door to wait. "There was a car across the street with two women and a guy in it . . . the three sat and stared while I waited. Then they started the car and went around the block, driving by where I was standing." Kathy G. said she recognized one of the women as a person she used to work with, but didn't know the other two. The car, with the same passengers, would also drive by her apartment.

Donna Taborsky, a friend of Kathy G.'s, who testified for her at the trial and today works as a medical manager for Walden House, a drug-rehabilitation center, remembered meeting her friend that day. "I remember meeting her [Kathy] at the bus stop on Van Ness Avenue," said Taborsky, who hasn't seen or talked to Kathy G. for many years. "She was very panicky. She kept thinking somebody was following her."

Herrera also remembered being parked at one point outside the television station where Kathy G. worked, and that someone might have been with him. He said he remembered driving by Kathy G.'s apartment, but can't recall whether anyone was with him or not.

Danny, who was in custody during that time, said he knew nothing about anyone trying to approach the victim to drop the charges.

"Danielle . . . wanted me to go to Delancey Street [one of the drug rehabilitation programs], but I told her, 'No way,' " said Zugelder.

Instead, Danny was placed in Walden House, a drug-and-alcohol-rehabilitation center located in an old four-story Victorian mansion near Haight Street in San Francisco.

Although the ground rules of Walden House specified no visits with family or friends during the first thirty days, they did allow Danielle, with a drug counselor, to pick Danny up eight days after his arrest and drive him to the facility.

"Walden House was cool," Zugelder said. "I mean, it was a live-in drug program that you couldn't leave. You could walk out the door if you wanted to, but they would call the police. It was a more humane drug-treatment program.

"They operated on the reward system. You do this and that, be good, and you get telephone privileges. After thirty days, if you are still good, then you are allowed to have visitors. Then, after a certain amount of time, you could go out on passes and spend the night with your family."

Danny arrived at Walden House on February 13, only to be rearrested the next day, charged with assault in a totally different crime. This assault allegedly took place on February 1, three days before the rape, and hours after a verbal battle over his drinking with Danielle.

In addition, Zugelder said the police tried to pin a murder rap on him. He explained, "I had been rebooked, and they put a ten-thousand-dollar bail on the assault charge [over and above the twenty-five thousand for the rape] and the same conditions for Walden House. There were a couple of detectives from homicide, and they started to work on me. It's hard to intimidate me, you know. I'm scared but I won't let it show. Basically, I walked in, sat down, and they had a folder. They opened up this folder and threw out all these photographs."

The photographs were of Samuel Edelman's body. Edelman, an eighty-five-year-old retired jeweler who lived in a plush apartment at 1966 Pacific Avenue (just a block from Danielle's home) in Pacific Heights, had been found on January 28, 1974. Lying in his living room, surrounded by a pool of blood, Edelman had had his throat slashed with a sharp object and his home had been ransacked. His killer was never found.

"I glanced and saw this blood and dead bodies," said Zugelder. "I wouldn't look at them. In fact, I stood up and told them, 'You guys are nuts, and I have absolutely nothing to say to you. Take me back to my cell.' And they did.

"When I saw that, it was like 'Hot damn, these people are going to try to put me in the gas chamber.' I was pretty shaken up about the whole thing [but] I knew they didn't have anything on me."

Once again, Danielle raised the money to finance Danny's bail, and he was released on February 24 to enter the program at Walden House. Sometime before his release, Danielle would announce officially that she was once again pregnant.

"It [the pregnancy] meant a great deal to both of us," Danielle wrote in a June 3, 1974, letter to the San Francisco County Probation Department.

She also said that "for over a month" they weren't able to see or speak to each other.

Danielle's first "glimpse" would take place on Tuesday, February 26, when Danny appeared in municipal court for his preliminary hearing on the rape charge. She would be waiting outside, removed with the rest of the potential witnesses and spectators from the courtroom.

The victim, Kathy G., remembered her own shock at entering the courthouse prior to the start of the hearing and seeing Zugelder talking to a woman she recognized from the car that had driven by both her work and her apartment. "She looked at me with darts in her eyes, like she wanted to kill me . . . very unfriendly. That's when I put two and two together."

It wasn't until five years later, though, when Kathy G. picked up a book in a grocery store and saw the author's picture on the back that she actually knew the woman's name. "It was Danielle Steel," she said.

Danielle wasn't allowed in the courtroom for the preliminary hearing as Judge John J. Welsh heard testimony on the charges. The court would find "reasonable and probable cause to believe that the defendant is guilty" and would set Danny's arraignment for March 19.

Stressed, the already-petite Danielle was losing weight. "She was trying to juggle her writing, her job, her daughter, and her commitment to freeing Danny," said one of Danielle's friends. Under more pressure than she could handle, Danielle needed to make changes.

In June, Danielle would write the probation department, telling them she was moving to a "less expensive home" and giving up her job. She said Dan wouldn't have "a mammoth salary to compete with," and she was "much happier" not being "just a visiting executive."

Actually, it had been a mutual parting of the ways between Danielle and Grey Advertising. Warren Peterson, now executive vice president for Grey in San Francisco, had just come on board as creative director in January 1974.

He remembered Danielle as a very sweet, gracious lady. "She was an incredibly fast, voluminous writer and a quick study," he said, although not a natural at writing advertising copy. "She was a little long-winded and needed a lot of editing," he explained.

The clinching factor for both sides, however, was Danielle's reluctance to work full-time. "Danielle was working only three days a week and another person was working the other two," Peterson said. "We needed someone to be there all the time, and Danielle wasn't willing to do that. The other party was willing to come in five days a week, so that's how that decision got made. Obviously, advertising wasn't Danielle's real career goal anyway."

On March 19, Danny again briefly left Walden House for his arraignment on rape charges, and eight days later, on March 27, he was back in court, this time for his preliminary hearing on the assault charges.

With hair neatly clipped, wearing a blue sports jacket and tie, Zugelder listened as witnesses identified him as the man who attacked a woman the evening of Friday, February 1, 1974.

The victim told the court she had been returning from the symphony, walking home alone down Jackson Street, when "someone stepped out of an alcove as I was walking up the middle of the sidewalk and grabbed me by the left shoulder."

Emotionally, the woman told the judge that the man raised a wooden billy club in his right hand. Startled, she told the court, she looked at the man and said something like "What are you trying to do?" or "What are you doing?" She said that without answering the man struck her on the head with the club.

"He didn't answer my question, and I thought I better start screaming. So I began to scream and I kept on," said the victim.

"What happened after you screamed?" asked the assistant district attorney.

"He kept on hitting me over and over and over and over," the visibly shaken victim testified.

"And where were you when you were being hit by this individual?"

"Well, it started out right there in the middle of the sidewalk, because I wasn't able to move away from him."

"Was he still holding on to you at this time?"

"Yes. And he jostled me up—I think it was the next alcove—and the next thing I knew I had fallen on my back."

"Approximately how many times were you hit in the head area by the club?"

"So many times I figured it must have been about at least once a second. Must have gone on for more than a minute," she replied.

She then reported trying to stop the blows with her hands and, after she was knocked down, with her feet.

"I didn't really see his face at all," the victim said. "I— By the time I was on the ground and could see him again, my eyes were full of blood and I saw just a dim shape with his— He was standing and his billy club was still raised. He was reaching for me, and that's when I started kicking at him."

Hearing the woman's screams, a man in a neighboring apartment looked out his window and saw a man emerge from the alleyway and run up the street. The witness ran from his building and across the street to find the victim crawling out of the alleyway with blood pouring from her wounds.

The witness said that with other help arriving for the victim, he ran up the street where the assailant had gone. Rounding the corner, the witness saw the assailant crossing the street, looking up the hill as the witness was looking down.

"I was trying to get somebody to drive me down there so I could follow the assailant," said the witness. "And by luck a cab came by. I just stopped the cab and he took me down the hill after I asked him to follow."

The witness and the cabbie sped down the hill, turning right and then spotting the assailant in the middle of the block, still walking. The assailant crossed the street and walked to a white car at the corner, while the cab continued through the intersection.

"We went through a green light and took the license number," said the witness, who then drove away in the cab, without looking back. The witness later identified Zugelder from a lineup several days after his arrest.

The testimony of the victim and other witnesses was compelling enough for Judge Welsh. The court moved to have Zugelder arraigned on assault charges. At the same time, Assistant District Attorney Robert L. Dondero alerted Zugelder's attorney that he would be attempting to consolidate this assault case with the rape case. Meanwhile, Danny was moved back to Walden House.

"They had absolutely no proof that I did it," claimed Zugelder, shaking his head. "The police report stated that the assailant was five-nine, a hundred and thirty-five pounds, [with] short, curly blond hair. It was pretty obvious that I didn't fit that description." Even twenty years later, Zugelder still says he didn't commit the assault, nor was he guilty of rape. "The others [rapes that would follow in years to come] I was, but not that one."

Zugelder said he was only allowed to talk to Danielle a couple of times on the phone. Danielle admitted in a letter to the court that when she finally visited him at the rehabilitation center, Danny wasn't tied to her "physically or financially" and they were free of "victim/prosecutor/rescuer roles." She said he had examined what went wrong in the past and faced "the realities of his relationship with me." Thereafter, Danielle said she and Beatrix "visited Dan frequently at Walden."

During April, Zugelder secured his first "pass" from Walden House. "I think it was a twelve-hour pass. Anyway, we [he and Danielle] rented a car and headed to Sausalito. I stopped at a convenience store and bought a bottle of Squirt and a couple of those plastic champagne glasses, because I'm on the wagon, and we toasted each other."

Zugelder said the couple spent the first few hours driving through the country. "Chasing cows," Zugelder laughed. "She used to get all excited about this country stuff. We're driving and she saw a turkey. She started speaking in French. She's calling it a 'dindon.' I tell her, 'No, baby, it's just a turkey.' "

Finally, they rented a bungalow in Sausalito, staying there until it was time to go back. It would be Zugelder's last official pass before he faced trial at the beginning of May.

Then, in mid-April, Joan Patricia Tuttle, a neighbor and close friend of Danielle's, came personally to Walden House to give Danny the bad news: Danielle had miscarried.

Danielle revealed in her June 3, 1974, letter to the probation department that she and Dan "were both stricken by the loss."

In a May 1974 letter written to the court by Tuttle in support of Zugelder, she wrote about the experience of going to Walden to tell Danny that Danielle had miscarried. "He cried," she wrote, adding that Danny was "under such stress," they were all fearful he would resume drinking. "Instead," she wrote, Danny "spent the night consoling" Danielle.

"It was actually twins," Zugelder revealed, looking down at his hands.

Zugelder recalled that Walden House made a special exception so that he could be with Danielle. "They took me to her, and because of the circumstances, they let [me] spend the night there with her. One of them [a counselor] slept on the couch downstairs to keep an eye on me, to fulfill their legal obligations."

For Danny, it was an emotional roller coaster. "She might be physically going through it, but I'm sitting there planning on having children, too." Zugelder shook his head and sighed. "It was heavy."

The next morning, Zugelder returned to Walden House.

Danielle would later write to the court that this disproved they "only drew close in times of disaster." Instead, Danielle said, the "bond between us has strengthened."

In addition to posting bond, Danielle was also paying for Danny's legal defense, which included hiring a private investigator to tail Danny's accuser. "We hired him to find out everything we could about her because we were trying to figure out why this woman was pressing rape charges against me," Zugelder claimed.

With fees mounting, a prudent Danielle asked Danny to sign a promissory note to repay her the legal fees.

Then, as the trial date approached, Zugelder urged Danielle not to attend. "Danielle was in real bad shape emotionally. I tried to get her not to come for obvious reasons," Zugelder explained. "They were going to be discussing sexual habits, things that allegedly happened while I was with this girl. It wasn't going to be a pretty sight and I tried to convince her of that, but she hung tough through the whole thing." She wanted to be there, he said, to support him.

Twenty years later, Zugelder still stands by his version of what happened on February 4, 1974.

"I was cruising during lunch hour, sometime in the afternoon, in the company sports car," Zugelder recalled. "I had the top down and I'm just cruising around San Francisco. I pulled up to this red light and there are people at this bus stop. There was a woman there and she smiled at me and I smiled back. She was flirting with me and I was flirting with her. It was a mutual thing. So I circled the block and came around and pulled into the bus-stop area and asked her if she wanted a ride. She said, 'Sure.' She got in and, ah, we started cruising toward where she lived. We smoked a joint, and I had my old trusty vodka and grapefruit juice that I was sipping on. We were passing that back and forth and the joint back and forth, and we ended up in her apartment. We had sex and I left. She was pissed off that I left. It was a hit-and-run. You know I hate to say this, it was my way of getting even with Danielle for the things she was doing to me."

As jury selection for Danny's rape trial began, an impeccably dressed Danielle sat in the visitors section. She had asked several people to be with her, so the courtroom was packed with old friends like Bruce Neckels.

"Danielle was very cool and calm, but it had to have been eating her guts out," Neckels recalled. "A few friends showed up to give support, all dressed beautifully, even in fur coats. I kept thinking, If I'm the judge, looking down, no wonder that he [Danny] had to become a part of this."

Everyone rose as the judge entered the courtroom, the blond Zugelder towering above his attorney and, in fact, almost everyone in the room except for the assistant district attorney, who was an inch taller than Danny. Thanks to Danielle, Danny was neatly dressed in a blue suit and red tie.

From time to time, as he sat sideways in his chair at the defense table, he would look back at Danielle. "She would give me a big smile, anything to reassure me that she wasn't impressed with the testimony," he recalled. "She stayed with me one hundred percent. The girl was wonderful at that time. She would literally have to be helped in to the courtroom and helped out, she was so frail."

Sitting quietly behind him, Danielle would work on her needlepoint. "I loved to sail," Zugelder said. "And I think she was needlepointing a sailboat on an ocean scene with the sun or the moon as background. She would needlepoint during the boring parts and then put it down and pay strict attention when they were testifying or doing cross-examination."

Once the testimony from his accuser began, Danny didn't look back anymore; he couldn't bear to watch Danielle's reaction.

Demurely dressed, the plaintiff, Kathy G., was a pretty girl, five foot three and 103 pounds, similar in size to Danielle. On the stand, her voice was quiet as she answered questions about the alleged rape, trying not to look at Danny.

She would tell the court about waiting at the corner of Van Ness Avenue and Greenwich Street for a bus when a man in a sports car with a black top and white bottom drove up to ask directions. When the man offered her a ride, she accepted. After reaching her first-floor apartment, she told the court that the man asked to use the bathroom, and she agreed.

According to court transcripts, Kathy G. would describe what happened differently from what Danny remembered. The assistant district attorney would take her tediously through each detail.

"Then what happened when you got up there [to the apartment]?" Dondero asked.

"I showed him where the bathroom was, and I proceeded out into the kitchen," replied Kathy G.

"Did you do anything in particular when you first got to the kitchen?"

"I proceeded to change my cat's water."

"While you were there in the kitchen, was there a point where he came back to the kitchen?"

"Yes."

"Did you have some conversation there?"

"He asked where the light was."

"The light in what room?"

"The light in the bathroom."

"What did you tell him?"

"I went down and turned it on for him."

"Is there any particular unusual factor about the lighting in your bathroom?"

"It is just very dark in there. It is not unusual for somebody not to be able to find the light."

"After you turned on the light, what did you do next?"

"Went back out into the kitchen."

"What happened after that?"

"He came out. After the bathroom, he came out into the kitchen and asked if he could have a glass of water."

"What did you do at that time?"

"I poured him a glass of water."

"What occurred next?"

"He drank it and set the glass down."

"Then what happened?"

"Then he came from behind me and put his hands around my neck."

"In what manner did he do this? Well, did he do it in a gentle fashion?"

"No. He started to choke me."

"Could you describe how you felt at that time?"

"I thought he was going to kill me."

"Could you describe at all the degree of force which was exerted on your throat during this time?"

"It was enough force that I felt that I was going to black out."

"Were you having any difficulty getting air?"

"Yes."

"Did you feel at that time if he continued to hold your throat with the same degree of force, you would be able to get any air?"

"No."

"Now, while he had his hands around your throat, did he say anything to you?"

"Yes."

"Could you tell us what was said at that time?"

"He said we were going to perform a certain sex act."

"Now, did he use those words, 'We are going to perform a certain sex act'?"

"No."

"Would you be able to recall the words, to the best of your recollection, that were used?"

"Yes."

"What was said?"

" 'We are going to fuck.' "

"Those were his words, is that right?"

"Yes."

"Did he tell you anything would happen to you if you did not agree?"

"Yes."

"Could you describe what was said to you?"

"Yes. He said if I made any sounds or screamed that he would kill me."

"Did you reply to him in any way?"

"Well, the only way I could reply was by nodding my head. So I nodded my head, yes, that I understood."

"Did he ask you whether you understood?"

"Yes."

"Now, after he said that, did he take any other action in regard to you?"

"Yes. He told me to take off my clothes."

"At the time that you were taking off your clothes, was he holding you in any fashion?"

"Yes."

"And how was that?"

"In the same manner."

"Were you removing your clothes in the kitchen area?"

"Yes."

"What happened after you took your clothes off?"

"He started leading me into the bedroom."

"All right. Now, is there some type of hallway or something between the kitchen and the bedroom?"

"Yes, there is a kitchen and then a living room and a long hallway and then the bedroom."

"Between the kitchen and the bedroom, did anything happen?"

"My coin purse was on the kitchen table, and he opened it up and removed the money that was in it."

"Now, was he holding you in any way at this time?"

"By the arm."

"As to your coin purse, what did he do with it?"

"He opened it up and took out two dollars."

"Did he say anything at that time?"

"He wanted to know where the rest of the money was."

"Do you remember the words he used or close to it?"

"He said, 'All right, you'll have to do better than this.'"

"What did you say?"

"I said, 'That's all I have.'"

"What happened next?"

"We went into the bedroom."

"Now, when you got to the bedroom, what happened there? Well, when you got to the bedroom, did you just stand there?"

"No."

"What happened there?"

"He shoved me on the bed and stood over me and— Do you want the exact words, or what?"

"Well, was there something that he said at that time?"

"Yes. He stood over me and he had his zipper down and he told me to suck it."

"Now, at that time were you expecting anyone to come home?"

"No."

"Had he made any requests in that regard, or asked you anything about that?"

"Yes. He asked me when my old man was due home."

"What did you tell him?"

"I told him, 'Any minute.' "

"Now, was that true?"

"No."

"What did he say or do after you told him that your boyfriend would be home any minute?"

"He said, 'All right, button your robe, you are coming with me.' "

"Did he say he would do anything at all to your boyfriend if he came?"

"Yes. He said that he would have to kill him, too."

"Now, did you put on your robe?"

"Yes."

"Then what happened?"

"Well, I didn't want to go outside because I was afraid to. So I told him that if I made—I could make a phone call and detain my boyfriend for about a half-hour, and so he told me to go ahead and do it."

"Why were you afraid to go outside?"

"Because I was afraid he would take me, go someplace and rape me and kill me and leave me there."

"Did you make a phone call?"

"Yes, I did."

"Now, did you make the phone call to your boyfriend?"

"No, I didn't."

"Who did you call?"

"I called my sister."

"Now, did she answer the phone?"

"No."

"Who answered the phone?"

"My brother-in-law."

"What did you say to him, to the best of your recollection, at this time?"

"I told him to tell Jim not to come home for about another half-hour, because dinner wasn't ready, and I rambled on."

"What was your reason in making these statements to your brother-in-law?"

"My reason for saying that was to give him an idea that something was wrong, because he knew that my boyfriend was in jail."

"Now, what did your brother-in-law say at that time when you told him about Jim?"

"He said, 'What's wrong?' He kept asking me, 'What's wrong?' And, obviously, I couldn't tell him, and he finally got the message, and he said he would be right over."

"Now, did you then hang up the phone?"

"Yes."

"At the time that you made the call, were you in the bedroom or some other room?"

"In the hallway."

"At the time you made it, where was the defendant, Mr. Zugelder?"

"Right next to me."

"Did you know his name at the time?"

"All I knew was that his name was Dan."

"Is this the name that he had given you?"

"Yes."

"Did you go back to the bedroom?"

"Yes."

"Now what happened when you got back to the bedroom?"

"Well, he put me back on the bed again and proceeded with different sex acts."

"Well, I think you might have to tell us in a little more detail. What was the first sex act?"

"Okay. Well, first of all, he had me—he put it in my mouth."

"Okay. By 'it,' are you referring to a particular part of his body?"

"Yes."

"What part of his body are you referring to?"

"I am referring to his penis."

"Did he say anything to you?"

"At this particular moment did he say anything?" asked the DA.

"Well, did you indicate that he had you put his penis in your mouth?" the assistant district attorney clarified.

"Yes."

"Now, did you desire to do this of your own free and voluntary consent?"

"No, no."

"All right. And why did you do it?"

"Because I was afraid he was going to kill me."

"Did he say anything to you originally to indicate what he wanted you to do?"

"Yes."

"Could you tell us what he said?"

"He said, 'Put it in your mouth.'"

"Did he make any other comments in that regard?"

"While the act was going on he commented that I wasn't doing well enough and I should do better."

"How did you feel at that time?"

"I was scared to death."

"Were you having any difficulty in breathing under the circumstances?"

"Yes. I was choking."

"Was there at some point that this particular sexual act stopped?"

"Yes."

"After the sexual act you have just described stopped, what happened then?"

"Then he proceeded to commence the act of sodomy."

"Now, did he say anything to you before he began."

"Yes. He said, 'Put it in.'"

"Did he tell you to put it in any particular place?"

"'Put it in your ass.'"

"Now, did you say anything to him when he said that to you?"

"Yes, I did."

"What did you say to him?"

"I told him I had just had an operation and I couldn't do that."

"Did you tell him what the operation was for?"

"Yes."

"What was the operation for?"

"Hemorrhoids."

"Now, did you actually have at the time this occurred hemorrhoids or a condition of your rectal area?"

"Yes."

"Had you actually had an operation?"

"No."

"Okay. Was there a reason that you told him that you had had an operation?"

"Yes."

"What was that?"

"Because of the condition of hemorrhoids, and it is very painful."

"Now, when you told him that you had this operation for hemorrhoids, did he say anything to you?"

"He said, 'That's too bad, isn't it?'"

"And what did he do next?"

"He proceeded to put it in."

"Now, by 'it,' what are you referring to?"

"I am referring to his penis."

"Where did he put it?"

"He put it in my ass."

"Now, actually, would this be a word which you would normally use or was it his word?"

"It was his word."

"Did you feel any pain at the time?"

"Yes."

"Is there some point when he withdrew his penis from your rectum?"

"Yes."

"What happened then?"

"Then he proceeded to just have regular intercourse."

"By that do you mean sexual intercourse?"

"Yes."

"Just so the record is clear, are you talking about any particular organs in relation to this act, sexual organs? Did he put his penis somewhere?"

"Yes, in my vagina," said Kathy G., now visibly upset.

"All right. Now, just relax. Okay. Now did he say anything to you at that time?"

"He said, 'You can do better than that.' And this was said various times throughout each act."

"Was there some point where the act of sexual intercourse terminated, stopped?"

"Yes."

"Did he withdraw his penis?"

"Yes."

"Did any other sexual acts occur after that?"

"Yes."

"Could you describe again what was—what occurred? I am sorry."

"Another oral sex act."

"Did you do anything in relation to his body at that time or did he do anything to you?"

"Just—he was just holding my head."

"Did he put any part of his—any part of his body into your body?"

"Yes, he put his penis into my mouth."

"Was this after the act of anal intercourse and the act of vaginal intercourse?"

"Yes."

"And how did you feel at that time when he did it?"

"Sick to my stomach."

"Just so we are clear as to the four sexual acts that you have described, did you enter into any of these acts of your free and voluntary consent? Do you understand my question? Did you desire voluntarily to engage in any of these acts?"

"No, I did not desire it, no."

"Is there any—is there a reason why you allowed them to occur?"

"I allowed them to occur because I was afraid he was going to kill me."

Through the six days of jury selection and testimony, Danielle sat in the courtroom, listening and needlepointing.

"I don't know how Danielle felt deep in her heart—we certainly were hoping Danny was innocent—all of us," Neckels recalled. "After I heard the victim's testimony, I felt Danny was guilty. I can't speak for Danielle's feelings."

Zugelder still remembered sitting in the hallway of the courtroom after his case had gone to the jury, sincerely believing he would be found not guilty. "She didn't know whether I was circumcised or not, or if I had tattoos on my body," explained Zugelder on why he thought he would be freed. "There was a University of Berkeley law student that covered the whole trial for a term paper. The jury went off and he came up to me in the hallway, came up to all of us, and shook my hand and said, 'There's no way you committed this rape.'

"We were all out in the corridor pitching pennies, discussing where we were going to go have our celebration feast," said Zugelder, explaining that his attorney came back to tell him the jury had returned after only two or three hours. "The lawyer said, 'That's a good sign.'"

Back in the courtroom, as Zugelder stood before the judge, he was shocked as the judge pronounced him guilty of the crime of assault with force likely to produce great bodily injury. Guilty of second-degree robbery. Guilty of rape. Guilty of oral copulation by force, duress, menace, or threat of great bodily harm. Guilty of sodomy. And guilty of false imprisonment.

Stunned, a tearful Danielle watched as Danny was handcuffed and removed from the courtroom, on his way back to prison. There would be no appeal bond.

In December 1976, Danielle would complete the manuscript of *Now and Forever*, the story of a man who is wrongly accused of rape, goes to trial, and is sent to prison, and the woman who loves and stands by him.

Danielle's current attorney, Charles O. Morgan, Jr., maintained in a recent letter sent on her behalf that none of her works were "based on Danny or any part of his life."

Yet the story of Danielle's fictional character, Ian Clarke, in *Now and Forever*, bears much more than just a passing resemblance to Danny Zugelder.

In the book, Clarke is described as "tall, thin, blond, blue-eyed, with high cheekbones and endless legs," a description remarkably close to the actual likeness of Dan Zugelder, with the exception of the eye color. In this case, her heroine, Jessica Clarke, shares the same eye color with Danielle: green.

The fictional Clarke, like Zugelder, was not known for his marital fidelity:

> And so what if now and then Ian had a fling? It didn't happen often, and he was discreet. It didn't bother her. Men did those things when they had to, when their wives were away. He didn't use it, or flaunt it, or grind it into her heart. She just suspected that he did it. That was all. She understood. As long as she didn't have to know. She assumed, which was different from knowing.

Still, as the days wear on to weeks, it becomes increasingly wearing on Jessica. She confesses to a friend:

> I don't even know at this point what the hell we had, or if it's worth wanting back. What did we have? Me supporting Ian, and him hating me for it, so much that he had to go out and screw a bunch of other women to feel like a man.

The similarities between the fictional encounter and the reality are endless:

Ian picked up a girl he didn't know on a street corner; Danny picked up a girl he didn't know on a street corner.

Ian had been drinking; Danny had been drinking.

Ian offered the woman a ride home in his sports car; Danny offered the woman a ride home in his sports car.

Though Ian was a writer, who used a manual typewriter, he wanted to tell the woman he picked up he was "a gigolo, kept by his wife"; Danny said he felt like a gigolo, kept by his girlfriend who was a writer and used a manual typewriter.

The Clarkes lived in Pacific Heights; so did Danny and Danielle.

Both Ian and Danny would claim they had sex with the woman through "mutual consent," not rape, although both would be charged with three counts of rape: rape, oral copulation, and sodomy. (Danny was also charged with false imprisonment, assault with force, and second-degree robbery.)

Both Ian's wife, Jessica, and Danny's girlfriend, Danielle, would use valued rings as collateral to post bond.

Both Ian and Danny would lose a jury trial.

Both Ian and Danny would not be granted probation between the trial and the sentencing hearing.

Both Ian and Danny would be sent to Vacaville.

Both Jessica and Danielle would stay on the ranch of an older woman friend when visiting their men in prison. Jessica's friend was "Beth" and Danielle's, with whom she stayed when Dan was in Lompoc, was Beatrice.

Although the dedication in *Now and Forever* would change from when it originally appeared as a paperback in February 1978, Danielle dedicated the first edition of the book "To special people, for a special time, with special love." Danny was included in the dedications. His dedication read: "To Dan for lessons learned and shared. For everything!"

And there were more lessons to come.

11

ۯ

*L*ike both the survivor and savior she had always been, Danielle sprang back into action. Although devastated by Danny's rape conviction, she now had the sentencing hearing to prepare for, scheduled for June 1974.

Again like her heroine, Jessica, in *Now and Forever*, Danielle was obsessed with helping Danny.

"Most of Jessica's efforts went toward Ian's sentencing," she wrote. "Twice she saw the probation officer detailed to the case, and she hounded Martin [the attorney] night and day."

In truth, as in fiction, they both hoped that Danny would receive probation and, in Danny's case, be returned to Walden House to complete his drug-rehabilitation program. To that end, Danielle once more activated what had been dubbed the Zugelder Defense League.

Well known for her attachment to telephones from as far back as her days with Supergirls, Danielle spent hours calling her friends and asking them to write letters on Danny's behalf. As requested, the letters started to pour into the county probation department, attesting to the fact that Zugelder would be a changed man if he were sent back to Walden House. Predictably, Jessica, in *Now and Forever*, followed the same path. Danielle wrote: "She also collected letters from a number of discreet friends, testifying to Ian's good character."

On Danny's behalf, letters were sent from experts in the penal-reform and drug-rehabilitation fields like Mark Dowie, director of Transitions to Freedom, Inc.; John Maher, president of Delancey Street Foundation; and Keith

R. Mathews, administrator of Walden House. Then Danny's employer, Francis L. Whisler of Whisler-Patri, and a secretary there, Prudence Freeman, sent letters, as did Richard Warburton, sales director, and Antoinette Mailliard, president, of Mailliard Design Consultants, where Danny had done some part-time work. Finally, Danielle called on friends and neighbors like Dan Talbott, Joan Patricia Tuttle, Gail Stewart Woolaway; and even an attorney friend of Danielle's from New York, Edward Tuck, who had never laid eyes on Danny. Finally, Danielle herself composed a revealing five-page letter, sent on June 3, 1974.

So anxious was Danielle to impress the probation department that she wrote about her recent engagement to Danny. She said they were "engaged in April" and planned "to marry in June, and that those plans have not changed."

Danielle, however, apparently "forgot" to tell the probation department about the biggest obstacle to her marrying Danny in June: she was still legally married to Claude-Eric. Due to the waiting period required by New York law, the Lazard divorce judgment would not be final until October 15, 1974.

Still, the letters in support of Danny were permeated with promise; her friends believed in Danny because Danielle believed in him.

Danielle's friend Antoinette Mailliard wrote the court, noting Danny had made excellent "progress," and saying she was sure he could become the "kind of man . . . he wants to be."

Gail Stewart Woolaway, a neighbor of Danielle's, also wrote on Danny's behalf, acknowledging the "struggle" he had been through trying to adapt to his new life. But after visiting Danny at Walden, she said he "seemed very secure and showed remarkable growth."

"There was a question in my mind whether he [Danny] was fairly tried," recalled Dan Talbott, talking about the letter he sent. "Nobody believed it [that he was guilty]. Danielle just didn't want to [believe it]. Mainly we didn't want to because of Danielle. But she stuck by him, and I will always admire her for that."

But others, in retrospect, were not so sympathetic. Mark Dowie, too, wrote a letter, even though by that time Danielle was no longer actively involved with Transitions to Freedom. He believed that Danielle was continuing to perceive Danny as salvageable, even though Dowie knew there was no way. "I always found that she had a problem with the truth," revealed Dowie. "And that's not necessarily to say that she was a liar. It's just that I don't think she knew the difference; I think that actually makes for a good romantic fiction writer, if you are able to blend truth and fiction, you can probably spin a pretty good tale. I always found that she was not totally in touch with reality.

"Danny was an example. Here was a guy who was just a brute. She could find that iota of goodness in a human being and blow it all out of proportion. The guy [Danny] did have some good qualities. She fell in love with that and ignored the other side."

In addition to the letters, Zugelder's counsel requested evaluations by three different psychiatrists to attest to Danny's mental stability, two of whom actually met with Danny and one with Danielle as well.

A prominent San Francisco psychiatrist interviewed Zugelder twice and Danielle once before issuing his findings to Danny's attorney on May 29, 1974. The psychiatrist wrote:

> Mr. Zugelder's recent crimes arose out of extreme psychological duress, but it would be a mistake to regard them as circumscribed events. They are part of a personality pattern, established since before adolescence. Certain anxieties arise, and Mr. Zugelder must impulsively obtain some gratification which will help ward off those anxieties. Usually, the first step has been to medicate himself with alcohol or narcotics.
>
> Typically, the anxieties to which I refer have their basis in Mr. Zugelder's highly conflicted relationships with women. Following the earliest experience with his mother, he has tended to become involved with women who are ostensibly engaged in reforming him, while covertly delighting in his wildness. Often, Mr. Zugelder becomes aware of feeling oppressed by the demands made of him. This somewhat hypermasculine stance, however, defends against his deep awareness of his overwhelming dependency on these women, and his fear that he cannot live up to what is required of him. The fear is mixed with a terrible resentment at being burdened with conflicting tasks. I believe he feels unconsciously that he is being encouraged to behave badly so that he may be controlled by being made to feel guilty. Also, he has some sense that women admire his bravado, and fears that they would not respect him if he became too tame.
>
> Eight months ago, he was tremendously perplexed and frustrated by the nature of his relationship with his current fiancée. She accepted his moving in with her, but he was not part of her public life. She seemed to want him to make something of himself, but would not put her own interests aside at all to cooperate in his efforts to establish himself. She seemed to be altogether too influenced by the demands of her former husband. Feeling hurt and emasculated, Mr. Zugelder left for Reno in an "I'll show you" frame of mind. He planned to take a job running a lodge which had been offered to him and to demonstrate his independence. Inwardly, of course, he

was frightened and angry. His plans for self-sufficiency soon degenerated, with the help of alcohol, to fantasies of scoring a big gambling win in Reno. When this fell through and he went broke, Mr. Zugelder impulsively snatched the purse of a woman he encountered in a parking lot. The desperate wish to get something from a femal [sic] figure, and the anger at being driven to tasks of which he felt incapable, are obvious in this act.

Reconciliation with his fiancée followed, but a similar situation soon arose. The couple had tried several times unsuccessfully to have a child, Mr. Zugelder's fiancée has a medical condition which disposes her to miscarriage, but he still felt defeated when another pregnancy failed after four months. In addition, because of his drinking, he was asked to move to his own place. Again, Mr. Zugelder was furious at his fiancée, and simultaneously in dread of losing her. Again he redoubled his drinking and drug use, went broke, and attacked a woman impulsively in order to get money. This time, I believe, the anger involved in taking something from a woman was closer to consciousness, and Mr. Zugelder was more aware of the displacement of his rage from his fiancée to other females.

The psychiatrist concluded that:

In addition to difficulties one might expect from this sort of beginning, and the obvious difference in backgrounds, there is no question that Mrs. Lazard, with her interest in penal reform and the particular character of her unsuccessful marriage, in some ways fits the pattern for the kind of woman with whom Mr. Zugelder frequently associates himself. At the same time, the two share a genuine and passionate mutual respect. Mrs. Lazard is in psychiatric treatment, and is in a position to work on those aspects of her personality which combine badly with Mr. Zugelder's problems. The relationship constitutes much more of an asset than a liability for either party.

Another psychiatrist, Dr. Richard Komisaruk, concluded in a May 21, 1974, report: "In summary, I see Mr. Zugelder as a neurotic criminal who has a drug-related early history, who has continued to have a drug abuse problem, at this time, involving alcohol, and whose offenses since his release from Lompoc have been directly connected, in my opinion, with his peculiar involvement with Mrs. Lazard."

In the meantime, Danny said he was having second thoughts about putting Danielle through another trial on the assault charges after having put her through the rape trial. "I'm sitting in jail, and I'm getting all these reports on Danielle from all of her friends," Zugelder recalled.

Zugelder said his attorney came to him with a deal to plead guilty to aggravated assault in the first incident involving the billy-club attack, in exchange for dropping some of the charges and giving him a lighter sentence. "My being a practical person, I said 'Let's get this over with.' In fact, at that time I tried to cut Danielle loose. I told her I would be in prison for a long time. She refused."

It was an emotional time, Zugelder remembered. Not only was Danielle dealing with Danny's problems, but medical problems of her own. "Danielle had just had another miscarriage," said Zugelder. "Her hormonal imbalance had to just be . . . well . . . it's a wonder she came out of it sane with all the miscarriages and traumas in her life.

"Our lives were so intertwined, our relationship so intense, we may have been rocky, but when you have two different personalities like that and then all the things going on that we had going on, it [the relationship] has got to be rocky. I just didn't have the maturity to deal with these things. I pled guilty to the assault charge. I told her she wasn't going to live through another trial. I think it would have killed her. She just couldn't do it."

On June 7, 1974, Zugelder was back in court for his sentencing. Even though he had been in jail since the trial, he was allowed to dress in street clothes for his hearing. He appeared in a tweed suit, light blue shirt, and striped red tie that Danielle had previously purchased for him. He had shaved and combed his hair neatly, but nothing could completely cloak his nervousness. He smiled at Danielle as he entered the crowded courtroom, a smile she returned with both her lips and her eyes.

Keith Mathews, director of Walden House, spoke first on Danny's behalf: "Of all the people that we have received in Walden House who come in to us for help, there are very few that progress as fast as Dan Zugelder has, or done as well, got into the family as quickly. As you can see, there are quite a few people here today. And they are all here because of Dan, and because of their love for him, and because of his love for them. They know he is hurting, and just want to be here with him."

Although Judge Donald B. Constine had no questions for Mathews, he did note, "I have had very few cases in the last several years that have had as complete an evaluation as this, with as many letters and documents and evaluations submitted to me."

Then Danny's attorney asked that Danielle be allowed to address the court. "I merely want to represent to the Court my willingness to stand by Mr. Zugelder," Danielle said. "If there were any possibilities for consideration of the suggestions by Walden House, I would appreciate it."

Judge Constine himself characterized the proceeding as the result of a real tragedy that was:

> tragic because of the violence and terror and injury suffered by the Defendant's innocent victims within a short period after having been released on parole for bank robbery. It is tragic because, perhaps, for the first time, within a very short period, the Defendant has gained some insight into his violence and dangerous behavior, and may have a real desire for rehabilitation. It is tragic, also, because of the effect this has on those who have come forward in his behalf, who wish to assist him, and have faith in his state of desire for rehabilitation.

Still, the judge believed the probation report summed up the matter:

> The Probation Office states that the Defendant, in substance, committed a robbery in Reno, a vicious street assault on a victim that he did not know, and a rape with force within a very short period of time. The Probation Office concludes in its evaluation that it would be an act of irresponsibility to release the Defendant on probation, and that it is possible that his participation in the Walden House treatment is sincere. The Probation Office feels that there may be some question that the improved behavior is as a result of a sincere personality change, or an effort to avoid further imprisonment. The Probation Office does state, accepting the fact that there has been a change in attitude, as such, nevertheless, the Defendant, according to the Probation Officer, "is far too dangerous to release on the community after this three-month experience."

Then, looking Danny in the eye, Judge Constine sentenced him to prison under "terms prescribed by law" for each of five counts against him, and remanded him to the Sheriff of San Francisco to deliver to the California State Prison at Vacaville. His sentence, basically, amounted to from five years to life. Ironically, in years to come, Danielle would meet this same judge again under a set of circumstances involving another convicted felon.

After watching Danny, cuffed and defeated, leave the courtroom, a tearful, frail Danielle, supported by her friends who had been with her at the sentencing hearing, adjourned to her house in Pacific Heights. According to a lawyer friend who was present, it was almost like a wake: "As this thing happened, Danielle went more and more into a fantasy world . . . a state of denial. She never stopped believing in him [Danny]." Yet if there was a complete turn-off for this attorney, he said it was when Danielle, who had been crying, said it was "a manly thing" for Danny to admit to the billy-clubbing assault.

"She was in love with danger and in love with being in love," believed the attorney, who said he walked out after that and never saw Danielle again.

Within a week, Danny was transferred to the California Medical Facility in Vacaville, near Sacramento. From June until late August Danielle would visit him, often with Beatie, on a regular basis.

Indeed, Danielle's description of that prison in her book *Now and Forever* shows her familiarity with it:

> Three days later, Ian was moved from county jail to state prison. He went, like all male prisoners in Northern California, to the California Medical Facility in Vacaville for "evaluation."
>
> Except for the gun tower peering over the main gate and the metal detector that searched them for weapons, the prison at Vacaville looked innocuous. Inside a gift shop sold ugly items made in prison, and the front desk might have been the entrance to a hospital. Everything was chrome and glass and linoleum. But outside, it looked like a modern garage. For people.

It was a trying time for Danielle careerwise as well. She had left her job with Grey Advertising in March 1974. And, even though her first novel had been released in October 1973, her New York agent, Phyllis Westberg, was having little luck marketing Danielle's next four books—*In the Fog, Savage Kind of Loving, To Kill a Son,* and *Drea*—and a screenplay, *Give Me Some Slack, Mama,* which were all written between 1972 and 1973. Danielle would later reveal that these books were rejected by fifteen publishing houses.

"One manuscript collected twenty-seven rejection slips," she told Pat Montandon in a 1981 profile. "But before I could get discouraged, I had already written my next book."

Danielle would later describe this period in her life to a reporter for the *San Francisco Examiner* as "a major emotional trauma that gave me literary constipation for a year and a half." And, although she didn't name Danny specifically, she would say it was related to their relationship. "In some ways," she said to the reporter, "I've had difficult experiences in my life."

Meanwhile, Danielle had also found a new apartment on Baker Street, in the Marina district. It, too, came furnished and without memories of Danny.

During her visits with Beatrice Baer the year before, Danielle had been exposed to Christian Science. Followers of Christian Science believe in the teachings of Jesus but also believe that sickness is an illusion and therefore can be dispatched through the power of the spirit. Generally, Christian Scientists do not take medicine or seek treatment from doctors.

"She was looking for something to fill that void left in her soul from the Catholic Church," Zugelder said. To that end, Danielle became increasingly intrigued with the teachings of Christian Science. "She really started getting into it after I was arrested. The more she found out about it, the more it fit her lifestyle and her beliefs. She was getting into the Bible for comfort and strength while I was in Walden House. She needed to find strength somewhere."

"I didn't like the guilt of the Catholic Church and the idea that adversity is God's will," Danielle told Glenn Plaskin in a 1991 feature he wrote for the *San Francisco Chronicle*, describing herself as a "very religious person":

> I now believe that there is no physical, financial, mental, or relationship problem that can't be worked out. That's a wonderful thing to teach your children—never to be defeatist. In Christian Science, they say: "If you hit a rock ten times, eventually it will break open." I believe that.

Then, in September, they both received another jolt when Danny was moved from Vacaville to San Quentin.

Zugelder explained, "At that time a lot of weed was coming in from the visiting room [at Vacaville] into the prison. I knew about it, but it wasn't my grass." Zugelder, who was working in the visiting room at that time, said he was "getting my cut of the grass, but I wasn't organizing it." Zugelder said he and an eighteen-year-old convict got "busted." "They sent him to Tracy because he was eighteen. It was like the gladiator school for the young kids, and they sent me to San Quentin, which was the gladiator school for the big kids. It was rough. San Quentin at that time was maximum security, and people were getting killed over there every week . . . people jumping off the tiers, people cutting throats. It was bad."

Closer to San Francisco, Danielle visited Danny in San Quentin and sent him almost-daily letters. Again, it would enable her to describe the prison with true authenticity in her book *Passion's Promise*, in which heroine Kezia Saint Martin goes to visit her convict lover, Lucas Johns: "They saw it as they rounded a bend on the freeway, San Quentin. Across a body of water, a finger of the bay that had poked its way inland, it stood at the water's edge, looking ugly and raw."

Danielle remembered San Quentin well, writing in her book:

> The mammoth fortress that was San Quentin took her breath away when they saw it again. It seemed to stand with its body jutting into

her face, like a giant bully or an evil creature in a hideous dream. One felt instantly dwarfed beneath the turrets and towers, the endless walls that soared upwards, dotted only here and there by tiny windows. It was built like a dungeon, and was the color of rancid mustard. It was not only fearsome, but it reeked of anger and terror, loneliness, sorrow, loss. Tall metal fences topped with barbed wire surrounded the encampment, and in all possible directions stood gun towers manned by machine-gun-toting guards. Guards patrolled the entrance, and people emerged wearing sad faces, some drying their eyes with bits of handkerchief or tissue. It was a place one could never forget.

"I give Danielle this," Zugelder complimented. "She was one tough lady. She also gave it her best shot. Visiting the prison, going through this, I gotta admit that was tough."

On March 28, 1975, Danny was returned to Vacaville to complete the rest of his sentence. Danielle would come "on Thursdays and Fridays when she could," said Zugelder, "because the visiting room was less crowded and more intimate." She would usually visit from eight-thirty in the morning until the close of visiting hours around three-thirty in the afternoon. Unlike Lompoc, where prisoners and their families could lounge and picnic outside, at Vacaville, families were relegated to the visitors' room, eating out of vending machines.

"In the summer, fall, and winter of 1975 and then into 1976, Danielle was getting more and more into her religion," said Zugelder. "She would bring the Bible with her during visits. It would have markers in it, and she would read it waiting for me to come.

"It was positive thinking, and it's amazing, but once she started getting into this stuff she quit having so many [health] problems," he continued. "She spent hours at Christian Science reading rooms and went to church every Sunday. She was constantly trying to convert me. She would send me literature, a Bible, books on Christian Science. She wanted me to embrace it the way she had."

Zugelder said she even quit her three-pack-a-day smoking habit, going cold turkey during this time (although later she would return to smoking), and also gave up Sanka for herbal tea.

"I remember she even used to send me herbal tea at Christmastime," Zugelder laughed. "The first time I got it, the guards weren't going to let me have it because they thought it was marijuana."

Ever since her divorce from Claude-Eric was final, Danny had been trying to convince Danielle to marry him so they could have conjugal visits. In August 1975, Danny applied for permission to get married, and they went about collecting the necessary forms. Once the license was ready, Danielle, at first, backed out. "She was nervous," Zugelder explained.

Then, a few weeks later, she said, yes to marriage and to becoming a prison bride.

12

※

*D*anielle's second wedding bore absolutely no resemblance to her first.

Instead of a ceremony in the somber holiness of a New York cathedral, witnessed by richly dressed aristocrats from around the globe, and feted afterward at a sit-down dinner and champagne reception in an elegant hotel ballroom, Danielle said "I do" to husband number two in the visiting room at the California Medical Facility prison at Vacaville.

It was September 13, 1975. Danielle had just turned twenty-eight. Danny was twenty-five.

As Zugelder remembered it, prison officials had "pulled out a few tables" in the waiting area. It was a grim, well-used room, with a linoleum floor, dirty blinds, scarred walls, and aluminum ashtrays scattered about. "I came in," he said, "and then she came in. We met in the middle, and my uncle married us."

Danielle's long beige gown and Southern-belle hat looked strangely out of place as she stood next to Danny, who was wearing blue jeans and a white shirt: formal wear for convicts. Their witnesses included a neighbor of Danielle's and an attorney who had handled Danny's defense in the Reno incident, for which he was ultimately not tried.

Neither Danielle's nor Danny's immediate family attended the nuptials. Donna Monroe, Zugelder's stepsister, remembered finding out about the ceremony the month before it happened. "None of us could attend except for Uncle Dale [Brown], a Baptist minister, who married them," Monroe said.

"I thought it was strange that they would marry," said Danny's sister, Sharlene Sweet.

Emmett Herrera was both surprised and disgusted when he heard about their prison marriage through mutual friends. "I thought that was such a weak choice that I decided to close the book on the both of them," Herrera said. "It was the first time I ever put her on the same plane with him."

Regardless of Danielle's motives, Danny said he pushed for marriage from the minute he heard about conjugal visits. The prison had two-bedroom mobile homes and full one-bedroom duplexes on the grounds. "They had nineteen-hour visits and forty-three-hour visits," he explained, which married prisoners got to use on a rotating basis every three or four months.

According to officials from the California Medical Facility at Vacaville, the facility has had the conjugal-visit program in effect since the early 1970s. At CMF, there are ten apartments, each of which has a kitchen, living room, and either one or two bedrooms. The units are fully furnished with color televisions, pots and pans, dinnerware, linen, and even games and puzzles for children.

"I wasn't really concerned about getting married myself, other than the conjugal visits. That was the key selling factor and the key buying factor in getting married," Zugelder said.

Ironically, there was no conjugal visit the night of their wedding; that happened "about a week later."

"We were on standby," claimed Zugelder. "A person in prison would arrange to have a conjugal visit and then the wife would decide she didn't want to come or couldn't make it. Danielle had call forwarding and everything. She kept a picnic basket packed with all the condiments. She kept a suitcase packed with all of her clothes and lingerie, and a full tank of gas. They would contact me within four or five hours of the time of the visit, and I would call her. Wherever she was at, she would immediately race home, throw the things in the car, stop at Safeway for some steaks and shrimp and chocolate cake, and come on out." Located east of San Francisco on the highway to Sacramento, Vacaville was a little more than an hour's drive for Danielle, which was a prerequisite, said California Department of Corrections officials, to being placed on the standby list.

"I can only think of one time she couldn't make it. She was really sick," Zugelder said. Otherwise, he said, during their marriage they averaged a conjugal visit "every forty-five to sixty days, ninety days tops." In between, Danielle would drive up weekly to see him in the prison visiting room.

In a letter written by Charles O. Morgan, Jr., Danielle's attorney, he claims that Danielle and Danny didn't have "regular conjugal visits." He said, "The program was new," there weren't many "facilities," and even then the visits were "stressful."

Responding to Danielle's statement, Zugelder said, "I'd been in Vacaville and San Quentin for over a year before we ever got married, and she had visited me regularly. If it was that stressful, why did she marry me in prison and why did she stay married to me for two years?"

Zugelder said they would alternate their conjugal stays. "One visit would be a family visit and the next time would be our lovers' visit. When Beatie was there we would play Parcheesi or watch television. It was important to me, and it was to her, that we maintain the family unit so we wouldn't become estranged from each other. It was tough on Beatrix, too." Indeed, pictures from that period, taken at the prison, show a growing, changing Beatie, who still appeared friendly with Zugelder.

Then, as it was in their beginning, Danielle got pregnant in prison, this time on a legally sanctioned conjugal visit.

Zugelder still maintained that he was against starting a family while he was in prison. "I didn't want to start a family until our lives stabilized. We still wanted children, but with the emotional stress of her visiting and all the things she had to go through, I didn't think she would ever be able to carry a child to full term. Now the best that we ever hoped for was that she would carry it long enough that she would get a premature baby that you could put in an incubator and have it live. I didn't want kids that bad."

Nor was Danielle thrilled about this pregnancy.

"She got pregnant and she did not want to have it," said Zugelder. "So she went to the Bible. She went through all this Christian Science stuff, got the faith healer, and had what they call in the medical books a one-in-a-million or one-in-two-million condition where the egg and the fetus was developing and then it just disappeared."

Although she doesn't explain when it happened, Danielle writes about just such an experience in her nonfiction book, *Having a Baby*:

> Once, a very long time ago, I discovered that I was pregnant (and I'll admit that I wasn't pleased—panicked in fact), and amazingly, after a very short time (I couldn't have been more than a few weeks pregnant), the symptoms stopped totally. I saw my doctor, and the pregnancy had literally disappeared—they call it reabsorbed. A short time later, I got my period, and the problem had resolved itself. I think that this is fairly unusual, but it does happen.

Ironically, Danielle, who liked to keep her private life quiet, announced in a *San Francisco Examiner* newspaper column one month after their marriage that she had wed Dan Zugelder.

The columnist also reported that Danielle was going to co-teach a seminar in November 1975 on the "Newly-Alone Woman." The seminar, she said, would deal with financial aspects of living alone that were customarily taken care of by the "husband." Danielle was quoted as saying, "There's help for the poor and the very rich, but no guidance for the upper-middle-class woman, who goes through as much trauma as anyone else."

Danielle didn't explain what had happened to her husband or why he wasn't living with her in San Francisco. A former acquaintance of Danielle's, Ann Dowie, was curious as to how she handled Danny's absence. "I remember her joking at the time she married him," recalled Ann. " 'Don't they want to meet him?' I asked, and she said, 'I just tell them he's in the shower.' She was very quick, very glib."

To help make ends meet, Danielle had begun teaching a creative-writing course at a private school in San Francisco called The Hamlin School, and she was still writing poetry for publication.

In between hitting the Christian Science reading rooms on a regular basis, teaching, and spending time with Beatie, Danielle continued to make time to write her novels. She would turn in the completed manuscript for *Passion's Promise* in December 1975.

When *Passion's Promise* finally reached the paperback bookshelves in January 1977, Danielle hadn't forgotten her Vacaville lover. She dedicated the first edition of that book: "To Dan with Endless [sic] love for making me so happy and so lukey [sic]. . . . "

Danny said the "lukey" was a private joke between the two of them, stemming from the time she misspelled the word "lucky" in a letter to him. "I'm pretty sure that she named her character Luke after the fact that we had this thing going with 'lukey' and 'lucky,' " he said.

In future editions, the dedication would be rewritten to reflect her new life. Danielle would rededicate later printings of *Passion's Promise* (as she has done with other books as well), switching her thanks from Danny to her daughter Beatrix.

Others would also believe the book's hero, "emerald-eyed" Lucas Johns, was a version of Danny. Even though he couldn't remember the title, Mark Dowie described the book "where the protagonist was a convict. She falls in love with this raunchy convict who is obviously partly Danny Zugelder," Dowie believed. "And in there [*Passion's Promise*] is a sort of guy who helps people coming out of prison . . . . but clearly, when I read the book, I was the character."

Zugelder said that during phone conversations and letters in between their visits, Danielle would discuss plot lines and talk about her books. In 1975 Danielle was still working on a book she had tentatively titled *Lizards and Ants*, which would later become *Now and Forever*.

Zugelder said Danielle started *Lizards and Ants* sometime after the trial. "That was cleansing her soul of all the trauma and everything," he believed. "When she started it, she told me she was writing a fictional biography of what we went through with the trial and everything."

Like *Passion's Promise*, *Now and Forever* was sold to Dell. The completed manuscript was sent to the publisher in December 1976, although it wouldn't be published until February 1978. After *Now and Forever*, Danielle started work on a book she titled *Season of Passion*, the story of a young woman married to a football player who is mentally impaired following an accident and placed in a nursing facility. The woman raises their son, born after the accident, while keeping the father's existence a secret from everyone. It would be the last book she ever discussed with Danny.

Financially, however, it was still a difficult time for Danielle. Even though Claude-Eric was still providing $900 a month in child support and another $1,500 in support under a property-settlement agreement, Danielle's expenses (an average of nearly $3,000 a month) outweighed her income (around $2,400 a month net). Her rent was $800 a month, and she was paying $250 a month for child care and household help. She also had accumulated substantial credit-card debt, and was sending minimum payments to Saks, I. Magnin, Sears, Wells Fargo, and Mastercharge, amounting to over $300 per month.

During the 1976–77 school year, Danielle started teaching a three-day-a-week creative-writing class at another private school, University High in San Francisco, using her maiden name of Steel rather than her married name of Zugelder. Only two years old, University High was described as a "pretty exclusive" private high school with about four hundred students in four grades, 9–12.

Katherine Conley, who now works for a publishing company in Eugene, Oregon, was a junior that year, and along with author Ethan Canin (*Emperor of the Air*), took the semester class from the woman they knew as Mrs. Steel.

"Her book *Passion's Promise* was published at the end of that semester, so she wasn't quite the famous person at that point," Conley said. And, although Conley said she was "just breaking into that realm," she still remembered Danielle wearing "fur coats and lots of jewelry to class. She did not look like a typical high-school teacher."

As a teacher, Conley thought Danielle "adequate." "I certainly wouldn't say she was a remarkable instructor. There were plenty of good teachers at that school, and I wouldn't rank her in the top ten. I thought she was pretty good at creating an atmosphere in the class where we felt comfortable sharing our thoughts and our work. We did a lot of reading out loud. She would discuss a technique and provide examples, and then ask us to write. She thought it was important to write every day and to write from experience. Not necessarily original writing tips, but certainly very valuable."

Conley, though, said she had a "fairly negative experience" with Danielle at the end of the semester, based on a miscommunication about due dates. In anger, Conley said she ended up writing a satire on romance novels. "It probably wasn't very good," Conley said, adding she probably did it because she felt betrayed. "Keep in mind that I was a struggling, obnoxious adolescent."

By the spring of 1977, Zugelder said he sensed that things were starting to sour between them, although he wasn't sure exactly why. "They always say you're the last to know; that's because you don't want to know. You see little signs, but you just don't want to know. For one thing, she wasn't coming up every single week. She would generally spend the night in the motel in Vacaville. At first she would come up with an excuse that she couldn't spend the night, and then she would come to the visitors' center and change her mind. When I would kiss her good-bye at the door, thinking I wouldn't see her for another week, I would see her the next day."

Danielle came for what would become their last conjugal visit in the summer of 1977. She was wearing, he said, a sleeveless, red print dress, two sizes too big and hanging to mid-calf or below.

"After that visit I thought back about it later," said Zugelder. "I knew she was screwing around. During this last conjugal visit she was really scared, really scared. I had never done anything to Danielle to make her feel physically threatened. She was extremely agitated, scared, nervous, and sick to her stomach. It was a two-day visit. In fact, she left a day early. She wouldn't admit to me consciously that there was something else going on in her life. I'd say, 'What's wrong?' and she kept saying, 'Nothing.'

"As soon as she went to sleep, she was talking in English, 'He's going to be so mad. He's just going to be so mad.' Like I say, when she talked in her sleep, she would hold whole conversations. She would say, 'He's going to be so mad,' and I would say, 'Who is going to be so mad?' and she would say my name. I'd say, 'Why?' and she would say, 'I can't tell you why—I can't tell you.' This went on for five or ten minutes."

Another telltale sign had to do with Beatie. "One week she would bring Beatrix and the next time it would be just her," Zugelder explained. "She quit bringing Beatrix down to see me about a month before [the last conjugal visit]. She told me that Beatrix was all 'hoped out' about me coming home.

"At the time I thought it was true," he said, because at that point he didn't know Danielle was seeing another man. "Now, looking back, I see the reason she didn't bring Beatrix is she didn't want her telling me.

"This was right after she moved to Green Street. I was the one who talked her into [renting] this house in the first place and told her to have Delancey Street move her. And the rest, as they say, is history," he said in reference to her next relationship.

"She creates the fantasy she wants to live," Zugelder believed. "And that's how she lives. And if any little thing doesn't fit into that fantasy, it either doesn't exist or she changes it to fit the fantasy. That's just Danielle."

Soon after the botched conjugal visit, Danielle came back to see Danny on a regular visit. "That's when we talked about it [divorce]," he said.

Several days following the visit, Zugelder called her collect, and she was crying. "Just really, really upset," he said. It was then she told Danny she wanted a divorce. Danny started to cry as well.

Just as she had been surprised by the marriage, Zugelder's stepsister Donna was equally surprised by the impending divorce. "My son was eleven months old at the time Jarrie and I went up to see Danny when he was in Vacaville," Donna remembered. "She [Danielle] told us to come stay with her, as we had the year before. When we got there [to Danielle's house], she shoved us right off into a motel. All of a sudden she was just completely changed. We had no idea they were having problems. She didn't say anything about them having problems, she just said that she was going to be too busy, she would put us closer to him. We had to follow her to the Motel 6 in our car, and she took off and that was it. I thought even if you are having trouble with the spouse, if you have grown close to the family, usually you don't write everybody off. All of a sudden we were just like dirt. She wanted nothing more to do with anybody. She quit writing and calling Mom and Dad. Everybody was just completely cut off."

Danielle had Danny served with divorce papers on October 13, 1977, exactly two years and one month after their prison wedding.

In the interlocutory judgment of dissolution of marriage, which wouldn't become final until April 14, 1978, Danny ended up with thirty dollars a month. His payments were to commence December 1, 1977, and continue until May 1, 1979, a month after his eventual release from prison. And, most important, he received a waiver on the $14,700 he owed Danielle for his 1974 legal expenses. In addition, she had her name legally restored to Danielle Steel.

Zugelder claimed he had no time or way to fight the process.

Instead, he had to give up any rights to what would one day be a fortune:

All rights [sic], title and interest in the novel *Seasons* [sic] *of Passion*, written by Danielle while they were still married;

"All rights [sic], title and interest" in novels Danielle wrote prior to the marriage, but many while they were living together, including

Going Home, Drea, In the Fog, Savage Kind of Loving, Passion's Prom-ise, Now and Forever (a/k/a Lizards and Ants); and Give Me Some Slack, Mama.

"It was like a joke," Zugelder said. "It takes money to live in prison just like it takes money to live outside. It would cost you thirty dollars a month just to have cigarettes and coffee. It didn't quite seem like enough when you're used to the previous four years, not having to worry about it. I just thought—for all the things that I've done for her—I felt it was only fair that she should have taken better care of me in the divorce. I was upset that she made no provisions for me to have any money to start my life with when I got out. I didn't ask for much, I asked for five thousand dollars. That was just so I could get an apartment, get a car or something to get me around, buy clothes; just so I could start my life over again. She wasn't prepared to do that."

Still, Zugelder admitted their marriage—their relationship—was doomed from the beginning.

"No," he said, shaking his head, "I don't think we ever could have made it. We had too many conflicting values. I was more apt to compromise and do the things that she wanted to do to please her, but she wasn't very willing to do the same for me. I liked the theater, but at the same time, I could sit on the dock fishing all day."

And Zugelder wasn't alone in believing their relationship was hopeless. Even though Dan Talbott, the former neighbor and friend of both Danielle and Danny, initially thought their marriage was good, he knows now he was mistaken. "We are talking about a major, major con man—a professional alcoholic," said Talbott, himself a recovering alcoholic. "Danielle had as much chance of survival in his world as he had in hers—none."

13

⬥

On a spring day in 1977, a phone rang in the offices of the Delancey Street Foundation moving company near downtown San Francisco. With only ten employees and three trucks, this moving outfit was no threat to United Van Lines, but it handled about fifteen homes a week, which pleased the founders of Delancey Street, John Maher and his wife, Dr. Mimi Silbert.

Profits were not the top priority when they set up this rehabilitative program for drug addicts, ex-convicts, alcoholics, prostitutes, and other outcasts in the city's Embarcadero District in the shadow of the Bay Bridge. Silbert, armed with a doctorate in criminology from Berkeley, and Maher, an ex-convict and recovering drug addict, started out small in 1971 with four residents and a thousand dollars from a loan shark. In time, they had acquired a live-in facility and several trade schools to give these so-called incorrigibles a fresh start in life.

"The point of Delancey Street is to get the underclass out of the world, out of the underbelly, and teach them to enter the middle class, and reach the top of the American dream," Silbert explained.

They did it by providing job training and teaching self-sufficiency, complemented by a counseling program that cut into criminal recidivism by adapting elements of Synanon and Alcoholics Anonymous. It offered a new lease on life for recovering heroin addicts like William George Toth, the foundation's thirty-year-old moving-company supervisor, the next man to enter Danielle's life.

Danielle, of course, was already fully aware of Delancey Street; she had supported them in a 1973 fight to house a residential treatment center in Pacific Heights. "She came over to Delancey Street and liked what we were doing and was an important friend," Silbert remembered. "One of the things about Delancey is that we teach people to interact with all kinds of people unlike them. You have to interact with a successful person to become one. Danielle was terrific about coming around and talking and making us feel important and like we belonged. Some people can get into prison reform and still not talk to an [ex-convict] as an equal. Danielle could do both. That's a rare quality."

And, although Silbert said she was never introduced to Danny Zugelder, she had heard a lot about him from Danielle. "Her support was both political and personal," Silbert recalled. "She was a good friend to us and still is, and I like her a lot. Her support was clearly a prediction of future success."

So, four years later when Danielle was thinking of moving out of her Baker Street apartment, she eschewed the conventional movers and phoned Delancey Street to get an estimate on moving her things to a new rental house on Green Street in Russian Hill. There seemed to be no hesitation about hiring a group of ex-convicts and recovering heroin addicts to haul away her furniture. What she didn't count on was having one steal her heart.

At the time, William Toth—Bill to his friends—had been drug free for two years, his longest period of abstinence since he got hooked on heroin back in 1966. When he entered Delancey Street in 1975, he was coming off a six-month jail stint for possession of stolen property. As a condition of his parole, he had to put in two years in a residential facility. More important, Bill Toth wanted to clean up his life.

"The profile of the general Delancey Street resident includes some violence in his background, with usually ten years of hard-core drug addiction," Silbert explained. "He's been in and out of prison several times, is unskilled, has no work habits, and comes from several generations of poverty."

It didn't matter where Bill had been. Delancey, he said, changed everything. He got counseling, took part in group therapy, and excelled in the work program. Slowly he regained his self-esteem.

By 1977 Bill was running the foundation's moving company and had completed the requirements for a Public Utilities Commission license. His responsibilities included directing staff and providing estimates for potential customers. Under his direction, Bill says the moving company turned a profit after being in the red for years. Life was good for Bill. Life had never been better.

So when Bill showed up at 2710 Baker Street and knocked on the door of apartment number five, he showed few battle scars from his troubled past. For the first time in years, he said he was feeling confident, self-assured, and convinced he had licked the tragic habit that had ruined his first marriage and turned him toward a life of crime.

The door opened and he smiled at the petite brunette standing before him. As Danielle showed him around the apartment, Bill was sizing up more than the task at hand. He was attracted by the dark brown hair, the dark complexion, the green eyes as big as saucers, and her full, sensuous mouth. She was very exotic looking, he thought. "There were vibrations, a mutual attraction. I don't know how else to describe it," Bill said of his first meeting with Danielle.

"He's no Adonis," a friend said of Bill, "but he was bright, friendly, and articulate." An ex-college football player, he was five foot eight and powerfully built.

"We were having a conversation," he said. "I was doing an estimate on moving her house, and just in the normal course of conversation, she told me she had a husband in prison."

Bill said he admitted to Danielle that he had been a drug user, but he had been drug free since coming to Delancey Street. "We hit it off," Bill recalled. "She was understanding."

He also learned she wrote novels for a living. Back at Delancey Street, he remembered picking up her most recent book, *Passion's Promise*, without its cover. He was surprised to find the book was about a relationship between a socialite and an inmate. "I remember reading this," he said. "It blew my mind."

Danielle postponed the move, and they didn't meet again until Bill took a deliberate detour down Baker Street on his way back from a job and spotted Danielle pulling up in her red Toyota wagon. He stopped and struck up a conversation, learning that her living arrangement had become unbearable.

In May Danielle's landlord, Paul Drymalski, had gone to court to evict her two basset hounds, Elmer and Maude, charging the dogs had defecated and urinated all over the apartment's mahogany floors and bedroom carpeting, causing in excess of a thousand dollars in damages. He demanded Danielle pay for the repairs. Drymalski claimed he feared this would happen in 1975, when Danielle moved in, and he agreed to rent the unit to her only after getting assurances that the hounds were housebroken. On April 3, 1977, while checking on a leak in Danielle's apartment, he discovered the dogs were using the apartment as "a toilet."

When Drymalski came by ten days later for another look, Danielle refused to let him in. What's more, his manager's key could no longer open the door because Danielle had changed the locks, claiming that he had entered the apartment without her permission.

It didn't take long for things to escalate. According to Danielle, Drymalski threatened to break down the door. Danielle called the police. When he finally did get inside for a second look, it was in the presence of Danielle and her attorney. Drymalski sued for $1,669 in damages and claimed that Danielle had withheld the June rent. Danielle denied the allegations and filed a countersuit, claiming Drymalski had wrongfully evicted her. She wanted $5,000 in damages for emotional distress and loss of income. A year later, a judge threw the entire case out of court.

On June 10, Bill's thirty-first birthday, two Delancey Street moving vans pulled up outside Danielle's apartment, and Bill and seven other men moved Danielle, Beatrix, and the dogs to a beautiful, two-storey stucco house at 1025 Green Street. Built in 1911 and set in fashionable Russian Hill, the 2,478-square-foot home had eight rooms and two bathrooms, including maid's quarters in the cellar.

Over the next few months, the novelist and the moving man began dating very heavily. Many passionate nights were spent at Bill's Delancey Street apartment in Sausalito. Years later, Danielle admitted in a court deposition that sex with Bill was the best part of the relationship. "It was great physical passion for a very short time."

Danielle began to integrate Bill into her life—they dined out, took in movies, and went for walks and long drives through rural Northern California. Bill recalled that most of the socializing was done with Danielle's friends—writers, lawyers, doctors, advertising executives. One of their favorite haunts was Robert, a Pacific Heights French restaurant. Its clientele was mixed; it drew not only the well-to-do of Pacific Heights but also the city's liberal young movers and shakers.

As time went on and they grew closer, Bill, a chronic self-doubter, was baffled by the relationship and privately wondered whether he was out of his league. He knew Danielle was an ambitious writer with expensive tastes, and he was a recovering middle-class junkie. He remembered, "The question that kept running through my mind was, What was a woman like this doing with a man like me?" A friend of Bill's believed he underestimated himself. "Sex may have started it, but she clearly loved him," he said.

Danielle's old friend Mark Dowie, who met Bill once, felt that Danielle's interest in Bill mirrored her relationship to Danny. "There's a syndrome that Waylon Jennings sang about: 'Ladies Love Outlaws,' " he said. "Danielle's part of that syndrome. I'm not surprised at all that she was attracted to Bill. She gravitated to that whole world. I was part of that world, and she gravitated to me. Remember, she married Dan after he smashed a little old lady in the face and after he got sent to prison. Danny Zugelder makes Bill Toth look like a saint."

In her 1981 book of poems, Love, there is a poem plainly titled "Bill," about a woman who falls in love with a man with a "macho swagger." Bill remembered that he also inspired "Jam," a romantic poem Danielle wrote about two lovebirds making breakfast after spending the night together. Danielle would go on to dedicate five of her best-selling novels to Bill, including sole dedications in two very significant books that marked turning points in her career. Those books, *The Promise* and *The Ring*, hadn't even been written when Danielle discovered she was pregnant with Bill's child.

The first stirring of life probably occurred in late summer. Bill suspected Danielle may have known she was pregnant when she made her last conjugal visit to Vacaville to see Danny.

"I wasn't happy about that," Bill said of the August 1977 visit. "But I wasn't about to stop her if she wanted to go see him."

By December, Bill was no longer bound to the drug-treatment program by the conditions of his parole. He was free to leave Delancey Street, but by no stretch was he ready to go. Most residents spend five years at Delancey before they venture out on their own under a strict set of guidelines; Bill had been there two and a half years when he felt it was time for him to depart.

"I asked to leave the program," he said, citing a difference of opinion between himself and the program administrators over the operation of the moving company. "It had reached a point of diminishing returns."

"Some people at Delancey didn't want Bill to go," remembered a friend of Bill's. "They didn't think he was ready. I thought Danielle would be good for Bill."

When Bill moved into Danielle's Green Street home in late December 1977, he was not considered a graduate of the program, Silbert remembered. Graduation requirements included finding a job and living on one's own without support from friends and family for six months before getting a formal release from the program. Moving in with Danielle didn't count, a friend of Bill's recalled.

"Bill did not graduate, so we must have felt he was not ready to go," Silbert believed. "There's a process, and he left. I can tell you in general we always make an effort to make sure people go when they're ready and not before, and that they do it in a way that gives them the best shot at their lives. When they don't do that, we do anything and everything we can think of—beg, cry, yell, to get them to do it the correct way, and at a time when they are truly most ready to make it."

If that effort included Silbert's lobbying old friend Danielle to keep Bill involved with Delancey Street, Silbert won't say.

It's a fair bet, however, that nothing could have changed Bill's mind, he said, adding he felt ready to get on with his life. Meanwhile, Danielle was pregnant with his child, so she thought she would give the new living arrangement a try. The relationship between Bill and Danielle was put to the test early. Within weeks, Danielle recalled noticing dramatic changes in

Bill's behavior. He became "very unpleasant, hostile and erratic," her lawyer later asserted. "He began disappearing for days at a time and would come home with strange-looking people. He was prone to explosions and rages. He never offered to pay for anything."

In fact, Bill kept asking for more and more money, which Danielle turned over to him because she was afraid. What Danielle didn't know was that Bill had returned to shooting heroin.

"I wanted to see what I was missing," he said. "I wasn't hostile. Had I been, why didn't she kick me out? I was using sporadically—every few days. We call it 'chipping.' I didn't want to ever come home fucked up, so I'd go to a friend's house for a few hours and come home late."

It was a way of life Bill knew only too well.

14

$\mathcal{B}$

$\mathcal{T}$he similarities between Danielle and Bill aren't apparent to the naked eye. Physically, her dark exotic features contrasted with his pale and pockmarked complexion scarred by years of acne. She liked designer clothes; Bill preferred jeans and sweatshirts. What they did have in common: they were only children in Catholic homes, and neither had completed college.

Bill's charm was his remarkable ability to warm up to people right away.

"He's the kind of guy who, in another time and place, I would have socialized with," observed Bill's former parole officer, Stephen Northrop, who has known Bill since the early 1970s.

Born on June 10, 1946, Bill was the only son of life insurance salesman Nicholas John Toth and his homemaker wife, the former Dorothea McKee. Raised a strict Catholic, he grew up in a modest two-bedroom townhome the Toth family still rents today in the middle-class suburb of Park Merced, about five miles southwest of downtown San Francisco.

Bill's fondest memories of his youth were the annual hunting and fishing trips he and his father took to Northern California. Each summer, they loaded up the car with two weeks' worth of supplies and headed for remote hunting and fishing grounds. They'd bunk in a cabin and angle for trout or salmon, or track deer through the wilderness. "Bill was a good shot," Nicholas said. "I spotted them; he shot them. He took three or four deer over the years."

Educated in parochial schools from kindergarten on, Bill was eventually accepted to prestigious St. Ignatius College Preparatory School. His old classmates remember him as conservative dresser: short hair, madras shirts, and khaki trousers. A mediocre student, he found his niche on the football field. His quick feet, strong upper body, and short legs made him a superb blocker, just as his father had been in his college days. "I had to be quick," Bill recalled. "I was small, but my short legs allowed me to get up under blocks."

In his senior year in 1964, he earned second-team all-city honors. "Bill was never the confident type," his mother said. "But the football helped boost his self-esteem."

"Bill was like an all-American boy in high school," recalled former football teammate Gerry Shannon, now a San Francisco firefighter who had a movie made about him based on a rescue he performed during the devastating 1989 San Francisco earthquake. "We'd all go to Saturday-night dances and ride around in pickup trucks drinking beer. Bill was popular and a respected football player."

After graduation, Bill went on to Santa Clara University, where he played on the football team. By now he was on the fringes of the drug scene that had pervaded the beach area near his home and was quickly taking hold in nearby Haight-Ashbury. Surfing and partying seemed to go hand in hand, and Bill blended right in with the crowd.

"He started leading a double life," Shannon recalled. "The surfers were a fast crowd that looked down on jocks. Bill played football at Santa Clara during the week and then would come home to party on the weekends. He was always the guy who could take more than anyone else."

After two years of life as a "hippie-jock," Bill took the road thousands of other rebellious teenagers traveled during the tumultuous sixties. First he smoked marijuana, then he graduated to speed, then LSD and, in the summer of 1966, heroin. He tried that drug for the first time during a trip to Mexico with friends.

"The hard drugs led to harder drugs," Bill said. During one stretch, Bill said he hallucinated on LSD once a week for eighteen months. After returning from Mexico, however, he contracted hepatitis, forcing him to drop out of school.

To Bill, getting a college education had turned into an "uptight" and square pursuit compared to the action of the fast crowd of day trippers he hung out with. He began injecting amphetamines into his veins, sometimes using homemade syringes made of hypodermic needles and eyedroppers. Bill used to carry them around in his pockets, sticking a pacifier on the needle tip so he wouldn't prick himself. "I was living a carefree, aimless existence, living strictly for the moment," he said.

After a while, Shannon didn't even recognize him. "It was a one-hundred-eighty-degree turn," he recalled. "His hair grew, and all he listened to were Bob Dylan tapes. He dove all the way, and I stopped seeing him."

While his high-school buddies headed in one direction, Bill went in another. Heroin would become his panacea.

In the summer of 1967, he and his twenty-nine-year-old girlfriend got arrested for selling opium, but later pled to a lesser charge of marijuana possession with an intent to sell. To avoid testifying against his girlfriend, Bill married her and instantly became a stepfather to her three children. Bill and his wife were sentenced to thirty days in jail and three years' probation.

The experience rocked his wife to her senses, Bill said. She eventually got the charges removed from her record after completing probation. Bill got into deeper trouble.

His parents tried to get him help, even sending him to a psychiatrist for four months in 1967. Bill would later say he thought it was a waste of time.

In 1970 Bill's wife filed for divorce. "The marriage fell apart as my rap sheet mounted," he said. "I was committing crimes to buy heroin and got arrested pretty regularly. In the early seventies, I was probably in jail more often than I was out."

Between 1967 and 1974, Bill's record mirrored the life of a minor criminal in search of money to support his drug habit, a lifestyle that set him back an average of twenty to thirty dollars a day and sometimes as much as a hundred and fifty dollars. There was a sixty-day jail sentence for breaking and entering, nine months in jail for burglary, three months in jail for receiving stolen property, and he was sentenced to the California Rehabilitation Center, a state prison facility, for the sale of narcotics and burglary.

"I was never into violence," Bill said. "I needed the money for drugs, and that's the only reason why I did it."

Twice he was caught in the act of burglarizing homes by the occupants, and twice Bill walked away without laying a finger on anybody. Both times he was arrested for the crime and convicted.

One of those incidents took place on July 17, 1973. Bill had just been released from jail and was in a work-furlough program when he decided to go back to burglarizing homes to get drug money. On that day, he approached an empty first-floor apartment on the 1400 block of San Francisco's Cole Street and broke in through the entrance. After climbing a set of stairs, he hopped out a second-story window and dropped down to an asphalt landing, giving him access to the apartment through an open bathroom window he had spotted from the street.

Biochemist Robert Webster, the tenant of the apartment, had left for work that morning at nine-thirty A.M. and decided to return home for lunch.

When he opened the door, Webster noticed his television set sitting by the bathroom door. Then he looked up and saw a man with long dark hair and wearing brown pants and a khaki jacket moving toward him from the hallway.

"What are you doing here?" Webster asked.

Webster didn't appear in the mood for many details, so Bill got right to the point.

"Well," Bill said, sweating profusely, "I guess you can say you caught me burglarizing your apartment."

"What did you take?"

"Well, just some small stuff, some pennies."

Bill dug into his pockets and offered to return the articles he'd taken. He handed Webster back a handful of coins, a pocket watch, and two rings belonging to Webster's wife.

"I suppose you want to see what's in the rest of my pockets," Bill said.

"Yes, might as well while we're at it," Webster replied.

Bill emptied his other pockets and returned Webster's pocket knife.

"Are you going to call the police?" Bill asked.

"No," Webster said, lying with a straight face. "You'd better leave right now, and I don't want to ever catch you here again, not this day, this week, or months from now."

Webster let him walk out the door. He had noticed that Bill's jacket pockets contained a number of tools of the burglary trade: a small crowbar, a prybar, and hammer. No sense getting hurt over a few pieces of jewelry, he thought to himself. Webster later testified that Bill never made a move for his gear or threatened him in any way.

After taking a moment to catch his breath, Webster hustled outside to look for help. Off in the distance, he spotted Bill walking down Cole Street casually, as though he hadn't a worry in the world.

Bill was later identified out of a photo lineup. On September 5, 1973, he was placed in a state prison facility in Vacaville, California, for ninety days of observation until the court could decide what to do with him. Bill was facing a stint in state prison this time, but his attorney fought hard to get him back into the California Rehabilitation Center, where he could get help for his drug problem.

Still, after his release from that facility on November 4, 1974, Bill was in trouble with the law again. He was arrested for receiving stolen property in late December and arraigned on December 31. Nineteen days later, he was busted for theft in Daly City, a few miles south of San Francisco.

This time the judge was harsh and sentenced Bill to six months in the county jail. By the summer of 1975, Bill was on the street again, but this time he was determined to clean up. He entered Delancey Street, where he would spend the next two and a half years in a rigid program for drug addicts.

It was here that he managed to stay drug free for the longest period of his life, and it was here he would meet the woman who would overlook his past drug problems: Danielle Steel Zugelder.

15

𝕰

*J*n the fall of 1977, Danielle got an offer for novelizing a screenplay for a film titled *The Promise*. Written by Gary Michael White, *The Promise* would turn out to be a bust of a film. Not many people saw the undistinguished 1979 movie about a girl who lost her face in an accident, got it back through plastic surgery, and found love when her old boyfriend fell for her new looks. Danielle's advance was ten thousand dollars, and there were no royalties. The advance was more than Danielle had gotten for any previous manuscript, but it was a veritable pittance compared to the sales the book racked up.

Danielle, who was pregnant at the time, took the job in part to defray the looming medical bills. The offer was attractive for another reason: Universal Studios was prepared to spend upward of $500,000 to promote the book in advance of the movie, Bill recalled. It was an unheard-of sum of money for a paperback, but the studio executives were banking on an equation that a hot book could stir up interest in the upcoming motion picture. The same formula had worked for *Love Story*, so it was worth a shot to make the book a success. It also would help put Danielle's name on the publishing map.

"I told her to go for it," Bill said.

Danielle would dedicate the book to Bill, referring to him in Spanish: "To Guillermo, With all my love, D.S." *The Promise* hit the paperback bestseller list in April 1978 and stayed there for months, launching Danielle as a name to be reckoned with in the growing field of romance writing. Almost a year after the book's release, *People* magazine reported that *The Promise* had gone through printings totaling two million copies. "She didn't make much money off it, but the book made her," Bill remembered.

Screenwriter White never spoke with Danielle about the book. What remains in his mind years later was that Danielle altered the ending. In the movie, the boyfriend's mother paid to have the girl's face reconstructed only after the girl agreed to get out of her son's life. He fell back in love with his girlfriend, but his relationship with his mother is left unresolved.

"Director Gilbert Cates decided to emphasize the darker aspects of the film," White recalled. The conclusion to Danielle's manuscript went from happy to happier. "In the novel, the mother and son are reunited and all is forgiven."

It was a formula that would serve Danielle well in the years to come. On January 2, 1978, the *San Francisco Chronicle* updated its readers on Danielle's writing pursuits. *Now and Forever* was due out in February and would eventually become a best-seller. Her last book, *Passion's Promise*, had reportedly sold 800,000 copies since January 1977.

Danielle delivered the manuscript for *The Promise* in December, the same month Bill left Delancey Street and moved into the Green Street house. They shared the master bedroom while Beatrix had her own room down the hall.

Though modest by Danielle's current standards, the Green Street home was located in one of the nicest neighborhoods in the city, boasting a panoramic view of San Francisco Bay. To the west, one could see the Golden Gate Bridge, and to the southeast, the Bay Bridge. Down the hill on Hyde Street, the cable car rattled through the neighborhood, offering access to scenic Fisherman's Wharf and the department stores in fashionable Union Square. Many neighbors became close friends, among them society columnist Pat Montandon and attorney Isabella Grant, who later became a superior court judge.

Living in tight quarters, Bill got a close look at the author's work ethic. Holing herself up in her office off the master bedroom, Danielle immersed herself in her writing, spending eighteen hours a day at her typewriter.

"She wore glasses and granny nightgowns when she worked," Bill said. "Her hair was disheveled and worn up in a bun. Sometimes she talked to herself. She never touched food, and I had to drag her out and make her sleep."

In many interviews, Danielle discussed her exhausting writing regimen. She has always started by blocking out her calendar for many days, letting nothing interrupt her concentration except her family and emergencies. "If you let anything infringe on your time, it will. And you won't get the writing done," she once told a group of authors at the Santa Barbara Writers Conference. "Taking one day off can cost me five days of getting back in the mood. Going out to lunch can cost me anywhere from five hours to three days, and for me it's not worth it. For my own sense of well-being, I have to finish my work before I can play.

"I sit at my typewriter and type until I ache so badly I can't get up. After twelve or fourteen hours, you feel as though your whole body is going to break in half. Everything hurts—your arms, your eyes, your shoulders, your neck, your hands. I've had cramps so badly that when I sat typing I couldn't move my hands for a couple of hours, but I usually keep sitting there and push through it for another five or six hours. . . . I have fainted when I stood up and fallen asleep face first in my typewriter and woken up the next morning with the keyboard marks on my face. . . . It's a little bit like a marathon or climbing a mountain."

In the early months of the relationship, friends who socialized with Bill and Danielle perceived them as a loving, affectionate couple. There was always an air of mystery about Danielle's men, a friend recalled. Danny's incarceration in Vacaville was a well-kept secret; only a handful of the author's friends were privy to the knowledge. To others, Danny was described as "a gambler and an alcoholic," a friend said. "I assumed he was always with her."

Al and Dede Wilsey, who became friends with Danielle later, said they knew she was once married to man named Dan, but the man she described wasn't anything like the convicted felon they read about many years later. "She said he was an architect who was incapacitated in an auto accident," Dede recalled. "He [Dan] had told her to get on with her life, to go ahead and divorce him."

When Bill entered the picture, some friends just assumed there had been a separation or divorce from Danny.

"I had met Bill before the [April 15, 1978] wedding," another friend recalled. "We went to each other's homes or went out to dinner. I liked Bill. He was nice and personable. His past was never brought up in detail, but I knew he was from Delancey Street because he talked about working for the moving company. He and Danielle were very loving around each other—a lot of hand holding and touching. Danielle is very loving to everyone she cares about. It was my impression that the relationship was good for a long time."

Their friends were unaware of the turmoil going on in the relationship. Danielle's recollection of that period is contained in a 1993 letter written by her attorney, Charles O. Morgan, Jr. In the letter she claimed that after Bill departed from Delancey Street, he moved in with her for a few days and then vanished, eventually turning up at a hospital stricken with hepatitis. When he was released, he persuaded Danielle to let him come with her to recuperate, only to fade from the scene again when he was back on his feet. Danielle claimed to her attorney that from that point on, Bill was only around for a brief period prior to Nicky's May 1 birth.

Those few weeks were miserable for the young couple. Bill suffered from nausea, diarrhea, high fever, jaundice. His stools turned white and his eyes turned yellow. As a precaution, Beatie and Danielle, who was seven months pregnant with Nicky, endured painful gamma-globulin shots because Bill "misrepresented that he had infectious hepatitis rather than serum hepatitis," her attorney contended.

While Bill was bedridden at the hospital, Danielle said she asked him not to return to the house. Bill said he had nowhere else to go, so Danielle let him return. He took over the master bedroom and had sole use of the only upstairs bathroom. Danielle and Beatie had to use the bathroom in the cellar.

To ward off possible infection, Danielle stocked the kitchen with plastic utensils and paper plates. Danielle cared for him for three weeks, then Bill started disappearing again, Danielle said.

Bill recalls being around for much of the time after his recuperation.

When Bill got sick with serum hepatitis, it was Danielle who admitted him to Mount Zion Hospital and paid for his one-week stay, she said in court years later.

He denied he was gone for days at a time, but he did vanish for hours. "I never wanted to come home loaded," he said. "So I'd wait until I was sober."

Looking back on his life, Bill realized he made a huge mistake in leaving Delancey Street. He didn't admit that to Danielle because then he would have had to confess he was using heroin. Danielle got her first inkling that Bill was on drugs again on March 20, 1978. While running an errand, Bill called home from a pay phone. "There's a little problem with the car," he said over the phone. Moments later, Danielle got a second and more urgent call from someone at the scene. Bill was acting disoriented and needed an ambulance, but he was refusing aid. Panicked, Danielle threw on a coat, ran outside, and hobbled her way down to the corner of Green and Leavenworth streets, covering the one-block distance as fast as she could carry her eight-month-pregnant body.

At the accident scene, she saw Bill was standing on the corner, dazed and confused. Her Toyota wagon was in worse shape—the car had been almost totaled and would cost $2,800 to repair.

"The minute I saw him it was very obvious something was wrong with him," Danielle said. "I thought he was drunk. But later he confessed to me he wouldn't let them call the ambulance because he was scared to death they would find out. He confessed and said it was a one-time thing. He had taken drugs and he didn't know what had happened to him. Later it turned out he admitted he had been taking them for months, but he didn't admit that to me until the middle of June."

Bill needed immediate help. He entered an outpatient drug-treatment program at the Haight-Ashbury Free Clinic. Danielle, wary about letting Bill back behind the wheel of her car, drove him there daily for three weeks. "When I went to the clinic, she went to a Christian Science reading room nearby," remembered Bill.

The treatment consisted of counseling and prescriptions for Darvon and vitamins. It worked for a while, but Bill said he returned to shooting heroin within weeks. "Danielle had no idea I had been on drugs for months," he claimed.

On Easter Sunday, the elder Toths joined Bill, Danielle, and Beatie for brunch at the ritzy Sheraton-Palace Hotel in downtown San Francisco. Bill's mother brought flowers for Danielle, and the two families enjoyed a relaxing day together. Dorothea also was overwhelmed by an impromptu gift from Danielle: a pair of antique emerald earrings that had once belonged to Danielle's great-grandmother. When Beatie saw the exchange, she was not pleased. Her mother had promised her the earrings when she was old enough to wear them, Dorothea recalled. Later, when Danielle was distracted, Dorothea pulled aside Beatie and promised to give the earrings to her when the time was right. That turned out to be a couple of years later.

As always, Danielle followed up with a thank-you note, telling Dorothea she was grateful for the flowers and the fabulous time they had together.

In April Danielle was leaning toward taking up Bill on his offer to get married. His mind was made up. "I loved her," Bill said. Danielle was ambivalent, and rightfully so. But pressure mounted from all sides to go through with a wedding, if for no other reason than the child's sake.

"A lot of us were pushing her to hurry up and get married because the baby was coming," a friend said. "What I didn't know was that her divorce from Dan wasn't final."

Signs of trouble were everywhere that perhaps this union was ill-conceived. "Danielle had told me Bill didn't want to get married, and then he said she didn't want to do it," recalled Dorothea. "I thought they should get married because of the pregnancy. I didn't know she wasn't divorced from her other husband."

Money was also a concern. Bill was still unemployed while Danielle's career was finally on the upswing after years of frustration. She even insisted that he sign a prenuptial agreement.

"It basically said what's mine is mine and hers is hers and that I wouldn't ask for anything if we separated," Bill said. "But I felt insulted."

On April 14—one day before the marriage was to take place—Danielle's divorce from Danny was finalized. The next day, as friends and family gathered nearby at the Norwegian Seamen's Church on Hyde Street, Danielle and Bill got into an argument over the prenuptial agreement, which Bill had yet to sign. Danielle finally gave Bill an ultimatum: sign the paper or she would call off the wedding, Bill remembered. He relented and they went to church.

And, for the second time in three years, Danielle took a husband with a fatal flaw. All the problems in recent months had been forgiven. "She married incredible people," Dowie said.

By Danielle's account, the abuse continued on their wedding day. The ceremony was held on clear and sunny Saturday with about thirty close friends and members of Bill's family in attendance at the church, perched halfway up Russian Hill with a spectacular view of Alcatraz Island and the Golden Gate Bridge.

The ceremony took place in the chapel, a small and simple room bisected by a red carpet and filled with rows of Scandinavian chairs. As cable cars rumbled up and down on Hyde Street, Bill and Danielle repeated their vows at the altar beneath an intricate relief engraved by Norwegian artist Dagfin Werenskjold. It showed Jesus walking on the water.

Dorothea and Nicholas sat near the front, bursting with pride over their son's success after so many years of failure. They had both taken a fond liking to Danielle, particularly Dorothea, who said she treated Danielle like the daughter she never had. Nicholas had become a huge fan, buying boxes full of Danielle's books every time one was released. He would bring them by, and she would sign them so he could hand them out to his insurance customers. Nobody from Danielle's family back East made it to San Francisco for the wedding. Her father, whom Bill said was suffering from arteriosclerosis and had recently undergone bypass surgery, was unable to make the trip. "The wedding was done at the last minute," added Dorothea. "There were no invitations."

After the ceremony, the wedding party moved on to the reception at Robert, the tiny French restaurant on Octavia and Bush streets. The wine flowed, the newlyweds nuzzled, and the guests mingled. Joining Bill's parents were Stan Buscovich, a San Francisco police officer and one of Bill's oldest friends; airline pilot Peter Eisenbarth and his wife, Nancy, who would later become Danielle's full-time research assistant; Isabella Grant, and restaurateur Robert Bitton, who gave Danielle away at the wedding.

Bill wore a dark navy blue suit and tie, while Danielle, eight and a half months pregnant with Nicholas, wore an oversized green, flower-print dress that hung loosely over her ample abdomen. Her long, dark hair flowed over her shoulders, contrasting sharply with the string of pearls decorating her neck. Later the merry couple stood over their three-tiered, white-frosted wedding cake as the beaming bride fed a piece to her happy groom. A picture chronicling that moment belied the underlying turmoil in the relationship.

On their wedding day, Danielle said later, drugs were uninvited guests. "He disappeared immediately after the wedding to use heroin with a friend," her attorney claimed later. "He came back the next day and asked for money. Between the date of the wedding and Nicky's birth, his activities were drugs."

Bill denied that he went out and got high. He said he and Danielle were exhausted after the day's events, went home after the luncheon, and fell asleep. Danielle, who had gained thirty-five pounds during the pregnancy, was tuckered out and Bill said he was groggy from all the medication he was taking to stay off heroin.

Though Danielle kept Bill's drug problems a secret, she wrote about her difficult marriage with Bill in her nonfiction book, *Having a Baby*. At that time, she wrote, she "had a very difficult marital situation on my hands, was tense, working too hard, and had to cope with a lot on my own. Just before delivering Nicky, my domestic tensions had come to a head only days before."

In the two weeks between the wedding and Nicky's birth, "things got steadily worse. The only time [I] saw [Bill] was when he showed up for money for a fix," Danielle claimed in court papers later.

However, he was at her bedside on the day Nicky was born. On the morning of May 1, 1978, Danielle was in labor and the contractions were coming hard and fast, she wrote in *Having a Baby*. Danielle wanted a natural delivery free of any medication. She had missed out on Beatrix's birth and didn't want to repeat the same mistake. First they made a stop at the doctor's office. The news was not what Danielle wanted to hear: the baby was huge and she might have to deliver by cesarean.

Once at the hospital, a technician took X rays and cracked that a truck could fit through Danielle's pelvis, Danielle recalled in her book. She was not amused with the joke or the dearth of decor in the labor room, which she described as ugly.

For most of the day, the doctors debated whether to perform a cesarean or wait for the baby to drop. They gave Danielle an enema and broke her water, but the baby didn't budge. Meanwhile, Danielle was in agony and Bill was losing his patience.

"[Bill] was extremely nervous and in need of drugs," Danielle asserted in court papers. "At one point, he blew up and told [me] to hurry up—that he had to go get something."

Danielle was thankful she had gone through the Lamaze training. The relaxation and breathing techniques made the pain bearable, but by late Monday, she was screaming and crying. An epidural lessened the pain but made it difficult for her to breathe. Finally, after twenty-two and a half hours of labor, the doctor ordered a cesarean. Danielle was asleep when the doctor made a vertical incision up to her navel—the same path doctors took years earlier when they removed Danielle's ovary. At 8:34 P.M., Nicholas William Toth entered the world without any complications.

While Danielle was asleep in the recovery room, Bill said he went out to use heroin and later returned to the hospital. The long labor had left his body starving for a fix.

Danielle felt groggy and ill, she wrote in her book. The incision hurt and her breathing was labored. Once again, there were regrets over the experience. She wished she had been more prepared for the cesarean; she wished the doctors had operated sooner and that she had been awake for the birth. Then she could have avoided the complications from general anesthesia.

Then Bill walked in and handed her a checkbook. He needed money right away, and a dazed Danielle scrawled her name across the bottom of a check. He kept making his wife do it over until she signed legibly. Then he left. It's true Bill made her write a check, but it happened later in the week, not hours after Nicky's birth, Bill said.

Danielle's spirits picked up when the nurse brought in her son. "They plopped him in my arms and I looked at the most beautiful little face, and I swear to you I did not feel a single ache or pain in my body. It all just stopped, and all I could see was the baby," she wrote. "It was one of the happiest and most beautiful moments of my life."

During her one-week stay in the hospital, Danielle hired a private-duty nurse to help her get around. "At the time there were twenty-one women in the maternity section, and nineteen of them had had cesareans. . . . And you could have died before anyone would have come to take care of you," she wrote. "Having my own nurse meant that every time I wanted to shift or go to the bathroom (all of which are major feats after abdominal surgery), there was someone right there to help me.

"We all have different areas in which we splurge, and mine is comfort," she wrote. "I can live without trips, without jewels, without first-class tickets to anywhere. I'll probably never own a sable coat (I know, get out your hankie). But what I like to spend my money on is my own comfort."

And the nurse was there when Bill was not.

"He came twice and was loaded both times. Once he almost dropped the baby," her attorney said in court papers. Bill recalled visiting daily. Danielle remained bedridden when she returned home and fed Nicky by bottle after two fruitless days of attempting to breast-feed the insatiable boy. Bill came and went as he had before, and was no help with Nicky. "He was frequently loaded, always wanted more and more money; he even stole money from Beatrix's piggy bank," Danielle claimed through her attorney. Bill admitted to taking the money from his stepdaughter, but he said he later paid it back. "When I wasn't working, I had to ask Danielle for money," he said.

For the next six weeks, Danielle relied on a baby nurse from Trinidad, a knowledgeable mother of six who taught Danielle everything she knew, Danielle wrote in her book. Beatrix also pitched in, and in June a nanny was brought in, but Danielle handled the bulk of the care. By mid-June, Danielle was back on her feet and eager to plunge into her next book.

Bill's behavior continued to worsen. Frustrated, Danielle said she asked him to leave again. Realizing his wife was at her wit's end, Bill finally told her the truth. "I admitted to Danielle I was using because she thought I was spending all the time away seeing other women. I never cheated on her."

He managed to talk her into giving him another chance, but only after he agreed to get help. That day they went to see Bill's former counselor at Delancey Street, who insisted Bill enter a detox program immediately. The counselor and Danielle drove Bill to Gladman Memorial Hospital in Oakland, where he stayed for a month in the detox unit undergoing therapy and methadone treatment.

The senior Toths were also alerted to the sad news and agreed to help pay the bills.

Over the years, Nicholas Toth estimated he loaned Danielle "eighteen to twenty thousand dollars" for Bill's care, adding that he had to raid his retirement fund to help finance the costs. "She needed the money and Bill was my son."

16

hile Bill was away at Gladman, Danielle retreated to the Ventana Big Sur Country Inn Resort, a coastal oasis of mountains, meadows, and a dense cedar forest overlooking the Pacific. It was located 152 miles south of San Francisco in nearby scenic Carmel, the famous resort town that once boasted a mayor named Clint Eastwood.

As Beatie attended a nearby summer camp, Danielle reinvigorated herself and then returned to San Francisco refreshed and ready to tackle her next book, published in 1979, called *Summer's End*.

During Bill's hospital stay, the romance writer and Bill's mother spoke frequently. On July 2, Danielle penned Dorothea a thank-you letter for all the love and support Dorothea showed in difficult times. Clearly, Danielle was feeling disconsolate over Bill and was pessimistic over their future, Dorothea remembered.

In time, Danielle shared some of her most intimate secrets with her mother-in-law. She talked about her lonely childhood, her disastrous marriage to Claude-Eric, and her future with Bill. "She was the nicest, sweetest person, very down to earth," Dorothea said. "I really liked her. She was very generous on birthdays and holidays and Christmas. She would give beautiful scarves, Gucci bags. There were always flowers on Valentine's Day and Easter.

"She had a difficult childhood," she went on. "Her mother left her father . . . when she was very young. Danielle spoke very highly of her grandmother, though."

During a trip East, Norma was introduced to Dorothea, who found Danielle's mother very warm and friendly. "She wrote me a letter later telling me Danielle was her whole life, that she admired her daughter a great deal," Dorothea recalled. "She had very high praise for Bill. It made me sad knowing how resentful Danielle felt toward her."

Bill's impression of Norma was that she was "very flirtatious."

Early in the marriage, Danielle and Dorothea became telephone pals. "A friend of Danielle's told me once that Danielle was born with a telephone on her shoulder," Dorothea said, chuckling at the memory in a warm, grandmotherly tone of voice. "When Bill was in the hospital, she was alone. She would call and talk for hours—sometimes as late as eleven-thirty at night. She would talk about Nicholas, her future. We went through Bill's problems. She was worried about Bill, and I sympathized with her. I do believe she loved him, and did not just marry him because she was pregnant. When the problems began, I always took her side. I blamed Bill for a lot of things."

After his release from Gladman in mid-July, Bill was ready to give it all he had to make the relationship work. With help from his old parish priest, he found a job counseling troubled teens at the Eddy Street Boys Home, a nonprofit organization for young runaways sponsored by Catholic Social Services. The pay wasn't much, about two hundred dollars a week before taxes, but the work was honest and honorable.

With Danielle's encouragement, Bill also enrolled at the University of San Francisco to complete his bachelor's degree. Majoring in human relations and organizational behavior, he wrote a series of sociology papers about his life experiences. He was awarded a degree in 1979.

Bill's old high-school pal Gerry Shannon recalled bumping into Bill at their old beach hangout, Kelly's Cove, in late summer. "I remember he was real exuberant about his kid," Shannon said. "He was real optimistic."

Shannon asked his old football chum if he had kicked the drugs. "I'm recovering and I have to stay with it because I'm a new dad," Bill said. Then Bill shook his head and wondered how he had survived all those years of carousing. "I guess I was way out there, huh?" he added.

Despite her misgivings, Danielle let Bill come home to try again, a pattern that was to repeat itself again and again during the twenty months they lived under the same roof. Dowie, for one, was not surprised by Danielle's ability to forgive and forget.

"The operative word here is 'rescue'—that's what she was into," he said. "She walked into my office in the whole spirit of rescue. There were a whole triangle of things going on here, and one way of getting out of dealing with your own dilemmas is by rescuing someone else. She couldn't just walk away. It happened with her over and over—way over the boundary of common sense."

A friend of Bill's said Danielle gave him every chance to recover. Another acquaintance recalled Danielle telling her she was willing to put Bill through law school. "She did try very hard. I felt that she wanted to make it work," Bill's friend said. "I think she really loved him. Sex may have started it, but Bill is a personable guy. He can be bright if he wants to be, and I think she would have set him up in any business he wanted. Bill could have been a very successful person, but he didn't have it in him. There are people in their thirties who act five years old. He's one of them."

Perhaps Bill simply kept tugging at her heart and she just couldn't give up on him yet. After all, Bill was her husband and the father of her son. "She's benevolent and kind and sincerely thought she could rescue these two guys. She loved them both," a close friend said of Danny and Bill in *People* magazine. "Danielle was naïve enough at the time to believe that romance and love conquered all."

"She was very forgiving of her men," another friend remembered.

Years later, Danielle recalled only the bitter memories from her years with Bill, particularly when it came to their son. "After [Bill] left Gladman, he was not interested in Nicky. He did not spend time with him. He didn't help and he had further problems with heroin," Danielle's attorney said in court papers.

Bill said he was drug free for a few months after Gladman, focusing his attention on his family, his counseling job, and school. "I was clean for a while," Bill said. "But then I'd use. It was like being an alcoholic—one drink and you're gone. When I was using a whole lot, I'd take a leave of absence from work."

His salary went mostly for drugs, and when that was exhausted, he made up phony excuses to get money from Danielle, telling her he had lost his paycheck or the car was in need of repairs.

Bill's ongoing battle with drugs was a well-kept secret from most friends and, certainly, the media. Besides coping with Bill, Danielle spent the summer mourning the loss of her father. John Schuelein-Steel died of a heart attack on May 17, 1978, shortly after Bill and Danielle were married.

Because of the baby, Danielle was unable to return to New York for the funeral, said Romelia Van Camp, the nanny who took over caring for Nicky when the baby nurse departed in June. Both the nanny and Dorothea remembered that Danielle took care of all the funeral arrangements from San Francisco.

"I remember asking her why John's wife, Kuniko, couldn't make the arrangements, and Danielle told me Kuniko wasn't up to it," Dorothea said. Romelia concurred. "Kuniko was in shock. Danielle had just had the baby and fixed everything by phone," she said.

"My feeling was there were a lot of unresolved issues in that relationship," said Bill, who got to meet Danielle's father only once before his death. " He seemed to epitomize the decadence of Berlin in the 1930s."

Over the summer, Danielle immersed herself in her work and caring for Nicky and by August she had delivered the manuscript of *Summer's End*. Then she went to work revising *Drea*, one of her earlier nonpublished manuscripts. She finished that in September but there were no takers. It was likely the last rejection letter Danielle ever would receive for one of her manuscripts.

"She would work twenty-four hours at a time. She worked very hard," Romelia said. Some of her fondest memories during the two years she spent working full-time for Danielle on Green Street took place on the second-story porch that Danielle had converted into a small office.

"I would sit with the baby in the office right there with her," she said. "If she heard a noise, she would be right there to find out what was going on. When he cried, she was there right away. At night, she was the one who got up with the baby. She never left him alone when he had a cold. She was a great, great mother."

Danielle later wrote about how important it was for her to spend quality time with Nicky after missing out on Beatie's early years. In those days she ceded the caretaking to the nanny and regretted that her daughter developed a tighter bond with the nanny than with her. The author clearly reveled in caring for her son.

"He was fat, happy, beautiful, and he laughed all the time," she wrote. "He never seemed to cry. He was happy and easy and a joy in every way."

One of Romelia's primary jobs was teaching Nicky Spanish. "We used to bring him Spanish kids to play with," Romelia said. "He was speaking so good. He was a very smart boy."

Around Danielle's house, all the hired help had specific chores. Romelia did not clean, another Latin woman came to the house two to three times a week to do that. A third person took on the daily duty of walking the two basset hounds. When Danielle needed her makeup and hair done for a publicity photo, beauticians came to the house to do the job. Caterers did her parties.

"I like bringing the mountain to Muhammad," Danielle later wrote in *Having a Baby*.

To save on time, Danielle also used the telephone to buy clothes. "She was a phone shopper," Romelia said. "She did everything by phone. Most of the things came from New York. She didn't go out much—she was always at home and working. She was a concentrator. She would sit down at the typewriter and wouldn't remember what she had to eat. I would bring food and make her eat.

"It was important to her because she had to make the money to live and survive," she said. "I was trying push her to stop working so hard, and she wouldn't."

Bill claimed to pitch in when Danielle hunkered down to write. He "didn't even mind changing diapers," he told *People* in 1978. For the same article, Danielle said her husband was "the only person I know who packs his days as full as I do."

Relating to Beatie was another story. Bill said that he and his stepdaughter maintained a cool relationship, but occasionally the family did things together as a group. Beatie tried very hard to please Danielle, Bill said. One outing that came to mind took place at the Golden Gate Park equestrian stables. Danielle outfitted her daughter to a T: breeches, a riding jacket, a helmet, and boots. "Beatrix was bouncing all over that horse, she looked scared to death, but she kept at it," Bill said.

The senior Toths were regular visitors to the Green Street house. Nicholas was the epitome of the doting grandfather and dropped by at least once a week to visit, Bill said. One night when Danielle was getting ready to go out, Dorothea remembered, Beatie showed them both a school paper she had written on President Jimmy Carter. Dorothea approved and then Danielle asked to see it. "This is a lot of crap," Danielle told her daughter.

"But Mrs. Toth said it was all right," Beatie replied.

"I don't give a shit what Mrs. Toth says. It's crap—do it over!"

"Danielle had the mouth of a stevedore," Dorothea remembered. "She always used four-letter words in casual conversation, and in front of Beatrix." And, in fact, correspondence from Danielle to her second husband was peppered with similar four-letter words.

Resistance was the word Bill used to describe Danielle's level of interest in his passions, such as the outdoors. "Roughing it to her is spending a weekend at the Awanee," he said, a joking reference to the luxury resort hotel in Yosemite National Park. In contrast, Bill spent many weekends fishing in Northern California, driving hundreds of miles to remote rivers filled with salmon and trout. Friends of the couple recall how Bill used to show up on their doorstep bearing a gift of a line full of fish. "Danielle tried to fish just once," he said. "I tried teaching her how to cast, but she gave up. She never came fishing with me. I always went off by myself."

If there was trouble in Bill and Danielle's marriage, it went unnoticed by some of the friends who socialized with them. Others knew precisely when they walked in on the heels of a fight. At dinner parties, "Bill would sulk and clam up when he was angry," said one acquaintance. "Danielle would pretend there was nothing wrong."

A talented hostess, Danielle was able to work a room "like a butterfly. She was eager to please," said the friend.

There were disagreements about more than Bill's behavior. When Nicky was ready to be baptized in September, Danielle and Bill fought over the church. Though a practicing Christian Scientist who even carried around inspirational tapes in her car, Danielle lobbied for an Episcopal christening, while Bill stood firm for a Catholic celebration.

"Danielle wasn't real happy about that, but I was insistent," he said. The ceremony was held at St. Brigid's Church in San Francisco. Claude-Eric and Policeman Stan Buscovich were the godfathers.

Beneath it all, Bill always felt Danielle had an understated need to be cared for. "She ran her father's house until she was nine, and deep down I think she wanted to be taken care of, just like the heroines in her books," explained Bill. "I couldn't live up to her notion of romance—notes, flowers. I'm not a romantic. My father was an orphan and had trouble expressing his emotions. My mother is a devout Catholic. I spent my whole life in parochial schools. I'm not a hugs-and-kisses type of guy."

One recurring scene seemed to manifest their incompatibility. "I had to tell her I loved her, not once but what seemed to be like fifty times a day," Bill said. "Every time I passed her, she said, 'I love you,' and I had to say it back. When I didn't we got into arguments."

Sometimes Bill just cut her off—sexually and verbally. "She hated that," he said. "She's a control freak. She needs people who will let her call the shots," he once told a reporter.

By early 1979 Danielle's personal life and career were going in opposite directions. *People* magazine came to the house to do an interview to find out who the young woman was behind the incredible success of *The Promise,* which was still selling six thousand copies a week when the story went to press in February 1979. Dell Publishing had also just reportedly signed Danielle to a six-figure contract to write three more novels; this deal was referred to again in a *San Francisco Examiner* article a month later.

Danielle reveled in playing the part of the glamorous author. The *People* article showed her posing in a floor-length fox fur at a Union Square fur salon where she was a customer. Another photo showed Danielle sitting in her cramped office over her manual typewriter, smiling up at her third husband as he perused a letter. The lead shot filled an entire page and showed Danielle staring pensively, with a curled lower lip and her hair tied up in a bun.

Photographer Michael Alexander, who took the photos, considered Danielle a difficult subject. Over lunch at the Stanford Court Hotel, one of Danielle's favorite settings in which to conduct interviews, the chatty and jovial Alexander tried to loosen up his subject. "What I remember is that we never broke the ice," he said. "I bantered on and on and there was no connection."

They met the next day at the Green Street house. Danielle introduced Alexander to Bill, and then they went to work.

"Can I go upstairs to look around for picture possibilities?" Alexander asked.

Her response was polite but firm. "No."

"Can I get a picture of you working?"

"I don't want any pictures of myself writing," the author said.

Alexander gently advised his subject that it would be very difficult to photograph a story about an author unless they had some photographs of her working. He was able to nudge his subject up to her office. Then Danielle suggested he join her on a shopping trip to her favorite fur salon. The next day, she posed in a floor-length fox.

"Her whole thing was to be in control," Alexander said. "She made it very tough. It seems like she turned down every idea, and everything we did do was carefully thought out."

For years afterward, Danielle would only permit photographer Roger Ressmeyer to shoot her portraits. These were the only photos she offered the print media for publication, save for the occasions she was caught at social events or the openings of the opera or symphony. Alexander later met Ressmeyer, and the subject turned to Danielle.

"How do you deal with her?" Alexander asked, recalling his painstaking session with her. "She was so negative with me."

"You have to keep telling her how beautiful she is," Ressmeyer replied.

In the *People* story, Danielle described herself as a compulsive shopper who never leaves the house without a hat. She doesn't cook, do charity work, or play sports. Her only passion is writing. Her craft is so all-consuming, it's almost impossible to pull herself away from a book after she starts, even for a bite to eat or to comb her hair.

Danielle also failed to explain the correct chronology of her relationship with Bill. It was reported that they is married in 1977 and that Danielle became "instantly pregnant." There was no mention of Danielle's second marriage to Danny, who was just two months shy of being paroled from state prison for the 1974 assault, robbery, and rape charges.

The domestic bliss portrayed between Danielle and Bill in the story once prompted Danielle to remark that the article was "the greatest piece of fiction of our time," adding, "I don't think Bill has ever seen a diaper, let alone changed one."

Still, it made for good copy. "Danielle Steel," the *People* headline read, "writes mushy paperbacks that are almost as exotic as her own life."

The headline writer was closer to the truth than he realized. Danielle herself told *People*, "I make a world peopled the way I want my life to be." A world where her heroines struggle in their relationships and are rewarded with something that had eluded Danielle's life up to this point—a happy ending.

The week Danielle's *People* story appeared on the newsstands, her fifth published novel, *Season of Passion*, hit the bookstores. Dedicated to Bill, Beatrix, Nicholas, and Danielle's Christian Science spiritual adviser, Nancy Bel Weeks, this contemporary romance about a young novelist who carries on a simultaneous relationship with a mentally disabled former football player and a talk-show producer is filled with tidbits from Danielle's own life, including elements of her relationship with Danny.

"I made a lot of decisions about my life when I wrote that," Danielle told the *San Francisco Examiner*, explaining that she turned in the manuscript just before meeting Bill.

Once again, the setting is San Francisco, and the heroine is a young debutante who dreams of becoming a novelist. Much to her parents' dismay, Kaitlin falls in love with and marries an aging professional football player ten years her senior named Tom Harper. Like Danielle, Kaitlin wears a frumpy nightgown when she writes and has a basset hound for a pet.

Tom's life turns into a tangled mess when he turns to alcohol and transforms into a beer-swilling, bar-brawling stereotype of a washed-up jock. In some ways, his downfall from booze parallels Danny's nosedive after he moved in with Danielle. Tom eventually loses his ability to walk and think after he botches a suicide attempt with a loaded gun.

Kaitlin then admits her husband to a mental hospital in Carmel and commutes three hours from Santa Barbara to see him. Unbeknownst to him, she is pregnant with his child, bears a baby boy, and raises him alone. While Danielle was writing this manuscript, she was living with Beatrix and commuting to prison to see Danny.

Success arrives for Kaitlin when she pens a novel based on her tumultuous relationship with Tom, a relationship she decides to keep secret from the public and the press. Kaitlin lives in constant fear someone will discover her secret.

There were some similarities to the book and her life as she was making her transition away from her second husband. In the book, Kaitlin falls in love with a television producer named Nicholas, the name Danielle chose for her second child. She gets pregnant by him while still married to the institutionalized Tom. In real life, Danielle became pregnant by her lover, Bill, while legally married to the institutionalized Danny.

Danielle's heroine eventually gains the resolve to leave Tom and move on to her new life with Nicholas, just as Danielle was coming to terms with the end of her five-year relationship with Danny when she met Bill.

Early in 1979, Danielle, Bill, Beatie, and Romelia took a trip to New York, where Danielle met with her editors and publisher. The journey was not an easy one, since Danielle had suffered from fear of flying since divorcing

Claude-Eric in 1974. A class helped her cope with the phobia. "She used to hold my hand and not let go the whole flight," Bill said.

On that trip, Bill said they had to get a second car for all the luggage they brought along. "I felt like a human clothes-tree walking through the airport," he said. He was introduced to Danielle's agent and they paid a visit to Kuniko, who showed Bill some of the souvenirs Danielle's late father had brought back from his travels. "There was a shrunken head and a Japanese samurai sword," Bill recalled.

In March, an interview of Danielle was published in the *San Francisco Examiner*. In that article, she compared Bill to "one of the dream men in my books," telling the reporter how impressed she was that her husband had recently stayed up all night counseling a troubled youth. "I thought, 'I sit here with my little sense of importance while this man is working with real people.' "

That day Bill certainly played the part of a romantic spouse, arriving home with a special gift: the soundtrack for the theatrical production of *They're Playing Our Song*, which they had seen during the Manhattan trip. Bill told the reporter he had read a few of Danielle's novels, but not all, explaining they weren't the sort of books he read for pleasure. "That's our biggest bone of contention," he said.

Their biggest bone of contention was really Bill's drug problem. Bill was still hooked on heroin; he had become increasingly ambivalent about his wife's success and uncertain of his own status. With her top-selling book making headlines, Danielle began to get invitations to social events and parties. Columnist Pat Montandon was a big fan and friend of the romance writer's, inviting Danielle to participate in Montandon's regular "round table" seminars, in which prominent writers, lawyers, doctors, politicians, and celebrities gathered at Montandon's exquisite penthouse for an afternoon of lunch and intellectual discussion on the issues of the day.

Meanwhile, Bill said he started feeling like a kept man. Danielle attired him in three-hundred-dollar Bernard La Vonne suits, silk shirts, and silk ties. Once, she bought Bill a Mustang convertible as a birthday or anniversary gift, but he told her to return it. He later went out and bought his own car: a used Volkswagen Beetle. Another time, they were shopping at a Union Square furrier, and Danielle laid eyes on a full-length coyote men's coat that cost five thousand dollars. She thought it would look great on Bill, but he vetoed the purchase. "All I'd need is a hat and a pair of platform shoes and I'd look like a pimp," he told her. "I never lacked for anything."

Danielle loved to shop, Bill said. He felt she shopped to cope with stress. Shoes were a particular passion. Danielle had taken twenty-two pairs for the ten-day trip to New York. "She loved Bruno Magli shoes, and she usually bought three or four pairs at a time. When she didn't want them anymore, she gave them away to friends."

Danielle's rising star was too much for Bill's ego to handle. "I had a wife making more money than me, and a baby. It was a big change. If Danielle had been a secretary, maybe we'd still be together."

That spring, Danielle began getting strange phone calls, and she suspected Danny was the culprit. One time he called the house and spoke with Beatie, Bill said. Not one to take chances, Danielle headed to court on April 4, with attorney Isabella Grant, to file a restraining order against Danny. Granting the order notifying police was Superior Court Judge Donald B. King.

According to Danielle's petition, Danny had been in Vacaville for five years and had been convicted of assault, robbery, and rape.

"He has exhibited violence in the past toward women and has a history of violence when he is drinking," she said.

Danny was scheduled to be released from prison on April 5, and Danielle was concerned he might start drinking again. Though Danielle had changed her name to Toth when she married Bill, she signed the document "Danielle F. Zugelder (or Steel)."

Danielle was uncertain how Danny would react to the news that she had remarried and had had a child. There had been only minimal contact after the divorce, usually desperate calls from Danny asking for money.

Once again, the romance author seized control of the situation and took every safeguard possible, including hiring a bodyguard for a three-day period after Danny's release from Vacaville. Bill called his old parole officer, Stephen Northrop, inquiring about a gun and whether it would get him in trouble. He eventually settled for keeping a baseball bat by the front door.

The fear subsided in a few days, after Danielle received a call from Danny. "Danny Zugelder never threatened me and never did anything threatening to me," she said. "The only time I was concerned about [Danny] was when he came out of prison many years ago and I had remarried Bill and I wasn't sure how he would take to that. And my only contact at the time was that he called to tell me that he understood perfectly that I had left him and he wished me well and wished me no harm, and he didn't call me again."

On April 5, 1979, Danny was paroled from Vacaville back to San Francisco.

Danny said, "It really hurt me that she put a restraining order on me, because I had never done a thing to indicate to her that I would harm her or Beatrix. That's when I realized she was casting me aside completely and totally. Nothing we had in our relationship would have meant anything at that point.

"I had every intention of going straight. I arranged to get a job with Whisler-Patri. I arranged to borrow some money to get an apartment and to get my life together. I had big plans for going to work, getting an education, and working in a career that I could enjoy. If you would have asked them back then who is the guy least likely to return to prison, it would have been me.

"You have plans of what you want to do, but nothing ever does go the way you planned. You don't realize this because you believe that everything you put together in your mind, that when you walk out that door, all you have to do is follow the steps."

This time, instead of a house in Pacific Heights, Danny's steps led to a tiny apartment downtown, within walking distance of Whisler-Patri. He didn't have money for a car.

"I was a model citizen for about a month," recalled Danny, who said he moved in with the girlfriend of someone he knew in Vacaville. "She was just a roommate," said Danny, explaining that later it developed into a romance.

"Every day I would get off work, come home, and pick up a six-pack of beer," he said. "We would split the six-pack between us and have dinner, and that would be the extent of my evening."

Danny stayed away from Danielle and the house on Green Street for almost a month, even though he admitted he thought about her often. Then around the beginning of May, while running an errand for Whisler-Patri in the company car, he drove by the house and saw Beatie out front pushing Nicky in a stroller and Danielle bending over talking to someone in a car. The blissful domestic scene was too much for Danny.

"As soon as I saw Danielle," recalled Danny, "I went to the nearest liquor store and got a quart of vodka, one hundred proof. Then I got some grass and some speed. I was on a death mission."

For literally the next month, Danny said he kept himself high on vodka and speed. He paid for his habit by reverting to an earlier profession: robbing banks.

"All my life people were telling me what I was going to end up doing," Danny said. "A rapist is the lowest form of life [in prison] other than a child molester. It wasn't like I set out to be this. But I thought, 'This is what you [society] want me to be, what you want me to do with my life, so I'm going to become this nation's worst bad man.' "

By May 14, 1979, just thirty-nine days after his release from Vacaville, Danny's parole had been suspended. The law, he said, was on his tail for both bank robbery and rape.

Once during that period, while he was on the run, Danny said he called Danielle from Dublin, a suburb of Oakland. "It was the day the cops were coming to arrest me [at Whisler-Patri]. I had a hell of a time getting out of San Francisco because of the gas crunch, and I was taking BART. I had to get a gun. It was a crazy day, I remember that."

He told his ex-wife "the shit had hit the fan and I was on the run again. One of her favorite expressions was 'I've got too much on my plate right now and I can't handle your problems,' and that's basically what she said to me. She sounded rather distant and detached. Looking back, psychologically, I understand that I really called her to say, 'Look what you made me do now.'"

Danny drove to Los Angeles, where he scored some coke and made plans for his getaway. "I decided to cool it in Minnesota," he said. "I started doing coke in Los Angeles. I left L.A. with an ounce of coke, a pound of grass, a thousand whites [uppers], an ice chest sitting behind the bucket seat with fifths of whiskey and vodka. I was shooting coke, smoking dope, popping whites, driving with a twelve-gauge, semiautomatic shotgun across my lap."

Zugelder said it probably didn't help his frame of mind that the police contacted his roommate in San Francisco and told her he was "too big and too mean, and that they were going to shoot on sight if I didn't turn myself in. I said, 'Whoa, they're going to shoot me? I'll show them who is going to shoot who.'"

Arriving in Glenwood Springs, Colorado, a lush mountain resort town two-hundred miles west of Denver, Danny was completely strung out. Spying a young girl leaving a house where a police car was parked out front, Danny stalked and then raped the girl.

"I had a death wish," he said, but instead of death, he would get life in a different kind of hell. Danny was arrested on June 4 in Glenwood Springs. He had been out of prison for exactly two months.

Years later, Danielle told Bill's lawyer that her third husband was a bigger threat to her than Danny ever was, even after conceding Bill had never physically abused her or been convicted of any violent acts.

"The difference is Danny never threatened me and Bill has threatened me," she said in 1984. "There was always kind of an underlying violence with Bill. I mean, you never quite knew what he was going to do because he wasn't totally coherent or sober. Not at the beginning, but once he went back to drugs.

"Danny was always nice to me. He made a mess of my life, but he was one of the nicest people to me. And Bill was never nice to me."

Around the time of their wedding anniversary, Danielle came home one day and found Bill high on drugs. She told him to get out, and Bill decided to put himself into a drug-treatment program at St. Joseph's Hospital. He lasted one night.

"They wanted to detox me on something other than methadone, and I had to have methadone, so I left," Bill said.

Infuriated, Danielle refused to let him back in the house, so Bill headed for his old turf, the seedy Mission District. That night, Bill kept calling Danielle, pouring his heart out over the phone. He was depressed and still wanted help. "I felt sorry for him," Danielle said. "I thought I would try to get him to treatment."

She called on one of Bill's oldest friends, Police Officer Stan Buscovich, to go out and find her husband. It was three A.M. when Buscovich tracked him down in an empty lot, hanging out with an unsavory group of characters. He persuaded Bill to get in his car and go to Mount Zion Hospital, where he had been treated for serum hepatitis.

They were met there by Danielle and Bill's personal physician. He had been alerted by Danielle that Bill was on a bender and needed to be hospitalized at once. Gladman Memorial had no beds available in its detox unit, so he admitted Bill to Mount Zion.

"He didn't want any part of it; he wanted to go back on the street," Danielle later told Bill's lawyer. Bill was acting hostile and irrational. "He was very high and acting kind of freaky," she said.

In a rush of anger, Bill reached out and stuck a medical instrument in Danielle's ear. "Fortunately it didn't do any lasting damage, but it was not overly pleasant," she said. "It was the only time he had ever physically attacked me."

Bill has no recollection of that incident with the medical instrument, but he does recall being admitted to Gladman a few days later for a month-long attempt at methadone rehabilitation in the hospital's detox unit. Danielle and Bill's parents paid all the expenses. Once again, Danielle allowed him back home, and Bill was on his best behavior, for a while.

Later that summer, Bill escorted Danielle to Pat Montandon and husband Al Wilsey's annual summer costume ball at their lavish spread in Napa Valley. That year's theme was an old-fashioned Southern picnic. Bill dressed as a riverboat gambler, and Danielle wore a blouse covered by a red shawl. During the luncheon, they were seated at a table with Dede Buchanan Traina, a Dow Chemical heiress and former *Town and Country* cover girl, and her husband, John A. Traina, Jr., a cruise-line executive. Bill and Danielle's table companions were among the city's most fashionable and attractive couples, and they circulated in the highest circles of San Francisco society life.

"When I first met her," Bill said, "she had a whole different set of friends, but they got left out as she moved up. I didn't fit in either."

That fate arrived for Bill sooner than he realized. In the summer of 1979, unbeknownst to Bill, Danielle was about to fall in love with another man.

17

                                ॐ

The man Danielle would dedicate her eleventh novel to was a San Francisco firefighter named Thaddeus Anthony Golas. Though details are sketchy, friends recalled that the introduction was arranged by a mutual friend and took place at Danielle's house.

Thaddeus—Ted to his friends—presented a striking picture: at forty, he was a handsome, blond, five-foot-nine, 170-pound firefighter with the kind of rugged good looks that enabled him to have a modeling career on the side. Just before meeting Danielle, he had been the model for a national television and print ad campaign for Extra-Strength Tylenol capsules.

Born on August 7, 1939, Ted was raised in Syracuse, New York, by his steelworker father, John Golas, and his wife, Vera, a cook at a church rectory. Ted's mother had died of a burst appendix when he was a toddler.

After high-school graduation, Ted joined the Marines in March 1959 and served part of his stint in Japan. When his tour of duty ended in December 1962, he headed west, remaining a member of the Marine reserves until he was honorably discharged in March 1965. Later that year, he married a dental assistant and they stayed together for eleven years until their divorce in 1976. By that time Ted was leading a comfortable life, making $1,560 a month as a firefighter based at the San Francisco International Airport. He earned another $120 a month moonlighting as a security guard. For a time he considered a teaching career, but it was acting and modeling that became passionate hobbies.

In an April 1979 print ad for the Tylenol campaign, Ted's face was splashed across the pages of *People, Reader's Digest,* and *Woman's Day.* The words "It's good and strong!" were emblazoned across his forehead. Underneath the copy, in much smaller print, Ted was identified as "Thaddeus Golas, Airport Fireman." Friends said he would later go on to model for car companies, banks, and department-store catalogs. Quite the entrepreneur, he later opened his own coffee shop and produced a video called *The San Francisco Firemen's Video Cookbook.* Though his acting career never took off, he did garner a small role as first controller in the 1986 film *Star Trek IV: The Voyage Home.*

Among his fellow firefighters and friends, Ted had a reputation as a ladies' man. "He always seemed to have three or four girlfriends," said writer Thaddeus S. Golas, no relation to Ted. "Things came easy to him. He was attracted to beautiful, sexy women and was very good looking himself. I was envious of him."

Writer Golas, author of *The Lazy Man's Guide to Enlightenment,* met Ted shortly after the launch of the Tylenol campaign. "We both had the same unusual name. He got calls for me and I got calls for him, so we decided to get together," Golas remembered. The confusion was such that even *San Francisco Chronicle* columnist Herb Caen wrote an item alerting folks that the men were two different people.

When they got together, Ted fixed a lunch of all salads, no meat, Golas recalled. "He was on a real strict diet," he said. "There was hardly any food in the house."

On September 3, 1979, shortly after Ted met Danielle, his older sister, hairdresser Lillian Golas Franklin, died of cancer at age fifty-three. Ted flew home for the funeral. Lillian was the oldest of the six Golas children and had been close to Ted, the youngest. Though they had been dating only a short while, Danielle sent a flower arrangement to the funeral home.

"That made a big impression on everybody," remembered Ted's niece Sally Braunitzer, still living in Syracuse. Sally subsequently struck up a long-distance friendship with Danielle. "Ted had come home two weeks before my mother's death, and on the way to the airport he gave me a copy of Danielle's latest book, *Summer's End.* He told me: 'I'm dating the author.' "

The book was dedicated to "Bill, Beatrix and Nicholas, cherished people of my soul." On the inside back cover was a photograph showing Danielle in a dark skirt and light-colored blouse open at the collar. Pearls are draped around her neck, and her hair is pulled back and tied up in a bun.

On the day Lillian's body was laid to rest, Danielle called Sally's house looking for Ted. "I've heard so much about you," Sally told Danielle.

"She was a great lady—honest, loving, and down to earth. In our first conversations, she listened to me when I cried about my mother's death,"

Sally said. "And she talked about her life. She told me to pick up the phone and call any time I needed to talk."

For the next year, they spoke over the phone at least five times a week, Sally said. The conversations ran the gamut: relationships, children, and Danielle's desire to have a big family. "She really loved kids," Sally said. They also talked about Sally's uncle. "They hit it off right away and got close very quickly," she recalled.

During one phone conversation after Ted had returned to California, Sally let Danielle know just how serious Ted was about her. "He told me if he were to marry anyone, it would be you. He really cares about you," Sally remembered telling Danielle. For her part, the author appeared to be falling fast for the fireman. "She called me back later and asked me, 'Did he really say that?' All it seemed she wanted in life was a good relationship," recalled Sally.

Friends said Ted provided Danielle much-needed emotional support at a critical time in her life. Her relationship with Bill was failing, and Danielle needed a strong shoulder to lean on. "Ted was a rock for her. I know he was there for her," said a close friend.

And Danielle was there for Sally and Sally's younger sister, Kristine, now a twenty-seven-year-old triathlete, married and living in Upstate New York. Back then she was an impressionable young teenager working her way through the grief that comes from losing a parent.

Lillian's widowed husband, George Franklin, was crestfallen by her death. His parents and his previous wife had also passed away, and Danielle stepped in to help fill the void left by Lillian, becoming a surrogate mother of sorts for Kristine.

After weeks of telephone conversations, Sally finally got a chance to meet Danielle in person during a trip to New York over Halloween weekend. Danielle was in town on business and had brought Ted along.

"I remember meeting Danielle in the lobby of the hotel. I said, 'Oh, my God, you're little!' But she has a heart like gold," remembered Sally.

Danielle treated them to a first-class weekend. She put them up in her favorite hotel, the Carlyle, and treated them to dinner at two of city's best restaurants, the "21" Club and Tavern on the Green. They also saw the Broadway production of *Children of a Lesser God*. Sally and her husband left for Syracuse on Sunday, but Danielle and Ted stayed in New York for the week.

The phone conversations continued long after the trip. "We bonded because of Ted," Sally said. "They loved each other. She was a real down-to-earth person, even with all her money."

A couple of days before Christmas 1979, the doorbell rang in Sally's home.

It was a special-delivery package from San Francisco. Sally opened the package. The card said that "Everyone" should have a Rolls-Royce. Inside the package was a two-pound block of Godiva chocolate carved into a miniature replica of the British luxury car. Sally was flabbergasted. Another card arrived a couple of days later, describing Sally as "Best sister, best friend." And when Danielle sent Sally a copy of her first hardcover novel, *The Ring*, she signed it to "little sister."

Danielle's kindness and gestures were magnanimous, Sally said. Sentimental notes, chocolates, handcrafted candles would just arrive in the mail. Danielle even wrote the marriage vows for one of Sally's girlfriends. Once, after a long phone conversation, Danielle wrote a note thanking Sally for lending an ear. It also said that Danielle had fallen for the most terrific man on earth and his family. "She was so, so kind. We had a great friendship," Sally said.

Christmas of 1979 was bittersweet for Danielle. Her latest paperback, *To Love Again*, was being released and Danielle decided to throw a party for seventy-five friends two weeks before the holiday to celebrate the occasion. Danielle rented a downtown disco called Scruples, an appropriate setting given that a novel of the same name written by author Judith Krantz had been a best-seller. *To Love Again* was the fourth book dedicated to Bill, who was named along with Beatrix, Nicholas, and Danielle's literary agent, Phyllis Westberg.

Pat Montandon mentioned the upcoming bash in her society column, describing Danielle as a prolific young "writer of contemporary fiction." It was a title Danielle preferred to the despised "romance novelist" label that book critics frequently attached to her name.

At the Christmas party, dancers rocked to disco music under flashing lights and thumping music while other partygoers played backgammon. Danielle, Montandon wrote later, outshined her nearest fashion rivals by wearing a lavender lamé skirt with a deep slit up the back and a matching coat with shoulder pads. Underneath it all, she wore a red-sequined tube top. She was "terrific looking" and "enormously talented," Montandon gushed.

The news item was accompanied by a photo of Danielle strutting her stuff on the dance floor.

During a break in the action, Danielle flipped on a special record that had been produced by a local songwriter. The song was called "To Love Again" and was written specifically to accompany her novel. It was a slow and mellow tune, luring a crush of dancers to the floor.

Bill hosted the party with his wife, but there was no mention of their failing marriage in the papers. The day after the celebration, the years of tension that had been building up came to a head.

Claude-Eric Lazard, Danielle's first husband, from his Stanford yearbook, taken in 1961. (*Courtesy Stanford Quad*)

Danielle Steel in 1969 when she worked for Supergirls in New York City. (*Jonathan Richards*)

Danielle Steel staying on top of things at the Supergirls' office while her boss, Claudia Jessup, works the phone. (*Courtesy D. Zugelder*)

Above left, Gil Stone, Danielle's grandfather, in March 1947 before sailing to Portugal for a visit. *Above right*, Norma Stone, Danielle's mother, in center. On the left is Teckla Stone (Stone's second wife) and on the right is Teckla's sister Lillian. Taken in 1947. *(Maria Theresa A. Braga)*

A formal portrait of Danielle Steel taken in 1964.

A quick kiss between Danielle and Danny
Zugelder while picknicking at Lompoc
Correctional Institute in 1973. Danielle's
six-year-old daughter, Beatrix, sits on his lap.
(*Courtesy D. Zugelder*)

Danielle's second wedding. Danielle and Danny in
the visiting room after their wedding at the
California Medical Facility, Vacaville, California,
September 13, 1975. (*Courtesy D. Zugelder*)

Left, a family lineup at the California Medical Facility, Vacaville, California, in 1976. *Right,* Danny and Danielle in front of one of the wall paintings in the California Medical Facility, sometime between 1976 and 1977. (*Courtesy D. Zugelder*)

Danielle with her third husband, Bill Toth, in an interview done with the *San Francisco Examiner* in March of 1979.
(*Katy Raddatz,* San Francisco Examiner)

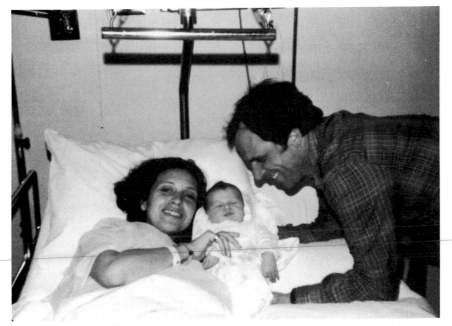

Danielle and Bill Toth are all smiles shortly after the May 1, 1978, birth of their son, Nicholas (Nicky) William Toth, at Mount Zion Hospital in San Francisco. *(Dorothea Toth)*

Clockwise: Baby Nicky, Bill, Danielle, a Lazard cousin, and Beatie celebrate at Nicky's September 1979 christening at St. Brigid's Church in San Francisco. *(Dorothea Toth)*

Nicky, Danielle's child by Bill Toth, in one of a
series of controversial photos taken by Dorothea
Toth, this one showing him cavorting with a pair
of rubber monster paws. *(Dorothea Toth)*

Danielle Steel with husband number four, John Traina, at a San
Francisco society event called 7th on Sale, September 9, 1992.
(Craig Lee, San Francisco Examiner*)*

1907 Pacific Avenue, the Pacific Heights duplex
that Danny and Danielle shared in 1973 and
1974. Notice third-story bay window on the
left—this was the room where Danielle
did her writing. *(Lorenzo Benet)*

2710 Baker Street, the apartment house Danielle lived in from 1975 to 1977.
Moving man Bill Toth met Danielle here, moved her to Green Street, and
then married her. *(Lorenzo Benet)*

The chapel where Danielle and Bill were married on April 15, 1978. (*Lorenzo Benet*)

A view of 2510 Jackson Street, on the right, from Alton Plaza Park. Danielle and John lived here from 1981 to 1990. The house on the left is owned by singer Linda Ronstadt, who painted her home lavender, much to the chagrin of many of her Pacific Heights neighbors. (*Lorenzo Benet*)

This view of 2080 Washington Street looks north. The Spreckels Mansion is a 1913 Beaux Arts residence designed by George Applegarth to please original owner Alma Spreckels's fondness for French grandeur. Danielle and John purchased the mansion in 1990 for $6.7 million. (*Lorenzo Benet*)

On December 18, Bill was admitted to Gladman for a third time, and praying Danielle would give him yet another chance. Her goodwill, however, was exhausted after years of paying his hospital and doctors' bills. "It was destroying [her] life and [her] children's lives," her attorney contended. This time, Bill was not allowed back. After his month-long stay at Gladman, Danielle rented her husband a room at the El Drisco Hotel in Pacific Heights.

While Bill was detoxing at Gladman, Dorothea stopped by Danielle's house over the Christmas holidays to visit with Nicky. Sitting in the kitchen with Danielle was a blond-haired gentleman named Ted. "She introduced me by name," remembered Dorothea. "He wanted to go to the Sonoma Mission Inn for the weekend, and he went and made reservations while I was there."

Dorothea said she offered to baby-sit for Nicky while they were away, but Danielle didn't take her up on the offer.

In January 1980, Danielle turned in the final manuscript for *The Ring*, her first hardcover novel and the last book dedicated to Bill. Though the marriage was in serious jeopardy, she chose to dedicate the book solely to him.

"To Bill, who said I could. With love, d.s.," it read.

The words relate directly to the support Bill showed for his wife's battle with Dell to get her books published in hardcover, a fight Bill backed her on all the way. She even gave him a signed copy of the book for his birthday later in the year, addressed to "Dearest Bill," concluding with "I love you, D."

"The only nice thing [Bill] ever did for me, which I gave him credit for, was he encouraged me to push my publishers to do a hardcover, which they had been violently opposed to," Danielle told Bill's attorney years later. "This is not any declaration of undying love. One of your secretaries just came up to me downstairs and asked me to autograph a book, which I did: 'With warmest regards and kindest personal something-or-other.' And I had never met her before.

"If he had kept all the correspondence I had written to him during our brief involvement, there were some anguished letters about how he was ruining my life and how unhappy he was making me that would certainly offset this . . . [The note] was no sign of any great relationship because we never had one. It's not a sign of any great love affair. It was great physical passion for a very short time."

The book, Danielle added, was no longer dedicated to Bill. She changed it to honor her paternal grandmother: "To Omi, with all my love, D.S."

Compared to Danielle's paperbacks, the hardcover edition of *The Ring* was somewhat more sophisticated looking. The back cover featured a glamorous black-and-white portrait of the author wearing giant pearl earrings and an antique choker and brooch. The inside flap read: "The novel her fans have waited for . . . " Gradually, Dell was moving away from the glossy Harlequin-style covers done up in heavy script, lace, and flowers, and was choosing to promote Danielle herself.

"Always she has had to push her career," said Charles Flowers, a friend from her New York days. "Take the publication of *The Ring*." Flowers recalled Danielle telling him that she was badgering her publisher to get her into hardcover. "They said, 'No, the kind of people who buy your words are beauticians in the Midwest, and they are not going to pay hardcover prices,' " said Flowers. "But she continued, and apparently they said, 'If you do a third book'—she was by then publishing two books a year—'if you do a third book by January first, then we will give you a hardcover.' Of course for Danielle that was no problem."

During a December visit with Danielle, she told Flowers, "I'm very busy on this Christmas vacation; I'm writing a novel." "And indeed," said Flowers, "that was *The Ring*."

For an article in the January 6, 1980, edition of *The New York Times Book Review*, Danielle told book critic Ray Walters, "There's more prestige in hardcover."

Walters's story was about the enormous sums of money romance writers were commanding from publishers, noting that Bantam Books had recently paid $3.2 million for the paperback rights to Judith Krantz's *Princess Daisy* while it was still in manuscript form.

Danielle wasn't in that league yet, but her popularity was growing tremendously. Dell had given *To Love Again* a first printing of 1.1 million and sent its young author out on the road for a book tour—something Danielle had avoided until now.

Incidentally, the romance novelist was referred to as Mrs. William Toth, and Bill was referred to as the author's second—not third—husband. The article also stated that her father descended from a Munich beer dynasty and that her mother was the daughter of a Portuguese diplomat.

In the previous three years, Walters wrote, "Mrs. Toth has published six paperback originals about the glamorous life she lived and observed on her way to Russian Hill." In an April 1993 interview, Walters confirmed that Danielle told him that "her books were inspired from her own experiences."

Palomino, Danielle's eleventh published novel, was no exception. The trade paperback was delivered in manuscript form in April 1980, one year before its release. The dedication was to Ted alone. "To Thaddeus, With all my love, And all my heart, And all my thanks, For all that you have given me. d.s."

That dedication was trimmed down in later editions to read "To Thaddeus, with love. d.s.," until finally Ted was written out altogether in favor of one of her children.

The heroine in this novel is an advertising executive named Samantha, and the setting is a ranch run by an older woman in California. Samantha ends up a paraplegic after a fall from a horse, and later, after inheriting the ranch from the owner, turns the spread into a horse camp for disabled children. That's how she meets a little wheelchair-bound boy named Timmie, the six-year-old son of a mother who beats and neglects the boy. She also shoots heroin. It was the first time that Danielle introduced a character with a heroin problem. It would not be the last.

"Why is she allowed to retain custody? Why don't the courts take him away from her?" Samantha asked a social worker. "Can't he be adopted by decent people?"

"Not unless she gives up custody, and you can't force her to do that," the social worker replied in Danielle's book.

Samantha falls for Timmie as she would for a son of her own, then goes to court to wrest Timmie away from his drug-addicted mother. When Samantha sees her for the first time on the day of the hearing, she finds herself feeling sorry for the woman whose child she wanted to take.

"One wanted instantly to love, cherish and protect her," Danielle wrote. "It was part of why Timmie had always felt sorry for her after she beat him. Because she looked so hurt and so distraught herself. It always made him forgive and made him want to help her, instead of expecting her to help him."

The woman, who is nameless, had completed a state-run drug-treatment program and had all her arrests removed from her record, just as Bill had done after completing his parole requirements at Delancey Street. After a tense and emotional trial, the judge sides with the natural mother. Two weeks later, the mother overdoses, and Samantha ends up with Timmie after all.

Danielle would find out later that the solution to her problem would require a lot more depth and thought.

As Bill gradually faded from the picture, Danielle began to emerge as one of the town's most eligible women. Yet in a 1993 letter from her attorney, Charles O. Morgan, Jr., Danielle failed to recollect that she was linked to a number of men, and she claimed she had no society life, with Bill or any other men, until after she became engaged in 1981.

Bill may have indeed got his walking papers, but in 1980 Danielle was spotted around town at dinner parties and attending events like the opening of the San Francisco Ballet. Even her car-shopping exploits made the papers when she bought an antique black 1940 Ford deluxe opera coupe. According to press accounts, she was dating some of the city's social lions, like Christian de Guigne, III, her escort for a May dinner Danielle gave at Robert. De Guigne was an independently wealthy bachelor whose father owned a fortune in chemical stocks. His mother, Eleanor, was recognized as the grande dame of San Francisco society. An invitation to Christmas Eve dinner at Guignecourt, her magnificent Hillsborough home, was regarded as among the most coveted invitations of the holiday season.

"We introduced Danielle around," recalled Dede Wilsey, who at the time was married to John Traina. "Pat and Al had introduced her to John and me, and we became good friends. She was new on the scene and a lot of fun."

Though Danielle was seeing other people, Ted remained her primary love interest. Over the summer, Dede and John invited Ted and Danielle out to Napa to spend the day at Dede's home in Oakville. That summer, Danielle invited Kristine, then fourteen, to San Francisco for a month-long visit. Kristine treasured her time with Danielle, Ted, and Beatie.

"She was my fairy godmother," believed Kristine, who would name her firstborn daughter, Nicole Danielle, after the author. "I can't say enough good things about her. She was there for me emotionally. I could call her when I needed to talk to her. She was there for me when my parents weren't. It was hard for my dad, who had lost two wives to cancer. Danielle made me feel real secure."

Most of the stay was spent palling around with Beatie. On another trip, Ted took the girls on a ski vacation, but on this trip they went to the movies, hung out at The Hippo, and walked around Pier 39 down by Fisherman's Wharf. If Danielle couldn't take them herself, a driver served as an escort, Kristine said. At night, Danielle took them to dinner and the theater. Kristine also remembered shopping at Saks and I. Magnin. "Danielle was wonderful to me," she said. "I was the best-dressed kid at my public high school. You would never think Danielle was rich if you met her on the street. She did dress nice or [went around] in a limousine, but based on her personality, you wouldn't know. She is very kind and the wealth was just part of her. It wasn't who she was."

During one outing, Danielle treated Beatie and Kristine to some chocolate at a shop on Pier 39. As she handed the cashier a credit card, the cashier asked, "Are you *the* Danielle Steel?"

The author became flustered. Instead of realizing that she had been recognized, Danielle thought the cashier was questioning whether she was the rightful owner of the card. "Oh, of course I am," she said.

"That's what I mean by down to earth," Kristine said, chuckling at the memory. "Beatie and I were laughing because this girl was overwhelmed by meeting Danielle, but Danielle didn't make the connection."

On August 1, Danielle became a homeowner, buying the Green Street house for $410,000. According to property records, she put down $80,000, and the sellers agreed to take back a $330,000 mortgage. Bill signed a quit-claim document deeding the entire house over to Danielle as her sole and separate property. A couple of weeks later, Danielle got a surprise from her publisher. They had decided to publish, as a birthday gift, a book of poems Danielle had completed back in October 1979. That same month, Danielle asked Bill to come over for a visit.

"I remember coming over to the house and she told me she wanted a divorce," said Bill, recalling that Danielle embraced him and then burst into tears. "I remember thinking, 'She's dumping me, and she's the one who's crying.' "

Bill may not have showed it, but he was heartbroken. He had spent five months in a methadone maintenance program and had gone to marriage counseling with Danielle in hopes of reconciling. But his wife was ready to move on. After the separation, she told Bill's lawyer later, her husband seldom came by to visit Nicky, and when he did, he harassed her for money and hardly paid any attention to his son. The tension between them had exploded during a confrontation over money the previous Easter at Danielle's rental house in Stinson Beach.

"I begged Bill to come visit Nicky because I felt he needed his father," Danielle told Bill's attorney. "And I told Bill's father that Nicky wasn't going to have his father around, because Bill didn't show up, he needed a man, he needed his grandfather. I begged Mr. Toth to come over. I use to beg Mrs. Toth to come over."

If Danielle had one regret after their separation, it was that she devoted the subsequent months to writing and put off seeking a divorce.

"She gave him a million-plus-one chances," said a friend of Danielle's.

Bill disputed Danielle's version of that period, saying he came by her house at least twice a week to see his son. Bill said the boy's new nanny, Lucy Westbrook, corroborated his visitation frequency to court officials.

On September 5, 1980, Danielle filed for divorce and submitted a three-page declaration asking Superior Court Judge Donald B. King for sole custody of Nicky and reasonable visitation for Bill—but only at her residence and in the presence of Nicky's nanny and the family bodyguard.

She also told the court that she had personal knowledge of Bill's use of heroin during five months in 1978, four months in 1979, and two months in 1980. "Although on each of these occasions [Bill] eventually sought medical treatment, he has refused to put himself in a long-term drug treatment program. [Bill] seems to have developed a pattern of heroin use and addiction every five to eight months," she said.

"When [Bill] is using heroin, he is irrational, irresponsible, paranoid, and unprincipled. He is a danger to himself and to others," she said. She claimed he was high during visits on Christmas 1979 and later during visits in April and May of 1980 and had been involved in two car accidents since she had known him. "During these visits he would often nod off with a lighted cigarette in hand," she said. Bill explained that what Danielle perceived as a heroin high was actually the effect of methadone treatment.

Danielle argued that other people needed to be around to watch Bill, or he could be a danger to their son.

That day, Danielle also successfully sealed the court file in the divorce case. Her attorney argued that public knowledge of Danielle's allegations regarding Bill's drug use "may subject the parties and the minor child to harmful and damaging publicity, public scorn and humiliation."

Her lawyer also pointed out that Danielle was a prominent public figure. "Petitioner is the author of popular novels and is a well-known public figure to a large segment of the book-buying public. She has been recently interviewed and featured in newspaper and magazine articles in the San Francisco Bay Area, and in other local and national media. Her public fame would attract further undue public attention to the highly sensitive nature of the family and personal matters to be litigated herein, all to the detriment of the minor child, and to the parties and their families."

That weekend, Danielle put all of Bill's remaining things in a couple of boxes and set them out on the porch for Bill to come and pick up. When he did, Nicky ran outside to see him, and Danielle immediately followed and blocked the steps leading to the street. She insisted they go inside, Bill remembered.

Later on, Danielle claimed Bill phoned the house and made a threat. He said, "One of these days my lawyer was going to die, and maybe he would have a hand in it," Danielle recalled later. Bill denied ever making the threat.

On September 10, 1980, *San Francisco Chronicle* society columnist Pat Steger reported that Danielle planned to attend the opening of the Performing Arts Center in San Francisco. The guest list included California Governor Jerry Brown and many prominent members of San Francisco society, including Mr. and Mrs. Gordon Getty, Mr. and Mrs. Prentis Cobb Hale, and John and Dede Traina. Self-made millionaire and benefactor Al Wilsey also was expected to attend, but he wouldn't be accompanied by his wife, Pat Montandon. They had separated the previous February and in the coming months would endure a messy and well-publicized divorce.

For this occasion, Wilsey would be escorted by his wife's friend Danielle Steel.

To friends and acquaintances, it was a perfectly platonic arrangement, since most people close to Danielle knew she was involved with Ted. What many people didn't know was that Danielle had a crush on Wilsey, twenty-eight years her senior.

"She was crazy about him and wanted to marry him," said one friend, who was surprised to learn Danielle would fall for a sixty-year-old man. "Then again, she wrote about falling in love with older men in her books," the friend said.

Wilsey, though, was no ordinary sexagenarian. A college dropout who left school to take over his late father's company, he made his first fortune in the wholesale butter business and then a second, larger fortune developing residential and commercial real estate. An avid pilot, he loved to cruise the skies in his own helicopter and airplane.

On one memorable date, Danielle on a whim asked Wilsey to marry her. The story goes that he was flattered by the spur-of-the-moment proposal, but declined politely. "I'm old enough to be your father," he reportedly told her.

Danielle was embarrassed and later told a second friend that she felt foolish for even bringing it up.

"I did date her for a time," Wilsey said. "It was very brief. I was very fond of Danielle when I was seeing her—she was bright and attractive, and had a lot of good qualities."

Wilsey hedged on the proposal story, but then admitted the offer of marriage "could have happened."

"You know people sometimes say things that are half serious and half in jest, and by the time they get repeated by two or three others, it's always serious," he said. "But it was never really a serious issue. Our relationship had not gotten to that stage. We never had anything other than a platonic relationship."

"Danielle's a romantic," explained a friend. "It always seemed like she fell for every man she dated."

When Wilsey was dating her, he invited Danielle and her two children to his home in the Napa Valley. "Nicky was a charming little fellow. He was quite bright, a jewel of a boy," Wilsey said.

His rustic house, called River Meadow, was set on twenty-five wine-country acres, about sixty miles north of San Francisco in the Napa County town of Rutherford. River Meadow had been Al and Pat's dream house—a New England–style wood-frame home surrounded by sweeping lawns, a swimming pool, tennis courts, a footbridge, and fountains. There was even a hanger on the property for Al's helicopter. In 1977, Danielle and Bill had been among the two hundred guests the Wilseys invited out to celebrate completion of the home. As guests sipped cocktails on the spacious lawn and listened to a concert by swing legend Benny Goodman, Al was introduced to Bill for the first time. His only other encounter with Bill was a ballet fund-raiser at Armen Bali's disco, Scruples. "He was bizarre," Wilsey said of Bill. "He was intelligent, but his manner was strange. I never got to know him well."

In the fall of 1980, Ted was still very much in the picture. Sally said Ted kept his own place in San Mateo, a suburb about twenty miles south of San Francisco, but he was spending considerable time at Green Street. "He was a pleasant and nice guy," said Wilsey of Ted, whom he met once at a social gathering.

September was also the month in which Dell released Danielle's eighth paperback original, *Loving*, which she had completed back in July 1979.

That same month, Danielle sent off a card to Sally. There was no special occasion. Danielle always did things like that, remembered Sally. The card was only a couple of sentences long, but it spoke volumes about all the action in Danielle's life. "So much going on," it read in part. "Tons of Love, Danielle."

18

தை

September 25, 1980, would have marked Danielle and Claude-Eric's fifteenth wedding anniversary. On this day, the already-tense relationship between Bill and Danielle took an ominous turn.

Six days earlier, Danielle and Bill had spent an arduous day at the Office of Family Court Services with Jeanne Ames, the director of the agency. At the meeting, Danielle and her attorneys pushed hard for a particular stipulation that Bill submit to a drug test before his first scheduled visit with Nicky.

"That hearing was a full-court press," said Carroll Collins, Bill's divorce attorney. "Danielle had submitted lengthy declarations about all of Bill's [drug abuse], and she took the approach that she had to protect the child."

The outcome was detailed in letter Bill later wrote to Judge Donald King:

> It was decided that I could see my son twice a week if I consented to undergo a urinalysis. Upon the advice of my lawyer, and against my better judgment, I consented. My wife agreed not to have the bodyguard or nurse present in the room with me when I visited my son. The reason for the urinalysis was that my wife refused to let me visit my son because she claimed I was under the influence of heroin. I think I should point out that of all the allegations my wife has made against me, the only one I have agreed with, was that I have had a problem with heroin in the past, but not the present.

Following the recommendation from family court services, Judge King signed an order giving Danielle temporary custody of Nicky, while the larger issue of visitation was turned over to child psychiatrist Dr. Morton Neril for further evaluation. Danielle, who was at the time paying Bill's monthly rent of three hundred dollars, made no demand for child support since Bill was unemployed and she had refused to disclose her income, "which is reported to be in excess of a million dollars a year," Collins asserted in court papers.

The judge also said that Bill could not see Nicky if he was using drugs, or under the influence. Bill couldn't merely be sober during visits—any trace of drugs in his system could cause suspension of visitation. Clearly, if he wanted temporary visitation, his best recourse was to quit using heroin. It was decided that a final visitation plan would be settled at a later date.

"Bill always denied to me that he was using drugs," Collins said. "I wanted to believe him, but I had my suspicions. He denied that he was using drugs at that hearing and felt he shouldn't have to submit to tests."

The day before a scheduled September 23 visit with Nicky, Bill went to a lab to take the urinalysis. "The lab attendant insisted that he remain in the bathroom with me to witness my urinating in the bottle," Bill wrote in his letter to King. "It was at this point I refused to take the test in that lab, left, found another one and gave a urine sample which turned out to be drug free."

But the results were unacceptable to Danielle. With the backing of the Office of Family Court Services, the test result was ruled invalid and the visit with Nicky was canceled. There would be no visits unless the urinalysis was witnessed.

"Why is it that the accusations and allegations my wife has made concerning me are accepted as true and at face value, while I have to prove whatever I say?" Bill asked in his letter to King.

On September 25, the day King signed the temporary visitation order, Danielle was in her bedroom when she got a telephone call from Bill. He demanded money and Danielle refused.

"He said to me that if he ever had the chance, when I least expected it, he would take Nicky," Danielle later told Bill's lawyer. "I would never see him again, and I would never know if he was dead or alive. That has stuck in my mind to this day, and I have always acted on that."

"You are aware," Collins said, "that Bill has had numerous involvements with the criminal-justice system?"

"Yes," Danielle said.

"Are you aware of any crime that he has ever been charged with that has been of a violent nature?"

"No," Danielle responded. "But I don't believe that somebody under the influence of drugs is entirely somebody who you can totally, totally trust. You don't trust their control or judgment. Those drugs are very corrosive over the years."

"Do you consider Bill's makeup to be of a violent nature?"

"I don't think I can judge that anymore," she said. "The person that he was when he was clean, when I met him, would be harder on the person he is now than any one of us. That person I would totally trust, and I would have no problem with totally trusting Nicky with him. But he is not that person. He is a person affected by the drugs, and the stakes are too high. The child is too important."

Bill admitted that in the heat of the moment he may have impulsively threatened to take Nicky on that fateful day, but only because he was angry and wanted to hurt Danielle. Bill said he later tried to explain to Danielle that he didn't mean any harm, but Danielle never believed him. Danielle denied that Bill ever took back what he said and claimed he made the threats again.

"There could be a first time," she said, noting that a marriage counselor she had been seeing with Bill once told her drugs could harm the brain. "Maybe he'll reach a point where it suddenly happens to him. I don't want to be the first where everybody says, 'Oh, gee, he never did this before.' Also, one of the things I have been concerned with are the associates he has who may be more violent than him."

Bill said he would never allow anyone to hurt Nicky, and that he never posed a threat to his son. "What was I going to do?" he said incredulously. "Hide him at my mother and father's? I knew he was much better off with Danielle than with me. All I wanted was to see him and have some input in his growing up."

Danielle, he claimed, overreacted and blew the entire incident out of proportion. "She transferred all her kidnapping paranoia onto me. She wouldn't let Beatrix in pictures [for publicity purposes] because of kidnapping. It was a phobia, to say the least."

Over the years, Danielle has told journalists that bodyguards had become a necessary evil because of her wealth and fame. During publicity interviews, her children were off-limits.

A publicist working for Danielle's publicity firm recalled that Danielle was indeed preoccupied with kidnapping. During a visit to Chicago to attend the American Booksellers Association convention in June 1980—three months before Bill made his threat—Danielle expressed concern over the safety of her children, Beatie and Nicky, who had joined her for the trip. "She was very concerned about security," the publicist said. "She worried a lot about her kids being kidnapped. She said it was the kind of thing that happened in Europe."

Kidnapping was a preoccupation that would play out on the pages of many of her books, including *To Love Again* and the 1987 title, *Fine Things*. *To Love Again* had been released five months before the Chicago trip. The manuscript had been completed in March 1979.

The heroine of *To Love Again* is a fashion designer named Isabella di San Gregorio, the "queen of Roman couture." Her husband, Amadeo, runs a fashion empire that Isabella inherits after Amadeo is kidnapped for ransom and killed by his captors. Isabella becomes totally focused on her job and her son, and her fear of reprisal transforms her into a recluse. From the moment her husband is killed, neither she nor her five-year-old son, Alessandro, goes anywhere without bodyguards.

Eerily, bodyguards were already a part of Danielle's life when she filed for divorce, and they were about to become a permanent fixture in her son's day-to-day existence for many years to come.

Nicky's first bodyguards were off-duty San Francisco police officers, but Danielle didn't like them because they packed pistols and seemed uncomfortable around kids. She eventually settled on a clean-cut, well-educated, martial-arts expert who had served in the Israeli Army.

"Because of [Bill's] threats, Nicky never goes anywhere without him," Danielle said in 1984. "I took those threats very seriously. And one of the most frightening things was the thing about 'when you least expect it.' That line kind of stood out in my head."

A kidnapping plot emerged again in Danielle's 1993 best-seller, *Vanished*. Set in the 1930s, the novel "brings to life the story of a man and woman faced with an almost-unthinkable tragedy: the mysterious abduction of their young son," the book jacket reads. Danielle dedicated the book to her husband John and her son by Bill.

The dedication reads in part: "To Nick, For the pain of having a mother who follows you everywhere, and the agony of so many years of not being able to do what you want, when you want to . . . "

The impasse over the drug-testing procedure as a condition of Bill's visiting his son continued into January. By then Bill was in a methadone-maintenance program that required weekly testing, but he feared that if he took one supervised urinalysis Danielle would insist on that condition forever. Danielle felt her concerns were legitimate, and she wanted verifiable results.

There also was some legal maneuvering going on. "Her first tactic was to get an annulment so there wouldn't be an issue over the community property," Collins said. "But we used the *People* magazine article and Nicky's existence to show there was a relationship. They got blown out on that one."

Bill and Danielle met with Dr. Neril in January to try and resolve their differences. A child psychiatrist, Dr. Neril had outstanding credentials, but no amount of education could have prepared him for this meeting. Bill lashed out at Danielle for keeping him from seeing Nicky. Danielle accused Bill of being on drugs at that precise moment. "He was intoxicated with drugs or he was under the influence of something," Danielle said. "And I objected because he was very messed up and nodding out. I told Dr. Neril it was an affront to sit there and pretend to discuss serious subjects with a man who was practically falling off the couch."

Recalling the incident, Bill said he had taken methadone earlier in the day. "When you relax, if you sit down, you can fall asleep," Bill said. "That's what was happening that day."

As they got up to leave, a small knife slipped out of Bill's pocket and onto the floor. Bill claimed it was an accident, and though Danielle admitted he didn't threaten her or wave it around, she felt it was an obvious attempt "to get everybody back in line," she said.

There appeared to be no simple solutions and Neril sensed the impasse as he prepared his January 27, 1981, report for Judge King. The problem, Neril reported, was the conflict between a mother's concern over the father's drug history and a father's concern that the mother was trying to get him out of the boy's life.

Neril recommended that Danielle keep legal and physical custody of Nicky and that it would be good for his development if visits resumed at home with Bill, but under close supervision by a neutral third party. Seeing Nicky "was one of the few high spots in [Bill's] life," Neril wrote. "There was intense anger at his wife for depriving him of visitation with the boy." Still, Neril decided, "I share the mother's concern about the father visiting the boy while on heroin."

At the next court appearance in late January, the drug-testing dispute was put to rest temporarily. It was decided that the testing would be handled by the methadone program Bill was enrolled in, but the matter was far from over.

By February, Danielle's love life was in as much turmoil as her custody battle with Bill. A new man had entered her life, and another was about to leave.

Back on November 20, 1980, Danielle had opened the *San Francisco Chronicle* and read a society item that Dede and John Traina had separated after fifteen years of marriage. They had been separated twice before and almost broke up in 1977 when Dede filed for divorce. They patched things up then, but this time there would be no reconciliation.

Five days after the news of the split broke, *San Francisco Examiner* columnist Pat Montandon reported that not only was the marriage kaput, but Dede had already selected her next husband. She only gave a hint as to who the mystery man was. "Good friends often seem to figure in marriage breakups as we all know by now," she wrote.

Society watchers could have guessed what Montandon meant by that remark. During 1980 some people had noticed the heavy flirtation going between thirty-six-year-old Dede and Al Wilsey during social functions. And now it was official: Dede was leaving forty-nine-year-old John Traina for Pat's ex-husband and Danielle's old dating pal, sixty-one-year-old Al Wilsey.

When Danielle read about the split, her heart went out to both John and Dede, parents of two teenage boys who were close in age to her daughter. The oldest boy, Trevor, took ballroom-dance classes with Beatie and even developed a schoolboy crush on her. Danielle phoned the Trainas to offer her condolences.

"I had my eye on him for a long time, but he never noticed me," Danielle told *Woman's Day* in 1990. She said she feared that like "all good houses he would never come on the open market." Danielle was too shy to ask him out. John took the initiative and asked her to lunch.

Though Danielle's interest in John was sparked, there was still some unfinished business with Ted. She was still very much involved with her fireman. They even took a trip together to New York in the winter of 1980, where they met with Dell so Danielle could discuss the cover design for *Palomino*, due out in April 1981. Over lunch, Danielle took one look at the frilly cover, called it "fruit salad," and playfully tossed the book back.

Marriage was definitely being discussed. Danielle was pushing for a serious commitment from Ted, even though he was seeing an old girlfriend, much to Danielle's dismay. "Danielle was upset about that. She was thinking about them being together," a close friend recalled. "John became very persistent, but Danielle seemed nervous about breaking up with Ted. She asked me if it was the right thing to do."

On Valentine's Day 1981, her dilemma was still unresolved. That night Danielle and her publisher threw a dinner-dance party at Trader Vic's restaurant to celebrate the release of Danielle's book of poems, *Love*. The incorrigibly romantic Danielle did the entire party in hearts, one of her favorite decorations. Her master bedroom at home seemed more like a shrine to Cupid than a place to sleep, Bill said. The walls were done in red and dotted with tiny white hearts, and she could even lull herself to sleep looking at two small hand-painted hearts on her ceiling.

A similar look was adopted for the party at Trader Vic's, where the late designer Richard Tam redecorated the restaurant's Trafalgar Room entirely in red and white. Ten round tables for ten were draped with red tablecloths decorated with tiny white hearts. The party favors for the women were porcelain heart-shaped boxes from Tiffany, each filled with candy hearts. Men received red Ralph Lauren Polo socks.

The one hundred partygoers danced to an eight-piece orchestra and dined to the sounds of a musical revue. The hostess herself was appropriately adorned in a Halston couture red dress, bare at the top with a tiered ruffled skirt, the *San Francisco Examiner*'s Montandon reported. The *San Francisco Chronicle* got its own scoop: Danielle's date for the affair was none other than Ted Golas, who was showing off an autographed copy of *Love*.

But the time had come to close the book on her firefighter boyfriend; Danielle had waited around long enough.

"It was at that time Ted told her once and for all he didn't want to marry her," recalled Dede Wilsey, who was still friends with Danielle. "Danielle wanted to marry him very much and it was sad."

"She wanted to marry Ted but he didn't want to marry her," a close friend said. "Danielle wanted lots and lots of kids. That's all she ever talked about. Her children are so important to her. I think if she had to give away everything for one of her children, she would. Everything else was secondary. All she wanted in life was a good relationship and kids. But I think Ted was afraid to get married and he didn't want to have kids."

The ambivalence and confusion Danielle was feeling was evident in a conversation with a friend at the time.

"John wants to be with me," Danielle said.

The friend had her own opinions, but kept them private. She didn't think Ted loved Danielle enough to marry her, and she didn't like the fact that Ted seemed to be dangling her.

"I think you have to go with the man who's treating you better," the friend believed.

John had been wonderful, and it was a word Danielle used a lot when describing the shipping executive. Bearing a striking resemblance to actor Roy Scheider, he seemed every bit like one of the Prince Charming characters who blaze in to rescue Danielle's love-starved heroines. The pace of their relationship picked up noticeably after Valentine's Day. The lunches turned into dinners. Flowers and sentimental notes showed up on Danielle's doorstep.

Ted, who was ambivalent about being tied down, didn't put up a fight. "He made it very easy for her," the friend said.

Not long after Valentine's Day, Danielle and John were secretly engaged. The gossip columns reported sightings all over town. They were spotted dancing at a fund-raiser for the San Francisco Museum of Art. In March they were seen emerging from a black limousine arm in arm for a cocktail party hosted by movie director Francis Ford Coppola and his wife, Eleanor. Later they showed up together at a party for author Gore Vidal, who was in town promoting his new novel, *Creation*. For that soiree, Danielle wore a pink organdy full-sleeved blouse with black silk pants. In late March, columnist Montandon was predicting wedding bells for the pair.

At some point, Ted reportedly had a change of heart. Apparently his interest in Danielle rekindled, and he tried to woo back the author.

"He told me he changed his mind," explained writer Thaddeus S. Golas. "He said that he missed her and cared for her and was willing to marry her and have babies. She said no. She told him she was already engaged."

Thaddeus recalls that Ted had few regrets. "I think he did miss the luxuries—riding around in limousines. But he didn't want the responsibility of a big family. He was having too much fun to be tied down to a family routine."

"He gave up a lot. I couldn't understand how he couldn't love her," a friend said. "She was very wealthy at the time," said the friend, praising Ted for not golddigging. "I give him credit for that."

Kristine Mallory, Ted's niece, was upset by the news. "It was sad for me when they broke up," she said. "I knew I wouldn't see her as much, no matter what happened from that point on."

In February 1981 with everything else going on, Danielle turned in the manuscript of *Remembrance*. Years later at a writing seminar, she would call it the most difficult book she has ever written. What she didn't say was that part of this book drew heavily on her calamitous relationship with Bill Toth and his struggle with heroin addiction.

The heroine's name is Serena, a blond-haired, green-eyed Italian principessa who emigrates to the United States and marries an Army major named Brad Fullerton. He has a younger brother whom Danielle chose to name "Teddy," and Serena admires him from afar. "Yet Teddy had something special, and it was impossible not to see it," Danielle wrote. "It was almost a kind of glow, a kind of excitement that lit up his soul and everyone who came within his sphere."

Teddy is the shoulder on which Serena cries when Brad dies in Korea. He would try to rescue her later, when naïve Serena unknowingly marries Vasili Arbus, a suave British-Greek photographer who lives a secret life as a heroin addict.

His demeanor and composure change quickly after their wedding in London, where Serena, Vasili, and her young daughter, Vanessa, settle down to live. For forty pages, Danielle writes in great detail about Vasili's abuses, his attempts to clean up, and his inevitable return to the demon drug that undid Danielle's own marriage to Bill.

One day Vasili arrives home late from work looking filthy and disheveled. "His hair was all askew, there were deep circles under his eyes . . . and he was walking unsteadily toward her at a much too rapid pace, as though he were operating on the wrong speed," Danielle wrote.

The next day he apologizes, but the problems only escalate. In the next month, Vasili inexplicably disappears for long stretches, like Bill, and his erratic behavior continues. Then, one night, Serena wakes up to find her husband in the bathroom: "She walked in and let out a scream. On the sink, next to a blood-stained ball of cotton, lay a hypodermic needle, a match and a spoon. 'Oh my God!' She wasn't even sure what she was seeing, but she knew that it was something awful."

Serena wants to end the marriage, but problems arise when she discovers she's pregnant with Vasili's child. She bears her soul to Teddy and then decides to give Vasili another chance. Danielle wrote: " 'Maybe I owe it to him to give him a chance,' she said to Teddy. 'He says he'll be himself again when he gets out.'

" 'He's a rotten man. Face it, dammit. You've made a terrible mistake,' Teddy said."

Like Bill, Vasili is a changed man when he leaves the hospital. He returns home and confesses to Serena that he has used heroin on and off for ten years and swears he'll never use again. "For the next five months he was as good as his word," Danielle wrote. He was "doing everything he could to make up to her the pain he had caused her . . . "

But it is only a matter of time before Vasili falls off the wagon again, and this time he tries to clean up on his own. After Serena gives birth to their baby girl, he contracts hepatitis and goes into the hospital. She is on the verge of leaving him once more when she changes her mind: "She still loved him, and she owed the baby something, at least to try one more time. She knew she should take her children and go now, but his magic worked on her. He was still dug deep under her skin."

When Serena finally does leave, Vasili follows her to New York to reclaim her. When he confronts her, Serena tells him he's a "bloody junkie" and that he "almost destroyed me and my children," Danielle wrote. Vasili then takes her throat in his hands and squeezes, screaming, "I love you!" over and over until Serena breathes no more.

On March 6, 1981, Danielle's divorce from Bill became final. The terms of the divorce were never made public, but what Danielle wore to the hearings did make the papers: "Giorgio Armani and crystal and black onyx jewelry," the *San Francisco Examiner* reported, adding that the author was joined in court by four lawyers, two bodyguards, and her Christian Science practitioner.

Bill recalled that Danielle made a settlement offer during a court recess: a thirty-thousand-dollar marital settlement and nine hundred dollars a month alimony for one year. Bill accepted.

A final agreement was hammered out shortly afterward. Danielle kept the Green Street house, her jewelry, furs, the Toyota wagon, two antique cars, and the literary rights to her books. Bill would get a total of $40,800 and also keep his Volkswagen Beetle. Danielle would receive sole custody of Nicky, Collins said. All that was left to deal with now was visitation with Nicky.

"Bill loved her," Collins believed. "He didn't care about the money."

His client wasn't interested in waging a hard battle over property rights. "Bill bails easy," Collins said. "He wouldn't stand up to her. He admired her, and in the end that was his downfall. He was a loser, and when he was married to Danielle, it was the only time in his life he was around a winner."

In retrospect, Bill regretted not putting up a tougher fight. "I should have hired Melvin Belli or Marvin Mitchelson," he said. "But I didn't give a shit."

Sometime during this period, Danny Zugelder, sitting in a prison cell in Canon City, Colorado, facing imprisonment until the year 2005, also wrote Danielle a letter.

"I was sitting in a hole in Centennial [a maximum-security facility]. I'm locked up and I write her a letter. I tell her, 'Listen, I need to get a lawyer to try and get the time off of me so I can do something with the rest of my life.' I offered to sell her the rights to anything I might say in the future." Zugelder said Danielle didn't write back to him. Instead she informed the warden that Danny was attempting to blackmail her. "The warden said I couldn't write her anymore," Danny said.

"If I would have signed something like that, I never would have said anything to anybody," claimed Danny, who said he initially turned down the television program "Hard Copy" and the National Enquirer when they asked for an interview. "I figured it wasn't up to me. If someone was going to break it [the news of their marriage], it was up to her." In late 1991 and early 1992, after "Hard Copy" broke the story anyway, Zugelder allowed himself to be interviewed by The Star and the television program "Inside Edition," both of which paid his family for the interviews. In June 1992, Zugelder was also questioned by People magazine, which did not pay for the interview.

Meanwhile, John and Dede wrapped up their own divorce with little fanfare. Under an April 29, 1981, agreement, Dede got custody of their sons, Trevor and Todd, and kept two Napa Valley properties she had purchased herself and held in a trust: a twenty-two-acre vineyard property and the twenty-two-room Oakville Victorian home. She also kept the 1963 Stude-baker Avanti her father had given her for her high-school graduation.

John would pay five hundred dollars a month in child support and got the Mercedes 600 and the Model T Ford. There was no alimony because Dede was independently wealthy.

The only point of contention was the house they had shared at 2510 Jackson Street. The agreement stated it was to be sold and the proceeds divided equally. Until the sale, Dede and the boys would remain in the home, with the mortgage payments, taxes, and homeowner insurance pre-miums divided equally.

By now, John and Danielle, as well as Dede and Al, were planning their respective weddings. But a dispute arose over what to do with the Jackson Street house. It had been listed with four real-estate brokers since February at $1.5 million, but no offers had come in. Danielle was in the market for a new house, so she and John decided they wanted to buy out Dede's share. John made an initial offer of $600,000, which Dede rejected. John countered on May 8 with an offer of $645,000, including a $50,000 down payment.

According to court papers filed by John, Dede had told him that she was not going to accept the offer. John said that Dede planned on living at the home with Al after their May 23 wedding in Washington, D.C. On May 18 John served his ex-wife with a lawsuit demanding that she accept his buyout offer of $645,000. John petitioned the court to force Dede to accept his offer, buy the house herself, or put the house up for auction.

Dede and Al went to Washington, D.C., for their wedding at her parents' home and then returned to San Francisco in time for a June 4 court hearing over the house. By now, the newly married Wilseys had no interest in staying at the Jackson Street home, especially when the Spelman Prentice home up the street went on the market. That was Dede's dream house. So Al and Dede agreed to vacate the Jackson Street home by November 14, the amount of time the Prentice family needed to pack up and move.

Though Danielle wasn't thrilled about buying the Jackson Street house, John was still very attached to it, Dede said. According to court papers, Dede agreed to accept John's last offer of $645,000 in cash due November 16, less a nonrefundable deposit of $50,000 that was paid to Dede on June 8, 1981—the very month that Danielle sold her Green Street house for $560,000, making at least a hefty $100,000 profit.

Danielle's buyer for her Green Street house, Dr. Thomas Russell, vividly recalled the day he looked at the place. "There were private detectives around the house," he said. "The maid told us Danielle was concerned her kids might be kidnapped. It was obviously a turbulent and difficult time in her life."

During the walk-through, Russell was struck by the personal touches Danielle had applied in virtually every room: hand-painted roses on the hardwood living-room floor, red tulips on the kitchen walls, a floor-to-ceiling mural of an antique car and driver against a brown silhouette of the San Francisco skyline in the dining room, and the heart-decorated master bedroom.

In Nicky's bedroom, there was a mural of Superman flying over a rainbow against a blue sky; in Beatrix's room, bright flowers splashed over yellow walls.

"Her home was sparsely decorated, with old-fashioned pieces," a friend recalled, "but with the paintings she created a fantasy land in which to write her books."

Back in Pacific Heights, Trevor and Todd lived with Dede and Al at 2510 Jackson. After John and Danielle's marriage, the newlyweds, Beatrix, and Nicky temporarily rented a house on Spruce Street. By early 1982, John and Danielle were settled on Jackson Street, and Al and Dede had moved into the Prentice home, just a few houses up the block. On November 16, the day John and Danielle took possession of the Jackson Street house, John deeded a 50 percent share of the home to Danielle.

Columnist Herb Caen wrote:

> It was Dede who bought the Spelman Prentice house at Jackson and Pierce—Spelman's mom was a Rockefeller—with money she got from selling her other house, on the same block, to Danielle Steel, millionaire author of romantic best-sellers, who is now married to Dede's ex-husband, John Traina. You don't think San Francisco society is too ingrown, do you?

19

⸙

$\mathcal{A}$s Danielle and John's June 14, 1981, wedding day approached, friends were tripping over themselves to honor the happy couple. The bride and groom were merely tripping up. At a June party given in their honor by Gordon and Ann Getty, Danielle was wearing a brace around her neck to nurse a pulled muscle, which ached so much she had to remove a pearl necklace John had given her as a wedding gift. The groom wasn't faring much better. During a rowboat ride with his two sons after the Gettys' party, he fell on the oars and fractured a rib.

The ceremony, to be staged at Richard Tam's showplace villa in Napa Valley, would resemble a Broadway production compared to the modest affair that Danielle had pulled together on short notice three years earlier when she married Bill.

So much had changed in so little time. This wedding would garner coverage in both local newspapers, *The New York Times*, and *People* magazine. The bride and groom would don white, and guests were shuttled from the parking lot up to Tam's fabulous hillside home in a 1937 Rolls-Royce.

"It was the wedding I should have had fifteen years ago with the man I should have married then," Danielle said. After the ceremony, the bride and groom planned to fly to New York for a reception and a press conference for Danielle's new book, *Palomino*. During the trip, which included a stop in Los Angeles, Danielle reportedly toted along twenty-nine separate pieces of luggage, including one suitcase just for hats. The celebration was expected to continue through the summer and into the fall, with an August trip to Europe and a September reception for close friends.

As the wedding day approached, the one unresolved issue was whether John and Danielle would have any children together. They had talked about having a family, and though thirty-three-year-old Danielle may have felt she was getting on in years, John reassured her and told his fiancée he wanted more kids, too.

Danielle wrote in *Having a Baby*:

> And then, interestingly enough, within days of our marriage, he said he'd be just as happy not to have any more kids. I was crushed. As an only child with a very lonely childhood, I had always longed to have a lot of children . . . John revived the hope. And I dreamed of having more babies with him. I was so disappointed that he didn't want more children that I cried (a lot).

Wedding guests began arriving at Tam's hillside villa on the afternoon of June 14. Danielle and her bridesmaids wore Mary McFadden gowns purchased by Danielle, who had her own makeup artist and two hairdressers tending to her. Before the six P.M. ceremony, bartenders broke out sixty-six-dollar bottles of Louis Roederer Cristal champagne. The party favors were Tiffany tie clips for the men and large heart-shaped lace sachets for the women.

Danielle was attended by Beatie and friends China Nurey and Kaisa de Tristan. Kaisa's husband, Marc, a good friend of John's, gave away the bride to a beaming groom outfitted in a brilliant white tux. During the vows, Danielle was so shaky that John's wedding band slipped out of her hand. Dinner was prepared by two French chefs and served on tables spread out over an outdoor pavilion. Dancing to an eight-piece orchestra lasted late into the night.

"I was so happy for them," Montandon said. "John and Danielle have created their own fairy tale. They could be on the cover of one of her own romance novels."

"Writing is easy compared to finding the right man," Danielle told *Woman's Day* in 1990. "When I became Mrs. John Traina, it was the most exciting day in my life. I thought, 'Wow, I've really made it.'"

The only apparent blight on an otherwise perfect day for Danielle occurred when Dede called Tam's home to reach her sons, Trevor and Todd. Montandon said she heard about the incident from a very distraught Danielle. "Dede was having a fit, and she was feeling pangs of jealousy," Montandon remembered.

Dede says that's not the way it went at all. That very day, Sarabelle, Dede's beloved fifteen-year-old dachshund, had wandered off and gotten lost on Al's Napa Valley estate. Dede needed to reach her sons because she had to find the dog before returning to San Francisco and didn't want the boys stranded outside the Jackson Street house because it was locked up and the staff was up in the country. "Danielle and John had planned on taking them back home in a limousine, so that got spoiled," Dede said. Instead, the boys went to Al's home and spent the night there before returning to San Francisco.

Sarabelle was found dead the next day. John had been attached to the dog, too, so Danielle went out and bought the groom another dachshund. They named the puppy Sweet Pea, after the baby by the cartoon characters Popeye and Olive Oyl, John and Danielle's respective nicknames for each other. Sweet Pea was a favorite term of endearment Danielle also used for ex-husband Danny and old friend Bruce Neckels, among others.

In July Danielle delivered the manuscript for *Once in a Lifetime*. The dedication read: "To John, Forever, Olive." Published in April 1982, the book features heroine Daphne Fields, a prolific writer whose husband and daughter die in a fire. For a while, she's a member of the living dead, and even gets clobbered by a taxi, just as Danielle's stepmother Kuniko had in 1968. Daphne's son is deaf and is put in a special school. Searching for new horizons, the novelist retreats to Los Angeles to write a screenplay based on one of her books and meets a handsome, blond forty-two-year-old actor named Justin Wakefield.

This character was likely influenced by Ted. Justin was sensitive, a terrific lover, and showered Daphne with gifts and compliments. He was a superb actor and loved to ski, one of Ted's favorite activities. But in Daphne's eyes, Justin also had his faults: "There are some things that mattered to him not at all, and children were one of them," Danielle wrote. And Daphne "had the feeling that sometimes he was in love with only part of her, and there were other parts that he didn't know at all."

If there was a romantic void in Danielle's life, John filled it, friends said. As Danielle wrote this novel, she was clearly at a crossroads in her love life: a woman who had switched from rescuing alcoholics and drug addicts to choose a man more appropriate for her station in life. "They are the ultimate couple," a longtime friend of Danielle's told *People*. "They're very romantic and surprise each other with gifts, small and large. After what she went through, she was rewarded with John. He was God's gift."

John's ex-wife was happy for them, too. "It was a great solution for everybody," Dede said. "He wanted to get married, and she has been very nice to my children." Her only regret is that when Danielle married John, "I lost a good friend in Danielle."

John's friends quickly became Danielle's, and some of the old acquaintances who knew Danielle when were gradually let go. "Armies of people are now insulted they aren't seeing me . . . but I'm making priorities in my life. John comes first, the kids, my work," Danielle told *Scene* magazine in 1981.

As husband number four, John was cut from a very different mold from his previous two predecessors. Born at St. Francis Hospital in San Francisco on September 26, 1931, John Angelo Traina, Jr., was the second of two children and the only son of San Franciscan John Angelo Traina, Sr., and the former Lea A. Castellini, both now deceased.

John Traina, Sr., was born in 1893, one of three children of Mr. and Mrs. Angelo Traina, early pioneers of the city's Italian community. Angelo's father, a native of Italy, first settled in San Francisco in 1850 and later set up a confectionery business that became well known for its Traina chocolates.

Born in Perugia, Italy, on April 23, 1900, Lea was the daughter of Mr. and Mrs. Gustavo Castellini. At thirteen, she became music critic of her father's newspaper and went on to earn degrees from the universities of Perugia and Rome. In 1921 she emigrated to the United States and did postgraduate work at the University of California at Berkeley. Intelligent, popular, and vivacious, John's mother became a star in the city's cloistered Italian colony. She eventually became a naturalized citizen in 1937, long after her husband, John Sr., who got his citizenship in 1910 when his father became a naturalized citizen.

The romance between John Sr. and Lea blossomed in Italy in early 1925 and was followed by an engagement party that November in San Francisco. Lea, a dark-haired, dark-eyed beauty, wore a lavender chiffon gown at the flower-laden home of Mr. and Mrs. Ettore Patrizi, perhaps the city's most prominent Italian couple at the time. More than forty friends chatted over tea as two sopranos, a violinist, a cellist, and a pianist provided the musical entertainment.

After their January 6, 1926, wedding at St. Mary's Cathedral, the couple embarked on a motor honeymoon down the coast with stops at Santa Barbara, Los Angeles, and San Diego. Upon their return to the Bay Area, the couple rented an apartment and later moved into a house built by John Sr.

Like their grandfather, John Traina, Sr., and his brother, Joseph, got their start in the food business, working in the family café-candy shop located in the city's bustling financial district, recalled Dede Wilsey, John Jr.'s former wife. The brothers sold the confectionery business in the 1920s and concentrated on real estate. John Sr. was able to retire at the young age of thirty-five but his fortunes dwindled during the Great Depression, John Jr. told reporter Glenn Plaskin in 1984. "We could hardly pay taxes on the land we owned," John Jr. remembered.

John's mother, Lea, was interested in music and fine arts. She channeled her energy into teaching foreign language and literature at the Kathryn

Delmar Burke School, among the city's most prestigious private schools for girls. In the 1940s, the Traina brothers ran an insurance business and John Sr. and Lea bought a three-bedroom home in Pacific Heights.

World War II changed life dramatically for the Trainas and many other Italian families across the country. As Benito Mussolini's fascist regime rose to power in the 1920s and 1930s, a surge of Italian nationalism swept through Italian neighborhoods from Boston's North End to San Francisco's North Beach. As one longtime San Franciscan put it, Blackshirts were a commonplace sight in those days.

After the bombing of Pearl Harbor, the United States entered the war and President Franklin Roosevelt ordered the arrest of all Japanese, German, and Italian aliens deemed dangerous to American security. Within three days, the FBI had rounded up 3,846 aliens, including 212 residents of San Francisco, and shipped them off to internment camps in Missoula, Montana, commencing one of the saddest chapters in American history.

John L. DeWitt, the general in charge of the Western Defense Command, urged the deportation of all enemy aliens fourteen years or older to inland camps, away from sensitive security zones. In San Francisco, Italians, Germans, and Japanese were issued I.D. cards and had to obey a dawn-to-dusk curfew, with their travel restricted to commuting to and from work.

Months passed, and the Japanese emerged as the group that would suffer the most as established German and Italian lobby groups back East fought against the relocation of their West Coast brethren. On Columbus Day, October 12, 1942, President Roosevelt announced that Italian nationals would no longer be classified as alien enemies, which came as great relief to the 600,000 unnaturalized Italians in the United States.

But the U.S. government did move against people suspected of being or associating with Fascist and Nazi sympathizers. In North Beach, scores of Italians were hauled before a board of military officials to show cause why they should not be removed from the command area. Among those expelled by the Army was the man who hosted John Sr. and Lea's engagement party, Ettore Patrizi, the seventy-three-year-old publisher of several local Italian-language newspapers and a leader of the North Beach Italian community. Accused of being a local press agent for Mussolini and other profascist activities, Patrizi was deported to Reno, Nevada, in October 1942.

John Traina, Jr.'s, mother, Lea, also appeared before the exclusion board on September 20, 1942, just six days before her son's eleventh birthday. She was labeled a protégée of Patrizi and was accused of profascist activities like hosting parties for people with Fascist and Nazi connections.

At her exclusion hearing, it was reported that Lea appeared timid and evasive about her prior associations, but the board felt that the evidence supported her expulsion. She was ordered to leave San Francisco by midnight, October 30. That morning, after saying good-bye to her husband and children, Lea left on a Southern Pacific train bound for Reno, where she lived at the El Cortez Hotel and Yori Apartments. The expulsion order was lifted a year later, and Lea was allowed to return to her family.

Lea's forty-four-year-old brother, electrical engineer Edgar A. Castellini, made newspaper headlines when he failed to enter the draft. He was expelled from the city in January 1943 but was permitted to return later.

The hard feelings still lingered a year after the war, when a *San Francisco Examiner* columnist wrote that Lea had been a supporter of Mussolini and the military authorities had ordered her out of the city because of her political leanings.

"John never told me about his mother," remembered John's former wife, Dede Wilsey. "Lea told me what happened. She started talking about it one day, about how she wanted to write a book, *My Life in Exile*. I could see John didn't want her to talk. I felt sorry for John about that."

John A. Traina, Jr., graduated from San Francisco's prestigious Lowell High School in 1949 and went on to Stanford University, earning an A.B. in social sciences in 1953. John's sister, Marisa, was an accomplished academician, attending Oxford University and the Sorbonne in Paris. Fluent in four languages, she wrote for European magazines and mingled on the fringes of Viennese, German, and Italian high society. She would eventually marry Carl Horst Hahn, a German executive with Volkswagen.

Marisa's wanderlust contrasted sharply with her provincial brother's tastes; her brother loved to travel but never severed ties with the city where he was born and raised. After Stanford, John went to work for American President Lines, pausing in 1955 to serve in the Army. He eventually worked his way up to the passenger sales manager of the APL's Northwest Division and then was promoted to a position as passenger traffic manager in the company's Washington, D.C., office. Over time, the six-foot-one, 165-pound shipping executive earned a reputation as a ladies' man, squiring around society women like Christine Lazard, the older sister of Danielle's first husband.

In Washington, John socialized with transplanted San Franciscans and cultivated the political capital's social elite. He took up a residence on fashionable Foxhall Road on the outskirts of Georgetown, sharing a two-story, three-bath guest cottage on the twenty-two-acre estate of Admiral and Mrs. Parke Brady. His roommate was Hayward Cushing Carleton, one of the Boston Cushings, and one of his neighbors was Nelson Rockefeller.

In a 1965 interview with the *San Francisco Examiner*, the handsome young bachelor noted the differences in social customs between the cities. In Washington, the cocktail hour is shorter, "time for one and a half drinks," John said. Everyone is home by eleven P.M. Dinner parties are planned down to the last detail—including displayed seating charts and small envelopes revealing seat location and dinner partner. There is also greater emphasis on punctuality, which John found out the hard way when he was reprimanded by a hostess for being fifteen minutes late for a dinner party. "You're not in San Francisco now," she told him.

As for the members of the opposite sex, the thirty-two-year-old bachelor said, "The girls are better looking out west. Frankly, I prefer the girls there and I hope to marry one."

It was a clever smoke screen. At that moment, he was in hot pursuit of one of the capital's most desirable debutantes, an effervescent young blonde, jet-setter named Diane (Dede) Dow Buchanan, the middle of three children of Wiley T. Buchanan, the former U.S. State Department protocol chief under President Eisenhower. Dede's maternal great-grandfather was Herbert Dow, founder of Dow Chemical Company.

As a Dow heiress, Dede grew up in a world awash with European royalty and Washington political leaders. Her father, a collateral descendant of former President James Buchanan, was a multimillionaire investment broker and a former ambassador to Luxembourg. Throughout the 1950s and 1960s, she and her family were frequent guests of European kings and queens. As protocol chief for Eisenhower, Wiley Buchanan once accompanied Nikita Khrushchev on a visit to San Francisco. Dede was educated by private tutors in Europe and at Washington's Holton Arms, a private school for girls. She later went to work as a receptionist in the office of Republican Texas Senator John G. Tower.

Dede's debutante party nearly caused an international incident in December 1961, when her family decorated the stately halls of the Pan American Union with giant cardboard peppermint sticks and red paper, transforming it into a replica of New York's chic Peppermint Lounge, where the Twist was invented. The main ballroom was decorated with papier-mâché peppermint sticks and a giant neon sign flashing "Dede's Peppermint Lounge." Some South American diplomats raised a fuss because they felt it was an undignified use of the building, but the seven hundred partygoers, including John Traina, didn't seem to mind as they rocked late into the night to the sounds of Bo Diddley's Twist Trio.

Later, *Town and Country* magazine selected Dede as its "debutante of the year" and put her on the cover of its June 1962 issue. By late 1963, John was courting Dede heavily, even visiting the Buchanans' stately Newport, Rhode Island, home, previously owned by Cornelius Vanderbilt. Dede then traveled to San Francisco with John amid persistent rumors that they planned to elope on the West Coast. Back in Washington, Dede's parents were denying that the couple was anything more than just good friends. John had indeed proposed to nineteen-year-old Dede, but she wasn't ready.

On Friday, June 18, 1965, John and Dede secretly eloped in a Washington church with only a few friends and relatives present: Dede's sister, Bonnie Buchanan Matheson, and her brother, Wiley, III. John's best man was Miles Carlisle, a transplanted San Franciscan. They honeymooned in Mexico and returned to the Bay Area. News of the marriage went out over the United Press International wire service.

The union occurred despite the public objections of Dede's parents, creating a rift between the Trainas and Buchanans that would last for almost the entire marriage. Dede's mother, the former Ruth Dow, told the *San Francisco Chronicle* that she and her husband had not been invited to the wedding and they didn't know when it had taken place. "We are not happy about it," she said. Husband Wiley was dismayed, saying the wedding came as "a shocking surprise . . . we are terribly upset."

The Buchanans' reluctance to accept John may have had something to do with age and religion, Lea Traina told the *Chronicle*, noting her thirty-three-year-old Catholic son was twelve years older than his Methodist bride. Dede's mother, Ruth, didn't hold a grudge against her son-in-law, but her father refused to speak to John for twelve years, Dede said. The tension between John and Wiley was such that John couldn't fly East with his wife when she went home to Newport.

"My father was upset because we came from completely different socio-economic, geographic, and religious backgrounds," Dede recalled. "There was a twelve-year age difference, and my dad and I had been close, and he was unhappy about me moving away. I must say that John was a complete gentleman and handled the situation beautifully; he never said a nasty thing about my father, who was so off-the-wall about it." Later in his life, Buchanan developed Alzheimer's disease. "My mother and I thought maybe his rejection of John may have been an early sign of the disease."

Settling in San Francisco, John worked his way up the ladder in the cruise-line business while Dede devoted herself to public service, working for the Ballet Guild Auxiliary, Telegraph Hill Neighborhood Association Auxiliary, the Opera Guild, and the Laguna Honda Hospital. She was profiled in a *San Francisco Examiner* story headlined "The City's Glamour Explosion."

On May 16, 1968, Dede gave birth to their first child, Trevor Dow Traina. Son number two arrived on October 22, 1969. He was named John Andrew Todd Buchanan Traina and was called Todd. Much of the Traina family life was chronicled in local newspapers, everything from their Far East vacations to the boys' Episcopal christenings to Dede's trips East to visit with her family.

John's career was followed closely as well. He was promoted to general sales manager for American President's passenger service and by May 1970 to general manager. In October 1973 John left APL after twenty years and jumped aboard Prudential-Grace Lines as vice-president of their passenger division. By then the family had moved into the stately Jackson Street house in fashionable Pacific Heights. Dede also bought two other pieces of property on her own: the twenty-two-acre Hermosa vineyard and a Victorian home in Oakville.

The first signs of trouble in the Traina marriage occurred in February 1975, when *San Francisco Chronicle* columnist Herb Caen reported that the couple had separated and John had moved into a penthouse on Broadway. They were back together by June, only to break up again in March 1977. This time Dede filed divorce papers, and the Jackson Street house was put up for sale. They reconciled and in August the entire family traveled to Newport to watch the America's Cup sailing competition from the Buchanan home. The icy relationship between John and Dede's father thawed when Wiley took the phone from his daughter's hand one day and asked John to come East for a visit. "John was wonderful about that," Dede recalled.

John changed jobs again in 1978, moving over to Delta Steamship Lines as vice-president of their passenger division. He went to work outfitted in conservative gray suits tailored by Wilkes Bashford and Jerry Magnin and was considered one the city's best-dressed men, wrote *Chronicle* society columnist Pat Steger. A size four, Dede showed a flair for style herself in outfits designed by Galanos, Giorgio, and Yves Saint Laurent.

John and Dede's friends were among the rich and famous of San Francisco. They threw lavish parties at their Napa Valley homes, took frequent European vacations, and entertained celebrity writers, actresses, and politicians when they came through town promoting their various projects. The two boys attended private school—prestigious Cathedral—and the entire family was listed in the *Social Register*.

Among their friends were Al Wilsey and Pat Montandon, but that all changed in late 1980, when Dede and Al fell in love.

On May 23, 1981, Al and Dede were married in an outdoor ceremony at Underoak, her parents' Washington, D.C., home. As fifty guests looked on, Edward Latch, the Methodist minister who had married Dede and John back in 1965, read the vows.

Looking back on the stir the breakups caused, Al Wilsey said, "It's never pleasant, but you have no recourse but to ride it out. It's like being on an airplane in rough and stormy weather; eventually it's going to stop."

These days, when he bumps into Pat at social functions, "We're civil to each other," Wilsey said. At parties, John has acknowledged him with a nod, but they don't speak. "From his demeanor, I would say he's still annoyed," said Wilsey. "He's not civil to me, which is bad because of the kids. But Trevor and Todd have kept a good balance. They were skillful in the way they handled it and never speak badly of any of us."

The same can't be said of their father, who has made disparaging remarks about his ex-wife and her husband to reporters years after the split. "A big day for my ex-wife was shopping at Saks," John told a reporter in 1984 as Danielle sat just a few feet away.

Dede has been known to make a few cutting remarks herself on the cocktail circuit. "What a difference a day makes" was a common refrain, referring to the fact that both men were born a day apart, John on September 26 and Al on the 27th.

Wilsey was quick to come to his wife's defense. "To say Dede spent all her time at Saks is sour grapes," Wilsey said in a September 1993 interview. "Dede has always been very active in public activities, volunteer work, and philanthropy. She spends as much time in public service as other women do at their careers, and it has always been that way."

John seemed deeply hurt over being dropped for Wilsey, and the wounds never seemed to heal. "Nobody expected it because my wife took off with a much older man . . . much older and much richer," Traina told the *Los Angeles Times* in 1988, seven years after the divorce.

"And I moved in and cleaned up," Danielle said.

20

ह≫

*N*ot long after the wedding, Danielle and John got down to the business of making babies.

"As soon as we did get married, I began calculating the dates, trying to guess when my most fertile period would be, and I became very insistent about our plans," Danielle wrote in *Having a Baby*.

By the end of the week, "John was looking wan," Danielle wrote. Danielle felt a pain in her right side and her doctor thought it was appendicitis. She was bedridden for four weeks while John and the boys went to Greece and Italy for a seventeen-day vacation. People around town began wondering whether the marriage was in trouble because John had left Danielle behind.

Danielle dismissed the rumors, saying she was too ill to travel with her husband and stepsons.

On August 13, the day before her thirty-fourth birthday, the doctors finally figured out what was ailing her. Danielle was pregnant. Thrilled, Danielle quit smoking that very day and phoned John in Europe, expecting an equally enthusiastic response. It was the middle of the night and there were only stars—not fireworks—flashing over John's head. In *Having a Baby*, Danielle wrote about John's reaction:

" 'That's nice,' he muttered, aroused from a deep sleep.

"I repeated the news, sure that he hadn't understood," she wrote. "Cannons were not going off in the background, trumpets were not blaring, he was not singing or telling me how much he loved me. 'I'll call you tomorrow,' he said."

Their children didn't react any better when Danielle broke the news to them. "They were immensely threatened by the idea of this new child because it was 'ours,' " Danielle wrote in *Having a Baby*. "My daughter burst into tears, saying, 'That's the most disgusting thing I've ever heard.' "

The author worked the impromptu remark by Beatie into her 1983 novel, *Changes*, the story of a widowed heart surgeon with three kids who falls in love with Melanie Adams, a television anchorwoman with twin girls.

Submitted in manuscript in March 1982, the novel was dedicated to Beatie, Nicky, Trevor, and Todd, "and especially John, for all that you are, and all that you have given me. With all my love, d.s."

The similarities between what goes in Danielle's life and Melanie's fictional existence are remarkable. Melanie and her daughters move into the doctor's home, once the realm of his deceased wife. Danielle and her children moved into John's house, once occupied by ex-wife Dede.

Writer Danielle even loosely adapted the innocent romance that went on between Trevor and Beatie before they became a family. In the book, however, the fictional relationship between the stepchildren involves kids a few years older and takes a malevolent turn.

Melanie gets pregnant in the first months of the marriage and the kids go berserk, similar to the scenario that was played out in the Steel-Traina household. "Theirs became a house filled with grief, and hurt and anger," Danielle wrote in *Changes*.

The relationship between Melanie and her husband sours, and they have second thoughts about the marriage and the pregnancy.

In *Having a Baby*, Danielle writes that after she had announced to the kids that she was pregnant, she and her husband "went out to dinner that night, and as we drove away, we saw those grief-stricken little faces and immediately got into a big fight, at the end of which John told me that he didn't really think we were suited to each other after all and I collapsed in total hysterics, muttering darkly about abortions, and sobbing long into the night."

"It was an adjustment for them," remembered Montandon, looking back on the relationship. "Obviously, anytime someone gets married, there's an adjustment period. He had kids, she had kids. But I feel they adjusted really well."

One of the biggest adjustments Danielle had to make was coping with John's passion for party-going. "Poor John likes to go out once a day," Danielle told *Woman's Day* in 1990. "I like to go out once a year. . . . We were each convinced our way was better. Finally, we were too busy to argue and learned to trust. With trust, decisions are easy."

Not surprisingly, things turn out all right for Melanie and her surgeon husband, too.

In August, while John was in Europe, Pat Montandon sat by Danielle's bedside and interviewed the author for *Scene* magazine. When the article appeared in October, Danielle was an international publishing force: her novels could be read in eighteen languages, and more than 19 million of her books were in print. *Palomino* had been on the *New York Times* best-seller list for six months.

Danielle wouldn't tell Montandon what she commanded for an advance, but she did reveal to her friend that her fee was doubling with every new contract. "And there's a Brink's truck just outside the door," Danielle added.

Danielle had actually just finished the first draft of her 1982 novel, *Crossings*, producing an astounding seven hundred pages in just twelve days, one of the few times she ever admitted in print just how quickly she can churn out a manuscript. The final draft was delivered in October and was honed down to 433 book pages.

It was a surprisingly candid admission for the secretive author. Later she told Bill's lawyer Carroll Collins that she doesn't write all the time, usually just "two to three times a year in very brief bouts."

How brief? Danielle was reluctant to say. "I am not about to have people pay nineteen dollars for a book and find out how long I take to write it," she said.

In many interviews, Danielle has described her writing regimen as a painstaking process. The one-hundred-page outlines can take "six months" to "a year" to complete. Parked at her typewriter for up to twenty-two hours a day, she has said it takes her a month to knock off a first draft, and another six to eighteen months to complete the rewrites.

She confided to Bill's attorney, in a deposition taken in their divorce proceeding, that writing and editing a book takes less time than she's willing to let on to her fans. "The outline of a book . . . takes me about eight months. It doesn't take me time in my office. It takes me eight months to a year to think up the plot of a book, but that happens up here," she said, gesturing toward her head.

"The books take me anywhere from ten to fourteen days to write. Quick," she joked. "Somebody call Herb Caen.

"When I do that, usually it takes me honestly about ten to eleven days, and in those ten to eleven days I always say it is like I take a trip . . . I sit there in my nightgown in my office and I write. I still stop to see the kids. They come in and talk and bring their pictures and drawings. If they have a problem, I am there.

"The rewrite of a book takes me two to four days, and once in a while five days. That is an eight-hour-day process. The longest, hardest thing is the outline, but that is not something that requires me sitting at a desk. I do about five hours of desk work a day, but I also go to bed late. I get up fairly early. I get up between seven and eight A.M. every day, and I go to bed anywhere from two and four A.M. I am going to look ninety when I am forty."

Danielle said she keeps her social life to a minimum by society standards, venturing out only one to two nights a week. She doesn't lunch out because she could wind up wasting five hours in a day. "I would rather be with my children or doing my work," she said. "I don't do charity."

Meanwhile, the thirty thousand dollars Bill had collected from Danielle in the divorce settlement was almost gone. He had lost his job at the Eddy Street Boys Home and couldn't get by on Danielle's monthly nine-hundred-dollar alimony checks. In desperation, he turned to crime.

"I was on a bender," Bill remembered. "The breakup destroyed me." On the night of September 4, 1981, nearly one year to the day after Danielle filed for divorce, Bill was arrested again, this time for shoplifting.

The arrest was a huge setback for Bill. He had been punctual for all his visits with Nicky, and his attorney was feeling optimistic that a permanent visitation could be arranged once they got their day in court.

A month after Bill's arrest, Danielle abruptly changed the location of Bill's visits with Nicky from her home to a therapist's office a few blocks away. Nicky would see Bill there in the doctor's office, with the nanny and a bodyguard waiting in another room.

Meanwhile, Danielle's life continued to flourish. She had told only a handful of friends about the pregnancy because of her tendency to miscarry. But in late September John shared the news with a group of friends over lunch in the Napa Valley, and before long, reports of the pregnancy appeared in the local newspapers.

The pregnancy went relatively smoothly until the fall, when Danielle took a business trip to Los Angeles. But after a week of meetings and business lunches and dinners, she began cramping and spotting and feared she was about to have another miscarriage, she wrote in *Having a Baby*. Afraid the nightmare would happen all over again, she canceled all her appointments and stayed in her hotel room. Two days later, John drove her back to San Francisco, Danielle stayed prone the entire trip. The bleeding didn't stop until she slowed down. There would be no more traveling during the pregnancy, and she would have to start eating regular meals to reduce the tension and exhaustion.

It was only a small pause for the fast-rising queen of romance. In October *Remembrance* had climbed to number seven on *Time* magazine's best-seller list, giving Danielle three best-sellers at once. *Life* magazine even arrived in town to include Danielle in a spread on the seven most popular women writers in America.

Once upon a time, Danielle swore to a friend she would never splurge on a fancy car, but times had changed. That fall Danielle treated herself to a new Mercedes diesel wagon.

Meanwhile, Bill was showing up regularly for his visits with Nicky. On December 3, 1981, he was scheduled to meet with his son for their regular two-thirty P.M. appointment at the therapist's office. Bill had just come from the Bayview-Hunter drug-treatment center and had just swallowed twenty milligrams of methadone. Arriving a few minutes early, he parked his car at the corner of Webster and Washington streets and waited for his son's arrival.

Unbeknownst to Bill, while Danielle was in the kitchen getting Nicky ready to go, the phone rang and was answered by Nicky's part-time bodyguard, a narcotics officer with the San Francisco Police Department. Danielle recalled that the message said there was going to be "some kind of trouble" outside the therapist's office. The call, Danielle assumed, had possibly come from another police officer. She then phoned her lawyer, Suzie Thorn, chairwoman of the State Bar of California Family Law Section committee and rated among the top divorce lawyers in the country, and asked what was going on.

"Don't send Nicky yet," Thorn reportedly said.

Nicky never did show up. However, two San Francisco police officers did. Kevin Gochet and Michael Lee worked as undercover narcotics cops and were well acquainted with Danielle's third husband. That fall, they had busted him for possession of a small amount of cocaine at a Mission District apartment, a charge that was later dropped. Bill alleged that Gochet and another officer had roughed him up during that arrest. Bill filed a complaint against the two men with the police department's internal affairs division, which was later dropped after they found no evidence of misconduct. A photograph of Bill had shown no evidence of an assault, and Bill had not requested medical attention when booked. However, as Lee and Gochet pulled their cruiser alongside Bill's Volkswagen, those charges were being investigated.

Bill was in trouble, and he knew it. Two days earlier, he had failed to appear in a Santa Clara County courthouse for a hearing on the shoplifting charges, and there was a bench warrant out for his arrest. Bill said he called the court to explain his absence on the morning of December 3. The court clerk told Bill there was nothing he could do until December 7, the day when the warrant would be issued in the computer. However, Gochet and Lee knew about the warrant as they approached Bill's car and asked him to step outside.

Inside Bill's car, the two officers discovered an open black attaché case on the passenger seat. It was filled with drug paraphernalia: three hypodermic needles and syringes, a razor blade, eight paper bundles, six spoons dusted with white powder, cotton balls, a cigar box, and a rolled red balloon containing heroin.

They also noticed the dark track marks on Bill's arms caused by frequent vein punctures. Bill's eyes were bloodshot, his pupils constricted.

Bill would later assert that the heroin was not there and the paraphernalia was not his.

Bill was immediately placed under arrest and booked at the Hall of Justice. Photographs were taken of his arms, and he submitted to a drug test, which would later reveal he had taken cocaine. He also phoned his mother.

"Call Dr. Riskind and let her know I won't be there to see Nicky," he said.

Justine Riskind was the therapist who monitored Nicky and Bill's visits. While relaying the message, Dorothea found out Riskind already knew Bill had been apprehended by the police, and that Nicky had never arrived. Later during a conversation with Danielle's attorney, Dorothea recalled Riskind's reply after she asked why her grandson had not shown up for the visit: she "became very confused and just said, 'Well, I had a phone call.' I asked her who and she wouldn't tell me," Dorothea said.

Bill had plenty of time to plot his course of action while stewing in jail for a few days until he could post bail. When he did, he headed for the Santa Clara County courthouse in search of some answers. He recalled approaching a clerk about the outstanding warrant. "I asked the desk lady about it," Bill told Danielle's lawyer. "She said, 'Oh, I remember that warrant. It was canceled before we ever had it in the computer because you had been arrested on it.' "

If the Santa Clara County warrant had never hit the main computer, Bill wondered how two San Francisco police officers in another county could possibly know about it. And how did Gochet and Lee know that Bill had a two-thirty P.M. appointment with Nicky on December 3? Did they just happen to be driving by? Though he was never able to prove it in court, Bill said he always felt he was set up by a private investigator employed by Danielle's divorce attorney.

"The whole thing smelled of a setup," recalled Noel Marcovecchio, a San Francisco criminal defense attorney who, as a public defender, represented Bill in the criminal portion of the case.

After the arrest, Danielle went to court to suspend visitation, charging that Bill had defied the court order by using drugs. Judge King postponed three visits and set a hearing date for December 17, 1981.

Asked in that court appearance about whether her attorney had hired a private investigator to follow Bill Toth, Danielle finally replied, "I think my attorney has made some arrangements in that area."

In years to come, Danielle would further admit that a private investigator was used to follow Bill, "to discover his drug involvement and whether or not he is using drugs."

At the hearing, Danielle raised another concern regarding contact between Nicky and his father. Danielle said she believed Bill was a health threat to her son. Citing his past bouts with hepatitis, she said she had repeatedly asked Bill not to share food or drinks with their son.

"He sucks on lollipops and hands them to the child [through] back and forth," Danielle told the court. "If he is using, I am very concerned about hepatitis, which is contagious for six weeks prior to manifesting itself. The child has had as much gamma globulin as he can tolerate as a result of constant exposure to his father."

Danielle also testified that the food problem was why she had moved the visits from her home to the therapist's office. "This was one of the reasons I wanted the visitation out of the home, because I feel he's a health menace and I don't want him near me [while I'm] pregnant. And I think he's less likely to eat—and I've asked him not to eat in the home when he visited in the home. And he continued to ask for meals when he visited and then shared them with the child."

In closing, Thorn asked Judge King to suspend visitation. The evidence was compelling: a positive drug test, drug paraphernalia in his car, pictures showing needle marks in Bill's arms, other arrests in Palo Alto and San Francisco.

Collins argued that Bill had been set up by a private investigator working for Danielle and the police. "It's very interesting that Officer Gochet should receive a phone call in a narcotics bureau regarding a warrant [unrelated] to narcotics," he said. "It seems logical that the private investigator in fact was the one who called them. The private investigator was the one who was able to get the police report the day after it was made, evidenced by the fact that [Thorn] received it on December the fourth from an arrest on December the third. Mrs. Steel Traina admits that she knew about the arrest before, so Nicky didn't even go over there. He [Toth] was set up.

"The end result is that we feel strongly that . . . [Danielle] was setting up my client just because she does not want him to be around her son. . . . We feel, Your Honor, that opposing party would like to be rid of my client," Collins concluded.

Thorn objected to the conspiracy allegations, but before she could finish, Judge King interrupted. "The key issue here is whether visitation should be suspended because of some potential harm to the child.

"I'm faced with a dilemma," he went on. "It does seem that the evidence indicates that Mr. Toth was in violation of the terms under which the visits were to be carried out. . . . But I can't ignore the previous reports from Dr. Riskind that the child enjoyed and benefited from visiting with his father."

The judge decided to resume visitation, but Bill was put on notice: he was forbidden to share any food or utensils with Nicky, and any violation of this order would result in a suspension of visitation.

King also expressed disgust for Bill's behavior. "If it were just you alone about whom I had to be concerned, I'd probably suspend the visits. But from everything that I've heard, there's a benefit to the child [through] his contact with you. The code provides certain rights to the child to be assured of frequent and continuing contact with both parents. And it's really because of that right that I'm not suspending the visits."

Years later, as an appellate judge with the California Court of Appeal, King reflected on the issue of substance abusers having visitation rights with their children: "One thing that's very important in making decisions in these cases is the relationship between the child and parent. If the relationship between the noncustodial parent and child is a good one, it's harmful to cut off all contact with the child, even if it's from a parent with those kinds of abuse problems. So what you try and do is make sure contact takes place in a way that the relationship is maintained and the child won't be harmed in any way."

21

The holiday season is festive around the Traina home, and 1981 was no different. Over Thanksgiving, John's sister, Marisa, and her husband flew in from Germany to spend the holidays with the senior Trainas. John and Danielle gave them a dinner at L'Etoile, one of the city's most fashionable French restaurants. The next morning, John flew to Hong Kong on business for Pearl Cruises of Scandinavia, for whom he was now working.

As Christmas approached, Danielle went shopping and decided to surprise John with an antique Model A Ford, one of the many automobiles he would receive as gifts from his devoted wife. This brought the total number of cars in the household to ten. The collection still included her beloved red Toyota, a car she has told friends she would never give up.

Danielle got nice presents, too. Late in the year, she was selected as one of the ten most influential women in the world by the University of Southern California Panhellenic Association. The survey had been engineered by her new publicist, Warren Cowan, co-president of Rogers and Cowan, at that time the General Motors of show-biz publicity firms.

There was one list published in late December that Danielle and John didn't make: the coveted *Social Register*, published by media mogul Malcolm Forbes. The omission of the newlywed Trainas from the fat black book was duly noted by the *San Francisco Chronicle*: "Oversights or overslights: Dede's former husband and his bride, John and Danielle Traina, aren't in this edition (John said he didn't send in the form)."

As Dede's husband, John had been listed before, but subsequent editions of the *Social Register* left John and Danielle out of the loop. Their neighbors, Dede and Al Wilsey, were listed in the 1982 book and have been in every edition since. Trevor and Todd were also included.

Danielle was five months pregnant in December, when she hosted a Christmas lunch at Trader Vic's restaurant; four of her guests were also expecting. Two of the women were collaborating with Danielle on a non-fiction book with four other pregnant women titled *Having a Baby*. The group had originally gotten together to work out in a private exercise class that met twice weekly at Danielle's home.

"The book was Danielle's idea," remembered Katherine Dusay, one of the book's authors. "We had all been moved by our birth experiences. Danielle wrote the outline and wanted us to be equal partners in the project."

Danielle was by far the most prolific of the seven contributors, who included therapist Dusay; local TV newswoman Jan Yanehiro; one of Danielle's divorce attorneys, Susan Keel; housewife Diana Bert; writer Averil Haydock; and skin-care specialist Mary Oei. The book covered every aspect of childbirth, from the agony of a miscarriage to sex during and after pregnancy.

Danielle's own pregnancy was moving right along. She wrote in the book that she was bothered by her appearance and tried to cover up her weight gain with baggy clothes, rather than maternity wear, which she didn't like. "Weight-wise, this was the most depressing time for me . . . it really upset me. Also I'm in the public eye to a certain extent . . . and there is nothing worse than being in the spotlight when you feel ugly," she wrote.

During this pregnancy, her weight topped out at 148 pounds, 45 pounds above normal. "I pigged out," she wrote.

Though Danielle had quit smoking in August when she found out she was pregnant, she resumed the habit because of all the burdens mounting around her—like moving into Jackson Street, work, and adjusting to a new husband. She held her ground at one and a half to two packs a day. "My vice is smoking," she wrote, explaining that she had given it up eight years earlier when she became a Christian Scientist. She avoided cigarettes for five years and then resumed smoking after marrying Bill. Though smoking went against the tenets of her religion, "I am not radical about my beliefs, and my children go to doctors, too. . . . But I will tell you that I basically have a certain mindset against drinking, smoking and drugs."

Another source of stress Danielle had put on herself was the remodeling of the Jackson Street home. The makeover of the 1895 mansion was chronicled by Danielle in a first-person story that appeared in *Architectural Digest*.

"What began as a few slight alterations eventually rivaled the building of the Boulder dam," she wrote.

No doubt 2510 Jackson Street, a Victorian neoclassical structure, was a lovely house. It had once been home to a clergyman, and Danielle and John set out to convert the mansion, without the aid of an interior designer, into a living space for a large family.

In the entrance hall, they put in a "dark green and white marble floor"; they decorated the living room with French furnishings and souvenirs from John's trips to the Orient; in the chapel room, they installed satin drapes and a magnificent chandelier; in the rosewood dining room, they decorated around a Biedermeier table big enough for twenty-four guests; in the cellar, they built a game room and a gym, complete with sauna, whirlpool, and exercise equipment.

The major remodeling took place on the second floor. The old master bedroom was transformed into a family room "all done in white," with a crystal chandelier and an "enormous mirror that reflects a large painting of clouds that we found in New York."

Danielle's tiny office was situated next to her husband's and filled with pictures of her kids and other family knickknacks. The master bedroom was decorated with a canopy bed done in stripes and English and French pieces. The bedroom also had a fireplace and two enormous his-and-her bathrooms with "double marble sinks and huge claw-foot bathtubs," Danielle wrote.

For the third floor, they commissioned an artist to paint murals in all the children's bedrooms. In the playroom, "a six-foot Paddington Bear presides gently over all," she wrote.

In February 1982, Danielle and John attended the annual Valentine Ball at the Museum of Modern Art, which included a fashion show featuring Halston's latest designs. The Trainas were trailed by a camera crew from the television show "Evening Magazine," hosted by *Having a Baby* coauthor Jan Yanehiro. As the svelte models strutted their stuff, the pregnant Danielle, elegantly attired in a blue and gold caftan, laughed and said, "I hate them all."

John rubbed his wife affectionately and reassured her, "You look beautiful."

Later in the week, Danielle went into premature labor and had to be rushed to the hospital. She wrote in *Having a Baby* that she may have taken on too much work during the move, with all the unpacking and redecorating chores. Danielle didn't give birth and she returned home to rest.

Danielle wasn't the only Traina embroiled in a custody fight with an ex-spouse. That very month, John hired Danielle's attorney, Suzie Thorn, and went to court to obtain joint custody of his sons, serving his ex-wife with court papers on February 11. The timing was terrible for Dede. Her husband was in the midst of the property settlement phase of his highly publicized court battle with Montandon. The divorce had been granted, but the trial over financial issues was in its third week. Even the *National Enquirer* was onto the story, reveling in Montandon's alimony demand of $57,000 a month. A judge eventually awarded her $20,000 a month through 1988.

"John wanted to hassle me," Dede Wilsey remembered. "He was still mad over my leaving him. There were no issues to argue over."

Central to John's case was his desire for equal time with the boys. A year after the divorce, he found the visitation arrangement—alternate weekends and Wednesday nights—unsatisfactory. "The children get very nervous toward the end of each visit with me," he said in court papers. "They are at an age where they need to spend large blocks of time with me as their father, as well as time with their mother."

Not according to Dede. She argued that the atmosphere around the Steel-Traina home was hardly conducive to raising two adolescent boys. A new baby was on the way, John had two stepchildren from two of Danielle's previous marriages to care for, and there was a full-time bodyguard on staff because of Danielle's problems with Bill, Dede said in court papers.

Dede also was irritated at her ex-husband's attitude, saying in court papers that John had a tendency to be cooperative one day while "flying into a rage" the next.

Donald B. King, the judge presiding over the Toth-Steel divorce, referred the case to the Office of Family Court Services and a resolution was reached in December 1983. John got joint custody, but Dede's home was set as the boys' permanent residence. The old visitation arrangement remained in place, with only minor alterations.

Although John's attempt to have the boys live half of their time with him fell short, it never stopped Danielle from describing Trevor and Todd as her own. In recent years, her press releases and books have touted her as a "mother of nine," and her nonfiction writings on motherhood have been peppered with phrases like "With nine children of my own, and my books to write, there is never a spare minute in the day to catch my breath," as she wrote in the 1988 book *After Having a Baby*.

In a 1985 story for *Cosmopolitan*, Danielle wrote, "And between cutting meat, fishing avocado slices out of glasses of milk, and accidentally sitting on a small wedge of chocolate cake, I actually managed to talk to my husband and our two oldest sons—one about college and the other about a new romance."

In these two publications, there was no attempt to explain that Trevor or Todd were from John's previous marriage.

When asked, Danielle has explained to some journalists that hers is a combined family, but some of her own writings have left a different impression, one that is not lost on Dede Wilsey.

"It's tragic a woman of her success is so insecure she has to claim someone else's children as her own," Dede said in a 1993 interview. "People ask me all the time about this, and I tell them, 'My sons know who their mother is.' "

Danielle does represent the roots of her children accurately in the 1984 book, *Having a Baby*. In writing about her first pregnancy with John, Danielle explained that one of the biggest problems she faced in early 1982 was dealing with Nicky. The three-year-old was worried about his mother going to the hospital and thought she might die. Danielle tried to alleviate his fears by taking him to the hospital and reading him a children's book that covered the complex subject.

Nicky's visits with Bill had resumed shortly after the December 17 court hearing, but the friction between the boy's mother and father grew. Bill's attempts to take Nicky outdoors during visits were met with heavy resistance from his ex-wife because she feared Bill would abduct him. Bill's later requests to call Nicky at home were also rebuffed because Danielle feared Bill would harass her. Nicky didn't like talking on the phone, she added. The tension really turned up a notch after Bill made an unannounced visit to Nicky's nursery school.

On March 25, Bill walked into the administration office wanting to know under what name his son was registered. He had heard from a friend that Nicky was using Traina or Steel.

"Up until that point, there had been no conversations about whether John Traina wanted to adopt Nicky, but I was beginning to wonder," Bill said. "I wanted to find out what was going on."

School administrators didn't release any information to Bill, and he said he left without incident. According to Danielle, school officials told her that her ex-husband appeared drunk. They were "rendered hysterical by the episode," Danielle claimed. "Whatever happened, he obviously frightened them and was very pushy, and they were very nervous about the whole thing."

Danielle took immediate action, going to court to file a restraining order against Bill. One of her attorneys submitted a declaration indicating that Bill had threatened in the past to take Nicky, and that may have been his true objective when he showed up at the school. Danielle wasn't letting Nicky back until a restraining order was in force.

Judge King went along and granted a temporary order requiring Bill to stay five hundred yards from Nicholas's school and five hundred yards from Danielle's Jackson Street residence. It stayed in force for many years afterward.

In the final weeks of her pregnancy, Danielle was prepared to leave for the hospital at a moment's notice. The nursery and layette were completed, and a packed bag was kept by her bed, she wrote in *Having a Baby*. She went out less and even needed John to sub for her at a baby shower because she didn't feel up to going.

"I worry a lot less about things if I'm well-organized, but that's me, and I've already told you I'm compulsive about things," she wrote in her book.

By her eighth month, the jitters from the earlier premature-labor episode turned to genuine fear. "Mostly I was scared to death I'd have a cesarean," Danielle wrote. "I was even afraid my three-year-old might be right and I might die. I was so scared I took out additional life insurance (which wasn't easy) and rewrote my will."

One of the things Danielle did to lift her sagging spirits was go on a little shopping spree. In the last few weeks of the pregnancy, she went out and bought three new dresses. "I looked like the *Titanic* in drag," she wrote. "Why not make yourself feel better. Go ahead, splurge, if you can!"

Danielle didn't limit the spending to herself. During a visit with Nicky at Danielle's home, she showed Bill's mother the surprises she had in store for Nicky when the baby came home.

"One of the things that changed with Danielle after she came into money was that she became excessive with gifts," Dorothea recalled. "One day I was over there just before the baby was born and she opened a full-size clothes closet. At the bottom of the closet was a brand-new baby buggy and piled on top of that all the way to the ceiling were these fancifully wrapped presents. I asked her who they were for, and she said, 'Nicky, so he won't feel jealous of the new baby.'"

Years later, Danielle told *Woman's Day* magazine that whenever one of her children celebrate a birthday, all the others receive a gift. "It makes everyone feel important and no one feels resentful or left out," she said.

By the morning of Wednesday, April 14, the anniversary of her divorce in 1978 from Danny Zugelder, Danielle was experiencing contractions, and she went to see her doctor. He ordered her to the hospital at once—no stopping off at home for her suitcase. Danielle went home anyway to grab her bags, and as she and John were pulling away from the house, she recalled looking out the passenger window during a squabble with Beatie over whether she could go out Friday night.

Danielle arrived at the hospital after eleven A.M. and spent the next several hours enduring heavy contractions, she wrote. After she was wheeled into the delivery room, everyone told her to push. Danielle recalled the pain and wrote that it was unbearable. Since the baby was in a transverse presentation, lying across Danielle's body crosswise, the doctor had to use forceps. He reached inside Danielle and turned the baby. John yelled, "Push!" and Danielle closed her eyes and their baby was guided out at eight-thirty P.M.

"I opened my eyes and there was this little purple ball squalling at me, and I could see she was a girl," Danielle wrote.

John stayed by his wife's side for the entire ordeal, and later rewarded Danielle with a jewelry piece of sapphires and diamonds.

They named their firstborn Samantha, after the resilient heroine in *Palomino*.

The aftermath was unpleasant. Danielle wrote that she required three blood transfusions and her body ached from the birth and the episiotomy.

"The night she was born, I told John, 'If I ever want to do this again, beat me,'" she wrote. By the fourth day, Danielle was already lobbying her husband for another baby, explaining, "I'm not crazy or masochistic. But it's all worth it!"

The very day Samantha Traina entered the world, Edith Allison's home at 1971 Ninth Avenue was burglarized. Among the items stolen were a silver punch spoon, a tea ball, a silver necklace, a letter stamp, and a gold pin.

Samantha's arrival was hardest on little Nicky, but there were adjustments for everyone to make, including John. About one week after the doctor gave her the okay, she and John had sex.

In *Having a Baby*, Danielle related what took place next.

> "Gee, umm, is everything okay? Is it the same as it used to be?" Danielle asked her husband.
>
> "No," he answered.
>
> "No?"
>
> "No, it's entirely different, as though you're a whole different woman now."
>
> Danielle felt a surge of panic. "Different how? Different bigger?"
>
> "Yes."

It wasn't something Danielle could shrug off. For a little while, she wrote that she even contemplated surgery, which John didn't seem to think was such a bad idea. However, common sense prevailed.

"I hadn't noticed that John was still coming back for more, 'different' or not," Danielle wrote. "I think he was unaware of how desperately worried I was, how frightened and hurt, or he would have been much more cautious about what he said. In any event, I went off the deep end."

In late April, Bill Toth and a friend walked into an antique store on Union Street with some jewelry to sell. The owner, Jack Novey, recognized Bill immediately. He knew him as Danielle's ex-husband. Novey and his wife even had dinner with them once. "Danielle use to shop in the store when she lived on Baker Street," remembered Novey. "We liked Bill. He used to bring us freshly caught trout from his weekend fishing trips."

Novey was aware that Bill had been a resident of Delancey Street, apparently for a drinking problem, or so he was told by Bill. On this day, Bill introduced his friend to Novey and they showed him some pieces that they said had belonged to the friend's grandmother. Novey paid them two hundred dollars for the items, and the friend, in turn, gave Bill sixty dollars for completing the deal.

Two weeks later, Edith Allison's neighbor Mary Jane Craig was shopping at Novey's antique shop, and several pieces of jewelry on display caught her eye: a silver punch spoon, a tea ball, a silver necklace, a letter stamp, and a gold pin. Only three weeks before, the jewelry had been in Allison's house.

On May 13, attorneys Collins and Thorn were back in court before Superior Court Judge Isabella Grant, Danielle's good friend, over whether the temporary restraining order against Bill should remain in place. It was decided that the order would stay in effect until further order of the court.

That same day, Bill was arrested and booked under suspicion of receiving stolen property that had been burglarized a month earlier from Allison's residence at 1971 Ninth Avenue.

The day of reckoning for Bill came on September 3, 1981, in a Santa Clara County courtroom. He had pleaded guilty to receiving stolen property as a result of his earlier arrest at a Palo Alto shopping center and was now facing a stiff prison sentence. Bill made one final plea to the judge.

"I would like to ask the court for a stay of execution," Toth said. "I'm out on bail, and my parents did put it up. I've shown up for all my court appearances. I've been at Walden House for about a little more than a month. And I do have some pressing family matters. I have a four-year-old son that, if I'm going to go away, I would like to tell him that I'm not going to be there for a while. It's very important. I would ask you to respectfully consider that."

The judge granted Bill a continuance until September. "When you come next time, be ready to go," the judge said.

As Bill prepared for prison, Danielle and John were getting ready for a two-week trip to New York to promote Danielle's new book, *Crossings*. Her traveling wardrobe was by Carolina Herrera, his by Ralph Lauren. Danielle was to appear on the "Mike Douglas" and "Today" shows, and she was considering taking Nicky along with her.

After his hearing, Bill phoned Dr. Neril, the child psychiatrist, and told him he was going to be sentenced to prison in two weeks for a period of one to three years, and he wanted to visit Nicky on September 8. He hadn't seen his son since early August because he'd been in the Walden House drug-rehab program.

By now Neril had replaced Riskind as the full-time visitation monitor because Nicky didn't like going to Riskind's office and because Danielle felt she was lax about enforcing the court order barring Nicky and Bill from sharing food.

"I know he flouted the food [court] order because Nicky would say stuff to me about how they had shared a lollipop or they had eaten this together," Danielle told Bill's attorney. "I didn't go looking for it, but Nicky would volunteer. I knew damn well he had violated that, and I was sensitive about that because I didn't want Nicky getting hepatitis from him."

Of particular concern were the lollipops Nicky shared with his father. "I complained about the eating, but [Riskind] never stopped it. I complained to [Suzie Thorn] and she sort of threw up her hands about it, but it bothered me more than anybody else. I remember feeling helpless because neither [Riskind] nor Suzie Thorn did anything about it and I was disturbed about it. I think Suzie felt there were more important issues to deal with."

At first, Danielle expressed doubts about whether Nicky and Bill should see each other one more time before her ex-husband went off to prison. She feared it might upset Nicky, and she didn't want him feeling bad just before they were about to leave town. Neril suggested that it would be better for the boy to hear the news directly from his father.

"The last time [Nicky and Bill] saw each other before he went to prison, Dr. Neril felt it was very important that they get together to say good-bye so that Nicky didn't feel he might have done something that had caused Bill to disappear without explanation," Danielle told Bill's lawyer.

On the afternoon of September 8, Bill arrived at Neril's office and found Danielle and Nicky sitting in the waiting room. A bodyguard stood nearby. The atmosphere was tense.

Nicky seemed excited to see his dad. He jumped on his father's back and they wrestled affectionately. Bill recalled that Nicky loved the physical contact.

As the visit drew to a close, Bill looked at his son and gave him the bad tidings. "I'm going to be away for a while," Bill said.

"Where?"

"Up north."

"For how long? A day?"

"No, maybe a hundred days."

Nicky was very quiet when he heard the news. Then he looked up at his father.

"It makes me sad. I'll call you," Bill said. "I'll see you when I get back."

Nicky walked up to his father and gave him a kiss and a hug, and then Nicky left the room.

Bill was distraught. He stayed and spoke with Neril. "It hurt," Bill recalled.

Danielle was already concerned that Bill's continual use of drugs might affect her boy; now she wondered what effect her ex-husband's prison stay would have on their son. It was a concern shared by Dr. Neril, who realized that Bill's comings and goings might traumatize Nicky.

"I was aware of that," Bill said. "I needed to work on these things. I always wonder what would have happened if I had straightened out."

In Neril, Bill had about as close to an ally as he could get. Despite Bill's numerous problems, Neril believed it was in Nicky's best interest to have a relationship with his father. However, he wanted to reevaluate the situation when Bill returned from prison.

In the meantime, he urged Bill to write and call Nicky while he was away. "I tried to explain to [Neril] that wasn't going to happen because Danielle wouldn't allow it," Bill said. Bill feared his letters wouldn't get through, though Danielle said later she never held back Bill's correspondence to his son. Bill sent Nicky a Christmas card from the Folsom minimum-security facility near Sacramento, but that was all.

On September 17, Bill was sentenced to sixteen months in state prison for receiving clothing stolen from a Palo Alto department store. He was later convicted of receiving stolen property from the sale of stolen jewelry to Novey's Antiques, the sentences to run concurrently.

Five days into his incarceration at Folsom and after a lot of soul searching, Bill felt compelled to write a letter from his cell. But it wasn't to Nicky or Danielle; he wrote to his former stepdaughter, whose fifteenth birthday was approaching.

Bill admitted that he and Beatie hadn't been very close during his marriage to her mother. They did kid around from time to time, and Bill remembered their tickling play in particular. "She was in need of genuine affection from a male father figure," Bill recalled. "I felt guilty about Beatrix. I'm sure my hostility toward Danielle affected her, and I didn't want her to feel bad. I may have ignored her after the divorce, and I wanted her to know it wasn't her fault."

Bill wrote in pencil:

Dear Beatrix,

Hello. It's been a long time since I've heard from you (or you me) and longer still since I've seen you. I've sent my love to you via Nicholas, but the little monster probably didn't pass it on. You should have heard the big lie he told about you breaking your leg in France, I went for it too!

So if my information is correct, you've lost your appendix and hurt your leg. Forgive me for not writing sooner but I'm a nerd! I hope you're better. Actually, I feel guilty about not contacting you—I really have no excuse. Whether you know it or not, I still love you very much and care about you but given the existing situation between your mother and me, I don't contact your house too often. Please don't take it personal!

You must be almost a grown woman by now—it's been so long. It would be nice if you gave my mother a picture (recent) of you so I could see how beautiful you are! I guess that means I can't tease you anymore. I'll miss it, as I do you.

I also hope you understand that the reason my mother isn't around too often is because she doesn't feel that she's wanted—if you'd like a more detailed description, I'll give it to you. If it's one thing you're not, it's stupid, and I think you know what's going on even if you don't know the reasons behind it! Again, if you ever want to know about anything, and I mean anything, ask me—the answers might not be pleasant and may be embarrassing, but I'll tell you the truth—I think you're old enough. Other than my love and care at this point in time, that's all I can offer you. Please be good, as I know you always (or most of the time) are, be good to Nicholas, even though he's a spoiled brat (sometimes) and remember me in your prayers as I do you. For even though my presence isn't with you, my love is. Por Vida, Bill.

Bill sent the letter to his mother, Dorothea, and asked her to pass it along to Beatie. Dorothea read over the letter before mailing it, and claimed she enclosed a note of her own saying that if Beatie wanted Bill's address, she would be happy to provide it if it was all right with her mother. Dorothea placed the letters in one of her husband's self-addressed business envelopes and mailed it off.

A couple of days later, on October 1, Dorothea arrived home from an afternoon of shopping to find a hand-delivered letter from Danielle waiting for her.

Dorothea recalled that Danielle's letter accused Bill of writing a sexually explicit letter and that if he ever attempted to contact Beatie again, she would call the police. "I couldn't believe she said Bill's letter was filled with sexual innuendo," Dorothea said.

Of particular concern to Danielle were Bill's remarks about Beatie's becoming a beautiful woman and Bill's request for a photograph. Danielle later told Bill's attorney she was outraged by the request "since he had never contacted [Beatie] and had never been pleasant to her while he was there, never wanted a picture of her while he was married to me. . . . The point that she was fourteen years old and was getting beautiful and [that] he wanted a picture of her was inappropriate and my daughter freaked out. And Mrs. Toth was a party to this inappropriate thing and I thought that was not good judgment.

"One of the biggest problems I had with Bill is that my daughter hated him with a passion and he hated her," Danielle went on. "They never had a civil word between them. She hated him before this, but when he ripped off her piggy bank, that was the end. But they just kept at each other."

Bill admitted there was tension between him and Danielle's daughter, but it never boiled down to hate. "But I always had a picture of her," Bill said, producing a small snapshot of Beatie he kept over the years. "That's why I wanted a new one."

Bill's attorney conceded later that writing to Beatie was "an incredible mistake," but that Danielle had distorted its meaning. If the letter was inappropriate, Bill's mother didn't think so. "You can read something evil into anything if you want to," she said. "If it were bad, I never would have shown it to Beatie. To me, it was a letter to a little girl. Bill didn't know what Danielle had told Beatie. He wanted Beatie to know the truth about his drug problem and that he was willing to talk about it. I knew what Bill meant by the letter, and that's why I sent it."

The incident opened some old wounds between Danielle and Bill's parents that had existed since the divorce.

"Danielle has never forgiven my not going along with her demands that I swear to it that Bill was using drugs after they separated," Dorothea later told Danielle's attorney. "I have never denied that Danielle tried to help Bill and was always kind and generous to my husband and myself. She forgets, or chooses to ignore, the fact that we contributed our share of the hospital expenses. She forgets the hours of phone conversations we had at all hours of the night over their problems and my giving her all the love and moral support possible."

The day Dorothea received Danielle's letter, she called her former daughter-in-law.

"I told her I could not believe what I was being accused of," Dorothea remembered.

Danielle explained to Dorothea that she was angry because she felt Dorothea had overstepped her boundaries by not sending the letter to her first.

"I tried to explain my reasoning," Dorothea recalled. "If Beatrix wanted to write, I was sure it would only be with her mother's permission, which was the main reason I did not enclose Bill's address."

In Dorothea's account of the conversation, Danielle launched into a tirade over Bill's numerous faults. "No other man has cost me so much," she reportedly told Dorothea. "I tried to help him," Danielle reportedly said of

Bill. "You're blind to your son's faults and are always helping him. But I understand your position. I would probably do the same for my son."

Dorothea said she tried to explain that the sexual connotations Danielle saw in the letter did not exist. "It's most likely he did it knowing it would annoy me," said Danielle, adding that she had shown the letter to friends and they agreed it was dirty.

Danielle also took the opportunity to criticize Dorothea for not taking more of an interest in her grandson and accused her of favoring Bill over Nicky in the hotly contested visitation dispute. Dorothea accused Danielle of making things impossible: the visits always had to fit in around Nicky's and Danielle's schedules, and they could never take the child outdoors or were allowed to be alone with him.

The visits were a constant source of contention between the elder Toths and Danielle. Dorothea felt Danielle didn't want them around either because they were a constant reminder of her ex-husband.

As the conversation drew to a close, Dorothea scolded her former daughter-in-law. "You should stop living life like one of your novels—just because a novel is finished, you close the book and make all the characters disappear. Real life doesn't work that way."

"That's the way I do things," Danielle reportedly said.

"Does all this mean that Mr. Toth and I could not see Nicky again?"

"We'll see."

In December Danielle returned to court to obtain a restraining order to prevent Bill from ever contacting Beatie again.

In addition to declarations submitted by Danielle and her attorney, Beatie made a declaration in support of Danielle's claims that her daughter was upset by the letter.

The restraining order was granted by Judge King and Bill never had any contact with Beatie again. Visits between Nicky and his grandparents resumed eventually.

"Our position was that it was a futile exercise to write or call," said Collins, referring to Bill's contacts with his son. "When Bill called, she'd say he was harassing her. And it was not like he could just call and Nicky would pick up the phone. There was a chain of command there: maids, bodyguards, and secretaries. And why send a letter that won't be read by Nicky or would be misinterpreted by Danielle? It was clear that Danielle would do anything in her power to keep them apart. Bill didn't write much or call, but he did want to see Nicky. He put up with the degradation of going to a psychiatrist's office for the visits. Bill's a loser, but his heart was in the right place."

Collins felt that the legal barrage projected from Thorn's office was an attempt to "create a collage of building blocks that Danielle was a fit mother and Bill was an unfit father. But that had nothing to do with reality," he said. "It was never established that Bill didn't have a relationship with his son. And she never proved Nicholas didn't love his father.

"Parents," Collins said, "look through rose-colored glasses as to what their relationship is with their children."

22

❧

*I*n the midst of the Beatie letter crisis, Danielle's publicity machine was in high gear for *Crossings*, the novel Danielle would later call her favorite. In a "Dear Friends" letter for the Waldenbooks chain, she said her third hardcover was the "most powerful book I have written." The characters form "bonds that you will undoubtedly identify with, and which will make the characters as real to you as they are to me."

During this period of her life, Danielle's characters were inspired by John, and possibly his ex-wife, Dede Wilsey.

"The shipping theme of *Crossings* was inspired by my husband, who happens to be in the shipping business," Danielle said later in a 1984 interview. "He became my researcher and that meant sixty books' worth of poring over facts and figures to get to the point where I could speak confidently and intelligently about the seas."

One of the characters in *Crossings* is steel industrialist Nick Burnham, who is trapped in a terrible marriage to a philandering wife named Hillary, a wealthy old-money debutante from Boston who not only cheats on her husband but rubs his face in it, too.

Hillary is very similar to a character in *Remembrance*, Danielle's first book dedicated to John. It was delivered in February 1981, the month John became engaged to Danielle, while in the midst of his divorce from Dede.

Danielle named the *Remembrance* debutante Pattie Atherton and made her the daughter of a "powerful Rhode Island congressman." The Athertons summered in fashionable Newport in a fourteen-room "cottage" and traveled the world in style. Atherton is blessed with terrific legs and *Vogue* magazine good looks, but she is also superficial, bigoted, and materialistic.

When Danielle's novel *Star* aired as a television movie, a friend approached Dede Wilsey. " 'My God!' the friend said. 'That was you on television!' " The *Star* character she meant was Penny Fuller, the sexy and wealthy daughter of a powerful Supreme Court Justice who steals the heart of a man longed for by the novel's sweet and innocent heroine, Crystal White.

"I've heard it from other people that she's written about me before, including from my mother," recalled Dede, who has never read a Danielle Steel novel. "But it doesn't bother me."

"Danielle likes to stick the needle into Dede but not too far," said a friend of Dede's. "Danielle once told Dede she would never write about her because she works too hard for her money and she would never take a chance on anybody suing her. Dede probably wouldn't have a case because the characters are disguised enough that she would never have a chance at winning a lawsuit. Besides, nobody associates Dede with those types of characters. Everyone knows her for her charity and good works."

During the 1982 *Crossings* publicity campaign, *San Francisco Chronicle* book editor Patricia Holt arrived at Danielle's Jackson Street home in October to profile the popular author. Although Danielle was now a full-fledged publishing phenomenon, recognition in her hometown was harder to come by. But the facts spoke volumes about her place in the publishing industry: some 20 million books in print and nearly all thirteen of her novels to date had been international best-sellers.

"There is a Danielle Steel fan club; there are publishers in New York who would give their right arm to publish her; she has become the subject of interview, of adulation, of applause in every city in the United States— except strangely enough, the town in which she has lived for a dozen years, San Francisco," Holt wrote.

The reluctance of the city to rally around one of its own might have had something to do with the type of books Danielle specialized in: the romance novel. "Original Paperback fiction. Pulp stuff," Holt wrote. Or maybe it was simply the inbred arrogance of the city's power structure. "This is an old-money town and it's hard for anyone to get established in any way," Holt said in an interview years later.

Even though Danielle's books were widely read, they weren't being gobbled up by devotees of the San Francisco Opera. Danielle took a lot of lumps, but she stood her ground. "Oh, our maid simply loves your books!" Danielle once heard at a party.

"Sometimes when people don't know who I am, I see that nasty glint in their eyes when I tell them what I do," Danielle told another interviewer in 1984. " 'Oh, have you been published?' they ask. I love it. 'Yes, seventeen books,' I reply modestly. That shuts them up for a while."

What Holt remembered about Danielle was that she was a good sport about it all.

"She has a good sense of humor," Holt remembered. "She has a splendid and deep knowledge of jet-setters' lives, and those details come into her writings. I sensed she wanted to be taken more seriously than as a romance writer. I find there's more heart in her books—like Jacqueline Susann—than you find in a book by Sidney Sheldon, though it's badly written heart."

Holt was actually gentler than most critics, who frequently savaged Danielle's work. The barbs hurt, particularly for someone who took great pains to fashion herself as an "author of contemporary fiction" in the same league as the Sheldons, the Krantzes, and the Micheners of the publishing world.

"She was very hurt by the criticism," said a friend. "She wanted to be accepted and never received critical acceptance."

Negative reviews, Danielle once said, were like "baking a cake with all the best ingredients and having someone sit on it."

She once admitted to a reporter, "I'm not a literary writer or Shakespeare, but I'm not a trash writer either. I'm a very serious person. I hate being portrayed as a frivolous jerk."

Critics aside, the thirty-five-year-old Danielle had already left an indelible mark on the publishing industry. "Romance readers can read up to seventy-five books a month and when Steel hit, she pulled them into the hardcover arena and opened up a field for many other women writers," Holt said. "She enabled people to make the transition to reading stuff with more substance. I'm glad she's out there."

In addition to the full calendar of publicity chores, Danielle and John were very busy on the social circuit during the fall of 1982. In September they occupied box seats at the opening of the San Francisco Opera, and in October they held a luncheon for fifty at their Jackson Street home in honor of baby Samantha's christening. In December they hosted a Saturday-night black-tie dinner dance at their home. Later in the month, they attended the formal Cotillion ball at the Sheraton-Palace Hotel to watch the 1982 parade of debutantes, one of the major events on the San Francisco social calendar.

Danielle also got pregnant. In November, about a month into the pregnancy, she began spotting and immediately headed for bed. "I would have tortured myself mentally if I hadn't known that I had done everything I could to keep it," she wrote in *Having a Baby*. Over several days, the spotting would transform from "pale pink" to "walnut brown" to a "brighter red," she wrote. Later, a sonogram provided a dire picture: a misshapen fetus. Danielle realized she might lose the baby, and by the seventh day, she was bleeding heavily. On a trip to the bathroom, she suddenly miscarried the fetus. Danielle wrote:

> It was a large, tightly woven mass, with the consistency of peach pulp, gelatinous gray and red, about three inches long and two inches wide and a half an inch deep, and there was no doubt about what it was. I was horrified, and I think I went into shock. It was there, it was over. I was heartbroken.

With the help of a friend, Danielle put the disgorged fetus in a plastic bag and the friend volunteered to deliver it to the doctor. For Danielle, the painful aftermath had only begun. Grief stricken, she kept to herself and avoided her friends. She wrote in *Having a Baby*:

> I felt as though the world had come to an end, and just then mine had. I consider myself a strong person and I have been through some very tough things in my life—loss, rejection, financial worries, major health scares, divorce, death of a parent and assorted other traumas which I will spare you here. But this is the first thing that has literally brought me to my knees, that I felt almost unable to cope with.

Longing to nurture something, Danielle adopted a dog. She chose a pure-bred pug because it was identical to the dog she had raised as a child. Danielle spoiled him rotten. She splurged on a blue doggy bed, leashes, collars, and more than a dozen toys. The pug was an ugly son of a gun, and Danielle wrote that he reminded her of a "gargoyle." The dog also may have reminded her of someone else. She named the pug Billy.

Now two dogs roamed the Traina household bearing the nicknames of Danielle's former husbands. How fitting, it seemed, that during Billy's inaugural tour of his new Jackson Street digs, he relieved himself on the carpet in one of the master bathrooms.

January 1983 ushered in a new season of promise and hope. Danielle would turn in two manuscripts in January and February: *Thurston House* and *Full Circle*. Fertile Danielle also was once again pregnant, conceiving a mere eighteen days after she miscarried. This pregnancy, however, would remain a secret from everyone except John.

The entertaining continued in grand fashion. When Parisian jewelry designer François Herail came through town, the Trainas hosted a cocktail party in which Herail proceeded to spread out $5 million in baubles across the Trainas' mammoth dining-room table. "I didn't know this was going to be a Tupperware evening," one amused guest remarked.

San Francisco magazine also put Danielle on its first cover of the year. The colorful glamour shot showed a dark, sexy, bare-shouldered author with flowing brown hair, accented by a stunning array of jewels.

The story inside, "Passion's Profitable Prose," was even more revealing than the cover.

It was perhaps Danielle's first major unflattering profile, but it could have been worse. The only reference to Danny Zugelder is a brief mention deep in the story where Danielle confided that she incurred writer's block "due to a second marriage that she doesn't choose to discuss but which is grist for the San Francisco rumor mill."

Danielle did briefly discuss third husband Bill Toth, but at one point she was quoted as saying the marriage had ended in "annulment." There was no mention that two of Danielle's ex-husbands were behind bars at the time.

That aside, the author Cyra McFadden captured the essence of the novelist-wife-mother perhaps more accurately than any writer before or since.

What the article described was a woman filled with contradictions, someone who made a fortune writing at least two novels a year, but said in her heart she would rather chuck it all and just stay home and take care of the kids. Then, in the next breath, Danielle seemed to indicate that she had no intention of ever checking out. "I admire women who are accomplishing something," she said, hardly sounding like a wannabe housewife. "There are so many dead-ass people out there, boring each other to death."

The reality was that her commercial success was about to catapult her into a financial league occupied by corporate CEOs. She was at the very least as well organized as any corporate head. During the interview, which had taken place in September 1982, Danielle said that she functioned by blocking out her days in rigid fifteen-minute segments. Her staff included a secretary, a baby nurse for Samantha, and a nanny for Nicky. There were two full-time housekeepers, a driver, and a part-time gardener.

Her day had begun at six-thirty A.M. with phone calls back East to change arrangements for an upcoming publicity tour. Next she called her agent. Then she phoned friends in Washington, D.C., to invite them to a birthday party she was giving there for John. At eight-twenty A.M., she drove Beatie to school and met with the bodyguard upon her return. At nine A.M., she took Nicky to nursery school, then came home and phoned three churches to arrange Samantha's christening. There were calls out to prospective godmothers, another to a Stanford physician to proofread her latest novel-in-progress, *Changes*. The rest of the day was filled with returning twenty-five to fifty calls, a clothes fitting for the upcoming book tour, shopping, and the interview with McFadden, which Danielle canceled twice. Then it took another thirteen calls to and from her publicist before a time was arranged.

That night, Danielle also was hosting a cocktail party with John. And at ten P.M., her work day really began when she sat down at the typewriter for several hours of uninterrupted writing.

"That's Danielle," said former mother-in-law Dorothea, referring to the *San Francisco* magazine story.

A *San Francisco Chronicle* story published later in 1983 shed more light on Danielle's affinity for business affairs and on life at 2510 Jackson. A former secretary revealed that her primary duties as an employee were handling correspondence, keeping an eye on home-remodeling projects, and scheduling play dates and arranging rides for Danielle's children. The author, meanwhile, personally tended to all money matters herself, including the bill-paying and check-writing duties.

Danielle watched her money closely. Once, when a repairman tried to cheat her, Danielle caught him red-handed. "People assume you're some kind of dummy," Danielle once told a reporter for *The Progress Bulletin*. "It boggles my mind when they believe a tooth fairy arrived with an enormous suitcase of money one day. Look, I've worked to have what I have, and it astounds me to be taken for granted."

The repairman raised her ire when he billed her twelve thousand dollars for one thousand two hundred dollars worth of repairs. When Danielle confronted him, he seemed surprised by her reaction. "Jeez, I didn't think people like you noticed these things," she recalled him saying.

As Danielle's star continued to rise, John's career in shipping struck an iceberg. After joining Pearl Cruises in 1981, John was routinely touted as a "shipping magnate," a description Danielle was using in her own press releases as late as 1988 in describing her husband, according to publicity agents who once worked for her. It's a title that stuck long after John had departed from Pearl Cruises. However, in some articles about his wife, John has been identified accurately as a shipping executive or shipping consultant.

Danielle herself has perpetuated John's image as a successful businessman with quotes like the one delivered to journalist Sindre Kartvedt, who profiled Steel in a June 1993 issue of *Scanorama*, a Scandinavian Airlines System magazine. Consider the Trainas' current home, the lavish Spreckels mansion the couple bought in 1990 for $6,730,975. Taxes on the house alone come to a whopping $77,406.20 a year.

"We live in a very big house, which I'm amazed to say, we've managed to fill to the rafters," Danielle said of her fifteen-thousand-square-foot home. "But I can't really say the house is entirely from my work; my husband's had a very big career and it's more due to him than to me, I have to admit. He's very clear about that." Today he splits his time between real-estate deals and the couple's Napa Valley vineyards. He and his wife have bought an abundance of personal property in Napa and San Francisco counties, including homes, vineyards, and other real estate collectively valued at $12.6 million. His business has been cruise lines, a career to which he devoted twenty-five years, until he finally became the figurative captain of his own ship.

That occurred the year he married Danielle, joining Pearl Cruises as its president and chief executive officer.

Pearl Cruises was a newly formed one-ship passenger line specializing in tours of the Orient. Its one and only flagship was the *Pearl of Scandinavia*, a converted ocean-going ferry with a capacity for 488 passengers. In his role, John oversaw marketing, publicity, itineraries, and the recruitment of well-heeled passengers from around the country to occupy the ship's lavish staterooms. The *Pearl's* primary draw was the Asian cruise, including mainland China, which had just opened its doors to tourism. This was no small task and brought John an annual salary in the $80,000 to $100,000 range, far below what his wife was reportedly earning at the time. John's new position was detailed in a very flattering profile by newspaper columnist Dwight Chapin in the February 12, 1982, edition of the *San Francisco Examiner*. In that story, headlined, "Starting All Over," the author wrote that people were constantly putting the "shipping magnate" title before or after John's name, and that he didn't mind being called a "shipping magnate" because he had looked it up and discovered it wasn't a synonym for Aristotle Onassis.

John was depicted as a man of action, confident enough to leave the security of a job as the vice-president of the passenger division at Delta Steamship Lines, willing and able to start "his own cruise line."

"He has backing from two powerful Scandinavian lines, but he's the chief executive officer," wrote Chapin, who said later his sources for the story were Traina himself and perhaps a press release.

John was clearly ready to take on a new challenge. "The three most intriguing things about starting this line are that it's new and exciting," Traina said. "It's going to open up the Orient, and its headquarters are right here in San Francisco."

Over the years, reporters have misidentified John as the owner of Pearl Cruises and have described him as a "shipping magnate."

"We all kind of got a chuckle over the 'shipping magnate' title," said Robert Carlsson, who worked on the Pearl Cruises publicity team and now is editor of *TravelAge West* magazine, a trade publication for the cruise-line industry. Carlsson said that his idea of a magnate was someone like Micky Arison, the owner of Carnival Cruise Lines, or the late Greek shipping tycoon Aristotle Onassis.

"I remember the article," said John Bell, then the general agent for Pearl Cruises. "We were all asking ourselves, 'What was a shipping magnate?'"

One thing a shipping magnate was not was John Traina, according to executives in the industry.

"That's not what he is my book," said Peter Weitemeyer, president of J. Lauritzen, the cofounder of Pearl Cruises.

"No, he's not a magnate. That's a journalism term," said attorney Richard Bank, the Washington, D.C.–based lawyer who recommended John for the Pearl job.

"No, no, no," said Erling Stangebye, the former vice-president of I. M. Skaugen, Pearl Cruises' other cofounder. Stangebye was the parent company's project manager for Pearl Cruises when John served as president. "He's never been close to [a shipping magnate]. He's never even owned a ship," he said.

"When you write about Pearl Cruises, make sure you say John Traina never owned the company," said Ann Kaar, the current vice-president and general manager for Pearl Cruises. "Almost everything I read about his wife says he was the former owner. He was just the president. We think it's funny that the media describes him as a shipping magnate. If he's a shipping magnate, there are an awful lot of shipping magnates around."

A much different story about John Traina's role at Pearl Cruises emerged from interviews with former employees and executives of the two Scandinavian shipping giants that launched the cruise line, J. Lauritzen of Copenhagen, Denmark, and I. M. Skaugen Management Co. of Oslo, Norway. Skaugen owned one of the world's largest tanker fleets and was part owner of Royal Caribbean Cruise Line. Shipbuilder Lauritzen owned Scandinavian World Cruises. Lauritzen and Skaugen teamed together and formed Pearl Cruises as a fifty-fifty joint venture, and did so long before John Traina was on the scene, sources from both companies said.

The original idea of establishing a cruise line off the coast of Asia belonged to I. M. Skaugen, Sr., remembered project manager Stangebye. Now retired, Stangebye spends much of his free time yachting off the coast of Spain.

"John Traina had no equity in the company at all," said Stangebye, who was surprised to read in the June 1993 issue of *Scanorama* that John once owned Pearl Cruises. The author of that article says he appropriated that information from previous stories about Danielle Steel.

"He was our media contact," Stangebye said of Traina. "They [the media] would refer to him as the originator, which is plain rubbish. If people say something long enough, lots of people will believe it."

In early 1981, partners Lauritzen and Skaugen went looking for a ship and decided to pay Finnlines $12 million for an oceangoing sea ferry, Lauritzen and Skaugen officials say. Christened the *Finnstar*, she underwent an extensive $20 million overhaul in the Lauritzen shipyards and was transformed into the *Pearl of Scandinavia*, complete with new suites, indoor-outdoor pools, saunas, a casino, shopping area, and theater.

The next objective was to hire a man to run the company, someone with experience in Pacific Rim shipping operations, Stangebye said. Realizing that most of their passengers would be Americans, the owners conducted an executive search in the United States and approached several candidates about the job. Some prospects passed because of the risk involved with a start-up venture. During the search, the Scandinavian team asked Washington, D.C.–based attorney Richard Bank to make a recommendation. Bank, who did legal work for Pearl, suggested his old friend Traina, whom he had known since 1972, when Bank was working for the U.S. State Department and John was an executive with American President Lines.

"John had a strong recommendation from Richard, which gave him an advantage," Stangebye said. "John was familiar with California and Pacific operations. He was a very good front figure for the company. He was charming, had a good appearance, and liked doing luncheons and dinners."

In October 1981, Pearl Cruises was introduced to the cruise-line industry with a flurry of publicity. John supervised the construction of new offices on San Francisco's Pier 27, and the trade magazines produced favorable write-ups that complemented the glossy six-page color advertising supplements that hyped Pearl's Asian itinerary: China, Japan, Korea, Malaysia, Borneo, and Indonesia.

The flagship itself appeared to have been transformed from a pumpkin to a golden coach. This "home away from home" featured all the modern comforts: air-conditioned staterooms with private baths and telephones, room service, gourmet cuisine, beauty salons, jewelry stores, and evenings filled with live entertainment and dancing. Trips ranged from fourteen to forty-two days. Fares for the China cruise ranged from $3,058 to $6,138. To fill cabins for the May 1982 inaugural voyage to China, travelers were lured by the catchy slogan "Cruise on the Pearl and the World Is Your Oyster."

TravelAge West placed a writer aboard the *Pearl* for its two-week maiden cruise. The reviews were decidedly mixed. While the *Pearl* was run by a hardworking and dedicated crew, and was a "friendly, comfortable way to see parts of China," it was beset by numerous problems: "Intermittent hot water, schizophrenic air conditioning, and numerous stewards who were not fully aware of how to render usual shipboard service."

A key problem was the language barrier between passengers and some of the Filipino stewards and waitresses. Others complained that the ship had been oversold as "new," citing the small bathrooms and cabins. Noise problems on one part of the ship forced the *Pearl* to drop its capacity to 435 passengers. The food was also not up to gourmet standards, and Carlsson recalled that there was near-rebellion on board because of the communication gap between the German chef and the Filipino staff.

TravelAge West urged agents selling the cruise to emphasize the "shore experiences" in China, but they cautioned that travelers should be prepared for a rigorous overland tour and warned of inferior hotel and train accommodations in that country.

In an interview, Traina told *TravelAge West* that there were a number of kinks to work out. The words "new" and "luxury" would be dropped from the brochures, along with a photo showing passengers playing roulette since there was no roulette table on board. The interior design of the ship also would change in response to complaints about the clashing Scandinavian and Far East motifs.

"We had a good first year, but there was a concept problem," Carlsson remembered. "The ship was not as luxurious as people thought, and we had problems selling it. It looked like a ferry."

"The owners wanted to see more of a profit," he said. "John did a good job promoting it and got society people interested, but too much money was spent on offices and overhead."

J. Lauritzen's Peter Weitemeyer said that Pearl Cruises was taking in water the moment it left drydock. When he joined Lauritzen in 1986, one of his first tasks was to unload the *Pearl*.

"It was a financial disaster from the start-up," he said. "They really needed to buy two more ships to cover the marketing costs. You couldn't operate this cruise line with a four-hundred- to five-hundred-passenger capacity. It was also a wrong decision to buy a cheap ferry and pour fresh money into the ship and come out with an old ship filled with costly upgrades."

By the time the *Pearl* was sold six years after its start-up, the company had absorbed enormous losses that Weitemeyer described as "two-digit million-dollar figures."

Though many of the problems appeared beyond John's control, he was out as president by December 1982. Coworkers said that Traina's strengths were in marketing and promotion, but he wasn't a numbers man, and the *Pearl* was losing too much money.

Publicly, it was reported that John resigned to spend more time with his family and concentrate on other business ventures. The boredom and bureaucracy of filling passenger ships had taken its toll, John himself told reporter Glenn Plaskin in 1984. The cruise-line business had changed dramatically since he traveled across the Atlantic aboard the great ocean liners of yesteryear, like the *Normandie*.

"In those days, boats were floating palaces filled with wood, brass, and leather, and I don't think the beauty of the *Normandie* will ever be equaled," John said.

Disgruntled with modern-day cruise lines, John complained they had been "middle-classed to death."

"Floating, eating, and two hours of shopping in St. Thomas isn't what I call a good vacation," he said. "Cruising nowadays is as commonplace as airplane travel and the ritual has become plasticized. Even some of the best ships today have plastic appointments, silver sparkle curtains, and purple upholstery. This is what the Europeans think the American public calls 'modern-deluxe,' which is pretty pathetic."

Apparently, one of John's former European bosses showed displeasure with John's performance on the job. "He likes to be the big boss," Stangebye said of Traina. "But on the whole he didn't fit in with a new task like this one. He left on a mutual understanding with the company. He had gotten married the year before, and his interest was in other places. The board would have asked him to go if he hadn't asked to resign."

Traina had no regrets about getting out of the cruise-line business. "It's a good time to be out of the ship-owning business—I prefer acting as a consultant to others and running my own little businesses on the side, which provide a greater variety of activity," he told Plaskin.

One of the projects John continued to oversee after he stepped down was arranging for an episode of "The Love Boat" to be filmed aboard the *Pearl of Scandinavia* during its May 21, 1983, voyage to China. At the time, "The Love Boat" was among the highest-rated series on television, and Traina handled the negotiations with Douglas S. Cramer, the show's coexecutive producer.

On the surface, it seemed like a great promotion and, to this day, former executives at Pearl said using the ship as a location site was a terrific idea. The production company forked over $500,000 to use the *Pearl*, and travelers lined up to spend a couple of weeks cruising the Orient with the affable Captain Stubing, played by Gavin MacLeod.

But the voyage was filled with snafus. What took place aboard the *Pearl* in those two weeks made *The Poseidon Adventure* seem like a leisurely sail across San Francisco Bay. The headline above a lengthy story published in a July 13, 1983, edition of the *San Francisco Chronicle* said it all: "The Love Boat Sounded More Like the Hate Boat." The stars squabbled over who got the biggest cabins, reporters complained about the cash-only bar, and passengers were miffed that the *Pearl*'s captain had given control of the ship over to the show's producers and directors. Moreover, unfavorable comparisons were made to the *Pearl*'s chief rival on the Pacific, the *Royal Viking*

Star. That ship was bigger and served gourmet-quality food while the *Pearl's* menu was "terrible," the *Chronicle* reported.

As the ship set sail, all the show regulars were threatening to commit mutiny because the guest stars, including Linda Evans, Lee Majors, and John Forsythe, got superior room accommodations. Since not everyone could have a luxurious suite, the cast rallied around MacLeod, who reportedly threw a tantrum by locking himself in his cabin and refusing to unpack until he got a new room, the *Chronicle* said.

John Traina was the person who gave up his stateroom to placate the cast.

About all that remains from John's day is the ship's official greeter, a seven-foot-five-inch wooden Buddha nicknamed Benny. The durable Scandinavian teakwood office furnishings purchased during the start-up are still in use, too, Kaar said. They now decorate Pearl Cruises' Fort Lauderdale headquarters.

Meanwhile, a couple of years ago, John held a reunion luncheon for the old Pearl Cruises team, chartering a Hornblower yacht for the occasion. He invited all the employees who worked in reservations and public relations to join him for four hours of sailing around San Francisco Bay. "He has fond memories of Pearl," Carlsson said.

In March 1983, John and Danielle took a trip to Los Angeles to attend a fund-raiser for the Los Angeles County Museum of Art. They also took in a private screening of *Now and Forever*, Danielle's first book to be optioned for a movie. The rights had been purchased by an Australian production company, and "Charlie's Angels" star Cheryl Ladd had been signed to the lead role.

That same month, Judge Francis Hart finally ruled on the heroin-possession charges against Bill stemming from the December 3, 1981, arrest. Thanks to Bill's attorney, the case had dragged on for fifteen months without a preliminary hearing. Had it gone to trial, Bill's public defender, Noel Marcovecchio, said he was prepared to pursue Bill's allegations that he had been set up, and he intended to call the famous author to the witness stand. Initially, he sought to subpoena a private investigator believed to have been working for Danielle's attorney, but the investigator's lawyer quashed the motion. Still, Marcovecchio was confident the case would never go to trial because, as he put it, "it was a can of worms."

George Beckwith, the assistant district attorney prosecuting Bill at the time, disagreed. He claimed that Bill had a reputation among San Francisco narcotics officers, and it wasn't for being a regular contributor to the policemen's ball. He was "a high-profile junkie" who had been nabbed with the goods fair and square. Both officers were prepared to testify against Bill, Beckwith recalled.

"I don't believe those allegations that Toth was set up," Beckwith said. Told that Bill had filed brutality charges against Gochet, Beckwith said, "There were a lot of complaints in those days against narcotics officers being overly aggressive, but those police officers are good men. They're the kind of men who'll put their lives on the line for you."

On March 9, 1983, Beckwith and Marcovecchio appeared at a hearing before Judge Hart. Bill was incarcerated at Folsom near Sacramento, and was demanding to return to San Francisco and face the charges from the December 3, 1981, arrest. Beckwith told the judge that since Bill was expected to be in prison another six months, city funds would be better spent on other cases.

The judge dismissed the case. As always, Danielle Steel's private investigator was in the courtroom to observe the proceedings, Marcovecchio noted in a letter to Bill dated March 16, 1983.

A week later, news of Danielle's pregnancy leaked out and was reported in the *Chronicle's* society column, along with the fact that Danielle would have three novels published that year. Friends had suspected she was pregnant, but their polite inquiries were usually met with rebuffs. When *Having a Baby* coauthor Katherine Dusay sent over congratulatory flowers, the secretive Danielle denied the pregnancy in fear of jinxing the baby.

"I not only denied it, I was extremely hostile about it, and I sent her a nasty note in reply," Danielle wrote in *Having a Baby*. "Can you imagine anything so rude?"

Danielle waited until she was four months pregnant before she ended her silent vigil with a celebratory party at home with her husband and children. Privately, she still wasn't sure. Only after a sonogram in which she saw the baby's tiny limbs move did she feel confident enough to acknowledge the pregnancy. The next day, she celebrated, buying a layette and a tribe of teddy bears for the coming child.

As Bill got news of the dismissal of his case at Folsom, Danielle had already fired her next salvo against the Toth family. While society may have felt that, behind bars, Bill wasn't a threat to anyone, Danielle feared otherwise.

A controversy had erupted on March 1 during a visit between Dorothea and Nicky at the Traina home. Danielle had been withholding photos of the boy from Bill and his parents, and Dorothea decided she wanted some of her own. On that day she took some snapshots of her grandson playing in his room.

The photos show a happy blond preschooler cavorting around in jeans, a blue tank top, and a brown leather jacket. His room is decorated with Mickey Mouse lithographs and two giant Raggedy Andy dolls sitting in a rocking chair. The snapshots illustrated the afternoon's activities: there was Nicky playing his toy guitar, cuddling his E.T. doll, posing in a monster getup, and swinging a toy sword.

On March 15, Danielle's attorney wrote a letter to Bill's lawyer demanding that Dorothea return the film and the pictures. If Danielle didn't get them back by March 23, she would take Dorothea to court.

The letter also made it clear that there was more at stake than a few photos. Attorney Suzie Thorn suggested that visits with Nicky were a privilege, not a right, and that her client had graciously volunteered to allow the elder Toths that opportunity. Dorothea was jeopardizing her contact with Nicky by taking advantage of the situation and by putting her grandson in danger.

Once again, the specter of kidnapping arose. Danielle's worst fear manifested itself again when Thorn raised in the letter that Bill had made repeated kidnapping threats. If Danielle had known of Dorothea's desires to take pictures, she never would have allowed it. Collins said he couldn't believe what he was reading. He returned Thorn's letter with an equally potent sense of outrage, scolding Thorn and accusing her of sinking to a new low by threatening litigation over a few photographs because of Danielle's "fantasies."

He berated Thorn for bringing up the child-stealing threats, noting for the record that Danielle could offer no proof that Bill had ever made them. Collins wrote that if Danielle had any information about such threats, he would like to hear about it. "Otherwise, I would suggest that your client stop living her romantic fiction. If she is planning to use this plot as a basis for a future novel, I may demand a royalty," he wrote.

Collins said in the letter that Danielle's real intentions were to damage any relationship her son had with Bill and his parents. The senior Toths, he reminded Thorn, love Nicky and have never done a thing to hurt Danielle. There was no evidence that Bill or his parents have harmed the boy, and that included taking pictures.

The last paragraph of his letter expressed his disgust at the absurdity of Danielle's demand. "Are you seriously suggesting that Mrs. Toth is planning to use these photographs as a basis for kidnapping her grandson? Is it your veiled threat that unless she returns the photographs that Dorothea will be precluded from visiting her grandson? Why did you even write this letter? I do not understand!!!"

Danielle was unmoved. Her attorney filed a court action on April Fool's Day. Thorn's and Collins's letters were entered as exhibits. Danielle wasn't joking. She was very concerned, and she filed a declaration on April 13 explaining her position.

She said that she permitted Dorothea to see Nicky as a way for her son to have indirect contact with Bill, but she never would have allowed her to take pictures.

Danielle believed that the photographs, if sent to Bill, could be used by someone inside Folsom to carry out Bill's threats—someone other than Bill who doesn't know what her son looks like. For this reason, she had not permitted Bill or his parents to have photos of Nicky for three years. No one, she added, is allowed to photograph her son, or her other children, because it would make them vulnerable to kidnapping. She said she didn't even allow them to be mentioned or named in the publicity about her work and success.

"I know from other people he blows off his mouth that he was married to me and I was very successful, and I didn't want him inappropriately showing the picture of the child in prison and ending up with somebody else grabbing him," Danielle later told Bill's lawyer.

"They [the elder Toths] came to the house and took a whole bunch of photographs," remembered Danielle, "which I can understand from a grandparent point of view, but they don't recognize the danger [Bill] presents. I felt very uneasy that they did that, and since that time they don't see [Nicky] alone and they don't see him outside of the house because I feel they will provide [Bill] access to Nicky that will endanger Nicky.

"They remain blind to their son's problems. His mother will tell you and believes it, I think, to her soul, that everything that's happened to him is mistaken identity or some sort of justice mistake. He never did any of it. She absolutely adores him, which I totally understand; he is her only son. And his father is fond of him, too. And I always told [Bill] how lucky he is to have parents as devoted to him as they are. If they were aware of the threat he poses, I would feel more comfortable."

Collins posed a question for Danielle: "Did she indicate or did you pick up from [Dorothea] that she would become an accomplice in a kidnapping?"

"I think she would inadvertently because I think she's innocent to the extent of Bill's problems and dangers. . . . I think it would be more inadvertent than malicious, but I do think that's a possibility. I also think they are real angry at Bill."

Years later, Dorothea has remained bitter over the confrontations with Danielle. "What were Mr. Toth and I going to do?" Dorothea said. "Carry [Nicky] down three flights of stairs from his bedroom?"

Judge William E. Mullins was not swayed by Danielle's arguments. At a hearing on April 22, 1983, he denied the author's request for the photos to be returned. "It took Judge Mullins thirty seconds to throw the case out of court," Collins remembered. "There are no laws saying grandparents can't have photographs of their grandchildren. Bill was always an easy target, but they made a mistake changing the focus to Bill's parents."

There were some changes made after the incident, recalled Dorothea. The senior Toths were never allowed to be alone with their grandson again outside the presence of the boy's bodyguard or nanny.

The photographs hearing turned out to be Suzie Thorn's last job as Danielle's attorney. Two weeks after Danielle's humiliating defeat in court, she replaced Thorn with a family-law attorney who also specialized in juvenile-court proceedings. His name was Christopher Emley, then a forty-year-old Hastings Law School graduate who was a respected lawyer, but not in the same league as Suzie Thorn, other attorneys said.

Bill and his attorney were taken by surprise at the change in lawyers. Collins speculated that the switch was instigated by Danielle, who perhaps was punishing Thorn for losing the photographs hearing. They didn't know it then, but the complexion of the case would change dramatically when Emley entered the fray.

One of Emley's first moves was to bring in psychiatrist John B. Sikorski to offer an independent evaluation of the case and provide some recommendations to Danielle and John.

Danielle said that Sikorski was concerned about the effect Bill would have on his son.

"He was disturbed about Bill's drug use," Danielle stated. "He felt very strongly that Bill's drug involvement was a very dangerous thing for the child and it was potentially very damaging to him."

Emley and Danielle also got to work preparing for Bill's release from Folsom. He was expected to be paroled on July 12, 1983, and Danielle was willing to allow him to see Nicky again—if Bill passed a drug test. When Bill sent back word he would not agree, Danielle went back to court to get an order to make him.

At court on July 20, Bill and Danielle saw each other for the first time since the September encounter at Dr. Neril's office. The judge hearing the case was familiar to Bill. A decade earlier, John A. Ertola had sentenced Bill to ten months in prison for burglary.

Bill asked for normal visitation, without the nannies, bodyguards, and psychiatrists. Judge Ertola granted him eight supervised visits spread over three months. His parents got four visits.

There was one other condition Bill had to meet. He had to provide a random urine sample sometime prior to October 25, the date Ertola set for the long-awaited visitation trial, which had been postponed in May because there was no courtroom space available.

The time and date for the urinalysis would be set by toxicologist Kenneth

Parker, who had been hired by Emley and Danielle in May to administer the drug test.

In court, Parker would later testify that he was paid a hundred dollars an hour for his services, and he remained on call for three months while Bill was kept under surveillance by a private investigator.

23

$\mathcal{J}$n 1983, Danielle's career took a dramatic turn. She fired longtime agent Phyllis Westberg and jumped to superagent Mort Janklow. With a stable of writers that included Judith Krantz, Jackie Collins, and Sidney Sheldon, the New York attorney was among the most powerful literary agents in the country. His reach extended beyond the publishing world, into the monied realm of motion pictures and television. Through these media, he added millions to his writers' coffers, not only by negotiating generous rights fees from the networks and studios, but also through the additional book sales that television movies and motion pictures can generate.

By 1985, Janklow's corps of novelists were churning out ninety hours of prime-time television properties, but Danielle wouldn't become one of his top suppliers for another five years.

Janklow's success in the literary field sparked the curiosity of John Traina, who began to devote more and more time to his wife's affairs after leaving Pearl Cruises. Danielle's books were enormously popular in the early 1980s, "but there was no real push behind me," she told the *Los Angeles Times* in 1988.

"She was a fairly established author already," Janklow told the *Times*. "But her instinct was not toward business."

This was the void John was able to fill. "John became involved in her career, and he perceived that she should be making more money," said a friend of Danielle's. "Her going to a new agent is directly attributable to him. He facilitated her career getting bigger and better. He's a very smart businessman, and that's what it's all about."

John helped with Danielle's entrance into another arena: films. His wife's desire to see her books on the big screen dates back to the late 1970s, when she approached movie mogul and fellow San Franciscan Francis Ford Coppola. Coppola's associate producer, Mona Skager, recalled reviewing at least two of Danielle's manuscripts, *The Ring* and *Palomino*, for potential motion-picture development.

"She was very sweet and charming, not aggressive at all," Skager said. "Danielle's attitude was 'Why not give it a shot?' We didn't feel there was enough stuff in her books for a Coppola film. Francis doesn't do romance-type movies."

John found someone who did. During the 1983 "Love Boat" cruise to China, he made a contact aboard the *Pearl* that would alter Danielle's career immeasurably. While filming went on, Danielle's husband asked "Love Boat" producer Douglas Cramer to read the manuscript of *Crossings*.

Cramer, who coproduced "Dynasty" with Aaron Spelling and helped develop such popular television series as "The Brady Bunch," "The Odd Couple," and "Love American Style," was a television powerhouse in Hollywood. He liked *Crossings*, optioned the movie rights, and three years later produced an ABC miniseries based on the novel.

Danielle has shown no reluctance about giving her husband his due. "I couldn't do anything without him," Danielle once said to a reporter. "He made it all happen."

Janklow focused his efforts on helping Danielle reposition herself away from the romance-writing ranks and onto the shortlist of "contemporary fiction" writers, a group Danielle had been trying to break into for years. The author detested the so-called candy box covers Dell insisted on using for her early books, but Janklow and Carole Baron, Danielle's new editor at Dell, worked to change all that.

"Let me emphasize that in the early stages of my writing career, publishers referred to my books as 'romance.' I classify myself as a contemporary fiction writer no different from Harold Robbins or Judith Krantz," Danielle said in a 1984 interview.

Janklow also got her a raise, though it's difficult to ascertain how much of a boost. There is much debate about the size of Danielle's advances in the early 1980s. A 1979 *People* story reported Danielle had already signed a six-figure contract for three books, thanks to the outstanding sales racked up by *The Promise*.

But in a 1993 letter from Danielle's attorney, Charles O. Morgan, Jr., it's asserted that Danielle didn't start making big money until after she had wed John and signed on with Janklow. At the time of her divorce from Bill in early 1981, the letter said, Danielle wasn't earning six-figure advances from her books.

In 1983, mass-market reprints of *Remembrance, Palomino,* and *Once in a Lifetime* were each released with a first printing of 1.5 million copies, Danielle's publishers told *San Francisco* magazine. The author of that article calculated if Danielle sold out the first printing of those books and two new books to be released that year, *Thurston House* and *Changes,* she stood to reap more than $3 million in royalties alone.

Reluctant to alienate the profitable romance market, Dell oscillated between publishing her books in hardcover and trade paperback. While *The Ring, Remembrance,* and *Crossings* had been issued in hardcover, one title had come out in mass-market paperback, and three others were released in trade paperback, including the July 1983 release of *Thurston House.*

Dell and its hardcover affiliate, Delacorte, preferred to groom its rising star gradually, a publishing insider remembered.

"The publisher built her in a concerted way," the insider said. "Her numbers were there—once they had the numbers, they ran with it and moved her into hardcover, and her readers followed because her readers were ready to move from a certain type of book to a more sophisticated book; they had matured and were making more money. She and her readers were in exactly the same place at the same time."

In late July, the matriarch of the Traina family, the former Lea Castellini, passed away in her home after a brief illness. She had just given a party for three hundred people to celebrate husband John Sr.'s ninetieth birthday. She was eighty-three. In her obituaries in both the *Examiner* and the *Chronicle,* she was eulogized as a patron of the arts, a supporter of the building of the War Memorial Opera House, and hostess to the opera stars in the 1950s and 1960s.

"Mrs. Traina was the wife of John Traina, a retired real-estate investor. Her son is shipping magnate John Traina, Jr., husband of novelist Danielle Steel," read one newspaper obituary.

In August 1983, Bill got a job working for a moving company and arrived for the first of his eight scheduled visits with Nicky. He was prompt for the first three appointments, but then missed two in a row because of work commitments. Once he called to cancel after Nicky had arrived for the visit and spoke with his son over the phone for fifteen minutes.

Father and son had somehow maintained a close rapport, even after Bill's eleven-month stay in Folsom, Dr. Neril observed in a written report to the Office of Family Court Services. Bill recalled lots of physical play with his son, who seemed excited to see him at each meeting. Bill remembered having brought Nicky a snakeskin belt he had made from a rattlesnake he killed in prison. During a September visit, Bill recalled, Nicky told him about his new sister, Victoria Lea Tobie, who had arrived on her due date of September 5, 1983, Labor Day.

The baby Danielle thought would never survive began yearning for freedom during the early-morning hours, Danielle wrote in *Having a Baby*. At first, Danielle thought it was another false alarm and she took a bath to calm the contractions. They kept getting stronger throughout the night, and a little after three A.M. Danielle was in labor at Children's Hospital. Three hours and two epidurals later, Danielle pushed Victoria into the world. She weighed eight pounds, two ounces, and had blonde hair and blue eyes.

"This time the baby has been a precious gift," wrote Danielle, "perhaps even more so because I was so reluctant to believe in her for so long. This baby that might not 'stick' not only stuck but has turned out to be the most beautiful little girl!"

In late September, Danielle and John began preparing for a cocktail reception for the screening of the Australian movie based on Danielle's *Now and Forever*. Earlier in the month, a critic from the *San Francisco Examiner* trashed the film, calling it a "drippy soap opera": "Believability isn't what this modern romance is all about. It's about horseback riding . . . designer dresses, couture jewelry . . . fevered glances and vows of eternal devotion."

Now and Forever had a very, very short life in the handful of theaters that showed the film in San Francisco. Danielle disassociated herself from the project. "You're not missing a great movie," she told a friend who couldn't make it to her party. "But the popcorn is four-stars."

The night of the September 29 screening, the Trainas stocked the Bridge Theater with hot dogs, pizza, and an open bar. Little Victoria, all of two and a half weeks old, made a cameo appearance, but even she was disappointed. She burst into tears shortly after the movie began, and her English nanny took her home.

Danielle's latest book, *Changes*, arrived at bookstores around the time that *Now and Forever* was nose-diving at the box office. The critics seemed gentler with Danielle's new book. One local critic described *Changes* as "delicious fluff, a perfect dessert if you're in a self-indulgent mood for something light and slightly naughty."

With the October 25 visitation trial approaching, Danielle's toxicologist still had not conducted the court-ordered random drug test. Bill was on parole and knew this was no time to screw up. He was aware he was being watched, and he knew that eventually Parker would confront him to collect a urine sample.

That day arrived on October 10, 1983. That evening, Bill borrowed the company moving van to help a friend haul a refrigerator across town. Unbeknownst to him, he was being tailed by two off-duty police officers who had been hired by Danielle's private investigator to follow him and observe whether he was under the influence of any drugs.

One of those officers was Cal Newton, then of the Berkeley Police Department. He was the first to observe that Bill was acting strange, that his body movements were staggered and awkward, and that his driving was careless. At eight-thirty P.M., Bill came to a stop outside a home on Prague Street and Newton watched as Bill unloaded the refrigerator. Bill's movements were still clumsy, so Newton decided to call toxicologist Kenneth Parker to come to collect the sample.

"I might have been high," Bill said, recalling the fateful night. As he visited with his friends, Parker arrived on the scene with a container. Shortly before midnight, Bill walked back outdoors and loaded the dolly into the van. Then three men appeared from the shadows.

There was some murmuring, and then Bill overheard one man say, "Yes, that's him."

Bill was nervous until he got a good look at Parker. "We want you to take a urinalysis right now," Parker said.

"You do? That's nice," Bill said.

"We'd like you to step over here and urinate into this bottle."

He pointed between two houses. Bill didn't want any part of this. "You would like me to step right over here in front of these houses, underneath these streetlights, and urinate in this bottle?"

"Yes."

"No, thank you."

Bill's excuse was he could get arrested for urinating in public, not to mention that it was unseemly. Moreover, he claimed to have used the bathroom indoors and had nothing left for the bottle Parker was holding in his hand. Parker asked again, suggesting that Bill climb into the back of the van for privacy.

Refusing once more, Bill got into his truck and left. Parker went home with an empty container. The next day, Bill wrote a letter to his attorney describing the events that had taken place the night before: "It was my understanding," Bill wrote, that "Mr. Parker was going to show up at my house sometime by himself. Not demand that I urinate and violate the law in front of two other witnesses. Urinating on public streets is against the law."

Two days later, Bill's fate was in the hands of yet another judge. Danielle had petitioned the court again to suspend visitation because Bill had refused to comply with the court-ordered drug test.

At a court hearing before Judge Robert W. Merrill, Carroll Collins went on the attack on behalf of his client, complaining that Danielle was having Bill followed and a midnight urinalysis on a public street was inappropriate as well as unfair because, at that hour, Bill couldn't obtain a second urine sample in case of a discrepancy. Emley, Danielle's attorney, told the judge that both Parker and Newton believed Bill was under the influence of narcotics, which Collins argued was untrue.

Disappointed that Bill had not shown up for his three most recent visits with Nicky, Judge Merrill sided with Danielle and suspended the remaining three visits left before the start of the October 25 trial.

Yet on October 25 there was no trial, and three days later counsel met in court with Superior Court Judge Donald B. Constine, the judge who had sentenced Danny Zugelder to state prison in 1974 for assault and rape. He urged the case back to the Office of Family Court Services in hopes that it could mediate a resolution. Failing that, the office was ordered to prepare an evaluation and investigative report to be submitted to the court prior to any future trial. Constine also kept Merrill's order suspending visitation in place for at least another thirty days.

The days turned to weeks and the weeks turned to months, and still there was no resolution, no report from the Office of Family Court Services, and no visits with Nicky.

Jeanne Ames, now a private mediator in custody and visitation disputes, was the person responsible for producing the report. Collins contended that during his conversations with Ames, she expressed to him the opinion that Bill did have visitation rights with Nicky. At the same time, Collins asserted, Danielle had waged a successful campaign stating that Bill was a terrible influence on their child. The conflicting views prevented Ames from doing her job, he said.

"Danielle didn't want to hear that Bill had rights," Collins said. "Jeanne always said she needed more time and information because the subject matter was complicated. She didn't want to bite the bullet and make the hard choice. I also felt she was taken in by Danielle's campaign and didn't want to get her mad. I always felt if Jeanne had done that report and Bill had passed a urine test, the outcome in this case would have been different. Justice was delayed and justice was denied."

Ames, who had been mediating the divorce since 1980, felt the case was problematic due to the complexity of the drug-testing issue and the lack of staff.

In late November 1983, little Victoria was christened at St. Mary the Virgin Episcopal Church. Danielle's mother, Norma Stone, and John's sister, Marisa Hahn, flew in from New York and Germany, respectively. For Thanksgiving, the Trainas headed for their Napa rental house for a few days of rest and relaxation.

During the holiday, John and Danielle went house hunting and came upon a small, quaint three-bedroom Victorian house that had once been part of a working farm, complete with barn, vineyards, and horse stalls. They both fell in love with it the moment they laid eyes on it, and by Christmas, the house was theirs. The Trainas immediately began a yearlong remodeling project that would transform the 1856 home into a showcase worthy of a spread in *Architectural Digest*.

The Trainas vacationed in Hawaii that winter and in February 1984 Danielle and Beatrix attended a fashion show at Saks. One of Danielle's favorite designers, Jacqueline de Ribes, was showing her spring collection and Danielle was spotted busily taking notes on four or five de Ribes gowns she wanted to try on. The Parisienne's designer gowns are pricey; a wedding gown and veil on display cost sixteen thousand dollars.

On Valentine's Day, Danielle and John attended the annual black-tie Valentine Dance at the San Francisco Museum of Art. That same day, Danielle had been quoted in a *San Francisco Chronicle* story about how she would have written the ending to *Gone With the Wind*. "The ending works," she said. "Scarlett was a twit—she was selfish and shallow. And Ashley was a wimp. Only if she had a lobotomy would she be right for Rhett. I probably would have written in another character for Rhett. A woman. I'd like him to end up happy."

Lawyers for Bill and Danielle also kept busy over the winter. Paralyzed by the lack of a report from the Office of Family Court Services, the attorneys tried to hammer out ground rules for another visit. On February 9, Danielle made a visitation offer that didn't require drug testing as a precondition, but when she didn't hear from Bill after the three weeks, the offer was withdrawn on March 1—the very day Collins said he wrote back that Bill had agreed to the proposal. Apparently the letters crossed in the mail.

Danielle was always put in a tough situation trying to explain Bill's absences. For two years, her pediatrician had been urging her to talk to Nicky about Bill's drug problem, but Danielle had resisted. "I feared [Nicky] would be tainted by association and that in some way he would feel there was some problem with him," Danielle told Bill's attorney. "I feared that particularly when he was older. I didn't know how Bill would feel about that. I also didn't want [Nicky] announcing this to the neighborhood."

Over the winter, Danielle saw an opportunity to broach the subject of Bill and drugs. After eight boys at Nicky's school were expelled from eighth grade when they were caught with marijuana, the school held a seminar for students to educate them on the dangers of drug use. "Nicky was very impressed by this," Danielle said. "It came up and all the kids were very shocked by this kind of thing."

Danielle later explained to Bill's attorney that she decided this was the ideal time to talk to Nicky about his father's involvement with drugs. She sat him down and brought up what had happened at school.

"This is Bill's problem," she told Nicky, explaining that his father had gotten involved with drugs a long time ago.

"It makes you do bad things," Nicky said.

"This is exactly his problem," Danielle said. "When you don't see him sometimes, it is not necessarily because he doesn't love you. It is perhaps [because] he is involved with drugs and that he goes away and comes back, but it has nothing to do with you."

Danielle added that her explanation "was not done in a judgmental way. It was not done in a negative way against Bill. I stressed the fact that [Bill] loved him and this has been something that has made [Bill] very unhappy. If Nicky ever talked to him about it, I'm sure [Bill] would say this is a very unhappy thing in [his] life. I said this is also why we didn't stay married, because it made things very difficult.

"I honestly felt that if Bill had been there, he would have been pleased by what was said, and he would have endorsed what was said."

Danielle was right about that. Looking back, Bill said he realized Nicky had to be told, sooner or later.

In April, Danielle went on the "Donahue Show" with the six coauthors of *Having a Baby*. She was about one month pregnant with her third child by John when the show was taped. One of the topics she chose to talk about was her desire to have a large family. "I find that very few people are supportive of having children and a lot of children," Danielle said during the show in response to an audience inquiry about how friends of the coauthors reacted to their pregnancies. "I find constantly people saying, 'You're not having another baby, are you?' As if we're expecting them to support them all. Most people are sort of horrified at the thought of other people having a lot of children. I think it's very threatening to a lot of people."

On April 9, Bill decided to take matters into his own hands and wrote a personal letter to Jeanne Ames, with a copy sent to Judge Constine.

In the letter, Bill chastised Ames for not completing the investigative report and complained he had not seen his son since September 1983. "Why does it appear to me that for some reason or another my [ex-wife's] defacto wishes are being granted?" Bill also wrote that he was working steadily and staying drug free. "I want to see my son . . . start interacting with him in some normal manner," he wrote.

In late May, Bill got his wish. Judge Constine ordered a ninety-minute visit for Bill and Nicky to take place at Dr. Neril's office on May 31. Bill also had to submit to a supervised drug test the day before the appointment.

Danielle would later inform Bill's attorney that she was cautious about telling Nicky he was about to see his father, and decided to wait until an hour before the visit to tell him about it. Her son hadn't seen Bill for eight months, and Danielle was uncertain of how her six-year-old might react.

"Guess who called? Bill called and he would like to see you. I think it would be nice if you went. It would hurt his feelings if you didn't go. You will probably have a nice time."

Nicky was initially reluctant but finally agreed.

Bill arrived promptly for the five-thirty P.M. appointment, and when he walked into Neril's office, the boy went to his father and gave him a hug. He showed him some toys and talked about his little sisters. Bill gave him a cookie, and they sat together on the floor to play. Nicky crawled onto Bill's lap.

"You've gotten so big," Bill said to his son.

There was a lot of catching up to do. Nicky told his father that tennis was his favorite sport now, but he also liked soccer and swimming. They talked about their dogs and the movies Nicky had seen.

"How long do you think it's been since I saw you?" Bill asked.

"Two months," Nicky said.

"It's been since September," Bill said. "I've missed you a lot."

"I wondered when you'd come back," Nicky said.

"It makes me sad that I can't see you more often," Bill said.

"Me, too," Nicky replied.

They talked about Nicky's kindergarten class, and Nicky told his father that he had just turned six, but people thought he was eight.

"We need to see each other more often," Bill said.

"Maybe we could go see *Gremlins*," Nicky said, referring to a recently released movie.

"How often would you like to see each other?" Neril asked.

"Every day," Nicky said. "But every week if it cannot be every day."

"I'd like it to be once a week, too," Bill said.

The time had passed so quickly. It was already seven P.M. "The visit has to stop," Neril said.

"I miss you," Nicky said to Bill.

"I miss you, too."

Nicky went out the door. Bill followed, and stepped out onto California Street into the cool San Francisco night. He hopped into his Volkswagen and drove away.

It was the last time he would ever see his son.

When Nicky returned home that night, he went up to his mother's room. Danielle was taking a bath, and Nicky sat down next to the tub.

"Did you have a good time?" Danielle asked.

He seemed calm and unencumbered.

"I had an okay time," he said.

Later, Danielle asked Nicky if he had said anything about drugs to Bill. "No, I thought it would embarrass him."

Danielle felt that was sweet. She also knew that if Bill failed the drug test, there was a chance Nicky wouldn't be seeing him for a while. She didn't want her son blaming himself for that. It was vital to alleviate any feelings of guilt her son had in his mind.

"Remember that it is always probable that after you see him, there could be a problem sometime and he may go away again," Danielle reminded her son. "If he does, he may come back again, but it has nothing to do with anything you do or say."

That night, Danielle noticed that Nicky seemed to need a lot of love and attention. She had set aside time to be with him alone in case he wanted to talk. "He can be a very loving child," she told Bill's attorney in a deposition. "He can, in the way of six-year-old boys, be very independent suddenly."

When Danielle climbed out of the tub, Nicky was already sitting on her bed cuddling with John as they watched TV together.

"I love you, Dad," he said over and over. "There was a lot of closeness with us that night," Danielle said later.

On June 8, 1984, just days after Bill's visit with Nicky, Danielle gave a deposition to Bill's attorney for the upcoming visitation trial. That very day, *San Francisco Chronicle* columnist Herb Caen revealed that Danielle's latest book, *Full Circle*, had hit number one on the *New York Times* best-seller list and that the first lady of romantic fiction also was pregnant. At the deposition, Danielle said she was feeling a little under the weather from the pregnancy, and reported to Collins that she was spotting. As she spoke, John was by her side, a request that Collins had agreed to a month earlier.

"Would it surprise you if I were to tell you that at the visit Nicky indicated to Bill that he would like to see him every day if possible?" Collins asked.

"No," Danielle said. "I think he may have gotten caught up in the spirit of the visit. He may have had a good time."

"Would it surprise you if I were to tell you that Nicky indicated at the visit that he loved Bill very much and wanted to see him a lot?"

"No. I'm sure he does love him."

"Do you feel that in some way you may well be depriving Nicky of that opportunity by your position vis-à-vis visitation?"

It was a question that surely ran through Danielle's mind over and over. As the custodial parent, the burden of what to do fell squarely on her shoulders. Now it seemed she had to do the thinking for all three of them.

"I think I'm in a very difficult spot, where it is a very painful decision to have to make," she began. "The person who is really depriving Nicky is Bill, by using the drugs. But I am stuck in the position of the responsible person doing what I feel is best under the circumstances. The whole issue always boils down to drugs. I mean, if Bill would stop using the drugs, life would be a whole lot simpler for all of us and especially Nicky and especially him.

"I think ideally if Bill conquers his drug problem that he could have normal visitation with Nicky and a very normal relationship with him. I think the whole thing hinges on how he deals with his drug problem.

"My ex-husband, Beatrix's father, is here now. He is with her constantly. He is spending the weekend with us. He is going to be in Napa with us. He is in and out of the house constantly. Beatrix has dinner with him every night. She has a totally normal relationship with him, but he is also a totally normal man who has never had any kind of drug problem. Bill has."

"Is it your position that Bill shouldn't see Nicky until such time as he has conquered his drug problem?" Collins asked.

"Basically yes," Danielle said. "I think he is dangerous to Nicky and himself when he is dealing with drugs."

Collins felt the animosity between Bill and Danielle ran too deep for compromise. "She always claimed everything would be okay if Bill got off drugs, but I never believed it," he said.

Bill never gave himself the chance to prove her wrong. In early June, the test results came back from the urinalysis he had taken the day before the visit with Nicky. From the time Judge Constine had ordered the May 31 visit, Bill had twelve days before the test to allow any drugs in his system to dissipate. Sadly, he continued to use drugs. The urine sample showed traces of morphine and cocaine.

"I kept saying all along we'd get our day in court," Collins said. "But when he flunked the urine test, it was devastating. Bill had always maintained to me he wasn't using. I took it hard, and I felt I couldn't go back to ask for more visitation unless he took a test and passed it."

Danielle knew all about what it was like to be let down by Bill. In her 1985 book, *Secrets*, Danielle once again explored a love affair between a sober person and a heroin addict. This time, the characters were two young actors: one a desperate and pathetic junkie named Sandy, the other a loyal, drug-free rescuer who tries in vain to clean up his wife's debilitating habit. Sandy's sad addiction would reek havoc in her marriage to Bill Warwick, her thirty-two-year-old actor husband.

Like Bill Toth, Sandy used "speedballs, a mixture of heroin and cocaine that kept her high but gave her the illusion of making sense, and the truth was she didn't," Danielle wrote in the novel.

Warwick abhors drugs, yet sticks by his addict wife, tolerating her arrests for prostitution, her deteriorating physical appearance, her disinterest in sex. He displays the same kind of loyalty and perseverance Danielle had once shown for Bill. Warwick refuses to give up on Sandy and never files for divorce. He even gives her money so she can buy drugs. When his patience runs out, Sandy steals from him.

In *Secrets*, Danielle writes from the viewpoint of Warwick, a man victimized by his wife's excesses. "The tension of living with her was unbearable," Danielle wrote. "There were days when he wondered if he'd survive it."

Warwick tries valiantly to save Sandy, whose life is seemingly crumbling before his very eyes. He offers to hospitalize her in a treatment center, as Danielle did for Bill.

"I'm taking you to the hospital right now. Right now!" Warwick orders Sandy. "And I don't give a damn if you never see me again, but you're not going to go on like this until you OD in some stinking shooting gallery or someone sticks a knife in you somewhere. Do you hear me?"

But Sandy doesn't go. Unable to help herself, Warwick is left frustrated and angry. She walks out of the house to meet her drug connection. Danielle's description of Warwick's feelings could have been similar to those she felt for Bill:

> She was gone, and this time, he didn't stop her. He knew he couldn't have anyway. There was nothing he could do. Nothing. [He remembered] how it had once been, how pretty she had been, how crazy they were about each other. They had met only two years before, and now it seemed a lifetime ago, a lifetime in the depths of hell with a woman he had once loved, and still did, although she was long gone.

However, Warwick didn't quit on her when a more sensible person might simply have changed the locks on the door and filed for divorce. He is really a codependent, a subject Danielle never explores fully. What was driving Warwick to stand by his wife? What made him cling to a vision of Sandy that had ceased to exist, a person he had little hope of resurrecting? Danielle probably asked herself the same questions, and the answers were just as difficult to come by.

Danielle had given up on Bill in late 1979 and filed for divorce in September 1980. Warwick simply endures and takes out his anger on everyone else around him. It is Sandy who finally severs their ties when she is shot to death by a drug connection. Warwick is accused of killing her, and after he is acquitted of first-degree murder charges, he goes on to stardom in a new hit television series and finds true love with a co-star who physically resembles Sandy.

Danielle's search for a suitable companion took much longer. In John, she found someone who could return the love and care she showed. "I have finally learned how to let someone love me, and to love in return," she told *Scene* magazine in 1981.

In the summer of 1984, Bill's attorney didn't make any more requests for visits with Nicky, and Bill didn't produce the negative drug test Collins believed was needed before asking the court to lift the visitation ban.

Instead, Collins set his sights on the visitation trial.

Meanwhile, the Trainas retreated to their new house in the wine country. While they were there, Glenn Plaskin, a writer on assignment for a national magazine, was invited to Napa for a profile on John he was researching.

The interview began on Jackson Street, where John met his guest in a gray linen Wilkes Bashford suit. John showed Plaskin his impressive collection of cigarette cases that he kept tucked away in a wall safe. There was a Cartier case of platinum and sapphires purchased from the estate of film director George Cukor, Fabergé cigarette cases of enamel, gold, and silver, and a gold and diamond cigarette case once owned by Czar Nicholas II. These collectibles don't just lie around in velvet cases gathering dust: John always carried one at social functions.

A regular on the San Francisco party circuit for years, Traina said he adored the city and thrived on the tight-knit social scene. But John confided that his wife did not share his enthusiasm for San Francisco. She "would move to New York in a second," he said.

From Pacific Heights, they were chauffeured in John's Mercedes 600 by the family driver to the Trainas' Napa retreat, arriving to the sounds of noisy young children, and construction crews busy building a swimming pool, sauna, Jacuzzi, a tennis court, and a new private road. With all the laborers, maids, and nannies running around, John was prompted to crack, "God knows how many we have in help."

Though Plaskin's article was never published by the magazine, the story revealed some intimate details about the Trainas' affluent lifestyle. John admitted he spent a hundred thousand dollars a year on clothes, and Plaskin observed during the house tour that John's closets were filled with designer wear, the price tags still attached.

"It's amazing how much you have to shop if you want things that everyone else doesn't have," John told Plaskin jokingly.

John also liked to spend money on Danielle. "I love to buy women jewelry," he said. At home in San Francisco, the Trainas had put their favorite jewels from South America and Hong Kong on display in the living room, including impressive collections of jade, topaz, and rubellite garnets. They owned eight late-model vehicles, ranging from Mercedes wagons and sedans to pickup trucks. The other cars in the fleet were classics: a 1940 maroon Ford deluxe sedan, a 1931 green Ford Model A sports convertible, a 1938

International Harvester fire engine, a 1930 Ford Model A coupe, and a 1944 Ford Opera coupe, Plaskin reported.

John also enjoyed the good life abroad. He said his favorite hotels were rated five stars: the Gritti Palace in Venice, the Vier Jahreszeiten in Munich, the Hassler in Rome, the Regent in Hong Kong, Claridges in London, the Carlyle in New York, the Ritz in Madrid, the Bristol in Paris, the Four Seasons in Hamburg, the Copacabana Palace Hotel in Rio. "When I go to a hotel, it's like picking a ship. I like the one with perfect service, gourmet food, and great atmosphere," he said.

John's lust for travel is not shared by Danielle, a homebody perhaps grounded in part by her fear of flying. More often, John is joined by friends or his two sons for more rigorous adventures: safaris along the Amazon, digs on Easter Island, and skin diving in Belize and Bora Bora. Later he remarked to Plaskin: "Why not enjoy the money when you're young? My wife and I work hard and we're not frivolous, though we get dressed up and go to parties; but then we disappear to the Valley for hard work and uninterrupted time with our children."

Amid all the affluence, John maintained that their children were not spoiled. "I'm an old-fashioned and a strict father," he said. "I demand a lot of study time from my boys. Aside from performing well in school, which is their main job, they have to grow up to be nice people."

In another interview years later, Danielle concurred with John. "John doesn't let them act like spoiled brats, and he can be tight with the money. Allowances are very stingy: a dollar a month for a five-year-old; two dollars a month for the nine-year-old; five hundred a month for the college kids, which must pay for everything—dating, gas, new sweaters, prescriptions."

Danielle also said that they have posted a wage scale at home for the more ambitious children: a dollar an hour for baby-sitting one kid, three dollars an hour for baby-sitting several kids; a dollar an hour for vacuuming, five dollars for cooking a meal, five dollars a night for having to give up a room for a guest, three dollars for washing the dog, five dollars for washing the car, and twenty dollars for waxing the car.

In a June 1986 *Architectural Digest* story written by Danielle, she described the remodeling work that transformed the farm into an eleven-bedroom, five-bath compound with all the luxuries and amenities of modern living. In the beginning, Danielle wrote, the main house had only two small closets with three bedrooms and one bath on the second floor and a tiny dining room, study, kitchen, and a larger living room on the first floor—hardly enough room for the growing Traina family. To create more space, they converted an old water tower into bedrooms for Beatie and John's two boys, with a sauna-bathroom on the ground level.

The caretaker's cottage was converted into four bedrooms for the smaller kids and their nanny, complete with kitchen and living room. A horse stable was made over into guest rooms. By the time the story was published, there were eight combined children in the Traina clan, and the main house would become Danielle and John's refuge from all the commotion.

John had a two-story porch erected around the perimeter of the main house to take full advantage of the marvelous views. The porch, decorated with wicker furniture, overlooked a yard surrounded by a white picket fence and gazebo, with a backdrop of rolling hills and vineyards of Pinot blanc, Chardonnay, and Cabernet varietal grapes.

Indoors, they expanded the kitchen by leveling the walls and adding on the back porch. They then laid down wood floors and purchased a new stove and yellow countertops. For atmosphere at breakfast time, the Trainas hung two Italian wood chandeliers and set up an entertaining player piano, Danielle explained in her article.

While the study was done in black, the living room was decorated in pastels and floral prints, with Victorian furnishings, a Persian rug, and a newly installed fireplace with a French sandstone mantel. Hanging above it was "a 19th-century English gilt-framed mirror," a piece Danielle described as "our very favorite." The dining room was dominated by a handmade round table that seated twelve, while the master bedroom was done in white wicker with blue carpeting and furniture.

"All in all, our country house was an enormous project, taking most of a year and a phenomenal amount of energy and hard work, but it was worth it," Danielle wrote. "In years to come, in the dead heat of summer, I'll undoubtedly be out in the fields, on the tractor with my husband."

In contrast, Bill's summer was spent working the graveyard shift at a printing shop and living at his parents' home. Still battling his drug addiction, he never bothered to turn in a clean urine sample, he said. As summer turned to fall, Bill wrote Collins a letter wondering about the visitation trial and when he would be able to see his son again. Worn down by the long, drawn-out legal battle with Danielle, Bill seemed resigned to defeat as he wrote this letter dated September 30, 1984:

> I'd like to see my kid, but I really doubt she's ever going to let me, and I feel like the courts are on her side, so I just don't know. My parents saw him last week. Same trip, bodyguard stayed in the room with them. Also she and John took Nicky to the opening of the "Hard Rock Cafe" the other night, so he could get some rock star's autograph. I wonder what would be the reaction if I ever took him to a bar and nightclub? But of course there's no double standard! Anyway, that's about the extent of my life. Work, sleep, work, etc.
>
> Like I said, I don't envision much hope for me, but I sure would

like to see my parents get a fair deal without it having to cost them any money.

Bill had not made a move to see his son in five months. The following year, Danielle's attorney asked Bill why he did nothing during that time span.

"What steps did you take in July of 1984 to secure visits with Nicky?" Chris Emley asked.

"Okay, all right. There was a period there of four or five months when I didn't do anything," Bill admitted.

"Why did you do nothing during that period?"

"Depression, feelings of hopelessness, that it was just too much, that she has too much money—"

Emley cut him off. "During that period, Mr. Toth, did you use any illegal drugs?"

"No," Bill said.

"Typically, substance abusers get better or they get worse; they rarely stay the same," said Donald B. King, now an appellate judge, in a July 1993 interview. King recalled presiding over the Toth-Steel divorce case until he was named to the Court of Appeal in 1982. "If they get better, of course it's helpful. If they get worse, they drop by the wayside, turn up at inappropriate times, or drift away and are not heard from again.

"These people have a considerable amount of guilt feelings themselves because they know they have a child, and somewhere inside they love the child, but they aren't able to control their habit," he said. "They feel guilty because they aren't providing a parenting role or support. It's difficult for them to see the child, though they love the child, when it reminds them they're not fulfilling their parental responsibility. A lot of these relationships don't go on long because that psychological dynamic occurs [in the substance abuser] and they drop out."

Collins did not contact Emley about renewing visitation until the day before the scheduled November 16, 1984, hearing before Judge Constine. But in October, Danielle had executed a legal strategy that would forever change the course of the custody dispute, a maneuver that Collins would describe as an "end run," but one he nevertheless should have anticipated.

Danielle had petitioned the San Francisco County Juvenile Court to declare Nicky free from parental custody and control of Bill Toth under Section 232 of the Civil Code. She attacked Bill on two fronts. First, she claimed Bill had abandoned his son by leaving him in Danielle's custody and control without communication, support, and with the intent to abandon, for a period of one year dating back to October 1983. Second, she alleged that his numerous felony convictions made him an unfit parent.

In her 1981 book, *Palomino*, Danielle wrote about an ugly custody fight between a heroin-addicted mother and an upper-class advertising executive—ranch owner who wanted to take the mother's son away from her to give him a better life. Life was now imitating art as Danielle prepared for her own courtroom battle with a heroin user, the father of her son.

Bill was not totally shocked by the move. In August 1982 he had told Santa Clara County court officials that Danielle was trying to have him declared unfit so John Traina could adopt his son.

But neither he nor Collins heard about the petition until Collins phoned Emley on November 15. That day, Emley informed Bill's lawyer that there would be no visits and that Danielle was going to court to sever Bill's parental rights.

The next day, Collins pleaded with Judge Constine to keep the case alive in family law court, where the issue was merely visitation, not Bill's custodial rights. Now the stakes had risen. If Bill lost in juvenile court, he would legally be prohibited from seeing his son. It also would permit what he had feared would come to pass all along: the adoption of his son by Danielle's husband.

Constine heard the arguments and suspended the visitation proceedings until Danielle's petition was heard in juvenile court. He had little choice: juvenile court takes precedence over family court.

The Office of Family Court Services still had not turned in the report that Constine had asked for a year earlier. And now it would conduct no investigation because juvenile court had its own investigative team: the Juvenile Court Probation Department.

The senior Toths had one more visit with Nicky in early November. A second visit was canceled when John's father passed away at the age of ninety-one. When the Toths contacted Danielle again about a visit, she told them there would be no visits until the legal dispute with Bill was resolved. Dorothea and Nicholas made one more try at a visit at Christmas, but were rebuffed again.

On November 5, 1984, a profile of Danielle was published in the Pomona, California, *Progress-Bulletin*. In this article, there was no mention of Danielle's previous marriages to Bill and Danny. Readers were led to believe that after Danielle divorced Claude-Eric, she didn't marry again until John. "With two children by her previous husband, his two children and their own two, the Trainas' household fizzes to visions of Jean Kerr's *Please Don't Eat the Daisies*," the author wrote.

By the time this story appeared, Bill's name had vanished from all the new editions of the five Danielle Steel novels that had been dedicated to him.

Bill Toth was being written out of Danielle's life.

24

&

On December 18, 1984, Danielle had a baby and a number-one book on the best-seller list. *Changes*, her eighteenth novel, was the top-selling hardcover, and the newborn was Vanessa Danielle Steel Traina, born at 8:39 P.M. at Children's Hospital. Vanessa was the seventh addition to the family: two hers, two his, and three theirs.

The new year heralded something more than a book and a baby, a feat Danielle had managed to pull off three years running. Years of hopes and dreams culminated in the signing of a contract with ABC to develop three of Danielle's novels into television movies and miniseries: *Crossings*, *Thurston House*, and the yet-to-be-published *Wanderlust*.

Crossings, which stayed on the best-seller list for twenty weeks as a hardcover and forty-two weeks in paperback, was optioned by producers Douglas Cramer and Aaron Spelling and aired as a three-night miniseries in 1986. The ratings were lukewarm, and subsequently Danielle's other two books were shelved by the network. The author would have to wait four more years before another one of her books hit the airwaves.

With entree into Hollywood came invitations to Los Angeles from the well-connected Cramer, whose dinner-party guest lists always included the likes of Joan Collins and her "Dynasty" costars. Not surprisingly, Hollywood would become a backdrop to two of Danielle's novels that were published back-to-back in 1985.

The first of these was *Family Album*, which follows a dysfunctional Beverly Hills family of seven through four decades of Hollywood mindlessness: infidelity, alcoholism, materialism, reckless spending, and financial ruin. And that's just the parents. The group is headed by philandering millionaire playboy Ward Thayer and his forgiving actress-turned-director wife, Faye Price Thayer.

The five children include one son who becomes a star college-football player and another who is caught nuzzling with his gay lover by his stunned father. One of the daughters is named Vanessa, the name Danielle and John chose for their newest child. But the most colorful child is the youngest Thayer daughter, Anne. She's a quiet, withdrawn girl who spends her formative years holed up in her bedroom reading books. When she hits adolescence, she rebels in a big way. At fourteen, she runs away to San Francisco and joins a commune, experimenting freely with sex and LSD. At fifteen, she falls in love with her best friend's father. He's forty-nine, but he's there for her unlike the elder Thayers, who are too busy winning Oscars and producing box-office hits to pay attention to their kids. Neglectful parents, older men, and communal living are three things Danielle experienced herself earlier in her life, and these sections of the book come alive.

Family Album was followed immediately by the release of *Secrets*, a novel about the trials and tribulations of the star-studded cast of a hot new television show. Book critics would speculate that *Secrets* was based on the hit television series "Dynasty," which Danielle denied, though she did admit to *USA Today* that *Secrets* was a "composite" of the primetime soap opera and that she had visited the "Dynasty" set on three occasions.

On March 29, 1985, John filed adoption papers for Nicky in court. He hoped to adopt Nicky if Bill's parental rights were terminated. Then the Traina family departed for their customary Easter vacation in Mauna Kea. The Traina family trips are quite a production. On this journey, two adults, seven children, nannies, and friends took up thirteen seats in the first-class cabin during the flight over.

Looming in the distance was the upcoming parental rights termination trial, set to get under way on May 1, Nicky's seventh birthday.

Two days before the trial began, the San Francisco Juvenile Probation Department submitted a twenty-page report on behalf of Nicky Toth, which it is required to do by law in all termination of parental rights cases. Probation Officer Cathie Clark interviewed sixteen of the twenty-eight witnesses who were expected to testify at the trial, as well as Nicky himself. The report also provided a lengthy summary of Bill and Danielle's relationship, the preceding divorce litigation, and background on Bill's drug and criminal history.

In the probation report, Clark reported that "Nicky remembers Bill Toth as always having been nice to him and describes him as his 'first father.' " When Clark asked Nicky whether he wanted to visit with Bill again, Nicky said, "Sure."

However, a 1993 letter from Charles D. Morgan, Jr., Danielle's attorney, written on her behalf, asserted that Bill's "only contact with Nicholas was to either endanger or threaten his life."

Clark also sought out an AIDS expert on Danielle's witness list: Dr. Richard Jacobs of the University of California's Moffit Hospital. Jacobs told Clark that someone can be exposed to AIDS through bodily fluids, including saliva, though the risk of contracting the disease without transfer of blood is extremely minimal. As an intravenous drug user, Bill was at risk for getting AIDS, and Jacobs pointed out to Clark that 18 percent of AIDS patients were intravenous drug users who were also susceptible to hepatitis B and other staph infections.

Another doctor on Danielle's witness list was an expert on chemical dependency, Dr. Joseph McCarthy, medical director of the Chemical Dependency Unit at Doctor's Hospital in Pinole, California.

After reviewing Bill's drug history, McCarthy met with Clark and told her that, as Clark later recounted in her report, "there is almost no possibility of Mr. Toth being drug free at this point in his life . . . the success rate of treatment programs, such as those in which Mr. Toth has participated, is only about five percent."

When Clark sat down with Danielle's expert in child psychiatry, Dr. John Sikorski, she found a doctor who believed that Bill's contact with his son should end. Sikorski had tried to meet with Bill, but his requests were ignored.

Dr. Sikorski felt that "Nicky does not see Mr. Toth as part of his life and Mr. Toth's negligence has contributed to this perception," Clark wrote. "Mr. Toth poses a threat to Nicky physically, for health reasons and due to the unpredictability of his behavior, based on his history of using illegal drugs . . . the interaction with Mr. Toth as described by Nicky is not what would occur between a child and a psychologically healthy, responsible adult. If this whole pattern is allowed to continue, it is inevitable that Nicky will suffer in some way."

Of the two doctors who observed Nicky and Bill together, Justine Riskind and Morton Neril, only Neril agreed to speak in detail to Clark about the case. He also would be the only doctor at the trial who had directly observed father and son interact.

"He does not think that the visitation has been detrimental to the child and that he favors limited, supervised visitation, if it can be established that Mr. Toth is not using illegal drugs," Clark wrote. Neril cautioned that if the court ended the visits, "it would be important for Nicky not to feel abandoned or rejected by Mr. Toth and the child should be given the truthful explanation as to why. He feels that if Nicky wants to see Mr. Toth and is unable to do so, he may become more curious at a later date."

Carroll Collins, Bill's divorce attorney, would also testify on his former client's behalf. For the termination trial, the court had appointed Greg Bonfilio to defend Bill because he was indigent. At forty-two, Bonfilio had fifteen years of juvenile court experience to lend in keeping visitation privileges for Bill.

Collins told Clark that Bill had been at a "disadvantage during these proceedings because he did not have Danielle's financial resources," Clark wrote. He said Bill faced an ex-wife who was "inflexible in her attitude about Mr. Toth having access to Nicky." Collins also felt some of the matters brought before the court should have been handled informally between the parties.

Bill also met with Clark and downplayed many of Danielle's assertions. He said that he and Danielle had a good relationship and lived together as a family. He denied that he was in constant conflict with Danielle over his need for money, his use of drugs, or his sporadic presence in the home during those years. After they separated, he saw Nicky at home twice a week until Danielle no longer permitted him to do so, Clark wrote in her report.

Providing his consent for the adoption was out of the question, Bill said, because it would place another barrier between himself and the kind of relationship he wanted with his child. He said he loved his son and felt they could have a relationship that would be beneficial to both of them.

Clark also interviewed Danielle, who went into detail with Clark about her relationship with Bill: the kidnapping threat, the demands for money, Bill's drug use and criminal activities, and his medical problems. "She worries that Mr. Toth is a poor role model and that during his visits he has encouraged Nicky to become preoccupied with monsters, blood and morbid stories," Clark wrote. "Mrs. Traina does not believe that Mr. Toth puts Nicky's welfare before his own."

After weighing all the evidence, Clark urged the court that it would be in Nicky's best interest if ties to Bill were cut and the adoption by John Traina allowed to go forward.

The final decision, however, would rest with recently retired Juvenile Court Judge Francis W. Mayer, the judge pro tempore hired to hear the case. He had been recommended by the supervising juvenile court judge as a fair-minded magistrate with experience in the field of juvenile law and termination-of-parental-rights cases.

What Mayer and the other players in this drama were about to witness was extraordinary. Jeanne Ames, the director of the Office of Family Court Services, would later testify that only five percent of thousands of cases dealt with drug abuse and she could recall only two cases which required one of the parents to submit to drug testing.

What wasn't said was obvious: this trial was pitting one of San Francisco's wealthiest and most prominent public figures against her ex-husband, a convicted felon and chronic substance abuser.

To speed the process along, Danielle elected to bear most of the costs of the trial, which would be closed to the public as is customary in all termination-of-parental-rights proceedings in the state of California. In addition to covering the legal fees for her two attorneys—Chris Emley and his partner, Theodore Winchester—she paid for Judge Mayer, Nicky's court-appointed attorney Margaret Coyne, the stenographer, the bailiff, daily transcripts, the expert witnesses, and other court costs. All told, it is estimated that the two-and-a-half-week trial cost Danielle approximately $75,000, according to attorneys familiar with such proceedings.

When the trial opened on May 1, 1985, Danielle showed up in a fourth-floor courtroom at City Hall with a bodyguard and her husband, who was given special permission by the judge to sit with her in court. The bodyguard remained in the hallway. Bill, outfitted in one of the old suits his ex-wife bought him in happier times, came alone.

The first witness called to the stand was Dr. John Sikorski. Of the three child psychiatrists expected to testify, Sikorski was Danielle's strongest advocate for severing Bill's parental rights.

Recalling the events that followed Bill and Nicky's last visit together on May 31, 1984, Sikorski was concerned about Nicky's future. Sikorski explained, as recounted by Nicky's attorney in his brief, that if for some reason Bill returned to prison, it would keep alive for Nicholas a pattern of expectation, disappointment, and unreliability about his father.

Furthermore, contact with his father would interfere with Nicky's integration into the Traina family, Sikorski said, adding that it was important that the boy feel confident about his place in the family.

To continue a relationship with Bill would be to the boy's detriment, Sikorski said. Continued visits would create anxiety and conflict in Nicky because he would experience a very different way of life. And further problems would result because of the intermittent nature of Bill's visits with Nicky.

The real problem, Sikorski testified, was Bill's drug habit. A father's heroin addiction, he said, causes problems for his children. The father is preoccupied with his own needs and emotionally unavailable to the child.

If Bill could quit heroin, he could salvage a relationship with his son, but for the present, the only option, in Sikorski's eyes, was to sever their ties. This would offer Nicky security that no visitation plan could ever provide.

Sikorski opposed giving Bill another chance. A trial period allowing time for Bill to clean up before resuming visits with his son would reopen a Pandora's Box, leaving Nicky in an untenable position.

In his four meetings with Sikorski, Nicky never said he was afraid of

Bill, nor did he say anything derogatory about his father, Sikorski testified. At some point in the future, added Sikorski, he expected Nicky would contact Bill, and at that time the boy would have the maturity to deal with whatever arose.

The second witness called to the stand was Danielle Steel Traina. As Judge Mayer listened, she recapped all the gory details of her two-and-a-half-year marriage to Bill and explained why she felt his visits with Nicky were unproductive and dangerous to their son. Of particular concern to Danielle was Bill's behavior during the supervised visits. She believed that by sharing food and utensils and being exposed to Bill's saliva, Nicky could catch a variety of diseases from Bill, ranging from hepatitis to AIDS.

John Traina took the witness stand after his wife, identifying himself as the person who began Pearl Cruises. He echoed many of Danielle's concerns about Bill posing a health risk to Nicky and testified that he wanted to adopt Nicky because he was distressed about Nicky's future, particularly if his mother died.

In attempting to prove that Bill was unfit to have custody and control of his son, Danielle produced a litany of damning testimony from five police officers and a toxicologist, all of whom said that Bill had appeared under the influence of drugs during three separate incidents spanning from 1981 to 1983.

Bill also took the stand and proceeded to admit that drugs and crime had plagued his life since the summer of 1967. He admitted that his contact with Nicky has been sporadic over the years and placed much of the blame on Danielle. Conceding that he rarely wrote or called, Bill said he had failed in this regard because he believed his letters and phone calls would never get through.

Emley also caught Bill lying about his use of narcotics over the past several years. Bill, however, said he was ready to change: that he wanted to play a role in his son's upbringing, and as a condition, would agree to drug testing and medical treatment.

Cathie Clark, the juvenile court probation officer who authored the twenty-page report, also was called as a witness for Danielle. She supported Nicky's adoption by John Traina for three reasons: John had lived with Nicky and had been a father figure to the boy for a longer period than Bill; Nicky himself desired adoption; and if he wasn't adopted by John, it might deprive the boy of the security needed to mature and deal with complex issues later in life. She also felt that there should be no uncertainty to Nicky as to where he would live if Danielle passed away.

She also opposed an open adoption allowing Bill some visitation, because Bill's drug problem could resurface. Bill's ongoing drug use, she said, influenced her decision urging the termination of his parental rights.

The best advocates for Bill were Dr. Neril and a court-appointed child psychiatrist, Dr. Henry Massie, director of child psychiatry at St. Mary's Hospital and Medical Center in San Francisco. Massie had been specifically appointed by the court to decide what was in Nicky's best interest. He reviewed all the documents and met separately with the parents and the boy.

Both psychiatrists testified that they supported Bill and Nicky continuing their relationship, if Bill could stay drug free and behave reliably. They also felt that it would be of no benefit to the boy to end his ties to Bill.

Massie even proposed a visitation plan requiring Bill to submit to drug treatment over an extended period before being allowed to see Nicky again. If Bill went back to drugs after visitation was resumed, those privileges would be suspended until he completed further treatment.

Bill could give up on this arrangement and forfeit having a relationship with his son. Or, as Danielle's attorney suggested, might Bill endure when he would otherwise quit if Nicky inherited a fortune? Massie conceded that was possible.

Massie knew there were drawbacks to this father and son relationship. He described Bill as depressed, impulsive, listless, and unambitious. There was a risk that Nicky might model himself after Bill's undesirable qualities, as children of the same gender often do.

But he also said in court that there was a danger to ending Nicky's ties to Bill. Down the road, Nicky might blame his mother for taking away his father, and could take retribution by seeking out Bill, or perhaps by taking on what he believed to be his father's traits, both the good and the bad.

On the whole, seeing Bill would not be as beneficial to the boy as knowing he will grow up as a full member of the Traina family, Massie said.

The behavior of Nicky's mother also came under scrutiny. Massie testified that her demands to control the drug testing increased the tension level, and that the urinalysis work-ups should be handled by a treatment center. However, he also told the court that it would be harmful to Nicky to keep up visitation if Bill was frequently absent.

The flaws in Bill's character were well-known to Neril. He testified that Bill was not a major influence in Nicky's life and had let his son down as a father. He also felt Bill had placed a higher priority on his own wants and needs than the boy's.

At the same time, Neril also worried about the long-term effects on Nicky if Bill simply disappeared from his life. "It would be bad for the father to drop off the face of the earth," Neril said, since Nicky viewed Bill as "one of his fathers." To abruptly cut off a child from his parent could have a detrimental effect on the youngster, he said in court.

While Neril agreed that adoption would enhance Nicky's relationship with John Traina, Bill shouldn't be dismissed. "In the boy's mind, there is an importance of Mr. Toth now and in the future in terms of knowing who he is and having involvement with him." Neril testified. "I don't feel we need to take Mr. Toth away from the boy unless it's clear that Mr. Toth is being emotionally or physically injurious to the boy, and for the here and now, I think we should continue to supervise the visits and reevaluate."

Midway through the trial, however, Bill and his attorney recognized that momentum was swinging toward Danielle. Bill swallowed hard and agreed with his lawyer that they should solicit a settlement offer from his ex-wife. In return for giving up his parental rights to Nicky, Bill requested a reasonable visitation plan for his parents. Danielle then submitted an offer: the senior Toths could see Nicky every other month, but only in the Traina home under the supervision of a bodyguard. Nicky would not be allowed out of the house. "It was an insult," Bill said. "She put the same kind of restrictions on them as she would with me. I could always understand her dislike of me, but my parents never did anything to her. We turned them down."

The trial concluded on May 17, and that very night, Danielle and John attended an evening benefit for the March of Dimes in the Grand Ballroom of the Fairmont Hotel. They sampled Texas quail, gravlax, and fresh fruit with Kahlua sauce before rushing home for dinner.

Three nights later, they made another appearance at a benefit for the San Francisco Ballet. The evening began with cocktails at Danielle's favorite jewelry store, Tiffany, and was followed by a five-course dinner. Danielle and John left early because they had a full calendar for the week ahead. The American Booksellers' Association convention was in town, and Danielle was the guest of honor at two luncheons and a dinner. She also planned on hosting a dinner party for her twenty-two foreign publishers.

On June 27, Judge Mayer rendered his decision in the Toth-Steel custody trial. Regarding the first cause of action—that Bill's numerous felony convictions made him unfit to be a parent—Mayer concluded that the case had no merit. Though state law permits the court to sever a convicted felon's relationship with his child, Mayer would consider only Bill's most recent felony convictions: the two receiving stolen property crimes he committed—in Palo Alto in 1981 and at Novey's Antiques in San Francisco in 1982.

"The court believes that at the time the petition was filed the commission of those two felonies no longer played any major role as to whether [Bill] could thereafter resume a proper father role with his son," Mayer said.

Nevertheless, Danielle was victorious. She won the case on her second argument: that Bill had abandoned Nicky.

The court noted that it has the authority to terminate the parental rights if it can be proved one parent left the child in the custody of another for one year, without any provision for support, without communication, and with the intent to abandon. If only "token efforts" are made by the parent to support or communicate with the child, the court can still declare the child abandoned.

That was a crushing blow for Bill. Judge Mayer deemed his efforts "token."

"The court is satisfied from all the evidence produced that [Bill] herein, since the child's birth, was never anything more than a biological father and not a father in fact," Mayer wrote in his decision. "This was a result of [Bill's] lifestyle both before the birth of the child and continuing up to the time of the filing of petition herein."

Mayer went on to state that the visits Bill had before and after his 1982 imprisonment were at most "token in nature; more of a series of play sessions than anything resembling a true father-son relationship."

The judge said he was aware "these visits were on a supervised basis, but as it turned out, the need for such supervision was indeed necessary. [Bill] contends he was never given the opportunity for a closer relationship, but again the evidence indicates clearly he could never get himself in condition so that the court could allow unsupervised visits to occur."

Mayer also rejected Bill's argument that others, particularly Danielle, "are responsible for his troubles and they, not he, are the cause of his failure to have closer ties with his son. In this court's view, the evidence points overwhelmingly to the fact that it is [Bill's] continued and deliberate use of hard drugs that has resulted in his present predicament."

The evidence also showed that Bill had his chances to clean up while married to Danielle, yet he seemed bent on destroying the family relationship through his use of hard drugs. While Bill was "stating to the court he was drug free and in no need of testing, he was in fact using hard drugs," Mayer ruled.

Bill's argument that he was denied a visitation trial had no merit, Mayer decided, because Bill had been offered visitation on many occasions as long as he could remain drug free, but he couldn't.

"The worst example of this was his last visit in May 1984 where the test showed he was in fact using just prior to the visit," Mayer wrote. After the last visit, Bill himself testified that he "blew it" and didn't do anything about another visit for five months. Prior to seeing Nicky in May 1984, Bill had been offered various plans for visitation that either were not acted upon or refused because of the demand for testing. Bill even wrote the court and said he wasn't on drugs at this time, but urinalysis on May 30 proved otherwise, Mayer wrote.

More lenient alternatives to termination were rejected because Bill never conformed to the behavior required that would lead to a better relationship with his son, Mayer ruled. For example, Bill had always argued that drug testing was an invasion of his privacy, but Mayer determined that wasn't the only reason Bill objected to testing. Mayer felt that made it impossible for Bill to continue on drugs and pass the tests.

There was Nicky to consider as well. Mayer stated he was more concerned about how future failures would affect Nicky's well-being and thus agreed with witnesses who testified that "continuing such token visits can only result in further detriment to the child."

It was the judge's conclusion that there was a pattern to Bill's behavior: he was unwilling to quit drugs to regain his relationship with Nicky until he "faced the moment of truth; only then did he fight tooth and nail, lapsing into his lifestyle once the crisis has passed."

Mayer proved prescient on the last count. Seventeen days after Bill lost his parental rights, he and an accomplice broke into a house on Sloat Boulevard in San Francisco. A neighbor spotted them forcing open the door and called the police. As Bill and his partner rummaged through some drawers and a closet in a first-floor bedroom, three San Francisco police cars pulled up in front of the house.

"She gave Bill every chance," a close friend of Danielle's told *People* magazine. "Only when he proved he couldn't be a responsible father did she end his parental rights. And she did it for the sake of the child."

In the aftermath of the May trial, Bill sat in his cell at San Francisco County Jail, believing that Danielle was motivated by something other than protecting her son. "I was an embarrassment to her," he said years later. "Here I was, this middle-class ex-con. So she got rid of me and pretends I never existed."

While Bill languished in jail after his July 14 arrest, Danielle retreated to the Napa Valley in August to begin another book after a yearlong sabbatical from writing. John went on a vacation with Trevor and Todd.

On September 5, 1985, five years to the day that Danielle filed for divorce from Bill, Bill's attorney filed an appeal in an attempt to reverse Judge Mayer's ruling. On October 25, Bill stood before yet another judge and pleaded guilty to the Sloat Boulevard burglary. He was sentenced to three years in San Quentin State Prison.

One book Danielle already had in the pipeline was *Fine Things*, a 1987 novel she liked to promote as a story about a woman who dies of cancer. But the book is about much more than death and dying. It's about child stealing and a vicious custody fight between an upper-middle-class department store executive and a convicted felon.

The hero's name is Bernie Fine. He's a manager for an upscale department store called Wolff's, which bears a striking similarity to I. Magnin and Saks, two of Danielle's favorite places to shop. Bernie moves to San Francisco to open a new store and falls in love with a blonde schoolteacher named Liz, the single mother of five-year-old Jane.

The girl's natural father is a dark and mysterious man named Chandler Scott. He is an actor and a con artist with a criminal record that included convictions for receiving stolen property and burglary. One year into his marriage with Liz, he disappears, and when Liz finds out he's in jail, she files for divorce and fortunately never hears from the scoundrel again.

Bernie marries Liz, they have a child together, and for two years they live happily together as Bernie becomes the doting father Jane never had. That is, until Chandler reappears on the scene, demanding to see his child. It turns out all he's after is money, and he goes away for ten thousand dollars. But after Liz dies suddenly of cancer, Chandler returns, looking for more money and threatening to reclaim from Bernie the daughter he says is rightfully his.

When the concerned stepfather calls his lawyer for advice, the attorney wants to know whether he adopted Jane.

"His heart sank at the question," Danielle wrote. "There was always something happening, the baby, Liz getting sick, the last nine months, then their adjustment . . . 'No . . . I haven't . . . I figured we'd seen the last of him for awhile.' "

Instead, Chandler goes to court, and the judge awards him temporary visitation. During an outing with Jane, he abducts her and flies to Mexico, where he holds her for ransom. Bernie hires bodyguards to protect his other child and private investigators to find his stepdaughter. They rescue her and bring her home, but Chandler goes back to court and wins custody of Jane.

In making his ruling, the judge says:

> There is no question here but that Mr. Fine loves his stepdaughter, and that is not the issue here, but the fact remains that a natural father belongs with his child, in the absence of the natural mother. With the unfortunate death of Mrs. Fine, Jane must revert to living with her father.

Bernie is infuriated by the decision and lashes out at his lawyer: "You're talking about my daughter, I know what's good for her and what isn't. One of these days that bastard is going to kill my kid, and you're all going to tell me how sorry you are."

But the evil Chandler never gets to have his daughter. On the day he is supposed to pick Jane up, the convicted felon from Liz's past is shot and killed by police—while robbing a bank.

25

ह्र

hree years after the court severed Nicky's ties to Bill Toth, he and Danny Zugelder had become distant memories that Danielle no longer chose to acknowledge. And the image she did choose to portray to her fans was shrouded more in myth than in fact. Consider the interview she gave to the *Los Angeles Times* to promote her 1988 book, *Kaleidoscope.*

"Then there's the exotic picture of her private life that's been presented by her Los Angeles publicity machine: daughter of a German 'nobleman,' wife of a San Francisco shipping 'magnate,' 'devoted' mother of nine. Even Ripley might not print that one without a smirk," wrote the *Times*'s Nikki Finke, injecting a note of cynicism into the January 1988 article because she was apparently wary of the romanticized background Danielle was claiming.

As the *Times* prepared to go to press with the article, journalist Finke reviewed her notes and discovered the number of children didn't add up. By now, the combined Traina-Steel brood numbered nine: two hers, two his, and five theirs. The latest two additions to the fold were Maximillian John Alexander Traina, born on February 10, 1986, and Zara Alexandra Teal Traina, born on September 26, 1987.

Danielle had reportedly told Finke she had nine children: one child by her first husband, five by John, and two stepchildren from John's previous marriage. But that added up to only eight. Where did the ninth child come from?

To resolve the discrepancy, Finke contacted Danielle's publicist, Warren

Cowan, explaining to him that there was a child whose origin was unaccounted for. Cowan told her that no one had ever brought this issue up before, and he promised to get back to her with an explanation. Minutes later, he called back and revealed to Finke he was shocked to hear from his client that she had been married briefly to an alcohol- and drug-abuse counselor between the unions with Lazard and Traina, and that they had a child together. When Finke interviewed Danielle later about the mystery marriage, Danielle refused to discuss her union with Bill Toth. "Alzheimer's has come on," Danielle said in the article reported by Finke. Since there were no children from Danielle's marriage to Zugelder, there was no way to know of that nuptial.

Withholding the facts was nothing new to Danielle. In a fall 1991 interview with McCall's magazine, Danielle apparently misstated her age by two years. When the author of the story later asked for clarification, Danielle replied coolly, "If I say I'm forty-two, I'm forty-two." McCall's went ahead and printed the accurate age of forty-four.

In the same story, John was reported as being fifty years old even though he had turned sixty-three months earlier. No one ever seemed to get John's age right. His age is even reported inaccurately on the birth certificates of four of his five children by Danielle.

One condition Danielle insisted on before cooperating with McCall's—or any other magazine, for that matter—was that it not identify her hometown as San Francisco. "Danielle asked me not to mention it," said Marc Meyers, who wrote the story. "Her biggest fear is that with nine kids, and given her wealth, there would be a kidnap or terrorist threat."

No exceptions were made, not even for an old friend like Fred R. Smith, one of the people mentioned in the dedication of her 1973 novel, Going Home. Smith had known Danielle from her Supergirls days, and when he called in 1988 asking for an interview for an airline magazine he was editing, Danielle wrote him a polite refusal. "She said she was so concerned about kidnapping [of her children] that she didn't want anybody to know where she lived," Smith remembered.

Danielle also demanded picture approval, and nowhere in the text could she be referred to as a "romance" writer. Reporters also were told not to ask questions about her previous husbands, recalled publicists who worked for her.

"People were usually okay about not mentioning her kids' names or the city she lived in because of security," remembered one former publicist. "But it struck us as odd because most of her books are dedicated to her children, and practically every book she writes is set in San Francisco."

After the ground rules were set, the writers who have interviewed the prolific author found her warm and congenial.

249

"She has a good phone voice," Meyers said. "I felt like I was talking withan old girlfriend. It was kind of a flirtatious voice, kind of like a canopy bed: a full, rich, feminine, earthy, consoling, maternal sound."

Until he brought up the subject of sex. The focus of Meyers's story, "How to Get It All Done," was to reveal how a busy person like Danielle organized her day to meet career and family demands.

"I faxed her the question, 'How do you find time for sex?' and she sent me back a tough note that said she found the question incredibly impertinent, highly irresponsible, and way too personal," Meyers remembered. "She told me that what her sex life was about was none of my business. It was an angry note."

Danielle also posed a question to him: If he were profiling novelists Stephen King, Sidney Sheldon, or James Michener, would he raise the same subject with them?

"Then the irony struck me," Meyers recalled. "Here's a woman who writes two books a year on sex and relationships, and suddenly sex is out of bounds? She was incredibly hostile about it. It was a hard question, but I didn't think she handled it with much grace."

Later on, Meyers dropped her a line saying he had hoped she liked the article. "She sent me back a handwritten card, saying she loved the story and she apologized for giving me a hard time," Meyers recalled. "She was very gracious."

Working on the other side of the publicity fence for Danielle was not an enviable task. For most of the 1980s, Danielle was a client of Rogers and Cowan, a leading show-biz publicity firm. Her publisher paid a handsome fee of five thousand dollars a month to the agency, whose co-president, Warren Cowan, was directly involved in all of Danielle's affairs, including mundane tasks he would normally delegate to an account manager. Setting up interviews for the author was frequently an exasperating experience, according to former publicists.

In 1986 Danielle admitted to USA Today that she hated doing book tours: "I hate leaving my children. To get me away from them for two days is a major psychotic event. I develop every malady in the world so I don't have to go.

"About once every two years they drag me out of mothballs for a TV show, but that's about it," Danielle once told Contemporary Authors. "I'm very shy. I'll do magazine things if they come to me, and I've been very fortunate in that the TV stuff has been coming to me in recent years. That makes it work."

Out of the limelight, Danielle was anything but shy. She made a point to stay on top of all the publicity campaigns for her books, remembered a publicist. She also kept an eye on the competition.

Once after a big article on Sidney Sheldon ran in the *Washington Post*, John Traina called Warren Cowan and told him that if the agency could deliver a story like that for his wife, she would be willing to travel to Washington, D.C., for the interview, though she would prefer a California-based writer so she wouldn't have to travel. For Danielle, publicity wasn't simply a means to sell books; she wanted placement in magazines that her friends read, such as *Women's Wear Daily* and *Town and Country*, a publicist said.

That same standard applied to Danielle's children. Despite the author's concern that her sons and daughters were kidnapping targets, she spared no effort to promote Beatie's introduction to New York society in 1986, asking Rogers and Cowan to place Beatie on the cover of *Town and Country's* December 1986 debutante issue. This was the very same magazine that had named John's former wife, Dede, as its debutante of the year twenty-four years earlier. Beatie, who was unable to debut in San Francisco because she was born outside the Bay Area, was rejected for the magazine's cover, but her New York debut did garner mentions in other publications.

One publicist felt Danielle's involvement in publicity bordered on being obsessive, recalling that the author and her husband frequently complained to Rogers and Cowan that the job they were doing was unsatisfactory. "We never seemed to do anything right," the publicist recalled. "We'd go through all this trouble setting up interviews, knowing in the back of our minds she probably would cancel out. She always told us she started Supergirls and knew more than we did about this business because she had done it herself.

"I asked her once, 'If you hate us so much, why do you stay with us?' " Danielle's response was blunt. "I like making powerful people squirm, and I make Warren Cowan squirm."

Over the years, there has been no shortage of local news about Danielle, particularly news she makes with her children. The society columns wrote her up when she breast-fed Maxx at a dinner party Ann Getty gave for Italian designer Valentino, who took one look at the earth mother and pronounced, "Look, she's milking the baby!"

In October 1987 Danielle took one-month-old Zara to a luncheon for designer Miguel Cruz, and the baby had her own table—and two nurses. "Papa John also had another new baby waiting for him outside the restaurant: a Bentley," the *San Francisco Chronicle* reported.

Everyone had a field day two months later after the annual Christmas dinner-dance at the M. H. de Young Memorial Museum. That night, Danielle arrived wearing a beeper. During the party, she was beeped when three-month-old Zara got hungry. Danielle didn't rush home to feed her. Instead, a driver spirited the infant over in a limousine, and Danielle breast-fed her daughter at curbside.

Children have been a big part of Danielle's life, partly because of her own childhood. Usually, Danielle's mother, Norma, absorbed the brunt of the blame for the author's lonely upbringing. Opinions of Norma Stone vary among the author's friends and acquaintances. Some find her warm and charming, while others believe mother and daughter are at odds. "There are scars, and she has never patched things up with her mother," one friend said. Regardless, Norma and Kuniko still visit once a year.

"She was an only child, and I don't feel she wants the kids to be alone," said Katherine Dusay, a coauthor of *Having a Baby*. "She wants them to have each other as friends. That's why she had a lot of kids, and I think she would have more if she could."

Attempts to add more children to the Traina brood didn't stop after Zara.

One former employee of the Trainas recalled that Danielle was devastated by another miscarriage in 1988 and subsequently had difficulty getting pregnant. "It was really an issue," the former employee recalled. "She began to see different specialists. She wanted more children; an even dozen." The experience also served as the inspiration for her 1992 bestseller, *Mixed Blessings*, about three women battling infertility.

John and the children are the focus of Danielle's life, friends said. Danielle keeps them out of the public eye, but she did write about each of them in the foreword of the 1988 nonfiction book *After Having a Baby*.

At nineteen, Beatie was described as a "gentle, determined, persevering, scholarly child . . . serious, quiet and definitely has her own mind." Perhaps her only pet peeve with Beatie was the teenager's messy room and that perhaps the Princeton sophomore didn't take enough time out from her studies to enjoy life a little more. After graduating from Princeton in 1990, Beatie worked as management trainee at the Gap fashion stores and in 1993 earned a master's degree in the field of health psychology education from Stanford University. Beatie turned twenty-six on January 10, 1994, and currently lives in San Francisco.

Stepson Trevor was "handsome and charming and debonair," and younger brother Todd, "full of mischief and fun," Danielle wrote.

Trevor, who was twenty-six on May 16, 1994, went on to graduate from Princeton with Beatie and today lives in New York while working for Seagram's as a product manager. Stepson Todd, who was twenty-five on October 22, 1994, earned a degree from Connecticut College and currently is a co-partner in a Los Angeles–based movie production company.

Danielle described nine-year-old Nicky as "an individual to the very roots of his soul." As a toddler, he hated "cute" clothes and as an adolescent "had dreams of life as a rock star . . . he is a nonconformist in every possible way.

We frequently meet toe to toe—and I'm not always sure I've won," she wrote. Nicky turned sixteen on May 1, 1994, and is now attending a private prep school in the Bay Area.

Samantha "wants to be a ballerina one day, and has a gentle soul. She is easily wounded and cares deeply about everyone she knows," Danielle wrote. She was twelve on April 14, 1994.

Victoria is "good humored and very shy." She was eleven on September 5, 1994. Vanessa "can be as tough as she has to be," and was ten on December 18, 1994. Maxx "is always laughing," and was eight on February 10, 1994. Zara, the youngest, was seven on September 26, 1994.

One story that didn't hit the local papers was John's secret adoption of Nicky. On May 4, 1987, three days after Nicky's ninth birthday, the San Francisco County Health Department sealed his birth certificate forever. Three months earlier, the California Court of Appeal upheld Judge Mayer's decision to sever Bill's parental ties to Nicky, thereby allowing the adoption by John to go forward. Nicky's name was changed from Nicholas William Toth to Nicholas John Steel Traina.

"Nicholas' mother and I have at all times treated him exactly as we do our own children, and we have taken extreme precautions to keep the facts surrounding his adoption and earlier life confidential," John said in a 1993 court declaration. "His younger brothers and sisters, for example, do not even know that Nicholas is adopted. Neither I nor my wife have ever spoken to any member of the media about Nicholas' status, nor will we."

Apparently John wasn't aware of the numerous stories about his wife over the years that clearly identified Nicky as Bill Toth's son. Danielle herself told San Francisco magazine's Cyra McFadden in 1982 that her marriage to Bill was "worth it, because Nicky's wonderful. . . . We decided to get married, and then after we decided to get married, we discovered that we had created Nicky, and then I wanted to get out of it but I didn't want to mess things up for Nicky. So we agreed to get an annulment."

Curtis Browning, an employee of the Trainas whose job included guarding Nicky and taking care of the family's fleet of automobiles, says the boy never mentioned Bill Toth to him when he worked for the Trainas in 1989. He got close to Nicky while accompanying him to soccer practice and outings with his friends. "He had no choice and Danielle never explained to me why I had to go," Curtis said. "The secretaries told me she was afraid of his father. He never said a word about his real father—and I never asked him, and we were pretty close. I was Nick's buddy, and I felt for the kid."

Danielle would arrange for Nicky and his friends to get box seats at San Francisco Giants games, and she would throw him lavish birthday parties. Once, Danielle rented out a bowling alley for ten thousand dollars and treated thirty of Nicky's friends to a catered pizza spread. "When the family went to Hawaii, she told me to get him the best Macintosh computer," Curtis said. "It cost ten thousand dollars."

One former employee who worked in the Traina home described John and Danielle as attentive and caring parents. "John was very good with the [small] children," the employee said. "He was around a lot and they would come in to see him in his office."

In a typical morning, the nannies would bring the kids into Danielle and John's bedroom, where they would play with toys on Danielle's bed and watch children's videos while their mother worked. In the late afternoon, the kids often gathered in the bathroom to talk about their day while Danielle relaxed in the bathtub. "She was very loving with the kids, and tried to be there when they came home from school for lunch," the employee recalled.

Her feelings of love could turn to fear when the young children didn't arrive home on time from school or activities. In June 1989, two nannies had taken Maxx and Zara to a shopping center and were delayed getting back. The fatal error came when they failed to call to let Danielle know they were going to be late. "I remember her yelling for me to get upstairs," the employee recalled. After climbing three flights of stairs from the cellar-based offices, the employee arrived in Danielle's room and found the author was frantic. "Call every hospital," she recalled Danielle ordering. "The nannies aren't back with Maxx and Zara."

"Danielle was sobbing, in hysterics," the employee recalled. "She felt they had been kidnapped. She found John and he had to come home from a luncheon. She totally lost it. It seemed like if the kids were ten minutes late, they were kidnapped."

Curtis recalled that he had to chase Nicky when he took off from the house without permission. He ran down Danielle's son in a park across the street and escorted him home. When they returned, the police had been summoned by Danielle, and Nicky had to sit in a squad car for a few minutes to teach him a lesson, Curtis said.

By 1989, Beatie, Trevor, and Todd were away at college, but there were still plenty of children to keep track of on Jackson Street, not to mention Danielle's staff, including two secretaries, five nannies, a cook, two housekeepers, a butler, a bodyguard, an accountant, and a groundskeeper.

"People think, 'Oh, she doesn't have to do anything because she has all those people to help her,' " Danielle told *McCall's*. "Who do you think manages them?"

Danielle's organizational skills are indeed extraordinary. Business writer Marc Meyers was struck by the similarities between the way Danielle ran her business and household and the tendencies of some of the country's foremost entrepreneurs.

"She's very controlling and doesn't delegate the crucial stuff," Meyers said, analyzing her management style. "And she probably wouldn't be as successful if she did."

"I am still not great at delegating work," Steel told Meyers during the interview, "and I have only come to do it as a matter of survival. I wish I could offer a tip for letting go, but I haven't found it."

Danielle traced her systematic ways back to her days as an only child living with a single father, she told reporter Glenn Plaskin for a May 1991 article:

> I buy birthday presents three months ahead of time and I use the telephone whenever possible, especially when buying the kids' clothes from two shops that know what I like.
>
> I spend an hour a day planning up to six months in advance. I keep elaborate books that tell me when everybody needs their checkups and shots, when I'm taking business trips, and when I'm blocking out writing time. Everything is lists! Endlessly. On Monday, I publish a schedule outlining where I'll be every day of the week—and I carry a beeper so that I can be tracked at any time I'm needed.

To help her keep organized, she has an elaborate system of more than seventy file cabinets in the house. Twenty of those cabinets are locked away in a vault where she stores her book manuscripts. Thirty-one-day accordion files are used for arranging daily affairs.

Danielle also prioritizes her time, declining to get involved in volunteer work, benefits, and school functions unless her kids are participating. "I will not string balloons, popcorn, and God knows what else at fairs. . . . No offense, but I'm just too busy," she told McCall's.

Danielle could be generous and congenial with her staff. She had this "folksy" way about her, Curtis Browning recalled. "There are redeeming qualities to Danielle. She's very generous with material things, she pays her nannies well, and she doesn't seem removed from her humble roots. She could be personable and connect with you in an empathic way."

But Danielle Steel the manager was another story. Former staffers have found her obsessive and controlling. Employee turnover was high and workers frequently left feeling that they had been treated badly.

"She runs a huge household—the staff numbered sixteen, including a nanny for each of the small children while I was there," said a former employee who worked closely with Danielle and her husband.

Danielle parceled out the work, but some employees felt she intervened unnecessarily when her underutilized staff tried to initiate any changes or deviated from the rules.

Reprimands frequently came down in writing. One worker remembered seeing nasty memos from Danielle, criticizing an employee for making a sandwich for a coworker in the family kitchen (lunches weren't provided for most staff) and for getting a visitor a glass of water from the wrong bathroom.

"I had [management] expertise, but she wouldn't allow me to use it; she would undermine things I did," a former employee recalled. "She has complete control—she writes every single check for every employee; everything is [communicated] in typed notes."

Danielle works on her books "just a couple of times a year when she shuts herself up in her office for a week at a time."

Around the Traina household, the hours were long, the work was hard, and the stress level was high, former employees said. Secretaries worked in a tiny office in the cellar and each morning climbed three flights of stairs to Danielle's bedside, where the nightgown-clad author doled out assignments. Sometimes, Danielle gave female secretaries instructions from her bathtub. "It was strange," Curtis said, recalling the bedroom visits. "I'd be up there in a suit and tie taking notes while Danielle would be in her [nightgown] giving orders."

While Danielle was coordinating the staff, John's morning routine was much more laid back. He frequently retired to the sanctuary of his indoor gym, located in the converted cellar. "He'd lock the door behind him and be very quiet," Curtis said. "He had his sauna, his VCR, and weights." During the day, John met friends for lunch at a restaurant and spent the afternoon tending to his extensive collections of Fabergé cigarette cases, cuff links, watches, malachite furniture, and antique model ships. Some of the cigarette cases are reportedly worth $10,000 to $25,000 each.

John also handles the day-to-day business affairs, for which Danielle pays him a salary. In 1993, his paycheck was more than $100,000 per month.

Annual salaries varied, but staffers said secretaries started at $30,000, and the base pay for nannies was the same, though they enjoyed incredible perks, including room and board, clothing, and jewelry. With the exception of one Latin woman, the Traina nannies were exclusively British and supplied by London-based nanny agencies. The job was high pressure, and sometimes the women fought among themselves, Curtis said.

"Camilla is the number-one nanny, and one day she made a cake for John's [fifty-eighth] birthday," he said. "Overnight, someone came in the kitchen and destroyed it. That was typical of the silliness and the antics."

Danielle tried to fix Curtis up with one of the nannies, but he had his eye on somebody else. "I went for the housekeeper," he said.

Curtis, now thirty-three, earned $29,000 annually working for the Traina family from January 1989 through January 1990. A graduate of the University of California, Berkeley, with a degree in economics, he served as Nicholas's bodyguard, chauffeured the young children to and from school, and maintained the family's fleet of twenty-eight automobiles, including two Rolls-Royces, a Bentley, and a Ferrari.

Browning's forty-six-year-old wife, the former Anna Maria De Mello, cleaned the Trainas' home from nine A.M. to nine P.M., six days a week. It was an exacting job. Danielle required that bath towels be replaced after each use, and once when Anna failed to make the master bed correctly, Danelle stood and watched as the secretaries demonstrated to Anna the proper way to do it. Anna took home $2,000 a month—under the table. Payment was in the form of an unmarked envelope stuffed with money or a check made out to "cash," Anna said.

A 1978 graduate from the Universidad de Brasilia, Anna emigrated to the U.S. in 1988 with her former husband, whom she subsequently divorced. In June 1989, she was recruited to work for Danielle by another Brazilian housekeeper who had previously cleaned for the Trainas.

Anna admitted she was an illegal alien while working for Danielle, but that was no secret to anyone in the household. She shared housekeeping chores with another Brazilian immigrant who worked the seven A.M. to seven P.M. shift. Curtis also supervised another undocumented employee.

"My wife was illegally working for Danielle, though she is now legal," Curtis said.

The Brownings and others said Danielle was suspicious of her employees and frequently tested their integrity. The tests usually occurred during the first month of employment, and involved leaving out valuable jewels and cash in view of the help. Anna recalled finding a ten-dollar-bill while cleaning one day, and after she turned it over, another employee later joked, "I hear you passed the ten-dollar-bill test."

Curtis believed his rite of passage involved a more complex scheme. In his first month on the job, Danielle asked him to run an errand, and when he went out to the car, he found an expensive emerald brooch in the backseat of the Mercedes. He promptly turned it in. "In hindsight I know it was a set-up," he said. "She sent me out to the car alone and it wasn't too hard to find."

"She was paranoid about kidnapping and stealing," a former employee said. "And yet you could say to her, 'I love that hand bag,' and two days later she'd leave one for you on your desk, but after a while it didn't matter."

The Brownings and others agreed that Danielle was in charge and controlled the purse strings. "One time I was buzzed on the intercom by both Mr. and Mrs. Traina," Anna recalled. "I went to see Mr. Traina first, and then when I went to see Mrs. Traina, she was upset that I had gone to see her husband first. She said, 'Who do you think signs your paycheck?' "

"She was in her world and he was in his, but they showed a united front," Curtis said. "She was in the driver's seat, without question."

That was never more evident than when Danielle interfered with instructions John had given the staff. At the Jackson Street house, the Trainas had adjoining bathrooms in the master suite, and one day John left a note for Anna to wash his tub with 409 cleanser. Danielle preferred Windex cleanser and she blew her top after she discovered the breech.

"Danielle called me and asked me why I used the 409," remembered Anna. "I told her John had wrote me a note to do it, but I had thrown it in the trash. And then, in front of her and me, he denied having written the note."

This didn't happen just to housekeepers. Another former employee vouched that the same thing happened to her over a business matter. "He would deny things to her to stay in her good graces," the employee said. "She could have such fits and tantrums; I imagine he did it to keep the peace."

Curtis, now a computer programmer working in the Bay Area, said he was fired after arguing with Danielle over his decision to send home the groundskeeper, whose mother had recently passed away. Danielle didn't believe the worker's story and Curtis said he was dismissed when he stood his ground. Anna was let go after four months. She was told she "didn't fit in." Anna believed it was because she got too close to the young children.

In the late 1980s, Danielle was also pounding the pavement in Hollywood trying to turn her books into movies. "That should be the headline of your piece," Steel told the *Los Angeles Times* in 1988. " 'Why Haven't Danielle Steel's Books Been More Commercial in Hollywood?' "

Danielle had soured on television, which had aired only one of the three books optioned back in 1985. "But now it's time for us to go to feature film," she said. "I want to be like the rest of the world and watch them on a big screen with a box of popcorn with my husband."

According to writers and executives in the entertainment industry, her books lack the conflict and controversy that would propel them into theaters. For now Danielle will have to settle for invading living rooms across America. "Her stories are perfect for TV," said Peter Lefcourt, the novelist and screenwriter who adapted *Fine Things* for television. *Fine Things*, Danielle's second television movie since *Crossings*, aired in October 1990. It came within three share points of beating out the opening night of baseball's World Series.

In the fall of 1989, Danielle met with producer Douglas Cramer and

Brandon Tartikoff, whose wife was a huge fan of Danielle's books. Negotiations dragged on for several months, but the television deal was finally completed in March 1990.

In the interview with *McCall's*, Danielle said the deal with NBC became a burden because it demanded too much of her time:

> At first we agreed that it wouldn't take any time from me. They'd turn the books into movies, and that would be the end of it. But the producer ended up needing tremendous amounts of my time to read, edit, comment, and write, which made me completely nuts.

Two writers who wrote scripts for NBC-produced Steel movies, however, said that the author was instrumental in the process from the start. Lefcourt, who scripted one of the first books under Danielle's new NBC deal, said he noticed that the producers and network executives were very "solicitous" of Danielle, unusual treatment for a novelist by a medium that ideally prefers to dispatch with the book writer.

"Brandon Tartikoff, Doug Cramer, and some network executives gave a lunch for Danielle and John in Los Angeles," Lefcourt recalled. "They treated her like she was visiting royalty."

Cramer then took Lefcourt to San Francisco on his private plane for another meeting with Danielle to discuss her book *Fine Things* and Lefcourt's outline. "Danielle was supposed to have creative input," he said. "She liked my script and put little smiley faces all the way through it."

Danielle was less charitable with writer Jane-Howard Hammerstein, a screenwriter who now lives in Connecticut. Hammerstein was hired by Cramer to write the script for *Daddy*. "I guess Doug got the completed script on a Monday or a Tuesday and he called me thirty-six hours later. 'Bless you, bless you,' he said, 'it's just wonderful. I'm not sure that Mrs. Steel is going to be crazy about it because the dialogue is not like hers, but she'll get used to it,' he said.

"Four days later, Doug called me again and said, 'You've been fired.' I said, 'I have to assume you didn't fire me, Doug, so who did?' And he said, 'Danielle Steel.' She apparently didn't like the dialogue because her characters don't speak like that at all. I said, 'Of course not. Mine speak in English.' "

As time went on, the Trainas began to outgrow 2510 Jackson Street, even with its nine bedrooms and nine bathrooms. Considering that the home also had to house John and Danielle's offices, workspace for Danielle's secretarial staff, and sleeping quarters for some of the live-in help, more space was required.

"We need a lot of room," John told the *San Francisco Examiner* in 1989. That year they put 2510 Jackson on the market for $5.5 million, and Danielle and John set their sights on a much larger and much more expensive house a few blocks east on Washington Street, the French baroque white limestone estate known commonly as the Spreckels mansion.

Built in 1913 by sugar mogul Adolph Spreckels and designed by Paris-trained architect George Applegarth, the mansion was set atop a one-acre hillside lot that spanned a half-city block in fashionable Pacific Heights. The front of the palatial home faced picturesque Lafayette Park to the south, while the back looked out over views of the Golden Gate Bridge and San Francisco Bay to the north.

The splendor of the baroque facade was matched by an interior "replete with marble floors, fireplaces, coffered ceilings and elaborate moldings and panelings," according to a sales brochure advertising the Spreckels as a twenty-seven-room residence with fifteen thousand square feet of living space spread over four floors. The home boasted twelve bedrooms, twelve-and-a-half baths, and eight smaller bedrooms and seven baths for the live-in help. There was also an indoor pool and a five-car garage on the property. The asking price: $13.5 million.

A controversy erupted in the summer and fall of 1989 as the Spreckels heirs attempted to stop a landmark designation from being attached to the property's lawn and gardens—apparently the largest single-family home backyard in the city. The heirs had no objection to the house on 2080 Washington Street being named a historical landmark, but putting similar status on the land below would prevent the Jackson Street side of the property from being developed into town homes or single-family residences, an option an owner might want to offset the purchase price or renovation.

That's precisely what the Trainas had in mind when they reportedly bid $12.8 million for the home, but the prospect of new construction fronting Jackson Street stirred the ire of neighbors and seventy homeowner's groups across the city. They rallied to the cry: "Save the Spreckels Slope!"

"People marvel as they walk by," neighbor Arthur Roth told the *Chronicle* in 1989. "It would be disgraceful. It would blot out the sky and ruin views of the house."

However, the Trainas launched a campaign of their own, explaining that they needed to sell the land to a developer to offset the restoration of the mansion itself, which was in need of roughly $2 million in interior and exterior work. That included transforming the inside of the home, which had been subdivided into three apartments, back into a single-family residence.

In June 1990 the San Francisco County Board of Supervisors and former Mayor Art Agnos voted to make the Spreckels mansion a city landmark.

That does not preclude development of the site, but any future changes will need to go through the Planning Commission and the city's Landmark Preservation Advisory Board.

Meanwhile, the Spreckels heirs fielded several offers from interested buyers and finally struck a deal with the Trainas. On October 10, 1990, they deeded a share of the property to John and Danielle, who subsequently moved into the house. Records show that the Trainas became tenants in common with four sugar heirs, including Dorothy Spreckels Munn, the daughter of the mansion's most famous occupants: sugar heir Adolph Spreckels and his flamboyant wife, Alma de Bretteville, the matriarch whose love of French grandeur inspired the design of the magnificent home, which now had been passed on to the French-inspired Danielle Steel Traina.

To close the deal, the Trainas borrowed $3 million from Wells Fargo bank and paid a total of $6,730,975, according to property tax and real-estate records. The assessee on the county tax roles is listed as John and Danielle Traina "etal/etc."

What county records do not show is how the Trainas and Spreckels heirs divided the property. Speculation in San Francisco real-estate circles is that the Trainas own the rights to the mansion while the sugar heirs hold the rights to the disputed land facing Jackson Street.

Nine months prior to the Spreckels purchase, the Trainas spent $1,390,000 for a piece of property at 2209 Jackson Street, around the corner from the Spreckels mansion. Two homes on the land contain twelve rooms and four bathrooms spread over 2,873 square feet. The house in the back is used for office space and guest rooms, but the tiny yellow house facing the street, with its tiny front yard surrounded by a white picket fence, serves as Danielle and John's getaway cottage. Calling it her "most outrageous luxury," Danielle told a reporter that the house was a place where she and her husband could spend time alone and create their own private hideaway.

"Sometimes we go there for twenty minutes just to have a cup of coffee. John calls it 'our yacht,'" Danielle told *McCall's* in 1991.

"I think these are fantasy fulfillments," agent Mort Janklow told *Women's Wear Daily* in 1986, though the remark seems apropos years later. "Except," he added, "that [Danielle] works so hard."

The hard work on the Spreckels interior began in earnest shortly after the Trainas purchased the property. The remodeling and renovation went on around the clock for more than six months, friends and real-estate sources said. So far, there have been no write-ups in magazines like *Architectural Digest* detailing the interior design, work Danielle apparently did without the help of a professional. Indeed almost nothing has been reported on the changes in the mansion since the Traina family moved in.

Much of what is known about the original interior of the home was published in *Big Alma*, the biography of Alma de Bretteville Spreckels written by San Francisco historian Bernice Scharlach. In her words, the 1913 Beaux Arts mansion was designed for "entertaining in grand style."

The tradition has continued under Danielle and John. During the 1993 pre-opera dinner in the spectacular City Hall rotunda, Trevor Traina surveyed the scene and said, "It's just like home, only smaller."

Trevor was kidding, of course, but not by much. When the mansion was built, the entrance was located in the center of the building facing out onto Washington Street. Visitors ascended a set of marble stairs and entered the "parlor floor." Facing north, they looked down a grand marble hallway of gold mosaics set in Italian stone that spanned the length of the house. It ended at the Pompeiian Court, a circular room at the north end of the mansion that contained a fountain and a ceiling decorated with cherubs and cupids. The view of the bay and the Golden Gate Bridge was spectacular from this vantage point. Guests now enter the main hall by elevator from the ground floor of the building, which is reached through a porte cochere that opens up onto a circular driveway on the east side of the property.

The first floor also includes the oval dining room, the oak-paneled library, a drawing room with an intricately molded ceiling and marble fireplace, and the living room, known as the Italian room, with its ornate coffered ceiling. But the most magnificent of all the first-floor rooms—the one possessing the grandeur of the City Hall rotunda—is the grand ballroom. Spanning the entire west side of the mansion, it has sixteen-foot-high ceilings, a marble floor, and a huge marble fireplace along the west wall in the center of the room—all the trappings of a European palace.

The second-floor living quarters include six bedrooms, six baths, a library, and a drawing room all connected by a grand hallway with marble floors and a Tiffany stained-glass ceiling. The third floor is a penthouse large enough for four rooms and three baths. On the roof, John and Danielle have set up a play area for the children. The ground floor contains the hotel-sized kitchen and offices for the secretarial staff, who work on word processors, a piece of technology that Danielle has no use for.

"A few Christmases ago John gave her a word processor, thinking it was a sensible gift for someone who writes, it seems, a novel a minute," old friend Charlie Flowers recalled. "She would have nothing to do with it. As we all said, 'If it ain't broke, don't fix it,' because what she prefers to do is write on her 1948 Olympia typewriter, which she calls 'Ollie.' "

When Danielle and John completed the renovation in 1991, they threw a housewarming party for fifty to seventy-five close friends and associates. Each guest received a party favor of a handcrafted chocolate miniature replica of the Spreckels mansion, neatly wrapped in cellophane and ribbon. San Francisco chocolatier Joseph Schmidt remembered the order well, describing it as his most difficult task to complete in his ten years in the chocolate business.

"I hate to bad-mouth a client, but I'll say she was extremely perfectionist and difficult to work for," said the Israeli-born chocolatier. "I'd have to think twice about working for her again."

The miniature houses, costing roughly fifteen dollars each and measuring five inches in diameter, weren't the problem. It was the ribbons they were wrapped in. Every time Schmidt sent over the order, Danielle's secretary called and said the ribbons were unacceptable—do it over. "She had different ideas and the order went back and fourth four or five times," said Schmidt. "She wanted satin ribbon and a lot of it, and we couldn't find it; it was always unacceptable. It was a big production over nothing."

After the fourth or fifth try, Schmidt sent Danielle a message along with the chocolate. "I told her if she didn't like it she could find someone else to do it. It was a small order with a big headache, but she's entitled to be a perfectionist."

Like the rest of her life, no detail is too small for Danielle to tend to, particularly when it comes to entertaining. For John's fifty-eighth birthday in 1989, guests were greeted at the Jackson Street home by white-gloved waiters pouring Cristal champagne as Danielle greeted her friends in a Bob Mackie black silk and velvet strapless gown with a train, "and diamonds twinkling everywhere," the Chronicle reported. John wore a Gianfranco Ferré tuxedo and emerald cufflinks from Tiffany. Guests filled seven tables of ten each, dined on caviar, and were entertained by two bands.

"She probably spent a hundred thousand on the party," a former employee recalled. "And then she probably spent another two hundred and fifty thousand on gifts—including antique cigarette cases, malachite furniture, clothing, artwork, and jewelry. And then he'd have to surprise her."

"Danielle's the engine and the director," said Katherine Dusay, an occasional dinner guest when the Trainas lived on Jackson Street. "The dining-room table could seat twenty and would be decorated with flowers and name cards, which were hand done. There would be boxes of chocolate and gifts on each plate. There would be servers and a special menu for the occasion."

The children's parties are also big productions. Neighbors say that Danielle and John often set up a huge tent on the Spreckels lawn and decorate with balloons and ribbons. "She'll bring in ponies, clowns, magicians, and face painters," said Dusay, who has a daughter and a son close in age to two of Danielle's children.

"When one of the children had a birthday, it was a major event," recalled a former employee. "We had to hire a full-time wrapper for a week straight. The birthday child would get a hundred and fifty presents, and all the other kids would get five presents each so they wouldn't feel bad."

These weren't small gifts either. Danielle was big on German-made Steiff ponies that retail for $1,100, bubble gum machines for $3,500, limited-edition dolls for $200, and motorized miniature cars for $5,000. Clerks at F.A.O. Schwarz, one of Danielle's favorite toy stores, say she showed up one day and purchased not one but two French-made life-size Jockline horses, which go for $5,000 and up. Danielle once reportedly bought eighteen Barbie dolls with custom-made, haute couture gowns and furs for daughter Zara's kindergarten graduation, at a price of nearly $20,000.

"The birthdays also included a catered party for thirty-five kids on top of that, and we put together goodie bags worth seventy five dollars each," the employee recalled. "She's quite excessive with the gifts and candy. It never seemed to be just one signature Barbie doll, but ten."

During one of Zara's birthday parties years ago, John was overheard saying to Danielle, "I think this is too much for a little girl."

But Danielle didn't agree. Every fall, another full-time employee was added to the lineup: Christmas gift wrapper. "During the holidays, this was a two-month-long position, and a very important position," Curtis said. "If you saw the number of gifts, you'd understand why."

Presents at holiday time would fill an entire apartment, Curtis recalled. And all the gifts had to be meticulously wrapped and color-coded for each child.

Then every few months or so, Danielle organized sweeps through the children's rooms to clear out the old toys. "I used to take the stuff to secondhand stores—and I always got a receipt for tax purposes," Curtis said. "Each load was about two hundred dollars and there were numerous loads throughout the year."

In June 1992, John and Danielle gave a party at the mansion for world-famous designer Gianfranco Ferré, who designed a gown for the house of Dior that Danielle wore to the 1992 opening of the San Francisco Opera. It was quite a show, one guest recalled. The young Traina daughters entered the dining room together all dressed in couture dresses, with their hair made up in French braids. "Then during the middle of the dinner, John toasted Gianfranco and announced that the designer had agreed to make Christmas dresses for all the Traina daughters," the guest said.

Designer couture dresses generally cost in the neighborhood of ten to twenty thousand dollars each.

Friends said that Danielle has always been one of the most generous people they've known, bestowing gifts ranging from Tiffany crystal to Paloma Picasso designer handbags to people in her inner circle. Over the years, John, the children, and her loyal cadre of nannies have been the biggest beneficiaries of her largess. Some of her nannies, friends said, have received furs and expensive pieces of jewelry. John is spoiled rotten on his birthday,

Christmas, and their wedding anniversary. On these occasions, he has reportedly received antique cars, sports cars, and recently a $145,000 Lamborghini four-wheel-drive LM002, which he later traded in for an easier-handling Range Rover.

At Danielle's disposal are department-store personal shoppers who have escorted her from floor to floor, pointing out new fashion lines and assisting her with purchases. Once at a neighborhood toy store in Pacific Heights, she swept through the shop collecting items for grab bags she was preparing for the annual plane ride to Mauna Kea, where the Trainas spend their Easter vacation. On her way out the door, she rattled off her credit-card number, leaving the toys behind for the family driver to pick up later. "She's always in a hurry," a clerk observed.

On another occasion, Danielle swept through a Pacific Heights kiddie shoe store with her three children and their nurses and bought twenty-four pairs of shoes, *Chronicle* columnist Herb Caen reported.

Danielle also shops by phone, working with specific salespeople who know her tastes. She even participates in overseas auctions by phone. In June 1993, during an auction from Geneva, Switzerland, she bid $750,000 on a diamond and emerald Panther bracelet, but returned it because she felt it was "too flashy." And when in doubt, the salespeople from her favorite shops and department stores—Tiffany, Hermès, Frank More shoes, Saks Fifth Avenue, and I. Magnin—will gladly pack up their wares and rush up to the mansion to show their latest jewelry, scarves, pumps, furs, and haute couture lines, apparently at all hours of the day and night. In 1994, Hermès even paid tribute to one of its biggest customers by introducing a large calfskin handbag called "The Danielle Steel Bag." The price: eight thousand dollars.

It was Curtis Browning's job to drive to all the stores Danielle visited and pick up the packages to bring back to the house. "She was out shopping four out of five days a week during the year I worked there," he said. "She'd put on jewels and a fur coat and leave, going out in her black Mercedes wagon."

Columnist Herb Caen wrote in 1990 that Danielle bought herself a customized sixteen-thousand-dollar desk designed in the shape of three of her favorite works: *Heartbeat*, *Daddy*, and *Star*. Earlier in the year, Caen had revealed that Danielle blazed through Ralph Davies's high-fashion boutique and spent $10,210, charging the clothes and accessories to American Express.

(Incidentally, American Express was the credit-card company Danielle's publisher and publicity team courted in vain to get the romance writer included in the firm's famous "Do You Know Me" campaign.)

However, Danielle needed no introduction to local merchants. "Danielle's a total shopoholic," a former employee recalled. "She had impeccable taste and money was no object." Not even her most ardent fans would recognize her when she's on the go. "She dressed very plain—jeans, a turtleneck, hair in a ponytail, no makeup. This allowed her to slip in and out of stores unobtrusively. She constantly collected things but never wore them. She had rooms full of dresses but walked around the house in jeans, T-shirts, and turtlenecks. She only went out when John wanted to, so she didn't dress up that often. She'd buy all these things—clothes, shoes, and bags—and end up giving it all away to Goodwill."

Jewelry is another passion of the writer's. When jeweler Nicola Bulgari came through town in 1991 to show a new line of baubles priced from three thousand to fifty thousand dollars, he was scheduled to give a dinner at Mason's Restaurant for his good friends. The woman who was penciled in to sit on his right was none other than Danielle, the *Chronicle* reported. The week before, Danielle had been seated next to Tiffany CEO William Chaney when he came to town to open a new store.

Back in 1986, when there was talk of boycotting diamond exports from South Africa, the U.S. government didn't get any support from Danielle.

"Danielle Steel Traina, who is one of the world's best jewelry customers, said, 'I don't think about diamonds coming from South Africa. They come from Tiffany,' " the *Chronicle* reported.

Danielle has seemed at odds with this part of her life, down playing her lifestyle whenever and wherever possible. She once told her publicist she didn't want to go on the TV show "Lifestyles of the Rich and Famous" because she didn't want to be portrayed as "rich." Another time, she told a reporter she had stopped doing interviews in her home because the writers tended to focus on the expensive paintings, "instead of seeing the applesauce dripping from my clothes. It makes you feel taken advantage of."

The vision she seemed most comfortable conveying is that of a homebody. "It takes an atom bomb to blast me out of the house," she once told *Cosmopolitan* magazine.

She was still singing the same anthem for a 1993 story published in the Scandinavian airline magazine *Scanorama*. This "glamorous Danielle Steel person doesn't exist," she said. "I'm sitting here in jeans and an old sweater, with my hair sticking up, waiting to drive my daughter to ballet class."

So perhaps there are many facets to Danielle Steel—the devoted mother and wife, the reluctant celebrity, the demanding manager, and the glamour queen who dazzles all on opening night at the opera and receives platinum-card treatment at shops across town.

"I met her in the mid-1970s, before she became famous," said Katherine Dusay, who has had only minimal contact with Danielle in recent years. "I knew her when she divorced Claude-Eric. I knew her when she was married to Bill. I don't think she has changed from the person I knew. I don't see her being arrogant. She's very natural and elegant and there's something down to earth about her."

As the years go by, observers of the San Francisco social scene say they have seen less and less of Danielle around town. Some acquaintances feel if she had her druthers, she'd rather move to Los Angeles or New York, where she could blend in more easily.

Some friends, though, feel Danielle is no different today from the woman of ten years ago. "She has never gone out a lot," said close friend Denise Hale. "She's very selective. She has her husband, her children, her work, and her friends; that's her life."

However, another acquaintance was always amazed by the attention Danielle received from her family and friends. "It was like a queen holding court," the friend said. "Everything was always focused around her. She would leave to go write, then take a break and come back into a room to open her mail. And everyone would stand around doting on her. There was a lot of hand-holding, fawning, people telling her she's great all the time. She's not at all secure. She wants approval, and I think that's the reason for all the presents she gives to friends. In a way, she buys people."

Pat Montandon disagreed. "She is one of the most generous people I know. And she never expected anything in return." Danielle's friend Charles Flowers also calls her generous. "She always makes you feel the center of attention whenever you're around her."

At the opening of the 1992 San Francisco opera season, Danielle stole the fashion show in her watercolor Dior silk gown with a nine-foot train. She wore the same dress to introduce the television movie based on her novel *Jewels*. A year later, she turned heads again at the opera opening in a black-and-white Chanel gown. While she routinely makes the unofficial best-dressed list for this major cultural event, the honor seems to obscure her absence from another closely watched list: the top of the donor list for the San Francisco Opera.

"She is not a devotee of the opera," said a San Francisco Opera spokesman. "She and her husband have been single-ticket buyers since 1984. They have made contributions over the years and they come to the openings, but they don't hold a season-ticket subscription. You need to contribute a minimum of five hundred dollars to get into the program, but in the 1992 program, their names appear nowhere on the list."

Marianne Welmers, the former assistant to the director of development for the opera, confirmed the spokesman's account. "The Trainas are not very generous contributors," she said.

She noted that serious opera devotees are "Series A" subscribers who dole out $1,585 per ticket for the nine operas and another additional contribution of at least $4,500. And the Trainas don't fall in that category, she said.

Danielle, however, did seek out and do a public-service radio spot for the National Committee for the Prevention of Child Abuse and the Advertising Council.

In early 1992 the media caught up with Danielle's secret past. The headlines roared: "Danielle Steel's Bank Robber Husband: Our Steamy Sex Sessions in Jail" read the January 7, 1992, edition of *Star* magazine. Its sister publication, the *National Enquirer*, had an equally compelling story the very same week: "New Danielle Steel Bombshell—She Divorced a Rapist to Marry Another Jailbird." "Hard Copy" and "Inside Edition" did their segments on the Danielle's secret past, and in June 1992, *People* magazine followed with its own story, calling the romance writer's marital history "Stranger Than Fiction."

Bill was paroled from San Quentin on April 24, 1987, but was back behind bars for a parole violation by the following February. He would spend the next three years in and out of prison until he was formally discharged on May 19, 1991. Today he lives in San Francisco, is newly remarried, and is still a recovering heroin addict. He was forty-eight on June 10, 1994. Nicholas and Dorothea Toth still make their home in Park Merced and have not seen their former grandson, Nicky, since November 1984.

Danny Zugelder, too, has been in prison since 1979 and does not come up for parole until 1998. He is serving his time in the Limon Correctional Facility in Limon, Colorado.

"I think probably the most distressing things in her life have been these trash TV and tabloid stories in the last couple of years, in large part because she fears the impact upon her children and their daily life," said Charles Flowers. "Tour buses stop outside their house in San Francisco now, trying to take photographs."

The war with the media was on. Since then Danielle has contended in court papers that she was stalked by reporters and cameramen, who have placed television cameras at their doors, climbed trees, hovered in helicopters as their children played on the roof, and pressed their cameras up against the family car windshields. Danielle also said she stopped doing the introductions to her NBC movies because it created "undue interest from the public."

In June 1992 Danielle claimed that *People* magazine was preparing a story on her and "reporters and photographers pursued my husband, children and me for two months, even following us as far as Hawaii and disrupting our vacation."

Jack Kelley, *People*'s Los Angeles Bureau Chief and senior editor, told a New York newspaper that Danielle's claims are "unequivocally false. I've checked our records, and we did not send a correspondent there or assign a stringer."

Writer Marc Meyers observed:

Danielle likes to hold the reins tight on her image, and the image she wants you have as a reader is that she is fabulously wealthy, incredibly glamorous, has a virile, successful husband, loves her kids and doesn't need this job writing. She wants you to believe she is really sweet and comes from an all-American background, although a hard Horatio Alger–type background. Those are the things that go into Danielle Steel and when you divert from that, when you tarnish that image, it's like setting up a hot-dog stand in Tiffany.

She's no longer that person who hooked up with a criminal; she is the successful, wonderful writer who has nine kids, and a wonderful husband. . . . I don't think she wants to hear from that other Danielle Steel; that person no longer exists. The Danielle Steel of today is someone who used to be somebody else. And she is spending the rest of her life trying to kill that person off.

Epilogue

Midway through her fifth decade of life, Danielle Steel appears to be ahead in the race.

She has battled through a lonely childhood, poor health, and three painful marriages to become what she always wanted to be: a wife, a mother, and a novelist with a flourishing career that helps pay for it all.

For her birthday in 1988, *San Francisco Chronicle* columnist Herb Caen said that Danielle's publisher, at her request, paid for a "supersized billboard" on Sunset Boulevard across from Spago, the exclusive Los Angeles restaurant. Along with her photo was the line that is her legacy: "America Reads Danielle Steel."

Her friends believe she deserves it all. Charles Flowers, a pal from her early days in New York, attributed Danielle's success as an author and as a person to her conviction. "In various ways," said Flowers, "[her books] do come from her own personal life and her own personal feelings, almost unfiltered, no matter where the stories take place. You can recognize the feelings Danielle has had about herself, family members, odd years of romantic love and odd years of having children. Those feelings she has had all her life and they infuse every book. That conviction, I think, is unmistakable to readers."

And perhaps therapeutic for Danielle as well. Her books, especially the more recent ones, appear to tackle her demons head on: fears of kidnapping, custody battles, and dealing with drug abuse. Even *Accident*, her latest book, taps into her fear of losing a child, and was reportedly inspired by the true-life story of a thirteen-year-old girl, a friend of Nicky's, who died after tragically being hit by a car. Danielle delivered a stirring eulogy at the girl's funeral.

"No one has ever held her hand and said, 'Let's do it.' At every major career step that has been advanced, it has been Danielle Steel," said Charles Flowers. "I have never resented her success at all. She earned it."

And, if success is measured in numbers, then Danielle is surely successful.

In the 1980s, publishers coined the word "megasellers" to delineate those authors whose hardcover books had sold somewhere in the seven-figure range—"numbers that in previous decades could be applied only to mass market paperbacks," explained *Publishers Weekly* in 1990. In a "decade of megasellers," Danielle was at the top. "Ten of the 13 million-copy novels [sold in the 1980s] were by three writers: Stephen King, Danielle Steel, and Tom Clancy," noted *Publishers Weekly*. *Daddy, Kaleidoscope, Zoya*, and *Star* had each sold over a million copies in hardcover.

If her 1992 hardcover sales are any indication, Danielle Steel should be topping the decade of the 1990s' megasellers list as well. *Publishers Weekly* researchers, who annually track book sales, show that Danielle had two million-plus best-sellers on its 1992 lists: *Jewels* and *Mixed Blessings*.

Seemingly a permanent member on both the *New York Times* and *Publishers Weekly* hardcover, trade paperback, and mass market best-seller lists, Danielle garnered "world's record status" in 1989 for having a book on the *New York Times* list for 381 consecutive weeks.

While Danielle's hardcover runs are around 1 million copies, her publisher prints from 2.5 to 3.5 million copies of her paperbacks for each book.

Danielle's series of children's books, launched in 1989, was so successful that *Adweek* said fifteen thousand additional copies of four of the six books were printed within a month after their first publication. Sherri Holt, associate marketing director for Delacorte's books for young readers, admitted to *Adweek* that the company's marketing strategy was to "sell the books to Danielle Steel readers."

In addition to her publishing empire, Danielle's deal with NBC reportedly earns her a fee in the mid-six-figure range every time one of her books is made into a television movie or miniseries. For example, *Kaleidoscope* and *Fine Things* had such high ratings (a combined viewing of 52 million) against "Monday Night Football" and the first game of the World Series, respectively, that the network used another of her books, *Changes*, up against the 1991 NCAA basketball finals. In that competition, Danielle was within two Nielsen rating points of what one reporter described as "outplaying the Duke Blue Devils."

Although no one but the Trainas and their accountants know exactly how much, Danielle Steel has assuredly forged a fortune from her writing. "They are making a fortune from her," Danielle's agent, Mort Janklow, said of Dell Publishing in a 1986 interview with *Women's Wear Daily*. Danielle's editor at Dell, Carole Baron, concurred: "She's supporting the house." Baron, however, indicated that "everyone's making money . . . including Mort Janklow."

"When I was there, she was making a million a month, and that was without the TV contract," said Curtis Browning, a former employee. "I saw the figures faxed from her publisher."

There is the occasional commercial flop, but for Danielle that simply means releasing a hardcover that stalls below the coveted number-one ranking on the fiction best-seller lists. In recent years, she has had only two books that stalled at number two: *Message from Nam* and *Vanished*.

Regardless, sources close to the novelist believe her advances now rival those of author Tom Clancy, who signed a deal in 1992 with his publisher, G. P. Putnam, Sons, to receive "between $13 million and $14 million" for his book *Without Remorse*. Clancy's was reportedly "the biggest deal ever for one book," but Steel cannot be far behind.

And this despite being an author who critics love to hate. Reviewing one of Danielle's books for *People* magazine in April 1989, Joanne Kaufman dubbed her "a Teflon novelist," because her books reach the best-seller lists even though "critics carp at her style, complain about her paper-thin characterizations, and laugh at her dumb plots.

"It doesn't matter," wrote Kaufman. "Steel's novels inexorably hit the best-seller list as if directed by lasers."

Through it all, Danielle has managed to plod ahead, seemingly undaunted by either the adversity or the odds.

As former friend and neighbor Dan Talbott concluded: "I would bet Danielle doesn't look at life as tough. I don't think her mind works that way. She looks forward to the happy ending, not where she has been. Look where she is now. Why would she want to remember the pain when she is living in the solution?"

Notes

The authors have made repeated attempts to interview Danielle Steel, the subject of this biography, and various close family members. Her attorney, Charles O. Morgan, Jr., has informed the authors through letters that neither Danielle Steel nor any of her family members want to talk with the authors.

Included below are references to the sources the authors used in writing each chapter. Not all-inclusive, it does, however, give an overview of the people who were interviewed, the documents that were obtained, and the publications that were utilized in researching material for this book. For detailed annotations on publications and books, please refer to the bibliography on page 291.

The authors wish to acknowledge and sincerely thank the individuals formally listed in what follows for their contributions to this work.

Chapter 1

Description comes from a composite of photographs taken of Danielle Steel over the past few years and printed in both magazine articles and newspapers. Figures on the number of books she has sold and the money she makes come from articles in *Entertainment Weekly*, *Woman's Day*, *Forbes*, *Publishers Weekly*, and industry sources.

Chapter 2

Records searched on the background of the Schuelein and Stone families include *New York Times* obituaries, immigration ship manifests, and, where possible, birth, marriage, and death certificates. (In New York, for example, laws prohibit anyone who is not a relative from obtaining documents on birth and death, and marriage certificates that are less than fifty years old.)

Information on Löwenbrau came from Wolfgang Rupprezht at the brewery in Munich, and from the book *Löwenbrau* by Wolfgang Berringer, which was translated by Tracy Emonds, a graduate student in German studies from the University of Colorado. Facts on Standard Brands came from editor Kathy Daley at the *Peekskill Herald* in Peekskill, New York. (The Peekskill facility closed in the mid-1970s.) Interviews with two key family members who wish to remain unnamed also served as the basis for some information.

Additional data on the Stone family came from interviews with Gil Stone's former assistant, Maria Theresa Braga, September 1993; Natalie Jordim Matinho, managing editor of *Luso Americano*, September 1993; and two longtime employees from the Portuguese embassy in Washington, D.C., who asked to remain anonymous, August 1993.

Most of Danielle's extended family is dead, including all of the Schuelein grandparents, granduncles and aunts, and her father, John Schuelein-Steel, and her maternal grandparents. We were unable to locate her mother, Norma, but Danielle's attorney made it clear that no family members wanted to speak with us.

Publication sources include the *Los Angeles Times* and *Cosmopolitan* and *Scene* magazine articles. The authors also read and analyzed all of Danielle Steel's novels to obtain comparisons between the books and her life. Books quoted in this chapter include *The Ring* and *Jewels*.

The authors were fortunate to have obtained 765 pages of personal correspondence written by Danielle Steel to her second husband, Danny Zugelder. While the authors did not quote from nor paraphrase those letters, they did serve throughout this book as corroboration of facts obtained from other sources. The authors followed the adage "When in doubt, leave it out."

Chapter 3

Publication sources include *Cosmopolitan*, *Scene*, *Women's Wear Daily*, *Woman's Day*, *People* magazines, and the *Los Angeles Times*. Also, excerpts are taken from Danielle Steel novels *Daddy*, *Loving*, and *Thurston House*, as well as her nonfiction book, *Having a Baby*, which was coauthored with six other women. Material on Colette came from *Contemporary Authors*.

Factual information about Lycée Francais was obtained from the president of the school in interviews during January 1993.

Similar information about Parsons School of Design came from interviews in September 1993 with former Dean of Admissions David Levy, who is now president and director of the Corcoran Museum of Art and School of Art in Washington, D.C., and Frank Rizzo, current chairman of Fashion Design for Parsons, who was a part-time teacher there in 1963. In that Danielle's schooling at Parsons lasted for only a short time and took place thirty years ago, neither the Dean of Admissions nor the then-chairman of Fashion Design or the current chairman remembered Danielle attending Parsons. Her actual attendance, however, was confirmed by admission records.

New York University provided the authors with confirmation of Danielle's attendance in December 1992.

Also, two family members, who asked not to be identified, provided information for this chapter, as did Danielle's second husband, Danny Zugelder. What Zugelder contributed was corroborated within the 765 pages of personal letters Danielle Steel wrote to him during the course of their relationship.

Chapter 4

Factual information about the Lazard family came from 104 newspaper articles in the *San Francisco Examiner* and *San Francisco Chronicle* over a period of more than two decades. Additional information came from a family member who wished to remain anonymous.

Other publications utilized included *People, Women's Wear Daily,* and *Ladies' Home Journal* magazines, as well as engagement and wedding notices in both the *Examiner* and the *Chronicle,* May 12, 1965, and September 27, 1965.

Claude-Eric Lazard would not return phone calls or respond to a certified letter sent to his home requesting an interview, so his side of the relationship between him and Danielle is unfortunately not included.

Interviews were provided by Charles Flowers, a friend of Danielle's from her days in New York, in April 1993; Danny Zugelder, Danielle's second husband (corroborated again by letters written by Danielle to him), in twenty-five hours of interviews from June 1992 to September 1993; Bill Toth, Danielle's third husband, in May 1993; Dorothea Toth, Bill's mother, in 1992; Mona Skager, who worked for Francis Ford Coppola and knew Danielle in the early 1970s, in December 1992; and by a friend of the family, who also asked not be identified.

Quotes were also taken from *Having a Baby,* and from her novels *The Ring, Crossings, Summer's End, Jewels,* and *Thurston House.*

Chapter 5

Books used in this chapter include *Having a Baby, Supergirls: The Autobiography of an Outrageous Business, Contemporary Authors,* and excerpts from Danielle Steel's novel *Going Home.*

Publications referred to include *Women's Wear Daily, Los Angeles Times, Associated Press,* and *San Francisco* magazine.

Extensive interviews were given by Genie Chipps-Henderson, April 1993; Jane James, September 1993; Claudia Jessup (written interview), April 1993; Fred R. Smith, September 1993; John Mack Carter, January 1993; and interviews (previously mentioned) with two ex-husbands, corroborated by personal letters (also previously mentioned).

Chapter 6

Danielle's extensive illnesses are corroborated by her second and third ex-husbands and mentioned throughout 765 pages of personal letters. Other taped interviews were conducted with Charles Flowers; Bruce Neckels, April

1993; Mark Dowie, December 1992; and Danny Zugelder, whose remarks are corroborated primarily by personal letters previously mentioned.

Publications used include San Francisco magazine and Ladies' Home Journal.

Chapter 7

Again, extensive taped interviews with Danny Zugelder, corroborated with the personal letters, as well as taped interviews with Dan Talbott, a former neighbor and friend, May 1993; Charles Flowers; Dr. Mimi Silbert, a founder of Delancey Street; Donna Monroe, Danny's stepsister, March and August 1993; Jarrie Monroe, Danny's brother-in-law, March 1993; and Sharlene Sweet, Danny's sister, March 1993.

Information about Lompoc Correctional Institution provided by Dennis Grossini, assistant to the warden at Lompoc, and Don Dunne, assistant Public Information Officer for the Bureau of Prisons in Washington, D.C.

The letter from psychiatrist Richard Komisaruk dated May 21, 1974, was part of Danny Zugelder's court file used for his sentencing hearing on June 6, 1974. (Written permission obtained from Zugelder to use his psychiatric reports, April 1993.)

Letter from Danielle Steel Lazard written to the San Francisco Probation Department on June 3, 1974, was part of Danny Zugelder's official court file used for his sentencing hearing on June 6, 1974.

Letter from Charles O. Morgan, Jr., was written to David N. Kaye on February 28, 1993, and was part of the official court record in a lawsuit by Nicholas Traina and John Traina against coauthor Lorenzo Benet and St. Martin's Press. (In that lawsuit, the Trainas asked for the return of a probation report that was given to Mr. Benet by Nicholas's father, Bill Toth. On January 13, 1994, the Superior Court of the State of California granted a summary judgment in favor of Mr. Benet and St. Martin's Press. In his decision, Judge William Cahill found that "[under] current Family Law Code S 7805, the parents can inspect the juvenile court probation office report. Those code sections place no restrictions on what a parent can do with the report, and therefore, those code sections are inapplicable to the press using the report after receiving the information from the parent."

Publications and books used in this chapter include the Los Angeles Times and quotes from Danielle Steel novels Going Home, Now and Forever, Palomino, and Passion's Promise.

Chapter 8

Interviews supplied for this segment come from Danny Zugelder; Dan Talbott; Primo Angeli, May 1993; Emmett Herrera, May 1993; Mark Dowie, and Donna Monroe.

Danielle Steel letter, June 3, 1974, to probation department mentioned in notes for Chapter 7.

Articles came from the *Rocky Mountain News* and from the *San Francisco Examiner*.

Chapter 9

Again, excerpts from Danielle Steel Lazard letter, June 3, 1974, that is part of court records.

Danny Zugelder's arrests are part of his police and prison records provided by the California Department of Corrections and the Colorado Department of Corrections.

Interviews with Danny Zugelder; Bruce Neckels; Emmett Herrera; Mark Dowie; Ann Dowie, freelance photographer, May 1993; Dan Talbott; and Carol Parker, former director of Connections, August 1993.

Danielle's book *Full Circle* is also quoted.

Chapter 10

Interviews with Danny Zugelder; Emmett Herrera; and Kathy G., victim of rape, August 1993; Donna Taborsky, medical manager for Walden House, October 1993; and Warren Peterson, executive vice-president of Grey Advertising in San Francisco, October 1993.

Newspaper articles from the *San Francisco Examiner* and the *San Francisco Chronicle* on Samuel Edelman murder.

Court records used include transcripts from the preliminary hearing in San Francisco Municipal Court, February 26, 1974, for rape charges; preliminary Hearing in San Francisco Municipal Court, March 27, 1974, and April 11, 1974, for assault charges; pretrial motions, April–May 1974; and Danny Zugelder police records provided by the California Department of Corrections.

Letters from court documents include one from Danielle Steel Lazard, written June 3, 1974, and one from Joan Patricia Tuttle, Danielle's neighbor and friend, who confirmed pregnancy and miscarriage in May 20, 1974, letter to probation department, which is also part of court file for Danny Zugelder's sentencing hearing.

Letter from Charles O. Morgan, Jr., February 26, 1993, is also used again (documentation provided in other notes).

Excerpts from Danielle Steel's *Now and Forever* are included as well.

Chapter 11

Letters, which are part of court documents for Danny Zugelder's sentencing hearing, were sent by persons mentioned on pages 96 and 97, and dated May–June 1974.

Psychiatric reports on Danny Zugelder are part of Danny Zugelder's court file for the sentencing hearing. Permission to use the reports granted in writing by Danny Zugelder on April 14, 1993.

Transcripts from Danny Zugelder's sentencing hearings on May 29, 1974, and June 6, 1974, were also used.

Interviews included those with Danny Zugelder, Dan Talbott, and Mark Dowie.

Publications included the *San Francisco Chronicle* and *Scene* magazine.

Books quoted: *Passion's Promise* and *Now and Forever*.

Chapter 12

Description of Danny and Danielle's prison wedding comes from photographs and from interview with Danny Zugelder. Confirmation of wedding comes from marriage license, obtained by parties in the County of Solano on August 18, 1975. The wedding actually took place on September 13, 1975, and was witnessed by Reno attorney J. Stephen Peek and Joan Patricia Tuttle.

Public notice of wedding was made in the *San Francisco Examiner*, October 23, 1975.

Information about the California Medical Facility at Vacaville came from the California Department of Corrections operations manual and other information provided by Lt. Scott Kernan, administrative assistant at the California Medical Facility at Vacaville in September of 1993.

Divorce records, which are part of the Superior Court of California court records, include: Petition (Marriage), October 3, 1977; Summons (Marriage) November 14, 1977; Request and Declarations of Default (Marriage), November 14, 1977; Financial Declaration, November 14, 1977; Interlocutory Judgment of Dissolution of Marriage, November 30, 1977; Notice of Entry of Judgment (Marriage), April 14, 1978; Dissolution, April 14, 1978; and Physical Restraining Order, April 4, 1979.

Interviews were provided by Danny Zugelder, Anne Dowie, Emmett Herrera, Mark Dowie, Dan Talbott, Donna Monroe, Sharlene Sweet, and Katherine Conley, former student at University High, September 1993.

Books and publications quoted include *Passion's Promise, Now and Forever, Season of Passion,* and *Having a Baby*.

Chapter 13

Factual information about the Delancey Street Foundation comes from articles found in the archives of the *San Francisco Examiner* and the *San Francisco Chronicle*. Additional articles and documents were provided by the Delancey Street Foundation.

Brief excerpts appear in this chapter from Danielle Steel's 1981 book of poems, *Love*.

Information on Bill Toth's criminal background provided by court documents on file with the San Francisco County Superior Court. Details on Paul Drymalski's lawsuit against Danielle Steel come from records on file with San Francisco County Superior Court. Factual information on Danielle's former home at 1025 Green Street obtained from San Francisco County property records on file in the Recorder and Tax Assessor's office. Information was also made available from real-estate property profiles.

Additional sources include records of the Danielle Steel–Bill Toth divorce and custody dispute. Those records are on file, but under seal, with the San Francisco County Superior Court and California Court of Appeal. However, Bill Toth, a party in all these proceedings, made the records in his possession available for the research of this book for the purposes of accuracy and fairness, and to substantiate and corroborate his recollection of the events. The records referred to in this section included Respondent's Reply Brief, July 18, 1986; Deposition of Bill Toth, January 27, 1985; Deposition of Danielle Steel Traina, June 11, 1984.

Interviews include Mark Dowie, Mimi Silbert, Bill Toth, Nicholas Toth, Dorothea Toth, Al Wilsey, Danny Zugelder, and a friend of Bill's and Danielle's who has asked to remain anonymous.

Chapter 14

Factual information on Bill Toth's criminal record obtained from court documents on file with San Francisco Superior Court and Municipal Court. Details from July 17, 1973, burglary on Cole Street taken from an August 2, 1973, preliminary hearing (case #86452) in San Francisco Municipal Court, Judge Samuel Yee presiding.

Psychological evaluations of Bill Toth by court-appointed medical examiners Jay Dee Wark, M.D., and John P. Glathe, M.D., were performed in December 1973.

Interviews include Bill Toth, Dorothea Toth, Nicholas Toth, Stephen Northrop, and Gerry Shannon.

Chapter 15

Danielle's quotes on her work habits from the book *The Complete Guide to Writing Fiction*. Danielle's views on Bill's disappearances from a February 26, 1993, letter from her attorney, Charles O. Morgan, Jr.

Danielle's other views and comments about Bill were obtained from her July 18, 1986, Respondent's Reply Brief on file with the California Court of Appeal. The material covered in those documents included Bill's contracting hepatitis; Danielle's learning for the first time that Bill went to prison;

Danielle's driving Bill to a drug treatment center; Danielle's being pressured to marry Bill; Bill's using drugs on their wedding day; marital problems with Bill; the hospital check-writing incident; Bill's behavior after Nicky's birth; Bill's admittance to Mount Zion Hospital for drug therapy.

Danielle's remarks on the March 20, 1978, car accident involving Bill were from Danielle's June 11, 1984, deposition taken in preparation for a pending trial over visitation privileges between Bill and Nicky.

Danielle statements on Lamaze, references to marital problems with Bill, missing out on Beatie's birth, and details of the cesarean birth of Nicky and aftermath are excerpted from *Having a Baby*.

The other Danielle Steel book referred to in this chapter is *The Promise*.

Interviews include Bill Toth, Dorothea Toth, Nicholas Toth, Gary Michael White, Dede Wilsey, and two acquaintances of Bill and Danielle's who requested anonymity. Isabella Grant declined to be interviewed.

Chapter 16

Interviews include Michael Alexander, Mark Dowie, Stephen Northrop, Gerry Shannon, Bill Toth, Dorothea Toth, Romelia Van Camp, Danny Zugelder, and several former acquaintances of Bill and Danielle who asked to remain anonymous. Roger Ressmeyer declined to be interviewed.

Danielle's views on the need to hire a baby nurse and Bill Toth's absence during the marriage taken from February 26, 1993, letter from attorney Charles O. Morgan, Jr.

Danielle's comments regarding 1979 *People* story, Bill's potentially violent nature, Danny Zugelder, and Bill's admittance to Gladman Hospital taken from her June 11, 1984, deposition.

Publications include *People* magazine and the *San Francisco Examiner*.

Danielle's views regarding missing out on Beatie's birth and Nicky's being a happy, healthy baby excerpted from *Having a Baby*.

Dates concerning the delivery of manuscripts and the publication dates for Danielle's novels provided by Phyllis Westberg.

Steel books analyzed and excerpted in this chapter are *Summer's End* and *Season of Passion*.

Some of Dorothea Toth's remarks about Danielle and Norma Stone are corroborated by letters from the author and her mother.

Chapter 17

Factual information on Ted Golas obtained from Screen Actors Guild, a Tylenol ad published in *People* magazine, the U.S. Marine Corps, the *San Francisco Chronicle*, and divorce records on file in San Mateo County Court.

Danielle's statements regarding *The Ring* dedication and visits between Nicky and the senior Toths were taken from a June 11, 1984, deposition.

Her comments on Bill's 1979 hospitalization, the Easter incident, and Bill's alleged threats against Danielle's lawyer taken from her 1986 Respondent's Reply Brief.

The author's statements on Bill's drug problems taken from a September 4, 1980, declaration in relation to her divorce action on file in Superior Court. Attorney David Stone's references to Danielle's celebrity and Bill's drug use were taken from his September 5, 1980, declaration in a motion to obtain a sealing order on the court file. These documents were also provided by Bill Toth, a party in the proceeding.

Books analyzed and excerpted include *The Ring* and *Palomino*.

Publications include the *San Francisco Chronicle*, the *San Francisco Examiner*, and *The New York Times*. Details from Danielle's 1979 disco party from an *Examiner* society column by Pat Montandon.

Danielle's views on the extent of her society life and Bill Toth's level of involvement from attorney Charles O. Morgan, Jr.'s, February 26, 1993, letter.

Interviews include Sally Braunitzer, Thaddeus S. Golas, Charles Flowers, Kristine Mallory, Bill Toth, Dorothea Toth, Ray Walters, Al Wilsey, and Dede Wilsey.

Despite numerous requests, Thaddeus (Ted) Anthony Golas, declined to be interviewed, explaining that he was asked by Danielle not to speak to the authors of this book.

Several of Thaddeus's relatives and a former wife also declined to be interviewed.

Chapter 18

Danielle's statements regarding kidnapping threats, her fear of Bill Toth, the need for bodyguards and details from the January 1981 meeting with Dr. Neril are taken from the author's depositions given on June 8, 1984, and June 11, 1984.

Bill Toth's fall 1981 letter to Judge Donald B. King provided his views on such issues as supervised drug testing and visitation. Other details from this period were contained in court declarations by Carroll Collins dated July 22, 1981 and January 9, 1985. The documents were provided by Toth.

Dr. Neril's comments on the Steel-Toth visitation dispute were taken from Bill Toth's Appellant Opening Brief on file with the Court of Appeal, and Neril's January 27, 1981, evaluation of the Toth family for San Francisco County Superior Court.

Books analyzed and excerpted include *To Love Again*, *Vanished*, and *Remembrance*.

Publications include the *San Francisco Chronicle*, the *San Francisco Examiner*, and *Woman's Day*.

Some of Danielle's views on her divorce settlement with Bill and his subsequent "threats" and financial demands were contained in Charles O. Morgan, Jr.'s, February 26, 1993, letter.

The November 16, 1981, "quit claim" real-estate transaction between Danielle and John Traina is on file with the San Francisco County Recorder.

Other information on Danielle's property at 1025 Green Street and the Trainas' 2510 Jackson Street home is on file in the San Francisco County Tax Assessor and Recorder offices. Additional information also obtained from real-estate property profiles. John and Dede Traina's divorce papers are on file with San Francisco County Superior Court.

Interviews include Carroll Collins, Thaddeus S. Golas, Kristine Mallory, Bill Toth, Dr. Thomas Russell, Dede Wilsey, and a former publicist for Danielle Steel who asked to remain anonymous.

Jeanne Ames declined to be interviewed, and Dr. Morton Neril did not return calls from the authors.

Chapter 19

Details of John and Danielle Traina's wedding from columns by the *San Francisco Chronicle*'s Pat Steger and the *San Francisco Examiner*'s Pat Montandon.

Books include *Having a Baby* and *Once in a Lifetime*. Steel's views on whether to have children with John Traina and buying the puppy from *Having a Baby*.

Details on the Traina family history were compiled from 110 articles and documents from the archives of the *San Francisco Examiner*, the *San Francisco Chronicle*, and the San Francisco Public Library. Special assistance was provided by the *Chronicle*'s Chief Librarian, Richard Geiger, and the *Examiner*'s Chief Librarian, Judy Canter. Special articles on the Italian relocation during World War II included Geoffrey Dunn's "Male Notte," published in *Santa Cruz* magazine in February 1992. Additional information was gathered from an unpublished manuscript titled "Gentleman of Napa Valley" by Glenn Plaskin.

Publications include the *Los Angeles Times*, *People* magazine, the *San Francisco Chronicle*, the *San Francisco Examiner*, *Scene* magazine, and *Woman's Day*.

Interviews include Pat Montandon, Bill Toth, Al Wilsey, and Dede Wilsey. Several family members related to John Traina, Jr., declined interview requests.

Chapter 20

Danielle Steel's views on marriage, children, pregnancy, family problems, and a near miscarriage were excerpted from *Having a Baby*. Steel's *Changes* was analyzed and excerpted. Danielle's remarks on the length of time it takes her to write a book were from her June 8, 1984, deposition taken for her dissolution proceeding with Bill Toth.

Information about Bill's September 4, 1981, arrest at Macy's department store from a report prepared by the Palo Alto Police Department.

Details of Bill Toth's December 3, 1981, arrest from interviews with Bill Toth, Carroll Collins, Noel Marcovecchio, and from court documents, including transcript of a December 17, 1981, hearing before Superior Court Judge King; deposition of Dorothea Toth, March 11, 1985; deposition of Bill Toth, January 29, 1985; deposition of Danielle Steel, June 8, 1984. Danielle's remarks about her use of private investigators from her June 8, 1984, deposition.

According to documents provided by Bill Toth, the San Francisco Police Internal Affairs office investigated Bill's allegations but found no evidence of wrongdoing by its officers.

Information on Bill's methadone intake on December 3, 1981, was corroborated by a December 21, 1981, letter from the medical director of the Bayview-Hunters Drug Treatment Center. These documents were provided by Bill Toth.

Publications include *Current Biography*, *Scene* magazine, the *San Francisco Chronicle*, the *San Francisco Examiner*, and *Woman's Day*.

Interviews include Carroll Collins, Appellate Judge Donald B. King, Michael Lee, Noel Marcovecchio, Pat Montandon, Dorothea Toth, Bill Toth, and Dede Wilsey.

Interview requests were refused by Suzie Thorn and Justine Riskind. Kevin Gochet did not return calls from the authors.

Chapter 21

John Traina's views on his custody dispute with Dede Wilsey taken from divorce documents on file with San Francisco Superior Court.

Danielle Steel's views on weight gain, smoking, going into premature labor, experiences leading up the April 14 birth of Samantha Traina, son Nicky's fears about his mother giving birth, and the Trainas' sex life after the birth were excerpted from *Having a Baby*. Danielle's statements about remodeling the Jackson Street home were excerpted from *Architectural Digest*.

The news of the omission of John and Danielle Traina from the 1982 *Social Register* appeared in a column by the *San Francisco Chronicle*'s Pat Steger. The authors reviewed every register published since 1982 and found no mention of John or Danielle.

Information on Danielle's resistance to allowing Bill phone access to Nicky and her objections to Bill taking Nicky outdoors during visits were documented in a July 20, 1982, letter from attorney Suzie Thorn to Family

Court Services Director Jeanne Ames. In the letter, Thorn objected to Bill Toth's calling her client's son because of Bill's history of harassing Danielle Steel and because Nicky did not like talking on the phone.

Danielle's depositions taken on June 8 and 11, 1984, described the following: her displeasure on Bill's March 25, 1982, visit to son Nicky's nursery school; her objections to Bill sharing food with Nicky; her concerns over Bill and Nicky's last visit before Bill went to prison.

Other facts surrounding the March 25 incident drawn from interviews with Bill Toth and relevant letters and court documents, including a March 29, 1982, declaration from Steel attorney Pamela Pierson and February 1983 letters to the court from attorneys Collins and Thorn. All documents were provided by Bill Toth.

Information on Bill's May 13, 1982, arrest for receiving stolen property taken from June 23, 1982, preliminary hearing transcript on file in San Francisco Municipal Court. Bill's statement about wanting to see his son from a September 3, 1982, transcript of hearing in Santa Clara County Superior Court. Other information regarding Bill's convictions from a December 15, 1982, transcript of sentencing hearing in San Francisco Superior Court.

Details of Bill's September 8, 1982, visit with Nicky come from interviews with Bill and observations by Dr. Neril in his psychiatric reevaluation of the Toth family, which was submitted to the court on September 22, 1982. The report was submitted to Judge Donald King and later became part of the court file for a subsequent termination-of-parental-rights proceeding between Bill and Danielle.

Bill's September 23 letter to Beatie Lazard provided by Bill Toth. Interviews with Carroll Collins, Bill Toth, and Dorothea Toth were conducted for this section. Relevant documents include Bill's letter, currently on file in San Francisco Superior Court as part of the Toth dissolution proceeding. Information about the October 1, 1982, phone conversation between Danielle Steel and Dorothea Toth taken from notes written the same day by Dorothea. Much of the information there is corroborated by an October 1, 1982, letter from Danielle Steel to Dorothea Toth, and an October 7, 1982, letter from Dorothea Toth to Carroll Collins.

Danielle's views on Bill's letter to Beatie taken from June 11, 1984, deposition. Other relevant documents used for this section include a November 9, 1982, declaration by Suzie Thorn, a November 5, 1982, declaration by Danielle Steel Traina, a December 1, 1982, declaration by Beatrix Lazard, and a December 28, 1982, restraining order signed by Donald King.

Publications include *Architectural Digest*, the *San Francisco Chronicle*, the *San Francisco Examiner*, and *Woman's Day*.

Interviews include Carroll Collins, Katherine Dusay, Bill Toth, Dorothea Toth, and Dede Wilsey.

Chapter 22

Danielle's comments on miscarriage and the aftermath excerpted from *Having a Baby*.

The assessed value and the annual tax bill for the Spreckels mansion at 2080 Washington Street is on file with San Francisco County Tax Assessor's office.

Information on the dismissal of heroin-possession charges against Bill Toth stemming from his December 3, 1981, arrest was taken from a transcript of a March 9 hearing in San Francisco Municipal Court, Judge Francis Hart presiding.

A March 16, 1983, letter from public defender Noel Marcovecchio to Bill reported the presence of a private investigator at the March 9 dismissal hearing. Both Marcovecchio and Assistant District Attorney George Beckwith confirmed that private investigators hired by Danielle Steel were present in the courtroom for all hearings related to Toth's December 3, 1981, arrest. Court records show that in May 1982, Marcovecchio attempted to subpoena the private investigator to testify, but his attorney quashed the subpoena. Analyzing the relevant documents, Marcovecchio recalled that his subpoena was quashed because the investigator claimed "privilege" and Marcovecchio failed to disclose his reasons for the subpoena.

John and Danielle Traina's property holdings are on file with San Francisco County and Napa County Recorder and Tax Assessor. The estimated value of $12.6 million was calculated on six individual pieces of property in both counties. All figures based on tax assessor records of current assessed values, except for 2510 Jackson Street. For this property we attached a value of $2.95 million, the published September 1993 asking price.

John Traina's salary range at Pearl Cruises was provided by Erling Stangebye. Though Danielle's income is unknown, Toth's divorce attorney, Carroll Collins, estimated in court papers that it was in the $1 million range at the time of her divorce from Toth.

The Stanford University office of the Registrar provided verification of John Traina's degree and attendance status.

John Traina's remarks on the shipping industry were excerpted from an unpublished interview written by Glenn Plaskin. The "Dear Friends" letter for Waldenbooks was reprinted from the January 1983 issue of *San Francisco* magazine. Many details on the 1983 "Love Boat" cruise come from a July 13, 1983, story in the *San Francisco Chronicle*.

Steel's *Crossings* is analyzed and excerpted. Publications include *Progress-Bulletin* (Pomona, California), the *San Francisco Chronicle*, the *San Francisco*

Examiner, San Francisco magazine, *Scanorama, Scene* magazine, *TravelAge West,* and *Woman's Day.*

Interviews include Richard Bank, Dwight Chapin, George Beckwith, John Bell, Robert Carlsson, Pat Holt, Ann Kaar, Noel Marcovecchio, Erling Stangebye, Bill Toth, Peter Weitemeyer, and Dede Wilsey.

Chapter 23

Information on Mort Janklow's relationship with Hollywood from a September 1985 profile on Janklow in *American Lawyer* and an April 1985 column by writer Liz Smith. Information on the death of Lea Castellini Traina from published obituaries in the *San Francisco Chronicle* and the *San Francisco Examiner.*

Details on Bill's visits with Nicky taken from interviews with Bill and observations by Dr. Neril in his November 28, 1983, evaluation submitted to Jeanne Ames, Director of Family Court Services. Information on the birth of Victoria Lea Tobie Traina from newspaper accounts and *Having a Baby.*

Some of the facts surrounding Bill's refusal to submit to urinalysis on the night of October 10, 1983, were taken from interviews with Bill and his attorney, Carroll Collins. Additional documents provided further details, including Respondent Minor's Brief, on file with California Court of Appeals; deposition of Bill Toth, January 29, 1985; transcript from October 13, 1983, Superior Court hearing, Superior Court Judge Robert W. Merrill presiding. Some details concerning the delay of the visitation trial taken from a transcript of an October 25, 1983, Superior Court hearing, Superior Court Judge Donald Constine presiding.

Facts concerning communication between attorneys Collins and Chris Emley regarding visits in early 1984 taken from Appellant's Opening Brief, on file in State Court of Appeal.

Danielle's June 8, 1984, deposition provided details of the following: Danielle and Nicky's conversation regarding Bill's drug use; Nicky's May 31, 1984, visit with Bill and the aftermath; Bill and Nicky's relationship.

The April 9, 1984, letter to Jeanne Ames from Bill provided by Toth. Details of Bill and Nicky's last visit together taken from interviews with Bill and observations recorded by Dr. Neril in an August 6, 1984, evaluation prepared for Jeanne Ames. This report, along with all of Neril's reports, later became part of the court file in the termination proceeding.

Results of Bill Toth's May 30, 1984, urinalysis taken from testimony by James Wright, which was published in Respondent Minor's Brief on file with California Court of Appeal.

Many of the details of life at the Traina home in the Napa Valley were excerpted from Glenn Plaskin's unpublished manuscript. Danielle's views on the remodeling the family's Napa Valley home from a June 1986 article in *Architectural Digest*.

Bill's September 30, 1984, letter to Carroll Collins provided by Toth.

The conversation between Bill and attorney Chris Emley about Bill's failure to secure a visit with Nicky during the summer of 1984 excerpted from Bill's January 29, 1985, deposition.

The information about Carroll Collins learning on November 15, 1984, that Danielle had filed a petition in San Francisco County Juvenile Court to sever Bill's parental rights came from Collins's January 9, 1985, declaration for the pending termination-of-parental-rights proceeding.

Details on Danielle's denying visits between Nicky and the senior Toths after the author filed her juvenile court action was excerpted from Dorothea Toth's March 11, 1985, deposition.

A review of early and current editions of Danielle's novels show that Bill Toth's name has been expunged from the dedications.

Steel books analyzed and excerpted include *Secrets* and *Palomino*. Publications include *American Lawyer*, *Architectural Digest*, the *Los Angeles Times*, the *Progress-Bulletin*, the *San Francisco Chronicle*, and the *San Francisco Examiner*.

Danielle's views on her income came from Charles O. Morgan, Jr.'s, February 26, 1993, letter. Information on Danielle's estimated royalty income for 1983 came from a January 1983 article in *San Francisco* magazine.

Interviews include Carroll Collins, Retired Superior Court Judge Donald Constine, Judge Donald B. King, Glenn Plaskin, Mona Skager, Bill Toth, and Dorothea Toth.

Reached in her office, Dell Publishing executive Carole Baron said she didn't have time to talk. Literary agent Phyllis Westberg declined comment for this section of the book. Mort Janklow did not return calls from the authors. Jeanne Ames also declined comment.

Chapter 24

On March 16, 1993, coauthor Lorenzo Benet, using common reporting practices, requested an interview from Juvenile Court Probation Officer Dennis Sweeney. Sweeney acknowledged the existence of the case and the probation report prepared by his office, but said he could not consent to an interview unless he had the permission of both parties, Danielle Steel and Bill Toth. Sweeney asked if coauthor Benet had the probation report in his possession. When Benet informed Sweeney that he had the report, Sweeney said Benet could go ahead and quote from it. On March 18, 1993, coauthor Benet received a phone call from Danielle Steel's attorney Chris Emley, demanding that he return the report, destroy it, or give it back to the person who gave it to him. On May 13, 1993, Nicholas Traina sued Benet, St. Martin's Press, and Time Inc. in Superior Court for possessing a copy of the probation report.

The information alleging that Bill Toth threatened or endangered Nicky Traina's life was contained in Charles O. Morgan Jr.'s, February 26, 1993, letter.

Books analyzed and excerpted include *Family Album* and *Fine Things*. Publications included the *Progress-Bulletin* and the *San Francisco Chronicle*.

The information that John Traina filed to adopt Nicky on March 29, 1985, was later contained in the April 29, 1985, Juvenile Probation Report.

The thirteen first-class seats purchased by the Traina family and their entourage for their Easter vacation was reported in an April 11, 1985, edition of the *San Francisco Chronicle*. Under state law, the Juvenile Court Probation Department is required to prepare a report for the court in all termination-of-parental-rights proceedings. For the Toth-Steel termination case, the investigating officer was Cathie Clark. Portions of her report are contained in this chapter.

Information on Danielle's arriving at court with her husband and a body-guard was gathered from interviews with Bill Toth and confirmed by other sources who asked to remain unidentified.

All trial testimony was taken from court papers filed in the California Court of Appeals. The documents include: May 23, 1986, Appellant's Opening Brief filed by Bill Toth's attorney; July 18, 1986, Respondent's Reply Brief filed by Danielle Steel's attorney; and the Respondent Minor's Brief, filed by Nicky Toth's attorney; Documents were provided by Bill Toth, a party in the proceedings.

John Sikorski's testimony compiled from Respondent Minor's Brief, Respondent Reply Brief, and the Appellant's Opening Brief.

Danielle Steel's testimony compiled from Respondent Minor's Brief and Respondent Reply Brief. Testimony by police officers from Respondent Minor's Brief. Bill Toth's testimony taken from Respondent Minor's Brief and Appellant's Opening Brief. Cathie Clark's testimony taken from respondent Minor's Brief and Appellant's Opening Brief.

Dr. Morton Neril's and Dr. Henry Massie's testimony taken from Respondent Minor's Brief, Respondent's Reply Brief, and the Appellant's Opening Brief.

The social activities of Danielle and John Traina immediately following the termination trial were documented in the *San Francisco Chronicle*.

Excerpts from Judge Francis Mayer's ruling on the termination proceeding from the Respondent's Reply Brief, Respondent Minor's Brief, and the January 18, 1987, decision from the California Court of Appeal, First Appellate District, Division Two.

Details from Bill's July 17, 1985, burglary arrest and subsequent conviction from court files and the transcript of an August 12, 1985, preliminary hearing on file in San Francisco Municipal Court.

Interviews included Bill Toth and sources who asked to remain anonymous.

Chapter 25

The discrepancy in reporting John Traina's age was noted in birth certificates obtained on each of the Traina children.

John Traina's statement regarding the secrecy of Nicky Toth's origin came from an August 11, 1993, declaration by John Traina on file in San Francisco Superior Court. It is part of a lawsuit Nicky Traina filed against coauthor Benet and St. Martin's Press.

Information on the number of Steel books in print comes from a Dell Publishing press release provided by a reporter who recently profiled Danielle Steel.

Details on the sale of the Spreckels mansion were culled from newspaper stories, real-estate sources, and public records on file with the San Francisco County Recorder and Tax Assessor's office. Specific documents include the Trainas' 1992 tax bill and the October 10, 1990, grant deed that was signed by the Spreckels' heirs and the Trainas, and standard real-estate property profiles. Information on other properties owned by Danielle and John Traina came from real-estate property profiles and records on file with the San Francisco County Recorder and Tax Assessor's offices.

Much of the information on the interior of the Spreckels mansion is documented in *Big Alma*, the biography of Alma de Bretteville Spreckels, written by San Francisco historian Bernice Scharlach. Additional details came from a Spreckels mansion sales brochure published in 1989.

Trevor Traina's remarks comparing the City Hall rotunda to home appeared in a September 13, 1993, column by columnist Herb Caen.

In gathering information about Danielle's shopping habits, coauthor Benet went to more than a dozen stores and shops frequented by the author and interviewed salespeople at the stores who have waited on Danielle Steel or who had intimate knowledge of her shopping habits. Many of these people preferred to remain anonymous, but their comments about Steel's preference for phone shopping and having clothes shown to her in person were corroborated by statements Danielle has made herself to the media over the years.

Danielle Steel's statements on being harassed by the media taken from a November 25, 1992, declaration on file in San Francisco Superior Court. The declaration was made in support of a motion to prevent a videotaped deposition in a lawsuit brought by her former secretary, Kathleen Mahaney.

Interviews include Curtis and Anna Browning, Katherine Dusay, Denise Hale, Charles Flowers, Peter Lefcourt, Marc Meyers, Pat Montandon, Arthur Roth, Joseph Schmidt, Fred R. Smith, Bill Toth, Dorothea Toth, Marianne Welmers, Jane-Howard Hammerstein, and several sources who asked to remain anonymous.

Steel's *Having a Baby* was analyzed and excerpted. Publications include *Cosmopolitan*, *Family Circle*, the *Los Angeles Times*, *McCall's*, the *National Enquirer*, the *New York Observer*, *People* magazine, the *San Francisco Chronicle*, the *San Francisco Examiner*, *San Francisco* magazine, *Scanorama*, *Star* magazine, and *Women's Wear Daily*.

The authors of this book interviewed three former publicists who previously worked on the Danielle Steel account. They were able to corroborate much of their information with internal memos and documents.

Epilogue

Quotes in this section were taken from interviews with Curtis Browning, Charles Flowers, and Dan Talbott.

Data about Danielle Steel's book sales came from *Publishers Weekly* and *The New York Times*. Other information on publisher prints and sales come from *Forbes* and sources within the industry who didn't wish to be identified.

Publications quoted include *Adweek*, *Women's Wear Daily*, *Entertainment Weekly*, *People* magazine, the *Wall Street Journal*, and the *San Francisco Chronicle*.

Bibliography

Books

Altner, Pat. "Steel, Danielle." In *Twentieth Century Romance and Historical Writers*. 2d ed. Edited by Lesley Henderson. Chicago: St. James Press, 1990.

Behringer, Wolfgang. *Löwenbräu: Von den Anfängen des Münchner Brauwesens bis zur Gegenwart*. Germany: South Germany Publishing House, 1991.

Bert, Diana, Katherine Dusay, Averil Haydock, Susan Keel, Mary Oei, Danielle Steel Traina, and Jan Yanehiro. *Having a Baby*. New York: Dell Publishing Co., Inc., 1984.

Bert, Diana, Katherine Dusay, Susan Keel, Mary Oei, and foreword by Danielle Steel. *After Having a Baby*. New York: Dell Publishing Co., Inc., 1988.

Conrad, Barnaby. *Complete Guide to Writing Fiction*. Cincinnati: Writer's Digest Books, 1990.

Falk, Katherine. *Love's Leading Ladies*. New York: Pinnacle Books, 1982.

Jessup, Claudia, and Genie Chipps. *Supergirls: The Autobiography of an Outrageous Business*. New York: Harper & Row Publishers, 1972.

Kingcaid, Renee. "Colette (Sidonie-Gabrielle)." In *Contemporary Authors*. Vol. 131. Edited by Susan M. Trosky. Detroit: Gale Research, 1991.

Ross, Jean. "Steel, Danielle." In *Contemporary Authors*. New Revision Series. Vol. 19. Edited by Linda Metzger. Detroit: Gale Research, 1987.

Scharlach, Bernice. *Big Alma: San Francisco's Alma Spreckels*. San Francisco: Scotwall Associates, 1990.

"Steel, Danielle." In *Current Biography Yearbook*. Vol. 50. Edited by Charles Moritz. New York: H. W. Wilson Co., 1989.

"Steel, Danielle." In *Something About the Author*. Vol. 66. Edited by Donna Olendorf. Detroit: Gale Research, 1991.

Steel, Danielle. *Accident*. New York: Delacorte Press, 1994.

Steel, Danielle. *Changes*. New York: Delacorte Press, 1983.

Steel, Danielle. *Crossings*. New York: Delacorte Press, 1982.

Steel, Danielle. *Daddy*. New York: Delacorte Press, 1989.

Steel, Danielle. *Family Album*. New York: Delacorte Press, 1985.

Steel, Danielle. *Fine Things*. New York: Delacorte Press, 1987.

Steel, Danielle. *Full Circle*. New York: Delacorte Press, 1984.

Steel, Danielle. *Going Home*. New York: Pocket Books, 1973.

Steel, Danielle. *Heartbeat*. New York: Delacorte Press, 1991.

Steel, Danielle. *Jewels*. New York: Delacorte Press, 1992.
Steel, Danielle. *Kaleidoscope*. New York: Delacorte Press, 1987.
Steel, Danielle. *Love: Poems*. New York: Dell Publishing Co., 1981.
Steel, Danielle. *Loving*. New York: Dell Publishing Co., 1980.
Steel, Danielle. *Message from Nam*. New York: Delacorte Press, 1990.
Steel, Danielle. *Mixed Blessings*. New York: Delacorte Press, 1992.
Steel, Danielle. *No Greater Love*. New York: Delacorte Press, 1991.
Steel, Danielle. *Now and Forever*. New York: Dell Publishing Co., 1978.
Steel, Danielle. *Once in a Lifetime*. New York: Dell Publishing Co., 1982.
Steel, Danielle. *A Perfect Stranger*. New York: Dell Publishing Co., 1982.
Steel, Danielle. *Palomino*. New York: Dell Publishing Co., 1981.
Steel, Danielle. *Passion's Promise*. New York: Dell Publishing Co., 1977.
Steel, Danielle. *Remembrance*. New York: Delacorte Press, 1981.
Steel, Danielle. *Season of Passion*. New York: Dell Publishing Co., 1979.
Steel, Danielle. *Secrets*. New York: Delacorte Press, 1985.
Steel, Danielle. *Star*. New York: Delacorte Press, 1989.
Steel, Danielle. *Summer's End*. New York: Dell Publishing Co., 1979.
Steel, Danielle. *The Promise*. New York: Dell Publishing Co., 1978.
Steel, Danielle. *The Ring*. New York: Delacorte Press, 1980.
Steel, Danielle. *Thurston House*. New York: Dell Publishing Co., 1983.
Steel, Danielle. *To Love Again*. New York: Dell Publishing Co., 1980.
Steel, Danielle. *Vanished*. New York: Delacorte Press, 1993.
Steel, Danielle. *Wanderlust*. New York: Delacorte Press, 1986.
Steel, Danielle. *Zoya*. New York: Delacorte Press, 1988.

Magazine Articles

"Are They Worth It?" *Entertainment Weekly*, 29 January 1993, 35.
Chin, Paula, Lorenzo Benet, and Vickie Bane. "Danielle Steel—With Two Criminals as Exes, the Romance Writer's Marital History Is Stranger Than Her Fiction." *People*, 29 June 1992, 90–96.
"Danielle Steel: Author of *Message from Nam*." *Bestsellers*, No. 4 (1990).
"Danielle Steel: Author of *Zoya*." *Bestsellers*, No. 1 (1989).
"Danielle Steel." *Ladies' Home Journal*, November 1990, 296.
Etra, Jon. "Power Players Reaching Millions." *Harper's Bazaar*, May 1990, 33.
Faber, Nancy. "Writing Is All I Enjoy." *People*, 5 February 1979, 65.
Farr, Louise. "The Romance of Danielle Steel." *Women's Wear Daily*, 3 July 1986, 12.
Goldberg, Robert. "Storybook Lives of Best-Selling Authors." *Cosmopolitan*, February 1985, 186–87.
Goldner, Diane. "Bestseller Practice." *The American Lawyer*, September 1985, 105.

Kartvedt, Sindre. "The Steel Industry." *Scanorama*, June 1993, 30–31.

Lesure, Paul. "Pearl's at-Home Atmosphere . . . " *TravelAge West*, 2 August 1982, 31.

Linden, Dana Wechsler, and Matt Rees. "I'm Hungry, But Not for Food." *Forbes*, 6 July 1992, 70–74.

Marchant, Sofia. "Woman of Steel." *Ladies' Home Journal*, October 1991, 46.

Marion, Jane. "Look Out Hoopsters." *TV Guide*, 30 March 1991, 7.

Maryles, Daisy. "A Decade of Megasellers." *Publishers Weekly*, 6 January 1990, 24.

McElwaine, Sandra. "Supermom, Superwife, Superauthor." *Woman's Day*, 16 January 1990.

McFadden, Cyra. "Danielle Steel—Passion's Profitable Prose." *San Francisco Magazine of Northern California*, January 1983, 50–54.

Meyers, Marc. "How to Get It All Done." *McCall's*, December 1991, 62.

Montandon, Pat. "Danielle Steel Traina." *Scene*, October 1981,18.

Plaskin, Glenn. "Babies and Best Sellers: How Danielle Steel Manages It All." *Family Circle*, 17 May 1988.

Sherman, Eric. "Danielle Steel: Her Toughest Challenge." *Ladies' Home Journal*, June 1987, 104.

Steel, Danielle. "Having Babies the Turning Tides: What Was Out of Fashion in the '70s Has Become Chic in the '80s." *Ladies' Home Journal*, May 1986.

Steel, Danielle. "Industrial-Strength Mom." *Cosmopolitan*, November 1985, 364–65.

Steel, Danielle. "Romantic Saga." *Architectural Digest*, April 1985.

Steel, Danielle. "The San Francisco Strutters." *San Francisco Magazine of Northern California*, July 1973, 40–41.

Traina, Danielle Steel. "An Eminent Victorian." *Architectural Digest*, June 1986.

"Two Rebuilt Ships to Enter . . . " *TravelAge West*, 12 October 1981, 12.

Newspaper Articles

Allsletter, Billy. "Made Over as Children's Book Author." *Adweek*, 8 January 1990, 21.

Bendel, Mary-Ann. "Danielle Steel." *USA Today*, 21 February 1986, 6.

Edwards, Cliff. "She Puts Hints of Truth in Danielle Steel's Fiction." *Los Angeles Times*, 10 October 1988, 4.

Finke, Nikki. "A Fantasy Named Danielle Steel." *Los Angeles Times*, 6 January 1988, sec. 5, p. 1.

Friedman, Mickey. "Inheriting the Mantle of Jacqueline Susann." *San Francisco Examiner*, 5 March 1979.

Holt, Patricia. "Women Who Love to Write About Abuse." *San Francisco Chronicle*, 22 February 1990, sec. E, p. 5.

Kaufman, Joanne. "The Face on the Back of the Book." *The New York Times*, 25 June 1989, sec. 7, p. 1.

Markfield, Allan. "The Love Boat Sounded . . . " *San Francisco Chronicle*, 13 July 1983, 13.

Noffsinger, Loretta. "American Style: Danielle Steel's Passion for Writing." *Associated Press*, 26 February 1982.

Plaskin, Glenn. "Steel Makes Up for Lost Childhood . . . " *San Francisco Chronicle*, 27 May 1991, sec. D, p. 3.

Rubin, Sylvia. "In Her Own Words." *San Francisco Chronicle*, 7 March 1991, sec. B, p. 3.

Singer, Linda-Marie. "Danielle Steel: Popular and Prolific Writer." *Progress Bulletin*, 5 November 1984, 6–7.

Smith, Laquita Bowen. "Miscarriages Leave Lasting Scars." *Rocky Mountain News*, 3 September 1993, sec. D, p. 42.

Walters, Ray. "Women of the World." *The New York Times Book Review*, 6 January 1980, 31.

Zorn, Eric. "Danielle Steel's Researcher." *Chicago Tribune*, 9 September 1988, sec. C, p. 1.

Index